THE POETRY OF CHARTISM

Between 1838 and 1852, the leading Chartist newspaper, the *Northern Star*, published over 1,000 poems written by more than 350 poets – as the readership of the *Northern Star* numbered hundreds of thousands, these poems were amongst the most widely read of the Victorian era. This book is the first full-length study of the *Northern Star*'s poetry column and offers a complete record of all the poems published. It asks a simple question: why did the writing and reading of poetry play such an important role in Chartism's struggle to secure fundamental democratic rights? It answers this question by analysing the interplay between politics, aesthetics and history in the aftermath of the Newport insurrection (1839), during the mass strikes of 1842 and the year of European revolutions (1848). Additionally, the book theorises poetry's political agency and examines the critical history of Chartist poetry.

MIKE SANDERS is Lecturer in Nineteenth-century Literature and Theory at the University of Manchester.

Nineteenth-century British literature and culture have been rich fields for interdisciplinary studies. Since the turn of the twentieth century, scholars and critics have tracked the intersections and tensions between Victorian literature and the visual arts, politics, social organisation, economic life, technical innovations, scientific thought – in short, culture in its broadest sense. In recent years, theoretical challenges and historiographical shifts have unsettled the assumptions of previous scholarly synthesis and called into question the terms of older debates. Whereas the tendency in much past literary critical interpretation was to use the metaphor of culture as 'background', feminist, Foucauldian, and other analyses have employed more dynamic models that raise questions of power and of circulation. Such developments have re-animated the field. This series aims to accommodate and promote the most interesting work being undertaken on the frontiers of the field of nineteenth-century literary studies: work which intersects fruitfully with other fields of study such as history, or literary theory, or the history of science. Comparative as well as interdisciplinary approaches are welcomed.

A complete list of titles published will be found at the end of the book.

THE POETRY OF CHARTISM

Aesthetics, Politics, History

MIKE SANDERS

CAMBRIDGE
UNIVERSITY PRESS

CAMBRIDGE UNIVERSITY PRESS

Cambridge, New York, Melbourne, Madrid, Cape Town, Singapore, São Paulo, Delhi

Cambridge University Press
The Edinburgh Building, Cambridge CB2 8RU, UK

Published in the United States of America by Cambridge University Press, New York

www.cambridge.org
Information on this title: www.cambridge.org/9780521899185

First published 2009

Printed in the United Kingdom at the University Press, Cambridge

A catalogue record for this publication is available from the British Library

ISBN 978-0-521-89918-5 hardback

In memory of my father
Terry Sanders
1943–2008

Contents

Acknowledgements

The seeds of this study were sown many years ago when my partner Cathy Cundy discovered a copy of Kovalev's Anthology of Chartist Literature in a second-hand bookshop in Derbyshire. From this chance discovery, a research project was born. In the course of writing about the intersections of literature and history in the nineteenth century, I have often considered how that same conjunction has operated in my own lifetime. Those meditations have convinced me of my extreme good fortune at having been born at the height of the welfare state (the finest achievement to date of the British Labour movement). The combination of a comprehensive secondary schooling and free higher education gave me opportunities denied to previous generations of my family.

The opportunities I have enjoyed are not just the product of educational structures – individual educators have played an equally crucial role and there are seven teachers in particular to whom I owe an incalculable debt. Mrs Johnson and Miss Cox taught me respectively to value the meaning of words and to relish their beauty. Mrs Harrington and Miss Wright schooled me in the vital connections between literature and the social order. Mr David Blair kept a sometimes obstreperous undergraduate on track, and his precise and subtle reading skills illuminated lecture hall and seminar room alike. At Birkbeck, that most remarkable of institutions, I was fortunate enough not only to find, in Professor Laura Marcus, a PhD supervisor who exerted a profound influence on my thinking, but also to learn from Professor Isobel Armstrong. Those of us working in the field of Victorian Poetry know the nature of the general intellectual debt we owe to her work. On a personal level her encouragement and support have been equally inspirational.

I have learnt much from friends, colleagues and students at the Universities of Exeter, Aberystwyth, Northampton, Lancaster and most recently Manchester. Particular thanks are owed to Florence Boos, Malcolm Chase, Ian Haywood, Helen Rogers and Roy Vickers, for their unfailing willingness to 'talk Chartist' whenever the opportunity presented itself. Special thanks are due to Alison Easton, colleague, landlady, mentor and friend, whose encouragement and example has inspired many academics.

Without a Research Leave award from the Arts and Humanities Research Council and accompanying study leave from the University of Manchester this book would have been even longer in its making. I am grateful to both institutions for their support. Thanks are also due to staff at John Rylands University Library, the Working-Class Movement Library in Salford, Manchester Central Library (where Jade Witherington was especially helpful) and Lancaster University Library. Chapters 3 and 7 have appeared in earlier versions. I am grateful to the following publishers for granting permission to reproduce in whole or part the following publications: University of Toronto Press for ' "A Jackass Load of Poetry": Re-constructing the Northern Star's editorial policy 1838–1854', Victorian Periodicals Review, 39:1 (Spring 2006), 46–66; West Virginia University Press for 'Constellating Chartist Poetry: Gerald Massey, Walter Benjamin and the Uses of Messianism', Victorian Poetry, 45:4 (Winter 2007), 369–89. I should also like to thank Linda Bree and two unnamed readers at Cambridge University Press for their helpful comments and suggestions.

Finally, more than thanks are owed to Cathy Cundy who has lived with this project as long as I have, and as a result has probably regretted ever finding the Kovalev anthology. More importantly she has lived amidst the chaos of my floor-based, horizontal filing system whilst remaining my first and best reader, my first and best critic, in fact my first and best everything.

Introduction

The *Northern Star*'s poetry column for 18 May 1839, carries a factory reform poem written by a woman known to history only as E. H., 'a Factory Girl of Stalybridge'. In this poem entitled, 'On Joseph Rayner Stephens', E. H. compares her position with that of the millowners' children and wives. The contrast she draws between their advantages purchased, she believes, at the cost of her own class's impoverishment is a common rhetorical device in early Victorian social discourse. Less familiar, perhaps, is the content of this trope, for E. H. protests her cultural deprivation as bitterly as any material deprivation:

> Their children, too, to school must be sent,
> Till all kinds of learning and music have learnt;
> Their wives must have veils, silks dresses, and cloaks,
> And some who support them can't get linsey coats.

Two stanzas later E. H. returns to the question of cultural entitlement – 'If they had sent us to school, better rhyme we could make, / And I think it is time we had some of their cake'. In this simple rhyming couplet E. H. attests to poetry's importance in the working-class movement. Here poetry is figured as a luxury rather than a fundamental necessity – cake rather than bread – but nonetheless it is something to which E. H. believes she is entitled. In her imagination, poetry equates with plenty; it signifies the desire for 'something more', the 'something better' which impelled Chartism.

Precisely because the history of all hitherto existing society is the history of scarcity, we have grown accustomed to hearing the cries for bread. In comparison the call for cake sounds anomalous. The inability to appreciate the difference between the two has entered popular consciousness as one of the causes of the French Revolution. If the call for cake seems outlandish as a popular demand, then the call for poetry seems equally improbable. To imagine a nineteenth-century workers' movement demanding the right to versify alongside the demand for the vote and better working and living conditions seems incredible. Yet for E. H. these demands were inseparable, and she ends her poem by returning to the subject:

> We factory lasses have but little time,
> So I hope you will pardon my bad written rhyme.
> God bless him for striving to get us our rights,
> And I wish the world over were true Stephenites.
>
> A Stephenite I am from the ground of my heart,
> And I hope from the same I shall never depart.
> May God spare your life till the tyrants are ended,
> So I bid you good bye, till my verses I've mended.

E. H. knows she is writing 'bad' poetry and wants to write better verse; aesthetic standards mattered to her as they did to the rest of the Chartist movement. A dozen years later, at the end of the period covered by this study, a similar note is struck by the better-known Chartist poet, Gerald Massey. Addressing a poetic comrade in the preface to his first collection of Chartist verse, *Voices of Freedom and Lyrics of Love* (1851), Massey simultaneously acknowledges and excuses his poetic shortcomings. He identifies a lack of education and limited exposure to poetry's 'great masters' as the causes of the intellectual and aesthetic weakness of his poetry which, he asserts, is nonetheless justified by its truthfulness and sincerity:

No one knows better than myself how unworthy [these poems] are of our common cause; no one knows so well as myself how far I have fallen short of what I had thought to perform; but the builder can only erect his edifice according to his material, and I have not much book lore . . . until of late, I have been quite shut out from the great masters of the lyre, and the mighty in the realms of thought. In my 'Voices of Freedom' I have endeavoured to utter what is stirring in poor men's hearts. The thoughts may be unripe, and the utterance crude, but what is written, is written in my own life's-blood; and you, at least, will not despise my earnest sincerity.[1]

E. H. and Massey assume that the political struggle to which they were committed, required not just poetry – but the best poetry. This study originates in a desire to understand the terms of this conjunction of aesthetics and politics effected by the Chartist movement. In addition, it

---

[1] Gerald Massey, *Voices of Freedom and Lyrics of Love* (J. Watson, 1851), i.

seeks to abandon the defensive formulations of E. H. and Massey by celebrating the aesthetic and political achievements of Chartist poetry – to join with *The Chartist Circular* in denying 'that the union of poetry with politics is always hurtful to the politics, and fatal to the poetry', and with *The Friend of the People* in affirming the value of those 'eloquent outpourings of the complaints of the people, passionate appeals for justice, [and] lofty dreamings of the great future, when SLAVERY and MISERY shall be no more'.[2]

Before beginning this study, I regarded Chartist proclamations of the importance of poetry with a large measure of scepticism and privileged the political over the aesthetic as the site of significant Chartist activity. This assumption fell away in the face of a prolonged encounter with the Chartist press in general, and its leading newspaper the *Northern Star* (NS) in particular, which convinced me that poetry played an active, primary role within the movement. Chapter 1, The Chartist imaginary: 'talking by turns of politics and poetry', is the result of the realisation that for the Chartist movement, the political and the aesthetic are not just closely related concepts but are thoroughly imbricated practices. The chapter provides the theoretical underpinning for this study's claim that Chartist poetry constitutes both a distinctive form of agency and a unique form of historical knowledge. The unity of these twin facets of Chartist poetry constitutes the realm of the Chartist imaginary.

Chapter 2 examines the reception and critical history of Chartist poetry over the past century and a half. It charts the fluctuating visibility of Chartist poetry over this period and discusses the work of the most significant critics working in this field. It notes that the existing critical tradition has tended to concentrate on the work of a handful of 'labour laureates' (most notably Ernest Jones, Thomas Cooper, Gerald Massey and W. J. Linton) who are atypical Chartist poets insofar as the overwhelming majority of Chartist poets enjoyed at best a limited, local rather than national reputation, and published their work in the periodical press rather than in single volumes. Therefore, this study takes the poetry column of a given journal rather than the individual poet as its object of analysis. Chapter 3 represents the methodological outgrowth of this argument. It provides an empirical analysis of the poetry column of the leading Chartist newspaper, the *Northern Star*, quantifying the number of poems and poets published on an annual basis as well as the ratio of

---

[2] *The Chartist Circular*, 11 July 1840, 170. *The Friend of the People*, 3 May 1851, 187.

Chartist to non-Chartist poetry in its columns. In addition, Chapter 3 seeks to reconstruct the poetry column's editorial policy, paying particular attention to its attempts to raise the quality of Chartist poetic production from 1844 onwards.

Chapters 4, 5 and 6 examine the *Northern Star*'s poetry column during the periods of political crisis which accompanied the presentation of each of the three national petitions in 1839, 1842 and 1848. Chapter 4 deals with the aftermath of the 'Newport uprising' in November 1839 and focuses in particular on the insurrection's ideological afterlife in the *Northern Star*. It examines the role of the poetry column in explaining and interpreting Newport and its treatment of the themes of exile and return following the transportation of the uprising's leader, John Frost. Chapter 5 deals with Chartism's resurgence in 1842 when a massive strike-wave in the aftermath of the rejection of the second petition constituted one of the most serious challenges to the British state in the entire nineteenth century. It demonstrates the crucial role played by the *Northern Star*'s poetry column both in the reconstruction of Chartist identity in the post-Newport period, and in the emergence of a more sophisticated economic and political critique. It examines the reworking of established Chartist poetic tropes in relation to the unresolved contradictions in Chartist strategy, before ending with an analysis of the role of 'nostalgia' in the Chartist imaginary in 1842. Chapter 6 examines the poetry column during the year of European revolutions, 1848. It traces Chartism's response to the revolutionary nationalism which swept both Ireland and continental Europe, and to the defeat of those same forces in the latter half of that turbulent year. It examines the consolidation of a new structure of feeling – 'red republicanism' – and analyses its accompanying new poetic, which consolidates the emergent political and economic critique identified in the previous chapter.

Chapter 7 differs from the preceding three chapters by concentrating on the work of an individual Chartist poet, Gerald Massey, rather than the *Northern Star*'s poetry column. It does so in order to capture the idiosyncratic qualities of late (post-1848) Chartist poetry, with its distinctive figuring of the relationship between forms of temporal understanding and political activity. In particular, this chapter seeks to differentiate between the 'messianic' (used in its Benjaminian sense) and the 'millenarian' in Massey's poetry, as exemplifying the ideological trajectory of the wider Chartist movement in this period. Massey's attempt to preserve hope at a moment of profound historical defeat provides a fitting coda for the Chartist imaginary:

> 'All's well!' saith the sentry on tyranny's tower,
>> 'Even Hope by their watch-fire is grey and tear-blind.'
> Aye, all's well! Freedom's altar burns hour by hour –
>> Live brands for the fire-damps with which ye are mined.[3]

---

[3] Gerald Massey, 'Our Symbol', *Voices of Freedom*, 10. This poem also appeared in the first number of *The Red Republican* under the title 'The Red Banner'.

CHAPTER I

The Chartist imaginary: 'talking by turns of politics and poetry'

> We became acquainted that evening, and, in the course of many
> subsequent years, I passed an agreeable half-hour in the shoemaker's
> garret, talking by turns of politics and poetry.
>
> Thomas Frost, *Forty Years' Recollections: Literary and Political*[1]

This chapter will follow Thomas Frost's conversational footsteps in 'talking by turns of politics and poetry'. However, it also posits the unity of politics and poetry in the form of the 'Chartist imaginary' which both underpins the agency enjoyed by, and constitutes the unique form of historical knowledge embodied in, Chartist poetry. This chapter, therefore, offers both a theorisation and a definition of the Chartist imaginary.

How can Chartist poetry be said to possess agency? What does a Chartist poem make happen? It is certainly the case, as Timothy Randall has shown, that Chartist poetry was performed in a variety of settings including, but not confined to, 'the mass open-air gatherings, the anniversary celebrations, the reading groups, the feasts, the evening teas, the workplace lunches, the public house meetings, the extempore singing in prison'.[2] However, in these contexts Chartist poetry serves either as a mood enhancer, confirming or consolidating the ethos of the gathering, or it is entrusted with a cathartic role, with discharging anger which cannot be vented in any other form.[3] In the first case it would appear to be the specific context (the mass meeting, etc.) which is the real locus of any agency, whilst in the second, the function of Chartist poetry appears to be the prevention of concrete action.

However, poetry also featured prominently in the Chartist press where, in addition to the poetry, reviews and literary miscellanies columns, it was

---

[1] T. Frost, *Forty Years' Recollections: Literary and Political* (Sampson Low, Marston, Searle & Rivington, 1880), 34.
[2] T. Randall, 'Chartist Poetry and Song', in O. Ashton, R. Fyson and S. Roberts (eds.), *The Chartist Legacy* (Rendlesham: Merlin Press, 1999), 172–3.
[3] *Ibid.*, 175.

quoted frequently in reports of speeches as well as editorials and readers' letters. Moreover, poetry permeated the entire movement, with both leadership and rank and file sharing a common belief in its value. This commitment is manifested by the numbers of rank and file Chartists who not only read but also composed poetry in their hundreds, and underscored by the close connection between poetic production and Chartist leadership at the local, regional and national levels. This relationship is exemplified by the careers of Thomas Cooper and Ernest Jones. At the national level they are joined by O'Connor, O'Brien, Harney, McDouall and Kydd – all of whom wrote poetry occasionally and all of whom (with the exception of O'Brien) published at least one poem in the *Northern Star*. In addition, Ulrike Schwab's *The Poetry of the Chartist Movement* identifies a further thirty-eight local and regional Chartist leaders who were also published poets.[4] This evidence suggests that the particular skills fostered by the writing of poetry may have played a vital role in the development of the Chartist movement.[5]

This chapter opened with Thomas Frost's recollection of his friendship with the Croydon Chartist shoemaker and poet, Jem Blackaby. Frost and Blackaby were leaders of local rather than national importance within Chartism and as writers neither enjoyed a significant reputation. Indeed, Frost credits Blackaby with publishing only two poems in his lifetime – one on the death of Lord Abinger in the manner of Byron's 'Vision of Judgement', printed privately in an edition of fifty copies, and another on the subject of the night-flowering cereus which appeared in *Reynolds' Miscellany*.[6] However, it is precisely the relative historical obscurity of Frost and Blackaby which underwrites their typicality and increases the value of their testimony.

---

[4] U. Schwab, *The Poetry of the Chartist Movement: a Literary and Historical Study* (Dordrecht, Netherlands: Kluwer Academic Publishers, 1987), 183–222. Given the extent of anonymous, pseudonymous and initialised publication in the *Northern Star*'s poetry column and the existence of figures such as Jem Blackaby (a local Chartist leader and poet unpublished by the *Northern Star*) there is a strong probability that there exists a meaningful correlation between Chartist poetry and Chartist leadership. However, in the absence of a systematic study of the Chartist localities, such a correlation remains a tantalising hypothesis.

[5] David Vincent argues that the skills developed by the autodidact, particularly literacy and a broader perspective, 'were indispensable to almost any working class organization' and notes that the overwhelming majority of his autobiographers made a 'practical contribution . . . to the cause of freedom, either as official or unofficial leaders, or as political writers and poets'. D. Vincent, *Bread, Knowledge and Freedom. A Study of Nineteenth-Century Working Class Autobiography* (Methuen, 1982), 176–7.

[6] Frost, *Forty Years' Recollections*, 122–3. Jem Blackaby's *A Vision of Judgement* (new version) was reviewed by the *Northern Star* (7 September 1844). A further poem entitled 'Moral Musings' authored by J. Blackaby was also published in the *Northern Star* (24 April 1847).

Of particular interest for this study is Frost's account of the continuous interchange and interplay between the aesthetic and the democratic in their conversation, 'talking by turns of politics and poetry'. Another of Frost's reminiscences of Blackaby highlights the way in which the 'political' could quickly become the 'poetical'. During 'a conversation on the land question', Blackaby comments on Frost's pronunciation of 'contrary' and 'quoted passages from *Henry IV* and *Samson Agonistes*' in support of his argument that Shakespeare and Milton placed the emphasis on the second syllable.[7] Indeed, throughout Frost's autobiography, *Forty Years' Recollections: Literary and Political*, the poetical and the political blend seamlessly. Frost recounts how as a sixteen year old he attended an Owenite entertainment at the Tivoli Gardens and found that his reading of Coleridge had already prepared him for socialism:

> I had just been reading Coleridge's 'Religious Musings,' and the brief address in which the philosopher of New Lanark had set forth the principles of his new constitution of society sent me to the poem again. The scheme of the philosopher seemed to be the due response to the aspirations of the poet.[8]

Frost records that his subsequent reading of Shelley confirmed his Socialist convictions and that later the combined influence of Coleridge and Shelley made him 'a Chartist, and something more'.[9]

Frost and Blackaby's interest in poetry was not an unusual feature of early nineteenth-century working-class culture. David Vincent's *Bread, Knowledge and Freedom* demonstrates that such readers 'inherited both a background of book ownership and a tradition, albeit a narrow one, of serious reading'. Moreover, as Vincent shows, the reading of Milton's poetry was central to this tradition of serious reading.[10] Robert Burns and James Thomson appear to have been the two most widely read poets after Milton.[11] Beyond these three, working-class reading lists became more eclectic and dependent on local circumstances. However, with determination and a degree of good fortune, the autodidact could complete a course of reading which would stand comparison with many a contemporary undergraduate syllabus. By his early twenties, Thomas Cooper had read (and memorised lines from) Milton, Shakespeare, Burns, Coleridge, Wordsworth, Scott, Byron, Moore, Campbell, Southey and Keats.[12]

---

[7] Frost, *Forty Years' Recollections*, 34.   [8] *Ibid.*, 14.
[9] *Ibid.*, 15 and 38. In similar fashion, W. J. Linton records the reading of Shelley's *Queen Mab* as one of his formative political experiences. W. J. Linton, *Memories* (New York: Augustus M. Kelley, 1970 [1894]), 26.
[10] Vincent, *Bread, Knowledge and Freedom*, 111–19.   [11] *Ibid.*, 186.
[12] T. Cooper, *The Life of Thomas Cooper* (Leicester University Press, 1971 [1872]), 64.

Although Cooper's reading was, probably, more extensive and more intensive than that of many autodidacts, nonetheless it exists as part of a continuum of working-class reading practices rather than an atypical aberration. Vincent notes that every one of the one hundred and forty-two autobiographers studied in his work 'read poetry, and a surprising number tried their hand at composition'.[13] In a number of cases the subject's first encounter with poetry is figured as a life-changing moment. Alexander Somerville, for example, records asking a harvester (as an eleven or twelve year old) what a poem was and being treated to a recitation from Burns' work. The harvester, seeing Somerville's 'delight', promises to lend him a book of Burns' poems on the following day. However, writes Somerville:

I was now so eager to see that famous book, from which he had kindled in me intellectual sensations so new, so delightful, and irrepressibly strong, that I could not go home to supper and to bed until I had accompanied him to his home, three quarters of a mile distant to get the book; I could not wait until he brought it in the morning.[14]

For Somerville, Burns' poetry produced 'sensations of pleasure entirely new' and 'so exquisitely delightful' that he 'continued to read everything of verse kind which fell in [his] way'.[15]

At a similar age to Somerville, Thomas Cooper had his first encounter with Byron's poetry:

in my thirteenth year, by some accident there fell into my hands one of the cantos of *Childe Harold's Pilgrimage* and the drama of *Manfred*. I had them in my hands for only a few hours, and I knew nothing of their noble author's life or reputation; but they seemed to create a new sense within me. I wanted more poetry to read from that time; but could get hold of none that thrilled through my nature like Byron's.[16]

A couple of years later as an apprentice shoemaker, Cooper was introduced to the poetry of Burns by his master. As with Somerville the effect was exhilarating – 'The pathos of Burns took possession of my whole nature almost as completely as the fire and force of Byron.'[17]

In both cases the encounter with poetry transforms the consciousness of the reader; Somerville refers to new 'intellectual sensations', Cooper to the creation of 'a new sense within me'. This transformation is qualitative and total. It does not alter any specific opinions held by its readers but is

---

[13] Vincent, *Bread, Knowledge and Freedom*, 185.
[14] A. Somerville, *The Autobiography of a Working Man* (MacGibbon & Kee, 1967 [1848]), 56.
[15] *Ibid.*, 57.   [16] Cooper, *The Life of Thomas Cooper*, 35.   [17] *Ibid.*, 42.

experienced by them as the acquisition of new powers in general. In both cases poetry increases the affective capabilities of its readers, producing 'new sensations so exquisitely delightful' for Somerville and 'thrill[ing] through' Cooper's being. The account of poetry's impact here clearly resembles the account of the 'emancipatory impact' of art offered by what Pauline Johnson describes as the 'felt, radical needs' school of Marxist aesthetics.[18] The principal proponents of this school, most notably the later Lukacs and Marcuse, argue that the richness of the aesthetic moment produces a cathartic experience in which the receptant recognises the creative potentialities and possibilities inherent in social-historical being, namely that life can be different. The cognitive rupture produced by the aesthetic moment is a necessary (but not a sufficient) condition for political action.[19] A sense of the potential political ramifications of the aesthetic is suggested by its appetitive function; the unleashing of an almost insatiable desire for more poetry is recorded by both Somerville and Cooper. It is certainly the case that the psychic structure of Cooper's desire for poetry (the need to find out more) is instrumental in securing his conversion to Chartism. Sent by his editor to report on a Chartist meeting in Leicester, Cooper begins to talk with some of the stocking weavers and is shocked when he discovers the level of their wages, 'I felt, therefore, that I must know something more about the real meaning of what they had told me'.[20] That desire for 'more' simultaneously generated by and initiating a combination of intellectual and emotional needs first unleashed by poetry would, in Cooper's case, also underpin his conversion to Chartism.

It would, however, be inaccurate to suggest that there existed an unproblematic identity between the aspiring writer and his (less frequently her) community of origin. The pursuit of literary knowledge sometimes required a degree of separation and self-alienation from the community. W. E. Adams, for example, records one such moment of choice:

One Sunday afternoon the usual call was made for a ramble in the fields. Word was sent to the callers that their old companion was not going to join them. I heard from an upper room, not without a certain amount of tremor, their exclamations of surprise. They wandered off into the fields in one direction; I, with a new companion, wandered off into the field in another. My new companion was Young's *Night Thoughts*. The old companions were never joined again. A new life had begun.[21]

---

[18] P. Johnson, *Marxist Aesthetics* (Routledge & Kegan Paul, 1984), 145.
[19] *Ibid.*, 43–4 and 99–111.   [20] Cooper, *The Life of Thomas Cooper*, 139.
[21] W. E. Adams, *Memoirs of a Social Atom* (New York: Augustus M. Kelley, 1968 [1903]), 107–8.

More than a century later, a similar scene occurs in Tony Harrison's poem 'Me Tarzan' which also opens with the author disobeying the gang's summons. Admittedly, in Harrison's poem the separation is less complete and the embrace of literary culture is more grudging, 'Ah bloody can't ah've gorra Latin prose'.[22] Nonetheless, both texts suggest the emotional cost which the gods of learning might exact. It is, therefore, unsurprising that Vincent notes that the reading of poetry often fostered the growth of an individual identity based on the persona of the 'Romantic solitary'.[23] Yet even this identification, which might be thought to be the antithesis of the communitarian/collectivist identity of the typical nineteenth-century working-class subject, could be integrated within working-class radicalism. As Vincent notes in the case of Chartism:

The writings and, in most cases, the personalities of Byron, Shelley, Bunyan, Wesley, Milton and Shakespeare were incorporated into a lively new radical culture which played an important part in uniting and sustaining the world's first mass working class movement.[24]

As will be shown in the next chapter, a broad consensus exists among scholars that Chartist poetry undertook what might be called 'ideological work' within the movement. This work ranges from the affirmation of shared values and aspirations, contributions to the debate surrounding Chartist strategy and tactics, through to the articulation of the movement's collective identity or consciousness. Such disagreement as exists concerns the extent to which the poetry actively shapes rather than passively reflects the movement's values, strategy and identity.[25] Accepting, for a moment, the stronger thesis which accords an active role to Chartist poetry in the realm of general ideological struggle – the contest over the meaning and interpretation of keywords, tropes and ideas – it remains the case that it is language rather than poetry which guarantees agency here.

Thus, the question arises as to whether there is a specific form of political work undertaken by poetry which could not be undertaken by any other form of language use. The answer to this question has important implications for the study of literature. For if poetry only performs the general political work of language, then a poem becomes a mode of ideological/discursive encoding which is ultimately reduced to a passive reflection of an already 'known' historical moment. This in turn generates

---

[22] T. Harrison, 'Me Tarzan', *Continuous* (Rex Collings, 1981), 11.
[23] Vincent, *Bread, Knowledge and Freedom*, 182–6.   [24] *Ibid.*, 193.
[25] To some extent this disagreement follows disciplinary boundaries with literary scholars according an active role and historians a passive role to literature.

a form of literary criticism in which poems are broken into to provide decorative illustration for a prior historical fact – a kind of ideological 'ram-raiding'.

E. Warwick Slinn in *Victorian Poetry as Cultural Critique* similarly laments current critical practices in which 'the intensive use of language in poetry appears to have become marginalized amidst thematic approaches to the politics of social discourse'.[26] This produces a situation, Slinn argues, in which value and meaning are 'always located in discourses from institutions outside literature – medicine, law, politics, public media'.[27] Slinn rejects this flattening out of poetic discourse and insists that attention must also be given to the ways in which 'literary writing' is non-continuous with those aforementioned discourses. Following Paul de Man, Slinn identifies 'referential aberration' as an essential characteristic of literature and argues that, in conjunction with the concept of performativity, it enables us to conceptualise a specific form of poetic agency whereby, 'Poetry reconstitutes or reshapes that reality in the very act of reiterating its norms; and the capacity of poetry for referential aberration, pointing in both directions – both inside and outside itself – draws attention to this double action.'[28]

However, despite noting Judith Butler's claims for the democratic potential of the performative insofar as it can '*establish* a political reality, not just ... describe it as if already existing', Slinn makes a far more modest claim for poetry's power: 'My claim for poetry as critique is not, therefore, a claim of consequential subversion ... poetry is more likely to expose, without necessarily subverting, [the] enabling conditions [of existing institutions and cultural practices]'.[29] Slinn argues that although poems engage with political issues, they 'do not resolve these issues but expose their complexities'. By defining poetry's political effectiveness in these terms Slinn returns poetry to its 'Arnoldian' function as the means of inculcating a broad-minded appreciation of the many-sided nature of truth.[30]

Overall, Slinn's model seems less applicable to Chartist poetry than to bourgeois Victorian poetry (poems by Barrett-Browning, Browning, Clough and D. G. Rossetti provide the objects of Slinn's study). In part,

---

[26] E. Warwick Slinn, *Victorian Poetry as Cultural Critique: The Politics of Performative Language* (Charlottesville: University of Virginia Press, 2003), 1.

[27] *Ibid.*, 13.   [28] *Ibid.*, 23.   [29] *Ibid.*, 22 and 29.

[30] *Ibid.*, 6. The account of the 'Arnoldian' function of literature is drawn from C. Baldick, *The Social Mission of English Criticism 1848–1932* (Oxford University Press, 1983), 60–3. See also T. Eagleton, *Criticism and Ideology* (Verso, 1978), 104–10.

this is because referential aberration carries a different value for Chartist poets, many of whom stress the referential nature of their work. In addition, where referential aberration can be said to occur – as, for example in the invocation of an assembled people who are not in actuality so constituted – it is often symptomatic of political crisis rather than political opportunity. Moreover, if we recall those accounts of actual Chartist reading practices, discussed earlier in this chapter, we find a radically different account of poetry's agency.

The most noticeable feature of those accounts is the wide spectrum of political work undertaken by poetry. As expected, poetry participates in general ideological struggle by exposing the working-class autodidact to new ideas. More surprisingly, perhaps, there is a much greater emphasis on the affective and sensual pleasures afforded by poetry, which is represented as increasing the reader's affective capacity and unleashing a desire for further, similar, sensations. The combined effort of these heightened emotional and sensual experiences is to effect a total, qualitative transformation of consciousness – Cooper's 'new sense' of being.

It is possible, therefore, to ascribe two distinct levels of political agency to poetry. There are the discrete interventions in specific political debates, which are readily identifiable and traceable (poems about factory reform, the new Poor Law, and the Corn Laws, for example, fall within this category). In as much as these texts belong to the realm of general linguistic struggle, their status as poems is an incidental rather than an essential aspect of their agency. However, the opposite is the case at the second level where we see the total qualitative transformation of consciousness wrought by poetry. Here, political agency arises directly out of poetry's creative capacities; its ability to imagine things differently.

In recent years, literary criticism wedded to the 'hermeneutics of suspicion' and committed to a politics of ideological unmasking has tended to be suspicious of affect and creativity.[31] Indeed, it is necessary to return to the work of the neglected 1930s Marxist critic, Christopher Caudwell, in order to begin theorising the political effect of poetical affect. In *Illusion and Reality*, Caudwell speculates that in early human society, poetry stimulated and channelled the collective emotions of a given social group. It achieved this, he suggests, through the creation of a 'phantastic object', an intermediate state between 'material reality' and 'ideal illusion'

---

[31] See, for example, Isobel Armstrong's discussion of these critical tendencies in 'The Hermeneutics of Suspicion and the "Problem" of the Aesthetic' in her study, *The Radical Aesthetic* (Oxford: Blackwell, 2000), 25–82.

which is capable of inciting and sustaining the social action necessary for its actualisation. (Caudwell gives the example of the harvest song which by 'phantastically portraying the granaries bursting with grain [inspires] the hard labour necessary to bring it into being'.) Thus, Caudwell identifies poetry's 'dynamic role in society' with 'its content of collective emotion'.[32] Elsewhere in *Illusion and Reality* Caudwell comments that '[a] poem's content is not just emotion, it is *organised* emotion, an organised emotional attitude to a piece of external reality'.[33] Therefore, Caudwell argues, poetry makes things possible by anticipating or producing the psychic structures necessary for their realisation. In this he anticipates Brian Maidment's observation that the Chartist lyric 'attempts to bring into being post-revolutionary consciousness'.[34] This dimension of Chartist poetry finds its most insistent formal manifestation in Gerald Massey's work which, as will be demonstrated in Chapter 7, continually imagines a future which is capable of reaching back and restructuring the present.

In addition, Caudwell regards poetry as a tool for the manufacture of new forms of consciousness. Poetry achieves this due to its ability to 'loosen' the subject/object relation and to separate space from time. These procedures, Caudwell suggests, inject 'plasticity' into consciousness, thereby preventing it from 'completely coinciding with external reality ... [and becoming] indistinguishable from perception'.[35] This capacity to imagine things other than the way they are, makes poetry an incarnation of the process of becoming, the means by which 'we catch glimpses of ourselves, not as we are, but as we are in active potentiality of becoming in relation to reality through society'. Furthermore, Caudwell credits poetry with a utopian function – like all art, it offers a momentary glimpse of a better world.[36] Indeed, in Caudwell's account, art joins labour as the expression of our species being:

[Art] exposes the endless potentiality of the instincts and the 'heart' by revealing the various ways in which they may adapt themselves to experiences. It plays on the inner world of emotion as on a stringed instrument. It changes the emotional content of [man's] consciousness so that he can react more subtly and deeply to his world. This penetration of inner reality, because it is achieved by men in association and has a complexity beyond the task of one man to achieve, also

[32] C. Caudwell, *Illusion and Reality* (Lawrence & Wishart, 1973 [1937]), 34–40.
[33] *Ibid.*, 240.
[34] B. Maidment (ed.), *The Poor House Fugitives* (Manchester: Carcanet, 1992), 38.
[35] Caudwell, *Illusion and Reality*, 204–5.   [36] *Ibid.*, 290.

exposes the hearts of his fellow men and raises the whole communal feeling of society to a new plane of complexity. It makes possible new levels of conscious sympathy, understanding and affection between men.[37]

A similar claim for the aesthetic as an integral part of our species being is made explicitly by Isobel Armstrong in *The Radical Aesthetic*:

[T]he components of aesthetic life are those that are embedded in the processes and practices of consciousness – playing and dreaming, thinking and feeling . . . These processes – experiences that keep us alive – are common to everyone, common to what the early Marx called species being.[38]

Although Armstrong focuses on the continuities between poetry and play rather than poetry and labour, nonetheless her account, like Caudwell's, stresses poetry's productiveness. For Armstrong both poetry and play make possible that 'essential cognitive leap which radically changes one's relation to reality' and hence both need to be understood as 'cognate' activities. Hence, for Armstrong as for Caudwell, the aesthetic is 'emancipatory' because it makes 'new kinds of knowledge' possible.[39]

There is a sense in which Chartist poetic production demonstrates Armstrong's claims regarding the quotidian *and therefore* democratic nature of the aesthetic. For, as will be shown in the succeeding chapters, Chartist poetry exemplifies Armstrong's definition of the artwork as 'a form of thinking, a request for knowledge, rather than as a privileged kind of creativity'.[40] To appreciate the full political significance of this conception of the aesthetic it is only necessary to consider Jacques Ranciere's distinction between 'strategic' and 'aesthetic' conceptions of the avant-garde. The strategic avant-garde understands itself as 'an advanced detachment that derives its ability to lead from its ability to read and interpret the signs of history'. Its exemplary political form, according to Ranciere, is that of the 'Leninist' vanguard party (of the sort to which Caudwell belonged). Ranciere might also have adduced the 'Romantic' poet as prophet or seer and possessed of superior insight as its cultural incarnation. In contrast, the aesthetic avant-garde refers to 'the meta-political idea of global political subjectivity, the idea of the potentiality inherent in the innovative sensible modes of experience that anticipate a community to come'.[41] Chartism understood the production of poetry by

---

[37] *Ibid.*, 174.   [38] Armstrong, *The Radical Aesthetic*, 2–3.

[39] *Ibid.*, 37–41.   [40] *Ibid.*, 79–80.

[41] J. Ranciere, *The Politics of Aesthetics* (Continuum, 2004), 29–30. I am grateful to Peter Howarth for first directing me towards Ranciere's work on the aesthetic.

its members precisely in these terms – as a demonstration of inherent human capacities which found their rational political expression in democracy. However, whilst the democratic and the aesthetic are both grounded in fundamental human attributes, Armstrong is careful not to collapse the former into the latter. Indeed, in her account the aesthetic is a necessary but by no means sufficient condition for politics: 'The aesthetic is not the political, but it may make the political possible'.[42]

The Radical Aesthetic moves beyond *Illusion and Reality* in respect of its theorisation of the forms of knowledge embodied in the poem. One of the limitations of *Illusion and Reality* is that as a result of its commitment to the 'strategic avant-garde', it envisages the effect of an artwork on its audience only as an attenuated version of its effect on its producer. In short, Caudwell privileges the producer over the recipient; the former has the superior insight which the artwork communicates (in a diluted form) to the latter.[43] Armstrong evades this hierarchy by focusing attention on the artwork rather than on its producer and, more importantly, by insisting on understanding that artwork 'as a form of mediation, a tentative, interactive form'. Drawing in particular on Gillian Rose's reading of Hegel, Armstrong invites us to consider not the particular knowledge generated by a specific artwork but the type (or form) of thinking made possible by the aesthetic:

Hegel [posits] mediation as a mobile, structuring *activity*, not a separable intermediary element, a relational movement, not an entity.

. . .

Mediation is a kind of three-dimensional thinking. It reconfigures experience and temporalities rather than creating an ever-new present.[44]

Elsewhere, Armstrong makes it clear that this form of thinking is one which understands that 'emotions should be included within a definition of the rational' and thus is able to integrate affect with analysis.[45] Rather than the 'flat' binary of concept/object (or sign/referent), mediation gives us concept/affect/object (sign/signified/referent). Moreover, it is clear that the artwork's ability to reconfigure temporalities in fact endows mediation with additional cognitive dimensions.[46] In short, the artwork

---

[42] Armstrong, *The Radical Aesthetic*, 43.   [43] Caudwell, *Illusion and Reality*, 224–5.
[44] Armstrong, *The Radical Aesthetic*, 59.   [45] *Ibid.*, 46.
[46] *Ibid.*, 68–9. Once more Caudwell partially anticipates this line of argument: 'We do not appear to take up an emotional attitude to a piece of reality; it is there, given in the reality: that is the way of emotional cognition. In poetic cognition, objects are presented already stamped with feeling-judgements. Hence the adaptive value of poetry. It is like a real emotional experience.' *Illusion and Reality*, 240.

constitutes an inescapably flawed attempt at totalisation and it is in this that its value resides. Similarly, the intelligibility of our experiences rests on a necessarily flawed apprehension of the totality; the very simplest acts of perception involve at least simultaneity and as we rarely achieve such a degree of single-mindedness, most of our conscious life involves the recognition of an extensive network of relations, agents and objects. (This is implicitly conceded by most forms of post-modern and post-structuralist thought which misrecognise the category of the sublime (that which exceeds our ability to represent it) and whose valorisation of fragmentation would lose all cultural meaning and force were it not for the continuing, but unacknowledged, presence of totality as the back-ground which throws the fragment into relief.) This conception of the totality owes much to Castoriadis' notion of the 'social' as that which is:

given as the structure – indissociable form and content – of human ensembles, yet which goes beyond any given structure, an ungraspable productive element, an unformed forming element, something that is always more and always other. It is something that can be presented only in and through the *institution* but which is always infinitely more than the institution.[47]

The artwork, despite its necessary inadequacy, provides us with both a sensible apprehension of totality and the opportunity to reflect on the concept of totality.[48] Returning to the concrete example of Chartism and Chartist poetry, one way of understanding the Chartist movement is to see it as a response of a significant proportion of the British working classes to the totality of changes being wrought by industrial capitalism. Chartist poetry can then be seen both as being enabled by its own imaginary, and as one of the means by which the movement sought to articulate (express and join together, hence totalise) its own under-standing of this process. In short, poetry shows us the very process of the movement 'thinking out loud'.

More recently, Jacques Ranciere has argued (like Caudwell and Arm-strong) that 'aesthetic acts . . . create new modes of sense perception and induce novel forms of political subjectivity'.[49] In *The Politics of Aesthetics*, he insists that since Romanticism, art has played a fundamental role in the constitution of human beings as historical agents: 'Politics and art,

---

[47] C. Castoriadis, *The Imaginary Institution of Society* (Cambridge: Polity Press, 1997), 50. Furthermore, Castoriadis argues, as human agents our relation to the social is one of '*inherence*' rather than '*dependence*', *ibid.*, 112.

[48] The concept of totality here is understood, following Fredric Jameson on Lukacs, as 'a metho-dological standard', see F. Jameson, *The Political Unconscious* (Routledge, 1989), 52.

[49] Ranciere, *Politics of Aesthetics*, 9.

like forms of knowledge, construct "fictions", that is to say *material* rearrangements of signs and images, relationships between what is said, between what is done and what can be done.'[50] Again, like Caudwell and Armstrong, Ranciere identifies aesthetic capability as our species being when, alluding to Aristotle's definition of man as a political animal, he declares: 'Man is a political animal because he is a literary animal who lets himself be diverted from his "natural" purpose by the power of words.' Indeed, Ranciere arguably makes a larger claim than either for the political significance of the aesthetic when he claims that the 'channels for political subjectivization are not those of imaginary identification but those of "literary" disincorporation'.[51] For Ranciere language 'is disincorporated when the only materiality that supports it is its own'.[52] In short ' "literary" disincorporation' strongly resembles 'referential aberration' except that where the latter facilitates an endlessly regressive analytics, the former enables multiple forms of agency.[53]

For Ranciere, aesthetics and politics are also mutually constitutive in a way which differs from both Caudwell and Armstrong. In *The Politics of Aesthetics* Ranciere defines aesthetics as 'a specific regime for identifying and reflecting on the arts: a mode of articulation between ways of doing and making, their corresponding forms of visibility, and possible ways of thinking about their relationships'.[54] Hence Ranciere identifies a 'primary aesthetics' (analogous to Kant's *a priori* forms) which through the 'delimitation of space and time, of the visible and the invisible, of speech and noise . . . simultaneously determines the place and the stake of politics as a form of experience'.[55] Thus, for Ranciere, 'aesthetics' plays a structural role in demarcating the 'political' (a proposition absent from Armstrong and Caudwell), whilst 'aesthetic acts' enrich 'politics' by generating new forms of experience and knowledge (a proposition central to Armstrong's and Caudwell's theorisation of aesthetic agency). Ranciere finds another affinity between art and politics insofar as both are 'contingent notions' (in that both power and individual artworks can exist independent of the categories of 'politics' and 'art').[56] Similarly, neither has a predetermined outcome: politics and art can contribute equally well

---

[50] *Ibid.*, 39.   [51] *Ibid.*, 40.   [52] *Ibid.*, 57.
[53] As Gabriel Rockhill notes in his 'Translator's Introduction' to *The Politics of Aesthetics*, 'Ranciere saw in the politics of difference the risk of reversing Marx's statement in the *Thesis on Feuerbach*: "We tried to transform the world in diverse ways, now it is a matter of interpreting it" ', *ibid.*, 1–2.
[54] *Ibid.*, 10.   [55] *Ibid.*, 13.
[56] *Ibid.*, 51. For a discussion of the three 'Regimes of Art' (the 'ethical', the 'representative' and the 'aesthetic') and the differing forms of politics therein, see 21–30.

to projects of domination or emancipation.[57] Likewise, Ranciere argues, there is no necessary correlation between artistic form and political practice – the meaning of form 'is often in fact decided upon by a state of conflict that is anterior to [it]'.[58] These are necessary correctives to the implicit optimism of Caudwell and Armstrong who are concerned with the emancipatory potential of the aesthetic. It also serves as a salutary reminder that Chartism and its poetry (which this study celebrates as a form of resistance undertaken in the name of an emancipatory project) were both ultimately overwhelmed by a more powerful conjunction of aesthetic and political forms.

For Ranciere 'primary aesthetics' are closely connected with the social division of labour. He argues, for example, that Plato's banning of artisans from government also provides the basis for his subsequent expulsion of the poets from his ideal Republic.[59] Similarly, his description of the artwork (in the 'aesthetic regime') as containing 'the power of a form of thought that has become foreign to itself', carries suggestive echoes of Marx's account of alienated labour.[60] The constitutive social role played by the 'aesthetic' in Ranciere's account suggests another reason why the Chartist movement made such an investment in poetry. Put simply, Chartism possessed a deep-seated, almost instinctual (and certainly a non-theorised) apprehension that the aesthetic was a necessary part of any resistance to utilitarianism and laissez-faire economics: both of which were blighting working-class lives in the 1840s and both of which were notoriously hostile to notions of aesthetic value. A complete articulation of the interplay between aesthetics, utilitarianism and economics in this period would require another study, but it is not difficult to see how ideas of craft and skill in the labour process might intersect with ideas of aesthetic value.[61] Certainly, later in the century, thinkers like Ruskin and Morris were to frame their respective social critiques on the need to substitute aesthetically satisfying 'work' for aesthetically degraded 'toil'.[62]

---

[57] *Ibid.*, 19.   [58] *Ibid.*, 62.   [59] *Ibid.*, 12–13.

[60] *Ibid.*, 23. In the *Paris Manuscripts*, Marx writes: 'the object which labour produces – labour's product – confronts it as *something alien*, as a *power independent* of the producer', R. C. Tucker (ed.), *The Marx-Engels Reader* (New York: W. W. Norton, 1978), 71.

[61] For details of the role which the defence of 'craft' and 'skill' played in the industrial disputes and social debates of this period, see M. Berg, *The Machinery Question and the Making of Political Economy 1815–1848* (Cambridge University Press, 1982); R. Gray, *The Factory Question and Industrial England, 1830–1860* (Cambridge University Press, 1996); N. Thompson, *The Real Rights of Man. Political Economies for the Working Classes 1775–1850* (Pluto Press, 1998).

[62] See in particular Ruskin's 'The Nature of Gothic' from *The Stones of Venice* and William Morris's 'Useful Work versus Useless Toil'.

Chartism's investment in poetry, therefore, represented an achieved, if unstable, synthesis of the emancipatory potential of individual artworks with an intimation that, due to its structuring role in what Ranciere calls 'the Distribution of the Sensible', the aesthetic underpins the most fundamental forms of resistance to the ideologies of capitalist modernity.

This hypothesis is bolstered if we pursue Castoriadis' contention in *The Imaginary Institution of Society* that reification rather than exploitation constitutes capitalism's central contradiction.[63] Reification is arguably the forgotten category of nineteenth-century labour history which tends to focus on the struggle against exploitation (wages, hours and conditions). Yet an era when bourgeois triumphalists such as Dr Andrew Ure, in works such as *The Philosophy of Manufactures* (1835), were explicitly theorising (and championing) the virtues of reducing the worker to the status of an appendage to the machine, and where 'hand' served as a metonym for factory worker, is clearly one in which the drive to reification is already underway.

Historians have often presented Chartism as the confluence of pre-existing forms of working-class protest: the coming together of social, economic and political discontents symbolised by the workhouse, the factory and the 'great betrayal' of 1832.[64] This conflux also brought together a variety of ideological formations. Tory-radicals and Tory-paternalists such as J. R. Stephens and Richard Oastler had played a prominent role in the anti-New Poor Law campaign and the Factory Movement, and they remained an ongoing ideological presence within Chartism.[65] At the opposite end of the spectrum, Owenite socialists also contributed to the ideological richness of the Chartist movement. Between these two poles many other variants of radicalism (Huntite, Cobbettite and even, in the movement's earliest days, 'philosophical') jostled for position, to say nothing of the differences in political outlook and temper between Chartism's various leaders (Lovett, O'Connor and O'Brien) and its different core constituencies (London artisans, trades in direct competition with the factories, and the factory proletariat).[66] Yet in spite of these differences (which did at times issue in internecine conflict

---

[63] Castoriadis, *The Imaginary Institution of Society*, 16.
[64] See for example, Edward Royle, *Chartism* (Longman, 1986), 6–17.
[65] For an outline of 'Tory Radicalism' see, for example, C. Driver, *Tory Radical: The Life of Richard Oastler* (New York: Oxford University Press, 1946).
[66] Benthamite Radicals such as the MP J. A. Roebuck (who assisted in drawing up the Charter) often described themselves as 'Philosophical Radicals'. For further details of this grouping see W. Thomas, *The Philosophic Radicals* (Oxford University Press, 1979).

between Chartism's leaders and, more rarely, amongst its rank and file), the movement somehow held itself together for more than a decade. In order to achieve this, there had to be a meaningful articulation between these different ideological trends, and it is the contention of this study that the Chartist imaginary (and, therefore, Chartist poetry) played a key role in securing that meaningful articulation. As will be shown in succeeding chapters, Chartist poetry contributes to this process in numerous ways. It does this partly by the 'simple' act of representing discrete fractions of the movement, thereby making them more intelligible to other parts. Moreover, precisely by representing these same fractions as fractions of the *same* movement, an underlying shared identity is adumbrated even whilst it remains undefined. The polysemic nature of poetry clearly assists in this; the creation of multiple points of identification, the ability of the word to carry shades of meaning, facilitates the process whereby group x comes to recognise aspects of group y as consonant with its own aspirations and values. Beyond this, poetry's affective capacity helps to generate the emotional bonds, the common feelings, which are as necessary a part of any movement's infrastructure as its organisational forms.[67] It is this dimension of language use which prompts Ranciere's declaration: 'The channels for political subjectivization are not those of imaginary identification but those of 'literary' disincorporation.'

If we pass from identification with the movement to a consideration of the movement's identity we find one irreducible component which expresses itself by means of two different signs: the 'People's Charter' and the 'Six Points'. Although at one level these signs can be seen as synonyms – the 'People's Charter' contains the 'Six Points', and the 'Six Points' comprise the 'People's Charter' – and are often treated as such, the relationship between them is more complex. As Miles Taylor has observed, although in Chartist discourse the term 'the six points' became widely used from around 1840, only the 1848 petition contained the demand; the 1839 petition contained five points and the 1842 petition eight points.[68] Conversely, Joseph Sturge's Complete Suffrage conference in 1842 foundered on the very sign of the 'People's Charter' itself, when Chartist attachment to and middle-class radicalism's distaste for this term

---

[67] Indeed, it might be argued that the role played by common feelings was particularly important in the earliest days of the movement, i.e. prior to the creation of a recognisable institutional infrastructure in the form of the National Charter Association (founded July 1840).

[68] Miles Taylor, 'The Six Points: Chartism and the Reform of Parliament', in O. Ashton *et al.* (eds.), *The Chartist Legacy*, 1.

constituted an irreconcilable difference.[69] Traditionally, Taylor suggests, historians have accounted for this discrepancy by arguing that the 'actual content of the Charter mattered less than its symbolic function'.[70] Taylor disagrees with this approach and demonstrates how careful attention to the Charter's content reveals the originality of the movement's analysis of the country's political ills.[71] In part, Taylor stresses this in order to avoid reducing the Charter to the status of 'a flag of convenience under which the various forms of protest could be mobilised'.[72] Yet if we turn to the substantive content of the Charter we find that thirteen of its twenty-two pages were 'devoted to proposed reforms in the registration of voters, the selection of election officials, and the actual means of taking votes'.[73] This degree of technical specification does indeed demonstrate the sophisticated nature of Chartism's political analysis, but it is not calculated to inspire and sustain a mass political movement by itself.

Rather than regarding the symbolic as an inchoate form of the political it is possible to pursue Slavoj Zizek's contention that 'poetic displacements and condensations are not just secondary aspects of an underlying ideological struggle but the very terrain of this struggle'.[74] Viewed through this lens both the 'People's Charter' and the 'Six Points' represent much more than their manifest content. To borrow from Marx's analysis of the symbolic dimension of proletarian revolt – 'here the content goes beyond the phrase'.[75] That this was widely understood at the time is attested to by contemporary commentators as diverse as Macaulay, Carlyle and O'Brien, all of whom identified a further, deeper meaning in the 'Six Points'.[76] The difference between the literal meaning of the 'Six Points' and the range of symbolic meanings which they generated and with which they were invested, simultaneously marks the operation and the field of the Chartist imaginary.

[69] For an account of the Sturge conference see R. C. Gammage, *History of the Chartist Movement 1837–1854* (Merlin Press, 1969 [1894]), 241–4.

[70] Taylor, 'The Six Points', 2.   [71] *Ibid.*, 1–19.   [72] *Ibid.*, 18.   [73] *Ibid.*, 11.

[74] S. Zizek, 'Afterword', in Ranciere, *Politics of Aesthetics*, 77.

[75] K. Marx, 'The Eighteenth Brumaire of Louis Bonaparte', in R. C. Tucker (ed.), *The Marx–Engels Reader*, 597.

[76] In the Parliamentary debate on the 1842 Chartist Petition, Macaulay said 'I am opposed to universal suffrage [because] we can never, without absolute danger, entrust the supreme government of the country to any class, which would, to a moral certainty commit great and systematic inroads against the security of property', quoted in A. L. Morton and G. Tate, *The British Labour Movement 1770–1920* (Lawrence & Wishart, 1956), 91. On the Chartist side, O'Brien was equally clear as to the significance of universal suffrage, 'The moment the people obtain a Parliament of their own, the whole of Society will undergo a rigid scrutiny', in M. Morris (ed.), *From Cobbett to the Chartists* (Lawrence & Wishart, 1948), 144.

Both signs, the 'People's Charter' and the 'Six Points', confer a dual identity; simultaneously marking an exclusion from the body-politic which is not only a demand for inclusion but also (and perhaps more importantly) a claim to universality, 'the stand-in for the Whole of Society in its universality, against the particular power-interests of the aristocracy or oligarchy'.[77] At the same time this claim is also an aspiration, a desire for a radically reconstituted social order which makes good the claim. This is not a programmatic manifesto. Rather, it is the expression of a 'not this'; a wish for something not simply different but better. (The desire for 'better' indicates the existence of things in the present which must be preserved and this prevents a slide into nihilism.) In short, it is a form of thinking capable of generating many different contents. The radically reconstituted social order is the underlying, ideal, totality which cannot be grasped in its entirety but whose structuring presence none-theless underpins specific contents (demands, aims) which function as synechdochal traces of the whole. An individual Chartist poem is just such a synechdochal trace and this constitutes the poem's unique his-torical knowledge.

The notion of the Chartist imaginary which this study seeks to elabo-rate describes a theoretical field which is derived, in part, from Althus-serian 'Ideology', Raymond Williams's 'Structure of Feeling', Fredric Jameson's 'Political Unconscious', as well as Castoriadis' work on the 'imaginary'. However, it must be emphasised at the outset that this is not an attempt at a grand Hegelian synthesis which sublates these prior the-oretical moments.

Insofar as the Chartist imaginary involves the imaginary representation of real conditions and the subsequent production of specific forms of action, it closely resemble Althusser's concept of ideology.[78] However, as numerous critics have observed, Althusserian ideology generates pre-determined, and thus essentially functionalist, forms of agency. Although Althusser's theoretical framework appears to contain the possibility of multiple and contradictory interpellations arising out of the plethora of 'ideological state apparatuses' and also does not rule out the possibility of resistance to specific interpellations, such contingencies are noticeably absent from his discussion of the actual operations of ideology.[79] In addition, Althusser's account is not so much ahistorical as atemporal. Both the past and the future with all their interpellatory possibilities are

---

[77] S. Zizek, 'Afterword', 70.   [78] L. Althusser, *Essays on Ideology* (Verso, 1984).
[79] E. P. Thompson, *The Poverty of Theory* (Merlin, 1978).

curiously absent and all interpellations occur in 'homogeneous, empty
time' (to borrow Walter Benjamin's phrase). This loss of alternative
temporalities drastically limits the possibilities for anti-hegemonic agency.
As future chapters will show, conceptions of both past and future constituted a crucial ideological resource for the Chartist movement. The
Chartist imaginary, therefore, includes both a sense of contingency and
of temporal multiplicity which is absent from Althusserian ideology.

   Different temporalities play a key role in Raymond Williams' thought,
where the concepts of 'Dominant, Residual and Emergent' are analogous
to, but not strictly identical with, the notions of past, present and future.
Nor is it an accident that arguably Williams' most important theoretical
innovation – the concept of a 'Structure of Feeling' follows on immediately from his discussion of these terms in *Marxism and Literature*. It
proceeds from Williams' recognition that:

Practical consciousness is almost always different from official consciousness . . . It
is a kind of feeling and thinking which is indeed social and material, but each in an
embryonic phase before it can become fully articulate and defined exchange.[80]

Williams makes it clear that his intention is to overcome the tendency of
criticism to '[reduce] the social to fixed forms' by redirecting our attention to the 'forming and formative processes' which actively constitute
culture (and society and history) rather than the 'formed wholes' which
are their residual product.[81] 'Structure of Feeling' indicates both that
'meanings and values . . . are actively lived and felt' and that this necessarily contingent process nonetheless constitutes a 'structure', 'a set, with
specific internal relations, at once interlocking and in tension'. Furthermore, the concept deliberately emphasises the importance of those
'specifically affective elements of consciousness'. In an anticipation of
Armstrong's work, Williams argues for the necessity of overcoming the
thought/emotion binary, 'not feeling against thought, but thought as felt
and feeling as thought'.[82] It also identifies a particular role for the
'aesthetic' as the realm of certain 'specificities' which can yield valuable,
perhaps unique, historical knowledge. He argues that these 'defining
forms and conventions in art and literature' need to be understood 'as
social formations of a specific kind which may in turn be seen as the
articulation (often the only fully available articulation) of structures of
feeling which as living processes are much more widely experienced'.[83]

---

[80] Raymond Williams, *Marxism and Literature* (Oxford University Press, 1977), 130–1.
[81] *Ibid.*, 128–9.   [82] *Ibid.*,132.   [83] *Ibid.*, 133.

Indeed, Williams ends his discussion of this concept by stressing the unique quality which the aesthetic embeds in the structure of feeling.[84]

For Williams the structure of feeling is a 'cultural hypothesis' and he offers a few tentative speculations concerning 'the complex relation of differentiated structures of feeling to differentiated classes'.[85] In part, this study is an extended application of this cultural hypothesis to a particular period of British history; an attempt to capture what Williams describes as 'social experiences *in solution*' and to retain a sense of 'the known complexities, the experienced tensions, shifts, and uncertainties, the intricate forms of unevenness and confusion' which distinguish 'practical consciousness' from 'world-view'.[86] However, the idea of the Chartist imaginary departs from the structure of feeling in two particular ways. Firstly, Williams privileges those artworks most closely connected with 'emergent formations'; it is here, he argues, that 'the structure of feeling, *as solution*' operates.[87] In contrast, this study is generally concerned with poetry that is more closely associated with the 'residual' rather than the 'emergent'. Although by a dialectical twist it might be argued that the residual elements of Chartism are also precursors of an emergent formation, in as much as the 'red republicanism' which emerges in the late 1840s anticipates the socialism of the late nineteenth century. However, this study is more interested (particularly in Chapter 5) in the ways in which the residual facilitates working-class resistance in this period.

Similarly, where Williams' privileging of the emergent suggests an affinity with the 'strategic' conception of the avant-garde (certain works are more valuable than others precisely because they constitute 'an advanced detachment' which anticipates the forward advance of history) – a suggestion bolstered by his explicit identification of the canonically secure Charles Dickens and Emily Bronte as exemplary figures – this study is interested not in a handful of great poems but in the generality of Chartist poetic production: good, bad and indifferent. This should not be seen as contesting Williams' insistence on the necessity of literary evaluation but rather reflects the different historical moments of the two texts. *Marxism and Literature*, written during a period of working-class militancy and advance, is understandably interested in the future, whereas this study, written during a period of profound defeat, is concerned with identifying those resources necessary for the undertaking of a journey of

---

[84] Williams refers to 'a mode of social formation, explicit and recognizable in specific kinds of art, which is distinguishable from other social and semantic formations by its articulation of *presence*', *ibid.*, 135.

[85] *Ibid.*, 134. [86] *Ibid.*, 133 and 129. [87] *Ibid.*, 134.

hope. Every Chartist poem, irrespective of aesthetic value, enacts a structure of feeling – bears witness in some way to the values and aspirations of
the Chartist movement. To adapt Walter Benjamin, each poem is an
image of the past threatened with an irretrievable disappearance if not
recognised by the present.[88]

At first sight Fredric Jameson's concern with narrative and narrativisation in *The Political Unconscious* appears unpropitious for the study of
poetry: a confirmation of Eagleton's observation regarding the reluctance
of Marxist critics to engage with poetry.[89] However, early in his study
Jameson suggests an equivalence between 'narrativisation' and 'text-
ualisation' in respect of their relation to the 'Real'.[90] This equivalence is
confirmed later when Jameson defines the 'political-historical' moment of
criticism as one which regards 'the production of aesthetic or narrative
form … as an ideological act in its own right, with the function of
inventing imaginary or formal "solutions" to unresolvable contradictions'.[91] There is nothing here (in theoretical terms) which prevents us
from positing the 'political unconscious' as a precondition for the generation of poetry. Rather, the question is whether the application of
Jameson's ideas produces a significant critical yield.

Clearly, Chartist poetry is on one level symptomatic of a set of profound social crises and thus evidences those 'unresolvable social contradictions' which, for Jameson, generate narrative. Similarly, Chartist poetry
abounds in 'imaginary solutions' of various kinds. More specifically, it is
not difficult to see that Jameson's conception of the political unconscious
itself, as consisting of the repressed knowledge of a sequence of modes
of production, is directly applicable to Chartist poetry.[92] As a result of its
co-existence with the consolidation of industrial capitalism (and as part
of this, the inexorable decline of certain occupational groups such as the
handloom weavers) Chartist poetry is produced during a historical
moment when different modes of production are all too painfully visible.[93]

---

[88] 'For every image of the past that is not recognized by the present as one of its own concerns
threatens to disappear irretrievably.' W. Benjamin, 'Theses on the Philosophy of History' in
Illuminations (Fontana Press, 1992), 247.

[89] '[P]oetry is the most searching test of a Marxist or para-Marxist criticism accustomed to dealing in
structural generalities and historical abstractions.' Eagleton, *Criticism and Ideology*, 36.

[90] Jameson, *The Political Unconscious*, 35.   [91] *Ibid.*, 79.   [92] *Ibid.*, 35.

[93] Whilst these are not modes of production in the classical Marxist sense, they do represent
significant transitions within the capitalist mode of production. More importantly, they serve to
illustrate Jameson's point about the historical co-existence of different moments of production (in
this case that of industrial capital with an older mercantile mode) and also, indirectly, to indicate
the necessity of repression insofar as the suffering of the industrial working class clearly requires an
investment in ideas of 'progress' and the 'future'.

For Jameson, the political unconscious is a conceptual tool with very particular methodological implications insofar as its elaboration requires a critical method based on 'three concentric frameworks' (or levels) of interpretation and analysis; 'political-historical', 'constitutive class struggle' and 'mode of production'.[94] The main features of the 'political-historical' level have already been discussed and the mere existence of Chartist poetry offers local corroboration of its positing of a generative relationship between social contradiction and textual production. At the second level ('constitutive class struggle'), Jameson calls for the text to be 'grasped as a symbolic move in an essentially polemic and strategic ideological confrontation between the classes'.[95] Once again, this is uncontentious with regard to Chartist poetry. Indeed, it is difficult to imagine a critical approach to such poetry which did not take cognizance of this dimension.

For Jameson, the second level is also the level of the 'ideologeme'; a notoriously slippery concept as suggested by Jameson's own description of it as 'an amphibious formation'. According to Jameson the ideologeme can:

manifest itself either as a pseudoidea – a conceptual or belief system, an abstract value, an opinion or prejudice – or as a protonarrative, a kind of ultimate class fantasy about the 'collective characters' which are the classes in opposition . . . as a construct it must be susceptible to both a conceptual description and a narrative manifestation all at once.[96]

Once more, it is not difficult to see how Chartism's internal debates over strategy, particularly those concerning the use of political violence or 'physical force', can be construed as ideologemes. As will be shown in succeeding chapters the vexed debate over the use of violence involved both 'conceptual description' and 'narrative manifestation' – respectively, the values and the circumstances which legitimated the use of such violence. Furthermore, Chartism's internal debates were simultaneously part of an ideological contest with external forces (middle-class reformers, Whig and Tory politicians) regarding appropriate forms of political behaviour.

The ideologeme as 'an amphibious formation' is surely intended to capture the sense of fluidity and flexibility with which Williams invests his structure of feeling. Yet it is also an unbalanced concept wherein the fluidity of the ideologeme as 'pseudoidea' (where it may be concept, belief, value, opinion or prejudice) is in stark contrast to its rigidity as

---

[94] Jameson, *The Political Unconscious*, 75–6.   [95] *Ibid.*, 85.   [96] *Ibid.*, 100.

'protonarrative' (where it is always a 'class fantasy'). In addition, the ideologeme (unlike the structure of feeling) has little to say on the question of affect, which may be vestigially present in 'prejudice' but otherwise appears entirely absent. Thus, although this study adopts Jameson's methodology by treating Chartist poems as symbolic interventions in a wider class struggle, it prefers Williams' conceptualisation of the nature of this intervention as a structure of feeling rather than as ideologeme. Similarly, the specific insight identified by Jameson's third level – the mode of production, wherein 'the individual text [is] restructured as a field of force in which the dynamics of sign systems of several distinct modes of production can be registered and apprehended' – is indicated in this study either by Williams' concepts of dominant, residual and emergent or by Benjamin's notion of different temporalities.[97]

Chartist poetry is understood here as a concentrated or specific manifestation of the general Chartist imaginary. As such, the individual poem is understood as being simultaneously an attempt to make meaning (its ideological/symbolic work) and to create agency (its aesthetic function). Its ability to construct forms of agency is crucially dependent on its ability to 'imagine otherwise', which is usually (but not invariably) bound up with specific conceptualisations of time. In order to achieve this the poem both draws on and manifests the imaginary, understood as:

a creation, the positing (institution) by the social imaginary of a figure or group of figures that are not real, which *makes* concrete figures (materializations, particular instances of the 'word-image') *exist* as *what* they are: word-figures, signs (and not noises or marks). Imaginary: an unmotivated creation that exists only in and through the positing of images.[98]

In addition to this political work, the imaginary also makes the poem the repository of unique historical knowledge which, following Williams, we can describe as 'social experience in solution'.

Having established (in theoretical terms) the political, aesthetic and historical significance of Chartist poetry, it is now possible to consider its literary significance. Generally speaking, Chartist poetry has been largely invisible for much of the past half-century and has only recently begun to appear in anthologies of Victorian verse.[99] In part, its visibility has been determined by the broader social-historical context. It was buried along

[97] *Ibid.*, 101.   [98] Castoriadis, *The Imaginary Institution of Society*, 247.
[99] V. Cunningham (ed.), *The Victorians: An Anthology of Poetry and Poetics* (Oxford: Blackwell, 2000). T. J. Collins and V. J. Rundle (eds.), *The Broadview Anthology of Victorian Poetry and Poetic Theory* (Peterborough, Ontario: Broadview, 2000).

with the cultural memory of Chartism in the second half of the nine-teenth century and neglected for much of the twentieth. The limited presence of working-class students in British academia has meant the absence of the archival-retrieval projects which played such a crucial role in establishing women's writing and women's history as important fields of academic study.

However, Chartist poetry presents a clutch of 'aesthetic' problems which have also contributed to its exclusion from the canon. Chartist poetry is often regarded as an aesthetic terminus, the last gasp of an exhausted romanticism which leads nowhere. As Florence Boos has remarked of nineteenth-century working-class writers more generally, their commitment to 'reformist romanticism' and 'populist' modes of poetry 'has also estranged them from other paradigms that have gene-rally guided *academic* taste, in the later twentieth century and beyond'.[100] The anachronistic, if not archaic, status of Chartist poetry creates diffi-culties of reading and interpretation which are multiplied by the addi-tional aesthetic challenges which it presents. In particular, the public and collective dimensions of Chartist poetry chafe against a subsequently established poetic tradition which valorises the private and the individual. Similarly, the straightforward oral register and the unambiguous political commitment of much Chartist poetry is sometimes felt to be rather crude and simplistic when measured against the linguistic complexity (and hence the political ambiguities and ambivalences) which are considered to be the characteristics of 'real' poetry. In short, 'Lines on the Conviction of the Glasgow Cotton Spinners' sounds incongruous as the title of a poem whilst 'Soliloquy of the Spanish Cloister' does not.

The difficulty of reading Chartist poetry has also been increased, albeit inadvertently, by the existence of a powerful critical tradition exempli-fied by E. D. H. Johnson's *The Alien Vision of Victorian Poetry* (1952) and Robert Langbaum's *The Poetry of Experience* (1957), which understands Victorian poetry in terms of what Armstrong calls 'an increasingly severe lesion between the poet and society'.[101] Unable to intervene in the public sphere, poetry instead becomes increasingly concerned with individual, subjective, psychological states: in Hallam's phrase 'that return of the mind upon itself and the habit of seeking relief in idiosyncrasies rather

---

[100] F. Boos, 'Working-Class Poetry' in R. Cronin, A. Chapman and A. H. Harrison (eds.), *A Companion to Victorian Poetry* (Oxford: Blackwell, 2002), 224.
[101] Armstrong, *Victorian Poetry*, 11.

than community of interest',[102] or, to use Ekbert Faas's pithy title, *Retreat into the Mind* (1988). Once again Chartist poetry does not conform to this pattern and its exceptionalism is underscored by its eschewal of the dramatic monologue, long seen as the quintessential Victorian poetic form.[103]

It is tempting to extend Disraeli's notion of 'Two nations; between whom there is no intercourse and no sympathy' in order to construct Chartist poetry as the (suppressed) 'other' of Victorian poetry. These 'dwellers in different zones' (to continue the Disraelian motif) – the one: collective, public, political and oral; the other, individual, private, psychological and densely textual – become the poetic counterparts of 'the rich' and 'the poor'. Having established this binary opposition it would be possible to re-orient its evaluation around the first set of terms thereby producing a situation in which Chartist poetry becomes aesthetically superior to its canonical antagonist. However, such an absolute opposition would be meretricious, for just as Disraeli was concerned to reveal the true identity of his 'two nations', so it is necessary to find a way in which Chartist poetry and Victorian poetry can be brought together in a mutually enriching dialogue.

Two recent developments within this critical tradition, Isobel Armstrong's *Victorian Poetry: Poetry, Poetics and Politics* (1993) and Matthew Reynolds' *The Realms of Verse 1830–1870: English Poetry in a Time of Nation-Building* (2001), offer suggestions as to how such a dialogue might be framed. Whilst not dismissing the 'psychological' tradition (of Faas *et al.*), both Armstrong and Reynolds seek to redirect attention to the various social and political engagements of Victorian poetry and in so doing, both find new ways of reading Victorian poetry which offer the possibility of including Chartist poetry. The key features of this approach are articulated in Reynolds' summary of his discussion of Hegel and Coleridge (both, and especially the former, important figures in Armstrong's study):

The striking overlap between the discourses of political and poetic theory in this period does not of itself tell us anything about poetic practice. But it does make clear a network of interrelations and correspondences which were available for poets to explore if they so desired.[104]

[102] Cited in Philip Davis, *The Oxford English Literary History. Volume 8: 1830–1880. The Victorians* (Oxford University Press, 2002), 460.
[103] *Ibid.*, 463. Armstrong, *Victorian Poetry*, 13; E. Warwick Slinn, 'Dramatic Monologue' in R. Cronin *et al.*, (eds.), 80.
[104] Matthew Reynolds, *The Realms of Verse 1830–1870. English Poetry in a Time of Nation-building* (Oxford University Press, 2001), 62–3.

For Reynolds, these 'interrelations and correspondences' include poetry's exploration of the national spirit, an anxiety regarding the relation between public and private, and the consideration of marriage as 'the fundamental social relation' and are exemplified in the mid-Victorian poets' quest to synthesise three forms of unity – 'marital, aesthetic and political'.[105] For Armstrong, the 'problems of agency, consciousness, labour, language and representation become central' to Victorian poetry as well as Victorian society.[106]

The expanded range of concerns identified by Armstrong and Reynolds provides a way of theorising Chartist poetry as a distinctive variant within, rather than other to, Victorian poetry. The particular nature of the inheritance from Romanticism, the construction of the 'nation', the need to establish a proper definition of (and a correct balance between) the public and private spheres, the constitution of fundamental social relations, questions of agency, labour, language and representation – all constitute the underlying cultural matrix which generated both Chartist and Victorian poetry. What Chartist poetry presents, therefore, is a different articulation of these historical pressures, which illuminates (and in turn is illuminated by) those other forms of Victorian poetry. The example set by Armstrong, who reads Clough alongside a number of Chartist poets, could be usefully extended.[107] Thus, for example, Reynolds' analysis of Tennyson as a nationalist rather than a democratic poet might be contrasted with an analysis of Ernest Jones as a democratic rather than a nationalist poet.[108] The Chartist invocation of the 'people' is not quite the same as Tennyson's invocation of the 'nation', although both may have their origins in the desire to imagine an internally differentiated but non-antagonistic collectivity. Similarly, the apparent difference between the two forms (such as the comparative absence of psychological introspection and an interest in marital unity, and the corresponding presence of a collective voice and a confidence regarding the public role of poetry, in Chartist poetry) might provide the basis for thinking about the relationship between history and aesthetics across class society as a whole rather than within a single class.

Ultimately, any discussion of Chartist poetry as Victorian poetry must engage with the most influential recent theorisation of the latter, in the form of Armstrong's concept of the 'double poem' as elaborated in

[105] *Ibid.*, 17–18, 49, 52 and 72. [106] Armstrong, *Victorian Poetry*, 7.
[107] *Ibid.*, 191–8. [108] Reynolds, *The Realms of Verse*, 26.

Victorian Poetry: Poetry, Poetics and Politics. This account emphasises the 'belatedness' of Victorian poetry, which finds itself (or more accurately is required to find itself) in a world which is simultaneously post-revolutionary, post-industrial, post-Kantian and post-teleological.[109] This historical condition, Armstrong argues, gives rise not only to a series of concerns regarding agency, labour, representation and power but also to a specific aesthetic form which she terms the 'double poem'. The dramatic monologue is the most obvious but by no means the only manifestation of the 'double poem' as her choice of paradigmatic examples – Tennyson's 'Mariana' and Browning's 'Love Among the Ruins' – makes clear. Arguing for the necessity of focusing on the double poem as a response to and an engagement with a particular matrix of historical-cultural problems (rather than attempting to codify its technical features), Armstrong defines the double poem as:

a deeply sceptical form. It draws attention to the epistemology which governs the construction of the self and its relationships and to the cultural conditions in which those relationships are made. It is an expressive model and an episte-mological model simultaneously.[110]

In addition, she argues that the double poem is 'inveterately political' precisely because it is 'founded on debate and contest' and that this requires (and assumes) an active reader 'compelled to be internal to the poem's contradictions and [who] recomposes the poem's processes in the act of comprehending them as ideological struggle'.[111]

There are some suggestive correspondences here between canonical Victorian and Chartist poetry. Indeed 'inveterately political', 'founded on debate and contest', concerned with agency, labour, representation and power, and requiring an active readership, seems to provide a blueprint for the ideal Chartist poem. Perhaps this is hardly surprising if we consider that Chartist poets were subject to similar historical and cultural pressures. Thus, the double poem offers a potential solution to the perennial challenge of finding the historical significance of a given literary form. The final part of this chapter seeks to articulate (in the dual sense of expressing and connecting by joints) the literary kinship between Chartist and Victorian poetry. It will do this by applying the concept of the double poem to three Chartist poems published in the *Northern Star* (the full text of which can be found in Appendix A).

[109] Armstrong, *Victorian Poetry*, 4.   [110] *Ibid.*, 13.   [111] *Ibid.*, 17.

Charles Davlin's 'Questions from the Loom' begins with a direct address warning the 'tyrants of earth!' of an impending revolution, 'the retributive hour'. It then asks two key questions concerning political legitimacy:

> What distinguishes noble from ignoble birth?
> Whence arises, what constitutes power?[112]

Whilst these questions are not answered directly, the very act of raising them calls the legitimacy of the aristocratic political order into question, and this uncertain legitimacy is underscored by the ominous image of an endangered ship which closes the first stanza:

> Now your bark is at sea, and your mariners sleep,
> Tho' the dark gloom of thunder half shadows the deep.

The second stanza amplifies this metaphor of the ship of state and offers storm and shipwreck as analogues of the approaching crisis warning that 'the raft of reform' provides the only safe way of reaching the shore.

The third stanza contemplates the consequences of continuing on the present course by means of synechdocal representations of revolution (the breaking of chains) and civil war – 'war's brazen trump' and 'the cannon's dread roar'. Once more, Davlin questions the ruling class; will they 'silence' the cannon or will they:

> . . . behold undismayed and with pitiless eyes
> Desolation's dark columns ascend to the skies?

These lines suggest both the horrors of a civil war and the uncertainty of its outcome, the 'dark columns' of the stanza's final line seem to prophesy as much 'the mutual ruin of the contending classes' as the eventual triumph of the working class.

The fourth stanza ends with a warning that adroitly turns the logic which connects property with political rights against its usual proponents:

> For the mob on the *grounds* you their franchise refuse
> Having nought to protect can have nothing to lose.

Once again the next stanza extends the idea contained in the closing couplet of its predecessor. Davlin recuperates 'the mob' as the producers of all property and warns the 'drone[s]' that they might be expelled from

---

[112] *Northern Star*, 28 July 1838.

the hive. The sixth stanza similarly develops the idea of working-class power as Davlin cautions the propertied classes against remaining:

> . . . so besottedly blind
> As to deem that the mob whom your manacles bind,
>   Cannot burst the vile bondage in twain.

These lines recall the third stanza with its image of chain-breaking as a synechdochal representation of revolution. The closing tetrameters similarly revisit and rework the ideas and images contained in the third stanza:

> Inoffensive shall fall the red blade of your trust
> And your cloud-cleaving citadel crumble to dust.

Significantly, where the third stanza imagined bloody reaction, the sixth imaginatively renders ineffective such a response, replacing the ascending 'dark columns' of desolation with the collapsing towers of the final line. In short, the sixth stanza imagines a non-violent revolution in which the united action of the working class effectively short-circuits violent reaction.

Is 'Questions from the Loom' a double poem? It certainly contains both 'sceptical and affirmative readings', it understands itself to be in a dialogue, and is certainly 'founded on debate and contest'. However, unlike Armstrong's paradigmatic double poems ('Love Among the Ruins' and 'Mariana') it contains no private dimension and no feminine presence. More importantly, 'Questions from the Loom' does not remain undecided between its sceptical and affirmative readings. Ultimately, it resolves what Armstrong refers to as 'the antagonistic struggle of dialectic'.

'Questions from the Loom', then, is not a double poem, rather its form is produced from a combination of negation, opposition and transformation. The poem proceeds in syllogistic fashion: it begins with negation, with images of shipwreck dominating the first two stanzas. It then moves into oppositional mode, imagining civil war, incendiarism and assassination in stanzas three and four before challenging dominant political definitions in the fifth. The four closing stanzas encode transformation. In stanza six this occurs at the macro level via the reworking of key images and ideas, whilst in the final two stanzas Davlin represents the desired political transformation itself.

Not every Chartist poem is as schematic as 'Questions from the Loom'. In another poem by Davlin – 'On a Cliff which O'erhung' – negation, opposition and transformation appear as dynamics rather than structures. This seems particularly fitting for a poem which incorporates sudden

changes of perspective and attempts the redefinition of existing ideological positions. Furthermore the poem's sophisticated rhetorical strategy
is complemented by its structural complexity. The rhyme scheme develops
unexpectedly (in the first instance) from alternate rhyme to a triplet
before folding back on itself in the final line whilst the metre oscillates
between anapaestic and trochaic tetrameters.

From its opening lines, 'On a Cliff which O'erhung' presents its readers
with an allegorical treatment of the contemporary political situation:

> On a cliff which o'erhung the huge billows that hove
> > Their white foam to the war waging skies;
> Sat Britannia consulting the daughter of Jove,
> > Rebel faction, how best to chastise.[113]

This setting not only gives a greater, almost cosmic significance to the
current struggle of the Chartists (thereby preparing the ground for later
verses which link Chartism to the Polish struggle for national liberation
and identify both as part of a European-wide movement for freedom), it
also requires an active readership prepared to draw the necessary correspondences between figure and event as well as undertaking more general
hermeneutic work. The use of 'rebel faction' to describe Chartist activity
is a bold, defamiliarising move which invites the readers of the *Northern
Star* to see themselves from the 'other side' as it were. That these words
are imputed to Britannia only increases the boldness of the move by
identifying the opponents of Chartism with an iconic emblem of patriotic
identity. Minerva responds by warning Britannia that:

> ... the gods had decreed hence that justice prevail,
> > That the millions, whose pacific arguments fail,
> > > Shall for death or liberty rise.

In this example, Davlin is searching for a way of forcing his Chartist
readership to apprehend the structural contradictions governing their
historical situation. He allocates anti-Chartist sentiments to Britannia to
remind his readers that 'Britannia' (the official state) possesses the power
to define Chartism as 'rebel faction' and that a higher power (God) is
needed to confer legitimacy upon the movement. The defamiliarising
move, therefore, provides the moment of negation (his readers have to
read themselves, albeit temporarily, as a 'rebel faction') whilst the higher
order divine discourse fuses opposition with transformation.

---

[113] *Northern Star*, 5 October 1839.

In similar fashion, the second verse invokes the idea of Britain as the ancient home of liberty, only to refute this historiographic tradition in its final verse, ''Twere delusion to deem e'er that freedom divine, / Blessed thy Peer and priest-ridden shore'. Instead, Davlin calls on the working classes to 'remember the feats of the fam'd Peterloo', to rely, in other words, on their own capacity to make history rather than on a dubious historical tradition. Here then the poem's final political significance emerges, not from the sequential ordering of negation, opposition and transformation, but rather from their interplay across the entire 'surface' of the poem.

Finally, to consider a rather different example of Chartist poetry – 'To the Dear Little Dead' by P. B. Templeton. An explanatory note at the end of Templeton's poem describes the tragic circumstances which gave rise to its composition:

> The occasion of these lines is the death of three lovely children who left Leeds, with their mother, in August last, for Canada, and who, dying on their passage, were committed to the deep. The mother of the children was the sister of the writer, and the only remaining member of his family in England. (*NS*, 19 January 1839)

My reason for choosing this poem is precisely because its content challenges conventional expectations of what constitutes a Chartist poem yet, in formal terms, it is consonant with the poems discussed earlier in this chapter. More specifically, it is a poem which carefully enacts a move from negation to transformation at the level of both content and structure. The first three stanzas describe the death and sea-burial of the children. The fourth stanza is the centre of the poem both thematically and structurally. It deals with the consequences of the absence of an earthly grave:

> On your grave the fond eye of a mother's affection
>   Ne'er shall gaze, – nor the tear of pity be shed;
> For no sod marks the spot where the sad recollection
>   Might restore to her bosom the dear little dead.

Yet by registering this absence, the fourth stanza also offers itself as a surrogate for the absent material site. This stanza then, is simultaneously the point of maximum negation (emphasised by its repeated use of negatives, 'Ne'er', 'nor' and 'no') and the point at which transformation begins.

It is noticeable that the following three stanzas are then able to forward the mourning process. This is achieved by revising the poem's first three stanzas in such a way as to wrest conciliation and compensation from the situation. In verse one, for example, the sea swallows the dead, but verse five looks to a time when the sea shall 'yield up the dead' (an echo of Revelation 20:13). Similarly, where the second verse is dominated by images of darkness, the sixth stanza features images of awakening; and whilst the third stanza emphasises the depth of the ocean, the final stanza (which begins 'Rise') describes the children's ascension to heaven, imagined as a place of familial reunion.

'To the Dear Little Dead' contains little by way of explicit comment on public matters. 'Questions from the Loom' and 'On a Cliff which O'erhung' contain no private dimension. It appears as if the constituent parts of the contradictions (between public and private, epistemology and expression) which give the double poem its particular force are invariably assigned to separate poems in Chartist poetic production. It is tempting to read this as evidence of the inability of Chartist poetry to articulate a meaningful link between these levels of human existence. I want to resist such a reading not least because it construes Chartist poetry as an inferior (or failed) form of Victorian poetry. Instead, I want to suggest that Chartist poets rarely produced a double poem because the indeterminacy of that form remained hostile to their needs. As the following chapters will show, the Chartist poem is drawn ineluctably towards 'resolution'. Chartist poetry needed to be definite; it recognised the 'antagonistic struggle of dialectic' and in many ways had a far more concrete under-standing of this term than its canonical counterpart. But the Chartist poet had of necessity to take sides, and this more than anything else militated against the elaboration of the double poem. Negation, opposition and transformation provide this cluster of poems with their own distinctive aesthetic unity, suggestive of the Chartist equivalent to the double poem, an analogous, perhaps even homologous, form which taken seriously will broaden and deepen our understanding of Victorian poetry.

CHAPTER 2

Chartist poetry and literary history

1848, John Saville's study of what is still thought of as Chartism's final flourish, examines the processes by which Chartism was destroyed both as a political movement and as cultural memory:

Chartism was finally broken by the physical force of the state, and having once been broken it was submerged in the national consciousness, beneath layers of false understanding and denigration. A radical movement draws essential sustenance from the inspiration of its past struggles and its past heroes; but who was to honour poor half-mad O'Connor on Kennington Common, leading his gullible followers to ridicule and execration? What was quite forgotten was the strength that continued in the Chartism in the months that followed the events of 10 April, and even the memory of the mass arrests and jailings were wiped from public memory. The contemporary agencies of the media were extraordinarily effective in traducing this greatest of all mass movements of the nineteenth century: but when all is said the almost complete obliteration of Chartism from public consciousness in the middle decades of the century remains a remarkable phenomenon.[1]

It is difficult to resist the conclusion that the cultural legacy of Chartism has been suppressed with even greater effectiveness.

At first sight the history of Chartist poetry appears as a sad tale of ever-increasing obscurity: a brief moment of florescence lasting little more than a decade quickly followed by oblivion. While such a history has its attractions for the literary scholar, allowing for the dramatic staging of archival work as discovery, a bringing to light of long-forgotten artefacts, a note of caution must be sounded. In the twenty-five or so 'quiet' years between the end of Chartism and the beginnings of the Socialist revival of the 1880s, Chartist poetry continued to appear in anthologies such as *The Reformer's Book of Songs and Recitations* edited by John Bedford Leno.[2]

[1] J. Saville, *1848: The British State and the Chartist Movement* (Cambridge University Press, 1990), 202.
[2] J. B. Leno, *The Reformer's Book of Songs and Recitations.*

The Socialist revival itself prompted a renewed interest in Chartism, particularly amongst those socialists keen to claim the Chartist heritage for themselves. This interest extended into the cultural field with publications such as *Revolutionary Rhymes and Songs for Socialists, No. 1* (published from the *Commonweal* office) and newspapers such as *Justice* reprinting Chartist poetry.[3]

However, it was not only the labour movement which retained a memory of Chartist poetry. The scholarly world also recognised its existence and contribution to the field of English literature. *The Poets and Poetry of the Century*, a mammoth nine-volume series edited by Alfred H. Miles (published between 1892 and 1897), which combined the functions of anthology and critical study, contains entries on W. J. Linton, Ernest Jones, Ebenezer Jones and Gerald Massey.[4] The entries on Ernest Jones and Gerald Massey are particularly interesting for the way in which they combine acknowledgement of the aesthetic achievement of each poet with an attempt to reassure a middle-class readership of the respectable nature of the poets' radicalism. Prior to its discussion of Jones' work, the reader is informed that he was jailed in 1848 'for making a speech which in our day would have attracted no legal notice'.[5] Miles' assessment of Jones' poetry recognises that the aesthetic specificity of Chartist poetry results from a particular conjunction of intention, mode of distribution and audience:

[Jones'] *Songs of Democracy* were also printed on fly-sheets, and circulated broadcast. It is difficult to imagine anything better for their purpose than these *Songs of Democracy*. They lack the bitter intensity of the *Corn Law Rhymes* of Ebenezer Elliott; but in their simple directness are much better calculated for popular use.[6]

Massey is hailed by Miles as 'a born laureate of the people, and one of the most thoroughly English poets of the century'. Not only does Miles consider Massey's collection *War Waits* to be amongst 'the most powerful' poetry written about the Crimean War, he also praises Massey's earlier Chartist poems as being 'full of good hope and sound teaching'.[7]

---

[3] *Revolutionary Rhymes and Songs for Socialists, No. 1* (T. Binning, 1886) reprints Ernest Jones, 'Song of the Low' as 'Song of the "Lower" Classes'. Kovalev notes that Massey's 'A Red Republican Lyric' was reprinted in *Justice* (1 November 1884).

[4] A. H. Miles (ed.), *The Poets and the Poetry of the Century* (Hutchinson, 1891–7). W. J. Linton is discussed in *Volume III*, Ernest Jones in *Volume IV*, and Gerald Massey in *Volume V*.

[5] *Ibid.*, IV: 548.   [6] *Ibid.*, IV: 550.   [7] *Ibid.*, V: 318–20.

His overall assessment of Massey's work stresses the national-patriotic essence of Massey's radicalism:

Gerald Massey is one of the most truly national of our English poets. His verse gives vigorous expression to the thoughts, feelings, emotions, and aspirations common to English hearts, and forcible representation to distinctive traits of the national character . . . He is before all things a patriot. He has an intense belief in the genius of England as the champion of liberty, and the pioneer of freedom. He glories alike in her old-time history and in her perennial potentiality.[8]

In contrast to Miles' enthusiasm, George Saintsbury adopts a more condescending tone in his 1896 study, *A History of Nineteenth Century Literature (1780–1895)*:

To the Spasmodics may be appended yet another list of bards, who can claim here but the notice of a sentence or a clause, though by no means uninteresting to the student, and often very interesting indeed to the student-lover of poetry: – the two Joneses – Ernest (1819–69), a rather silly victim of Chartism, for which he went to prison, but a generous person and a master of a pretty twitter enough; and Ebenezer (1820–60), a London clerk, author of *Studies of Sensation and Event*, a rather curious link between the Cockney school of the beginning of the century and some minor poets of our own times, but overpraised by his redis-coverers some years ago.[9]

Saintsbury's suggestion of a degree of affinity between the Spasmodics and the 'two Joneses' is tantalising (Isobel Armstrong hints at something similar in her *Victorian Poetry* where her discussion of the Chartist poets follows on immediately from her consideration of the Spasmodics) although the implication of immaturity and the trivialisation of Ernest Jones' political commitment are by turns patronising and offensive.

Fourteen years later in 1910, Hugh Walker offers a somewhat grudging assessment of Chartist literature in *The Literature of the Victorian Era*. He allows that the Chartist movement produced 'a small literature, both in prose and in verse, which is by no means destitute of merit'.[10] Walker concentrates on two writers, Thomas Cooper and Gerald Massey. Cooper is compared unfavourably, both poetically and politically, to Samuel Bamford:

Cooper in his *Autobiography* shows considerably less of the literary faculty than Bamford, and he appears to have been a man of altogether less sane and safe judgement than that very acute and sensible radical . . . The *Purgatory of Suicides*

---

[8] *Ibid.*, V: 317.
[9] G. Saintsbury, *A History of Nineteenth Century Literature (1780–1895)* (Macmillan, 1896), 307.
[10] H. Walker, *The Literature of the Victorian Era* (Cambridge University Press, 1910), 349.

has many faults. The Miltonic inversions and complexity of sentence, imitated by an ill-educated man, produce a deplorable effect. The style, in short, is inartistic and bad, and the tone generally too shrill to be dignified.[11]

In his discussion of Massey, Walker recognises his subject's remarkable achievement in writing verse at all given his family background and lack of schooling. However, Walker is quick to emphasise the inferior nature of Massey's poetic gift, '[h]is patriotic pieces are fervid and stirring, but a comparison with Tennyson shows that they fall considerably below excellence'.[12] Wyatt and Clay in their 1912 study *English Literature of the Nineteenth Century* offer a similar assessment of Massey's place in the poetic hierarchy – 'distinctly a minor poet' – whilst acknowledging his 'wide range of lyrical power' as well as his importance as a poet who gives 'expression to the democratic aspirations of the age'.[13]

Between the 1890s and 1910s Ernest Jones effectively disappears as a Chartist poet and his invisibility largely continues throughout the 1950s and 1960s. Writing in 1950, Sherard Vines somewhat idiosyncratically observes:

Poetry of the political Left Wing had appeared in the *Corn-Law Rhymes* (1828) of Ebenezer Elliot (1781–1849), Hood's *Song of the Shirt*, and work by the Chartist group, including Thomas Cooper and Capel Loftt . . . It remained for William Morris to conceive poetry on such political foundations, more grandly.[14]

A year later R. C. Churchill's *English Literature of the Nineteenth Century* makes reference to Cooper (whose *Autobiography* is praised as 'very interesting'), Ernest and Ebenezer Jones and Gerald Massey.[15] This study indicates a further waning of an already residual interest as the work of all four writers is mentioned but not assessed. By the early 1960s, in spite of renewed interest in Chartism in the field of historical studies (*Chartist Studies* edited by Asa Briggs appeared in 1959), the discussion of Chartist literature manifests a rather shaky grasp of the movement's composition. For example, Batho and Dobree in *The Victorians and After 1820–1914*, cite Elliot, Cooper and Massey as examples of Chartist poetry and

---

[11] *Ibid.*, 350.   [12] *Ibid.*, 448.
[13] A. J. Wyatt and H. Clay (eds.), *English Literature of the Nineteenth Century* (University Tutorial Press, 1912), 116.
[14] S. Vines, *100 Years of English Literature* (Gerald Duckworth, 1950), 52.
[15] R. C. Churchill, *English Literature of the Nineteenth Century* (University Tutorial Press, 1951), 73 and 144.

contend that the two latter poets were 'less centrally' in the movement than Elliot.[16] They consider Cooper's *Autobiography* to be his best work and their assessment of Massey is that his work is 'sometimes too poetical' although they also concede that 'he had a touch of the true fire'.[17]

The imprecision with which Batho and Dobree characterise the Chartist movement is symptomatic of the declining interest in Chartist literature in the early 1960s which, considering the intellectual milieu, requires explanation. The cognate discipline of history had seen the emergence of 'labour history' as a field of study with two highly influential works focused on the nineteenth century: E. P. Thompson's *The Making of the English Working Class* (1963) and E. J. Hobsbawm's *Labouring Men* (1964).[18] Richard Hoggart's *The Uses of Literacy* (1957) and Raymond Williams' *Culture and Society, 1780–1850* (1958) had begun to redefine literary studies both by reconnecting literature with the society in which it was produced (crucially conceiving this as an *active*, two-way relationship) and by introducing a democratic focus into what had previously been an elitist subject.[19] More specifically 1956 also saw the publication of the first (and to date only) anthology of Chartist Literature, Y. V. Kovalev's *Anthology of Chartist Literature*.[20]

Kovalev is the first critic to recognise that Chartism was a literary as well as a political movement. He is the first to compile a catalogue of the literary resources available to Chartist writers, identifying Godwin, Paine, Byron, Shelley, Methodist hymns and, rather less precisely, 'the best Radical poets of the 1830s and 1840s [and] popular working-class poetry' as key components of the Chartist literary tradition. Kovalev also draws attention to the importance of Chartist journalism as a literary genre, tracing its emergence 'out of political speeches' and discussing the continuing importance of oral modes throughout Chartism's history.[21] In addition, he considers the relationship between Chartist and 'mainstream'

---

[16] E. C. Batho and B. Dobree (eds.), *The Victorians and After 1830–1914* (Cresset Press, 1962, 3rd rev. edn.), 213–14.

[17] *Ibid.*, 214.

[18] E. P. Thompson, *The Making of the English Working Class* (Harmondsworth: Penguin, 1980); E. Hobsbawm, *Labouring Men* (Weidenfield & Nicolson, 1968). Both of these studies followed on closely from the formation of the Society for the Study of Labour History in 1959.

[19] R. Hoggart, *The Uses of Literacy* (Harmondsworth: Penguin, 1957); R. Williams, *Culture and Society, 1780–1850* (Hogarth Press, 1990).

[20] Y. N. Kovalev (ed.), *An Anthology of Chartist Literature* (Moscow: Foreign Languages Publishing House, 1956). Kovalev's introductory essay to this volume was translated into English by J. C. Dumbreck and M. Beresford and published in *Victorian Studies*, vol. II (1958), 117–38.

[21] *Ibid.*, 120–3.

literature as a two-way process in which Chartist writers contribute to the development of canonical writers and vice versa.[22]

Kovalev must also be credited as the first critic to recognise and discuss the historical evolution of Chartist literature. He describes early Chartist poetry as 'chiefly imitative' although he does note the relatively early development of 'satirical genres' as an exception to this rule. For Kovalev, Chartist poetry achieves aesthetic maturity only in the period after 1848 when:

> the very nature of Chartist poetry changed. Short poems, songs, couplets, and hymns gave way to vast poetic cycles and epic poems of monumental length . . . [as the necessity] of giving an artistic generalisation of their experience in the long social struggle, spurned poets on to master more 'capacious' genres.[23]

Although the development of Chartist poetry is rather more uneven than Kovalev suggests (Cooper's epic *Purgatory of Suicides*, for example, was written well before 1848), the historical irony which he identifies, whereby the most significant literary achievements of Chartist poetry coincide with the movement's terminal political decline, has subsequently commanded widespread critical support.

Finally, Kovalev is the first critic to give a detailed account of the aesthetic challenges which Chartist literature both faced and presents. In particular, he argues that the introduction of new themes (or content) by Chartist writers necessarily involved the elaboration of new literary forms – or to use Kovalev's term 'a new literary method'.[24] Although in Kovalev's 'Introduction' this notion of the dialectical relationship between content and form is asserted rather than demonstrated, Donna Landry's study of eighteenth-century plebeian women's poetry, *The Muses of Resistance*, has shown how the injection of new content into established genres is capable of generating 'innovative if not textually radical [results]'.[25] In terms of form, Kovalev argues, Chartist literature attempted a synthesis of 'revolutionary romanticism' and 'social realism'.[26]

The most important individual Chartist poets for Kovalev are W. J. Linton, Ernest Jones and Gerald Massey. Kovalev is in no doubt that Jones is the 'most significant Chartist poet' and praises his 'lofty emotional

---

[22] In particular, Kovalev argues that the 'new themes' of aspects of working-class life introduced into literature by Chartist writers contributed to the development of the work of, amongst others, Dickens and Thackeray, *ibid.*, 120.

[23] *Ibid.*, 124–6. [24] *Ibid.*, 126.

[25] D. Landry, *The Muses of Resistance: Laboring-Class Women's Poetry in Britain, 1739–1796* (Cambridge University Press, 1990), 13.

[26] Kovalev, *Anthology of Chartist Literature*, 129.

tone' and his ability to represent the 'people' as the 'powerful, collective hero' of his work. Indeed, Kovalev argues for the recognition of Jones as a major Victorian poet:

The artistic significance of his work far transcends the limits of Chartist poetry. Jones was an outstanding English poet of the nineteenth century, worthy of a place beside the most talented pupils and heirs of Byron, Shelley, and Keats.[27]

Massey is seen by Kovalev as a poetic talent betrayed by a combination of temperament and historical accident. He argues that Massey 'could have become a very considerable poet, given more stable convictions and a more independent view of reality' but considers that his entry into Chartism at the moment of its final decline effectively thwarted his development as a Chartist poet. Linton is viewed as the least talented of the three poets, with Kovalev describing his poetry as 'rationalistic and precise, and [lacking] emotional expressiveness'. The most curious aspect of Kovalev's 'Introduction' is his complete neglect of Thomas Cooper as a poet. No mention is made of Cooper's poetry and Cooper himself is only discussed (and dismissed) in the most cursory fashion as a writer of 'short stories asserting Christian morality'.[28]

A sixteen-year silence followed the publication of Kovalev's *Anthology*, broken only by Martha Vicinus's (1974) study *The Industrial Muse*, with its chapter on Chartist poetry and fiction. In many respects Vicinus concurs with Kovalev's assessment of Chartist poetry, identifying its descent from 'folk and religious sources' and noting the importance of Romantic poetry (especially Byron and Shelley). She follows Kovalev's periodisation, dividing Chartist poetry into two periods; the literature of the first period (from 1838 to 1848) is characterised as generally 'exhortative and inspirational', while that of the second period (1848 to 1853) is described as 'the richest period of working-class creativity until the dialect writers rose to prominence in the 1860s'. Vicinus also echoes Kovalev regarding the aesthetic challenges which faced Chartist poets; they were, she argues, 'given the responsibility of fitting a new subject – working-class ideals – into the traditional forms of English poetry'.[29]

What is new in Vicinus's assessment is her analysis of the significance of the poetry of Ebenezer Elliott, the Corn Law Rhymer, whom she describes as the 'single most important predecessor of Chartist poets'. For

---

[27] *Ibid.*, 132–3.   [28] *Ibid.*, 132–7.
[29] M. Vicinus, *The Industrial Muse: A Study of Nineteenth Century British Working-Class Literature* (Croom Helm, 1974).

Vicinus, Elliott's influence was ambivalent – whilst his example encouraged working-class men to write about their own experience, his poetry also bequeathed a mixed aesthetic legacy:

The virtues of concreteness, however, were offset by the accompanying emotional bombast. Elliott's fervid language and urgent appeals to God were appealing to those making their first attempts at verse. If reading Shelley encouraged personification and totalizations, Elliott encouraged ranting and exclamation points.[30]

Vicinus also draws attention to the, sometimes uneasy, relationship between oral and written forms in Chartist poetry. She distinguishes between 'Chartist song writers' and those poets who used established poetic forms (such as the sonnet and epic) which they considered to be 'more aesthetically important' than the oral modes. Vicinus identifies the complex cultural and political pressures at play in this process. Chartist writers, she suggests, were concerned with writing 'appealing and ennobling poetry that was intelligible to the working class' and with satisfying their own authentic aspirations and, in some cases, literary ambitions. Implicit in Vicinus's analysis is the assumption that the distinction between the 'intelligible' and the 'aesthetic' maps identically onto the oral/written divide. In her account, the quest for aesthetic complexity comes at the expense of readership; referring to those poets who worked in written forms, she comments:

Despite their passionate political message, the difficulty of reading their poetry limited the audience of all Chartist poets. The division between oral and written literature – songs and poetry – was only partially bridged by writers and readers.[31]

Vicinus offers a minor revision of Kovalev's assessment of Chartism's major poets where, despite describing *The Purgatory of Suicides* as 'virtually unreadable', she adds Thomas Cooper to the earlier triumvirate of Jones, Massey and Linton. A similar note of disapproval attends her criticism of the 'deliberately self-advertising display of information' contained in the poem, and in a judgement which dismisses any possibility of reading *The Purgatory of Suicides* as a specifically Chartist challenge to the dominant culture, she describes Cooper himself as 'trapped by his painfully acquired learning and his middle-class aesthetics'.[32] Vicinus also differs from Kovalev, both politically and poetically, in her assessment of Gerald Massey. She describes his politics as 'a diffuse form

[30] *Ibid.*, 96–7. [31] *Ibid.*, 98. [32] *Ibid.*, 110–12.

of revolutionary sentiment, unenlightened by any ideological comprehension' and detects similar failings in his poetry, criticising his over-reliance on 'extravagant language' as well as 'the command form, personification and exclamation points' and noting the 'peculiar sense of emptiness' which attends some of his more striking images, 'as if Massey were not quite sure whom he was addressing, or if anyone were listening anymore'.[33] Although Vicinus's account makes passing reference to the political context of the early 1850s, her analysis of Massey's career rests on a sense of his individual failings, unlike Kovalev who stresses the significance of the failure of the Chartist movement in his account of the poet's development. As regards Linton and Jones, Vicinus concurs with Kovalev in praising Linton for his adherence to Chartism and describing his 'Hymns to the Unenfranchised' as 'sophisticated and clear, albeit poetically stiff', thus exemplifying both 'the strengths and weaknesses of early Chartist poetry'.[34] Finally, she concurs with Kovalev in his view of Ernest Jones as the hero of Chartist poetry. Jones is praised specifically for trying 'to write verse that was accessible to working-class readers' and for understanding 'the importance of intangible feelings and emotions in galvanizing the oppressed'.[35]

Phyllis Mary Ashraf's *Introduction to Working Class Literature in Great Britain* (published in 1978 in what at that time was the German Democratic Republic) is the first full-length study of Chartist poetry and as such constitutes a significant moment in the critical history of the field. Ashraf is the first to begin the process of quantifying working-class literary production. For example, she examines the literary content of five Chartist and Cooperative weeklies over a two-year period in the 1840s and estimates that as each publication published, on average, between one and two poems per week, their total collective output annually is in the region of 300 poems, a figure which exceeds 'the life-output of most poets'. Ashraf also estimates that there are some two hundred 'worker and radical poets' requiring critical attention.[36] Ashraf's own study makes a strong contribution to this process of recovering 'lost' poets, as it discusses upwards of thirty poets and considerably more than thirty poems from the Chartist period (c. 1838–1855). Her study is both more extensive than the *Industrial Muse*, which contains a detailed analysis of six representative poems, and more intensive than Kovalev's 'Introduction', which

---

[33] *Ibid.*, 98–104.   [34] *Ibid.*, 99.   [35] *Ibid.*, 98–101.
[36] P. M. Ashraf, *Introduction to Working Class Literature in Great Britain* (German Democratic Republic, 1978), 66–68.

confines itself to statements regarding general trends within Chartist literature unaccompanied by any specific analysis of individual poems.

Historically, Ashraf's study has been neglected, due largely to the nature of her own political and ideological commitments. *Introduction to Working Class Literature in Great Britain* is written from within a teleological form of Marxism (confidently assuming an inevitable progress towards socialism) which was the official ideology of the former Soviet Union and its Eastern European satellites. Ashraf is confident that a similar teleological process is at work in literary history and that Marxism provides her with a theoretical method capable of discriminating between historically important developments and temporary diversions in the evolution of literary genres. This kind of theoretical and critical certainty is currently unfashionable (except in the negative formulation which confidently asserts the impossibility of making such judgements), but its presence in Ashraf's work should not be allowed to obscure the important insights contained in her study.

Ashraf revises the existing critical orthodoxy concerning the formative influences on Chartist poetry and also modifies the established hierarchy of Chartist poets. In terms of poetic influences, she notes the importance of Byron and Shelley but emphasises the influence of Burns on the development of Chartist poetry. It is Burns, she argues, who provided a poetic model which harnessed the existing cultural resources available to working-class writers:

[Burns'] service was to inspire workingmen with self-confidence to teach poets the aesthetic value of poetry for and about the common man in the regional vernacular or in a form and idiom not far removed from formal speech. The example of Burns opened the ways to using the resources of tradition in a contemporary context and the reworking of local song.[37]

When evaluating the achievements of the major Chartist poets, Ashraf dismisses Massey as a 'renegade', describing his work as consisting of 'highflown revolutionary phrasemongering, "poetic" archaisms and jumbled metaphor, which did little to advance revolutionary poetry'.[38] Ernest Jones is also criticised for failing 'to understand the common need for less ambitious versifying [which] also had its value in the lives of the common people', whilst Thomas Cooper is applauded as the poet 'who did most to encourage other writers'.[39] It is, however, Ebenezer Jones whom Ashraf identifies as 'the most significant pioneer of Chartist poetry' who anticipates many

---

[37] *Ibid.*, 118–9. [38] *Ibid.*, 191. [39] *Ibid.*, 107–9.

of the future developments in working-class literature. In particular, Ashraf praises the psychological depth of Jones' poetry, hailing him as:

the first of the new poets to go beyond the immediate externals of the class struggle and the claims of Justice. He confronts the complex human problems of established capitalism.[40]

However, the most significant aspect of Ashraf's study is her insistence on the primary role played by poetry within the Chartist movement. The sheer volume of poetry, she argues, provides compelling evidence of its importance to the working-class movement which assumed that 'the poet had a useful function and that his task was associated with . . . the moral, political and educational advance of the people'. In addition, Chartist poets were charged with 'the task not only of vindicating the rights of the working class but their potential culture, their capacity to use and develop art'.[41] The implication of Ashraf's analysis is that Chartism must be understood as a movement which was consciously engaged in a cultural as well as a political struggle. This cultural contest, moreover, was waged on two fronts simultaneously. On the one hand, Chartism proclaimed the right of the working class to its proper share in the cultural heritage of the nation (cultural deprivation thus joined economic privation and political exclusion as evils endured by the working class); on the other hand the Chartist poet stood as an emblem of the intellectual and moral maturity of the working class (and thus exposed the falsity of the argument that due to its lack of education the working class was as yet not ready to be trusted with the exercise of the franchise). This sense of the interlocking nature of the political and the cultural as *fundamental* aspects of Chartism (rather than treating the cultural as a secondary reflex of the political) constitutes an important breakthrough in the study of Chartist poetry.

Ashraf emphasises the continuities between working-class aesthetics and working-class organisation. Both, she argues, enjoyed 'sporadic and uneven development' and found it necessary to adopt and adapt elements of the existing culture and 'to invent what it could not find ready made.'[42] Furthermore, the desire for aesthetic experience is, contends Ashraf, a permanent aspect of working-class culture:

Working class poetry over the generations expressed aesthetic demands. It offered consolation. An oft-repeated aim was to fashion beautiful visions in words, to discover beauty in common things and unbeautiful surroundings, to compensate for poverty by noble ideas.[43]

[40] *Ibid.*, 153–61.   [41] *Ibid.*, 97 and 90.   [42] *Ibid.*, 16–17.   [43] *Ibid.*, 52.

This demand for aesthetic satisfaction is also reflected in the 'insistence that petitions, addresses, circulars etc., should be persuasive, eloquent, true and well-written' – in effect the aesthetic and the political were integrated within working-class culture.[44] Indeed, when Ashraf formalises her findings in a series of theses at the end of her study she insists on literature's political agency, arguing that it 'contributed to the growth of class and political consciousness directly, and helped to sustain militant and revolutionary traditions in periods of reaction'.[45]

Ashraf's single most important contribution is to demonstrate that it is the absence (rather than the presence) of aesthetic practice within the working-class movement which requires explanation. Accordingly, her enquiry is therefore directed to a careful consideration of the specific ways in which working-class aesthetic practice emerges out of and feeds into political practice. And this, in turn, introduces a number of fresh perspectives into the study of Chartist poetry. For example, the use of personification (especially of Reason, Brotherhood and Liberty) within Chartist poetry is often ascribed to the influence of Shelley. Yet Ashraf observes that these personifications can also be seen as examples of 'emblematical allegory' as practised in the pictorial tradition of trades union and friendly society banners and certificates.[46] The identification of an autochthonous source for this poetic practice is not to deny the influence of Shelley but rather to develop a more complex account of Chartist aesthetic practice which admits the dialectical interpenetration of 'popular' and 'high' cultural forms.

Ashraf also draws attention to the ways in which the specificities of working-class existence give rise to new categories and forms of aesthetic practice. She offers as an example the collective nature of working-class political and economic struggle:

The public meeting and demonstration are moments of experience which awaken special feelings, not shared by other classes. The treatment of mobs, demagogues, heroic leaders etc. in bourgeois literature is not only different in tone and attitude but in the aesthetic sense.[47]

Whilst the notion of the public meeting as an exclusively working-class phenomenon is questionable, Ashraf is surely correct in her analysis of the largely class-determined nature of its different literary representations. In similar fashion, she argues that working-class poets were much quicker at wresting 'imagery, metaphors and similes' from the 'industrial

---

[44] *Ibid.*, 56.   [45] *Ibid.*, 202.   [46] *Ibid.*, 58.   [47] *Ibid.*, 60.

environment' than their bourgeois counterparts who 'strained after the exotic, the medieval, eventually the bizarre to feed [their] starved imagination'.[48]

The relationship between the collective (or trans-individual) aspects of working-class life and working-class aesthetic expression is repeatedly emphasised by Ashraf: 'The worker lives in a crowd at home and at work. From this enforced identity come aesthetic values common to working-class writers.'[49] For the most part, she argues, neither these experiences nor the values which they generated were shared by middle-class writers. Perhaps the most striking literary manifestation of this is given in the very different attitude towards 'originality' displayed by working-class poets. Ashraf contends that many working-class poets were not interested in originality, preferring instead to concentrate on the efficient communication of ideas:

> Innumerable poems take up the same theme, clothe the same ideas in different words, use the same similes and metaphors repeatedly . . . Technique is subordinated to sense. Meaning is concentrated into a common phrase. Neat paraphrase is not regarded as plagiarism but as skill . . . There was always an attitude that regarded any poetry written or unwritten as a form of common property.[50]

Inspired by collective experience and unconcerned with originality, working-class poetry offends against the central canons of post-Romantic aesthetic judgement. Herein lies another clue to its degraded status in literary history, for the post-Romantic valorisation of originality and the expression of individual experience only permits a reading of working-class poetry as variously antiquated, old-fashioned, imitative, repetitive and clichéd.

The next major study of Chartist poetry is Ulrike Schwab's *The Poetry of the Chartist Movement: A Literary and Historical Study*, published in 1987. Schwab begins by excavating the critical history of Chartist poetry. In particular, she is interested in the critical neglect of Chartist poetry within British academia which she attributes to a combination of its inherent 'political and social explosiveness', an (aesthetically based) prejudice against 'political' poetry, and the fact that historians of Chartism are well-supplied with other documentary source material.[51] In addition, she argues that the study of Chartist poetry has been hampered by its hitherto

---

[48] *Ibid.*, 69.   [49] *Ibid.*, 172.   [50] *Ibid.*, 37–8.
[51] U. Schwab, *The Poetry of the Chartist Movement: A Literary and Historical Study* (Dordrecht, Netherlands: Kluwer Academic Publishers, 1987), 14.

ambiguous location in relation to academic disciplines. It evinces '[an] original affinity to literary scholarship on the one hand and an essential attachment to historical scholarship on the other'.[52] In short, Chartist poetry has been considered of historical interest (and consequently of marginal importance) by literary scholars and regarded with suspicion by historians due to its status as literary text.

Yet for Schwab it is precisely the dualistic nature of Chartist poetry, as simultaneously artistic and political expression, which requires both acknowledgement and explanation. Her study challenges the disciplinary assumptions of both history and literature. 'Why should a poem convey less, be less authentic, than a statute, a speech or a petition?' she asks historians, whilst literary scholars are challenged to recognise that Chartist poetry 'represents artistic language expression as well as historical statement'.[53] Furthermore, Schwab recognises that Chartist poetry presents the literary critic with a series of methodological and theoretical problems. In particular, she translates Ashraf's insistence on the importance of the collective dimension of Chartist poetry into a methodological tool, making genres and sub-genres of Chartist poetry rather than individual Chartist poets the focus of her study. Using thematic organisation, she discusses Chartist poetry in terms of its repertoire of identities – slave, patriot, freedom fighter/martyr, noble workingman, the People – and its treatment of such issues as the land, the state, industrialism, nature and natural law, Christianity and ethics, and education.[54] She lays the foundation for an approach which recognises (in both theoretical and methodological terms) the specificity of Chartist poetry.

Schwab's major concern is with the agency possessed by Chartist poetry as a whole rather than with the particular political/ideological functions performed by individual poems. More specifically, she identifies a genre of Chartist poetry consisting of songs/poems of praise/freedom and 'propaganda poems' which she describes as the 'nucleus' and which she considers to be central to understanding the role of poetry within Chartism. This nucleus, she argues, gives expression to inchoate experience thereby promoting the formation of a collective Chartist consciousness:

In the nucleus a socio-political consciousness, that is, a 'we-consciousness', becomes manifest. It arises from a collective state of feelings and wants . . . By anchoring the new consciousness collectively the authors make a decisive contribution to the constitution of the movement.[55]

---

[52] *Ibid.*   [53] *Ibid.*, 16–17.   [54] *Ibid.*, 117–23.   [55] *Ibid.*, 65.

In this sense, Chartist poetry performs the functions of an 'organic intellectual'.[56] Schwab observes that the Chartist poets:

act as an avantgarde without deriving from this a special position themselves. As speakers of their poems they remain part of the collective well into the late phase.[57]

She also argues that the communicative process enacted by these poems is doubly active because the addressee 'has to take an active part'. Finally, Schwab claims that the 'nucleus' 'is aimed at immediate objectives as well as long-term objectives'.[58]

In addition to this discussion of 'what' Chartist poetry did, Schwab is equally interested in the question of 'how' it did it. Her account recalls Caudwell's and Armstrong's insistence on the effect of affect: 'The nucleus creates consciousness through the rational and irrational portions of its message. In this the irrational portions have a key function.'[59] For Schwab the 'irrational' component of Chartist poetry includes its 'complex emotionality and psychological efficacy', which she sees as complementing its political message.[60]

The central weakness of Schwab's thematic approach is that it privileges the synchronic over the diachronic and thus flattens out the historically uneven development of both the Chartist movement and its poetry. By analysing Chartist poetry in relation to crucial moments in Chartist history, this study seeks to complement Schwab's more general study. In addition, this study seeks to pursue the question of the aesthetic specificity of Chartist poetry which Schwab's study recognises but leaves undeveloped. For example, she regards the aesthetic specificity of Chartist poetry as inhering in its content rather than its form – 'The poems of Chartism deviate from the ideas which commonly standardize poetry [and do] not bring forth any formal innovations'.[61] Yet later she returns to the question of form and briefly identifies, without analysing, two stylistic features of the nucleus. The first of these, 'a pronounced character of summoning', is marked by the use of 'imperative forms' (which, however, are not constituted as commands). The second consists of 'two basic structures [namely] positive-negative-positive, negative-positive-negative' (where 'positive' denotes statements about the 'desired condition' of society and 'negative' denotes statements about the 'actual condition of society'.[62]

[56] The term 'organic intellectual' is taken from the work of Antonio Gramsci, see *Selections from Prison Notebooks* (Lawrence & Wishart, 1971) for his elaboration of this concept.
[57] Schwab, *Poetry of the Chartist Movement*, 66.   [58] *Ibid.*, 67–9.   [59] *Ibid.*, 67.
[60] *Ibid.*, 68.   [61] *Ibid.*, 33–8.   [62] *Ibid.*, 111.

1987 also saw the publication of Brian Maidment's ground-breaking anthology of 'self-taught poets and poetry in Victorian Britain', *The Poorhouse Fugitives*. From the outset Maidment insists on the necessity of considering the 'literariness' of the poems included in his anthology. In particular, he emphasises their relation to the literary tradition and argues that they provide 'a complex commentary on how the British poetic tradition might be read – or rather re-read and re-interpreted – in relation to various emergent senses of class-identity'.[63] Maidment offers this insistence on the literary as a necessary counterweight to the 'narrowly political' focus of Kovalev and Ashraf, which, he argues, 'denies the importance of literary allusion and tradition, and in addition over-simplifies the complexity of literary discourse as an aspect of class for-mation'.[64] He cautions against a definition of Chartist poetry which rests *exclusively* on known authorial affiliation or perceived political content (an assumption shared by Vicinus as well as Kovalev and Ashraf) and argues that more attention should be paid 'to the ways in which radical or Chartist poetry might be defined largely by the poetic genres used, or by analysis of the very specific symbolic language widely found in the political poetry of the 1840s, or by examining the nature of the readership, audience, and occasion presupposed in such poems'.[65]

As part of his contribution to the elaboration of a literary definition of Chartist poetry, Maidment begins by listing a number of its common features:

a strong sense of orality [and] of communal occasion and the appropriate rhetoric, or a willingness to align the devices of popular literature – pathos, melodrama, refrains, and catchphrases – with quite sophisticated literary skills in order to convey ideas or abstractions by emotional as well as intellectual means.[66]

Later, when Maidment returns to the question of the literary specificity of Chartist poetry, he identifies the existence of a 'dominant literary strategy' which consists of the interplay of 'memorable lyric forms against quite complex *symbolic* modes of writing'. The use of 'extended symbolism', he argues, stems from the attempt to represent both 'dramatic political change' and the consequences of such a change. He notes a marked preference for symbols based on natural change (fire, flood, earthquake) which he argues are intended 'to stress the "naturalness" of the revolutionary process'. Finally, Maidment points to the way in which new content

---

[63] B. Maidment (ed.), *The Poor House Fugitives* (Manchester: Carcanet, 1992), 13.
[64] *Ibid.*, 24.   [65] *Ibid.*, 23.   [66] *Ibid.*, 23.

engenders new form (or substantially revises existing forms). He argues that Chartist poetry's attempts 'to bring into being post-revolutionary consciousness in and through language ... subvert[s] lyric assumptions'.[67] In a complex process (which is intimately connected with the peculiar representational power of language) Chartist poetry seeks to represent a better social order (a future state) as a way of arousing and consolidating a present consciousness which desires that future state. In its turn, this same present consciousness is a necessary precondition of any movement towards this future state.

Chartist poetry, for Maidment, also performs other political functions. He cites, for example, the creation and extension of 'group identity and political solidarity' and the translation of thought and feeling into 'political activism' as twin aims of Chartist poetry.[68] In respect of the perceived intentions of Chartist poetry, Maidment's account closely resembles that offered by Schwab. However, Maidment evinces a rather more sceptical attitude concerning the fulfilment of these intentions. In particular, he is doubtful whether Chartist poetry always acted as a direct stimulus to political action. He contends that 'the recitation of the poem often seems to have served a *cathartic* effect rather than a persuasive one, so that the social aggression in the poem was sublimated or acted out rather than developed into action beyond the poem'.[69]

In similar fashion, Maidment problematises the relationships between a text and its multiple readerships. In a section entitled 'The Metropolitan Response to Self-Taught Writing', he examines the middle-class response to working-class poetry. Earlier Ashraf had observed that the Chartist movement was consciously engaged in a cultural as well as a political struggle. Maidment extends our understanding of this contest by examining it, as it were, from the other side. He notes, for example, that the middle classes were equally conscious (at the very least) of the relationship between the cultural and the political:

there was a crucial link in the middle-class mind between cultural progress and social or political challenge. Writing poetry was inevitably read as a symptom of wider, more disruptive aspirations.[70]

Maidment emphasises the ambivalence of the middle-class response. On the one hand, he argues, they felt that working-class poetry ought to be encouraged (and they expended their own energies collecting, editing, annotating and arranging the publication of artisan writers), whilst

---

[67] *Ibid.*, 38.   [68] *Ibid.*, 37.   [69] *Ibid.*, 37.   [70] *Ibid.*, 282.

remaining fearful of the political challenge which they considered to be an implicit and integral aspect of such poetry. This ambivalence was resolved, he suggests, by formulating 'a version of working-class poetry which was politically harmless and culturally ambitious'.[71] This manifested itself in two major ways. Firstly, when writing the biographies of working-class poets, middle-class editors tended to downplay (or even omit) those aspects of working-class life most troubling or most offensive to the middle-class conscience, such as material hardship, preferring instead to emphasise 'achievement rather than suffering, genius rather than personal weakness, and local benevolence rather than general neglect'.[72] Secondly, Maidment notes that an aesthetic discourse was used to neutralise the political challenge posed by working-class poetry:

The social and political threat offered by proletarian or artisan poetic articulacy is constantly glossed over by focusing the discussion on the literary weaknesses apparent in the texts . . . The point at which this anxiety [regarding the political challenge] consistently surfaces is in the discussion of the *language* of self-taught writers.[73]

This strategy obviates the need to confront directly the political content of such poetry. Instead, the question of politics is approached circuitously by means of the literary. The implicit hierarchy of discourse here privileges the literary over the political and the discovery of failings in the 'higher' discourse simply invalidates the claims encoded in the 'lower' – the political challenge is subsumed within the poetic and perishes with the failure of the latter. This strategy is rendered all the more effective because most working-class poets, including the Chartist poets, also believed that poetry was a higher discourse than politics and wanted their work to be recognised as possessing literary value.[74]

Many aspects of this strategy are played out in a novel which purports to be the autobiography of a Chartist poet, Charles Kingsley's *Alton Locke* (1850). Early on in the novel, the eponymous hero discusses the significance of poetry in working-class life and concludes with a pithy summary of those middle-class anxieties identified in the previous paragraph. The working class, Alton reflects, 'must either dream or agitate; perhaps they are now learning to do both to some purpose'.[75] The connection between poetry and politics is further underlined by the titles of chapters nine and ten: 'Poetry and Poets' and 'How Folks Turn Chartist', respectively. Later

[71] *Ibid.*, 287.   [72] *Ibid.*, 284.   [73] *Ibid.*, 287–8.   [74] *Ibid.*, 289.
[75] C. Kingsley, *Alton Locke, Tailor and Poet: An Autobiography* (Oxford University Press, 1983 [1850]), 84.

in the novel a publisher (approached by Alton's patron, Dean Winnstay) expresses reservations about the political content of some of Alton's poetry. Tellingly he does not challenge the validity or veracity of Alton's observations but he does consider them 'somewhat too strong for the present state of public taste'. Dean Winnstay then tries to persuade Alton that politics has no place in poetry proper and feels certain that Alton will, upon reflection, concur with him in this judgement. Significantly, Winnstay bases his confidence on Alton's readiness to listen, and more importantly, on his use of language specifically, his 'pleasing freedom from all violence or coarseness in expressing [his] opinions'.[76] At first Alton resists and cites Milton, Shelley, Burns and Southey as examples of political poets before finally agreeing, somewhat reluctantly, to amend the offending passages in order to secure publication. The response to this decision (Alton is criticised by both his fellow Chartists and another of his patrons, the aristocratic Eleanor) suggests Kingsley's anxiety at such a crude method of dealing with political dissent. Kingsley's preferred method is demonstrated within the text by Lord Lynedale who reproves Alton for the tone rather than the content of his speech, 'Sir . . . your bitterness is pardonable – but not your sneer'.[77] Within the novel Dean Winnstay's method of outright suppression is productive only of increased violence, whilst the approach of Lynedale and Eleanor finally secures Alton's conversion to Kingsley's brand of Christian Socialism.

Maidment also detects a structural ambivalence within Chartist poetry with regard to its readerships. 'Chartist and radical poetry', he argues, 'is addressed generally to two audiences – upwards to the aristocracy and Government, which it seeks to challenge or threaten, and outwards to the already converted radical groups and followers, where its function is confirmation and uplift'.[78] This notion of what might be termed the 'double address' of Chartist poetry provides us with a category which is simultaneously political and aesthetic. The double address thus joins the question of the construction of post-revolutionary consciousness, and the complex of reading relations surrounding Chartist poetry, in demonstrating not only the possibility but also the necessity of reading the political in the literary and the literary in the political.

The next major critical consideration of Chartist poetry occurs in Isobel Armstrong's *Victorian Poetry. Poetry, Poetics and Politics* (1993). Although neither is made the subject of a discrete chapter, both Chartist and working-class poetry receive extended discussions in the second part

[76] *Ibid.*, 179.   [77] *Ibid.*, 141.   [78] Maidment, *Poor House Fugitives*, 14.

of her study where they are located in relation to the work of Clough and Arnold in particular; thereby breaking with the critical tradition which takes Romanticism as the main co-ordinate for the discussion of Chartist verse. Clough emerges as the poet most aware of, and responsive to, Chartist poetry with Armstrong arguing, for example, that the 'battle imagery' used in *The Bothie of Tober-Na-Vuolich* 'alludes to the imagery of struggle in radical, Chartist poetry' and that one of Clough's most anthologised poems, 'Say not the Struggle Nought Availeth', 'is clearly modelled on the rhetoric of Chartism'.[79]

Armstrong's analysis of Chartist poetry proper begins with an anatomisation of its masculinist and martial propensities.[80] However, once these reservations have been recorded, Armstrong moves quickly 'to salute the achievement of [Chartism's] critique'. This achievement includes the creation of 'a genuinely *public* rhetoric of collective action and affirmation, and a genuinely social rhetoric of community which derived from their own traditions – the ballad and refrain, the marching song, the Bunyanesque hymn, biblical imagery', and the elaboration 'of an impersonal language of hope and energy' which she identifies as '[p]erhaps the greatest achievement of Chartist poetry'.[81] Like Maidment, Armstrong recognises the importance of considering the intended audience of Chartist poetry when trying to assess its aesthetic achievements. She notes, for example, that 'because the songs would be learned and sung by the illiterate they could not be burdened with literary device'. This recognition of the studied simplicity of Chartist poetry avoids the pitfall of seeing such poetry as culturally unsophisticated, for as Armstrong acknowledges, this verse 'was simple and accessible but firm and powerful verbally'. Armstrong also praises Chartist poets for their ability to develop poetic forms and figures well-suited to their political and agitational requirements: 'Firm antitheses – between tyrants, priests and slaves, peer and peasant, cottage and throne, industrial lord and labour – and clear symbols of oppression – mitre and crown, crown, cross and sabre – provide lucid contrasts and *alternatives*'.[82] In other words these verbal structures simultaneously educate and seek to mobilise their audience.[83]

Maidment had argued that Chartist poetry could serve as a heuristic device within the movement, providing Chartists with a way of imagining

---

[79] I. Armstrong, *Victorian Poetry. Poetry, Poetics and Politics* (Routledge, 1996), 191–4.
[80] *Ibid.*, 192–3.   [81] *Ibid.*, 193–4.   [82] *Ibid.*, 194.
[83] This does not blind Armstrong to the risks attending Chartist poetry – 'didacticism, sentimentality or violence, simplifying or blurring the rigour of the deliberately banal material it worked with and generally transformed', *ibid.*, 195.

(and thus discussing) the process of social transformation and the nature of post-revolutionary consciousness. In this account, Chartist poetry unproblematically assists in the strategic development of the Chartist movement. Armstrong alerts us to the possibility that the figurative power of poetic imagery is also capable of retarding the movement's understanding. In particular, she draws attention to the 'potential within the battle image for the expression of violent militarism and phallic power which makes it such a dangerous and equivocal image except in the hands of exemplary writers of great integrity'.[84] Linton is praised as an example of the latter whilst the 'violence' of Massey's poetry is criticised. Armstrong's negative assessment of Massey recalls the equally hostile judgements of Vicinus and Ashraf. However, where Vicinus and Ashraf read Massey's poetic shortcomings as signs of his own limited political commitment and/or understanding, Armstrong's analysis suggests another possible explanation in which his poetry generates his political weakness rather than vice versa. Commenting on Massey's bloodthirsty support for the Crimean War, Armstrong notes that the 'logic of a rhetoric of freedom and united manhood which had consolidated Chartist poetry seemed to some to imply the logic of patriotism – it is almost as if the rhetoric of Chartism becomes pathologised in a literal war'.[85] The suggestion here is that favoured rhetorics and images possess a degree of autonomous agency which can assist in the determination of political positions.

Elsewhere Armstrong is far less circumspect in her assessment of the kinds of agency expressed and possessed by Chartist poetry. In a discussion of the differences between 'early' and 'late' Chartist poetry, for example, she writes:

Up to 1848 a poetry of protest, exhortation and millennial confidence was dominant. Martial imagery, certainty in the necessity of struggle and action and a shared definition of manhood and agency create a remarkable bond between different poems. After 1848 such poems are harder to find.[86]

Shortly afterwards, she offers an account of the particular use which Chartist poetry made of 'biblical, millennial and apocalyptic imagery', arguing:

It was necessary to generalise and secularise biblical imagery because the stress was on human agency and not on divine intervention: it was necessary to evolve a rhetoric of power to energise and enable a rhetoric of revolution and change which did not threaten immediate violence (or at least conceded its possibility) by shifting the mobilisation of force to an indeterminate utopian future.[87]

---

[84] *Ibid.*, 193.   [85] *Ibid.*, 229.   [86] *Ibid.*, 192.   [87] *Ibid.*, 194.

With regard to the question of agency, Armstrong overstates the degree of coherence and unanimity displayed by Chartist poetry. As later chapters will show, Chartist poetry contained the same divisions, uncertainties, dissonances and contradictions in relation to agency and strategy as can be found in the wider Chartist movement.

Anne Janowitz's *Lyric and Labour in the Romantic Tradition* (1998) once again situates Chartist poetry in relation to Romanticism. However, for Janowitz, Romanticism is not simply an aggregate of literary influences (Shelley, Byron) but is rather the cultural manifestation of a fundamental social antagonism. She contends that Romanticism must be understood as 'the literary form of a struggle taking place on many levels of society between the claims of *individualism* and the claims of *communitarianism*'.[88] It is the use of this latter category within a theoretical framework derived from Raymond Williams' concepts of 'dominant', 'residual' and 'emergent' which gives Janowitz's study its analytical power. Janowitz's adroit use of Williams' theoretical triad allows for a much more nuanced account of both the ideological and literary development of the working-class movement in the nineteenth century. For example, her insistence on romanticism-as-dialectic emphasises its ambivalent ideological significance (seen as a product of its historical location) – 'Chartist romanticism is made up of both emergent (individualist) and residual (plebeian communitarian) elements'.[89] This dialectic generates competing forms in the areas of lyric and landscape poetry. In the former, argues Janowitz, the 'individualist lyric' is counterposed to the 'communitarian lyric', whilst in the latter, landscape as a site of 'personal transcendence' is challenged by an understanding of landscape as 'natural instantiation'.[90] In essence, Janowitz argues that Chartist poetry constitutes a specific appropriation and development of this conflicted inheritance. In particular, Chartist poetry rests on a rejection of the 'individualist' or 'liberal lyric' in favour of the communitarian lyric. This choice has important consequences for Chartist poetry insofar as the communitarian lyric is essentially teleological (unlike the liberal lyric which is atemporal) and crucially dependent on rhetorics of 'temporality, solidarity, and futurity'.[91] Likewise, in Chartist poetry, landscape is charged with economic and political significance in a way which recalls the older tradition of topographical poetry. Janowitz is more interested in the ideological rather than the poetic implications of Chartist landscape

---

[88] A. Janowitz, *Lyric and Labor in the Romantic Tradition* (Cambridge University Press, 1998), 13.
[89] *Ibid.*, 143.   [90] *Ibid.*, 91.   [91] *Ibid.*, 26.

poetry and is particularly concerned with its deleterious effects on the attainment of class consciousness, more specifically its tendency to 'mystif[y] the relationship between a rural past and a proletarianised present'.[92]

Like Schwab, Janowitz emphasises the active role played by poetry within the Chartist movement: 'Chartist poetry was not merely a reflex of the movement, however, for the Chartists' desires to create a self-sufficient intellectual world urged them to formulate a poetic that would in turn fuel the political movement itself'.[93] However, where Schwab hypothesises the vital role of Chartist poetry, Janowitz provides concrete evidence. Janowitz also concurs with Schwab's assessment that the most important political work performed by Chartist poetry was its articulation of a shared Chartist consciousness or identity, and also identifies the ways in which Chartist poetry constructed this identity at both the collective and individual levels.

> Poetry was both a flattering mirror to a movement-in-formation, offering conventions for group identity, and a social matrix within which people could discover themselves as belonging to an on-going set of traditions, goals and expectations. The work of Chartist poetry was both to excavate and invent that sense of tradition.
> . . .
> My claim is that Chartism as a social and political movement made itself culturally intelligible to its constituencies *through* its use of poetry.[94]

For Janowitz, the prestige accorded to Chartist poetry by the wider movement is exemplified by the events surrounding Thomas Cooper's expulsion from the movement in 1846. The crux of her analysis is that the Chartist leader Feargus O'Connor did not dare to move against the author of *The Purgatory of Suicides* until he had secured as an ally a poet of equal status in the shape of Ernest Jones.[95] Furthermore, Janowitz is the first critic to recognise the historical development of Chartist poetry as it responds to the changing needs of the movement. Between 1838 and 1842, she argues, 'Chartist poetry was chiefly engaged in trying to formulate an independent people's poetic', and Chartist poetry of this period draws heavily on the oral tradition and is 'abundantly collective, often anonymous'. After 1842 there is a shift towards a much more 'literary' (as opposed to oral) poetics and Chartist poetry generally becomes 'less militant and more analytical'. Janowitz detects further changes in the late 1840s as Chartist poetry becomes increasingly elegiac and after 1851 there emerges 'a newly complex poetry of defeat and hope'.[96]

---

[92] *Ibid.*, 153–7.   [93] *Ibid.*, 28.   [94] *Ibid.*, 135–8.   [95] *Ibid.*, 173.   [96] *Ibid.*, 151–2.

Ernest Jones and William James Linton are, for Janowitz, exemplary writers of this 'complex poetry' and their work provides her with two different ways in which Chartist poetry attempted to reconcile the contending models of identity which it had inherited from Romanticism. Jones, for example, demonstrates (in both his poetry and his own life) that the free-willed, voluntaristic 'self' might not only choose to identify with the Chartist movement but might also find that such an identification is the precondition for the discovery of a truer and more authentic self. In addition, precisely because the act of affiliation is a conscious one which requires explanation (not least to the Chartist body itself), Jones is better placed to theorise the new class and social relations engendered by the consolidation of industrial capitalism. Janowitz summarises Jones' contribution to the development of Chartist poetry as follows:

[by transmitting] custom-based communitarian poetry into more obviously industrial and class-based poems, and endowing them with a firmer sense of the agency of the workers . . . Jones helped create a poetic of community which is voluntaristic rather than inherited . . . an unmooring of collective affiliation from either customary filiation or social origin – the family, the parish, the counters of the moral economy – and its recovery as choice and solidarity.[97]

If Jones offers a dialectical synthesis in which 'self' is initially negated by 'collective' only to re-emerge as 'affiliated self' (and as such truer to both 'self' and 'collective'), then Linton offers an arrested synthesis in which the competing claims of both moments are recognised but remain unreconciled without being figured as necessarily antagonistic. Thus, Janowitz argues, Linton's poetry is frequently riven by contending impulses, '[his] poetry searches for a way of highlighting the autonomy of the self, while being inflected by a strong sense of class-consciousness' and his best poetry is that which addresses 'the problem of finding a voice for the claims to collective civic subjectivity'. Janowitz attributes this to Linton's commitment to political liberalism (of a republican kind) and his rejection of economic liberalism, which produces a paradoxical, if not contradictory, position in which '[Linton's] liberal notion of self [is] deeply imprinted by the anti-liberal social ideology of his political milieu'.[98]

Lyric and Labour in the Romantic Tradition constitutes an important advance in the critical history of Chartist poetry. Janowitz not only offers a compelling argument for considering poetry to be a central rather than a marginal Chartist activity but also demonstrates how the particular

---

[97] *Ibid.*, 183.   [98] *Ibid.*, 203–9.

interventions made by that poetry could only be made through poetry. Janowitz greatly increases our sense of both the richness of the cultural resources on which Chartist poetry draws and the richness of the transformative work which it undertakes on those same resources. Janowitz's study is, perhaps, only limited by its concentration on individual authors; George Dyer, Allen Davenport, Thomas Cooper, Ernest Jones and William James Linton are offered as exemplars of various kinds of radical/ Chartist poetics. Yet, although these writers are indeed 'typical' (in the Lukacsian sense) they are not representative of the broad mass of Chartist poetic production.

The theoretical strength and historical sensitivity of Janowitz's work are made even more apparent when compared with another study published in the same year, Susan Zlotnick's *Women, Writing, and the Industrial Revolution*. Zlotnick devotes her final chapter, 'Nostalgia and the Ideology of Domesticity in Working-Class Literature', to an analysis of Chartist and dialect literature which she compares with the remarkable writings of the working-class women poets, Fanny Forrester and Ellen Johnston. Zlotnick's study is organised around a single, bold thesis, 'This book's main contention is that the female and male literary response to the industrial revolution was Janus-faced: while women writers were more likely to look to the future with hope, male writers frequently longed for an idealized (and often medievalized) past'.[99] In her account, Chartist and dialect writers do not so much challenge as reiterate the views and attitudes of the more established canonical male voices (Carlyle, Dickens, Ruskin and Arnold): 'the male-dominated traditions of Chartist and dialect writing . . . replay the male repudiation of modernity'. Indeed, in a rather unlikely symmetry, 'Chartist and dialect writings correspond to the two movements in the middle-class male canon: medievalism and culture'.[100]

The publication in 1994 of a collection of essays, *The Chartist Legacy*, edited by Owen Ashton, Robert Fyson and Stephen Roberts, provides evidence of the increasing recognition of the significance of Chartist literary production within labour history. Two essays on Chartist literature appear in this volume. One, by Kelly J. Mays, is concerned with Chartist autobiography: the other, 'Chartist Poetry and Song' by Timothy

---

[99] Susan Zlotnick, *Women, Writing, and the Industrial Revolution* (Baltimore: John Hopkins University Press, 1998), 1.
[100] *Ibid.*, 171–2.

Randall, examines what its author describes as 'Chartist verse'.[101] Randall begins by arguing that the 'primary need' for scholarship in the field remains that of retrieval rather than interpretation. In particular, he cites the necessity of recovering the specific functions of Chartist verse within its particular historical context and describes his own work as reconstructing 'in close detail a popular cultural formation within its historical context'.[102]

Randall identifies the many local contexts in which Chartist verse functioned. These range from large formal 'open-air gatherings' through to 'extempore singing in prison'. These contexts, Randall argues, remind us that Chartist poetry 'existed not only on the page as a literary text, but also as a social event and public demonstration'. He also comments that they are contexts of which 'literary critics are largely oblivious'. Randall demonstrates that the relationship between text and context is variable. He offers Robert Gammage (Chartism's first historian) singing in prison as an example of the synergy of text and context and also notes that more often there is a disjuncture between the two, 'the verbal expression of militancy was [frequently] mitigated by the ritualisation of a public occasion'.[103] The sheer variety of situations within which Chartist poetry was reproduced and the concomitant need to think of a poem as both printed text and public event has enormous implications in terms of both literary-critical methodology and aesthetic evaluation. For example, it is likely that a poem which is performed at a public meeting and printed in a Chartist newspaper performs significantly different political and cultural work in each context.

Randall identifies six major 'collective functions of Chartist verse within the movement': communal singing, the celebration of individual Chartists, the representation of political agency, a means of defying imprisonment, the exploration of utopian visions and the evolution of a 'distinctively Chartist stock of poetic imagery'.[104] It is clear from this list of functions which might be summarised as solidarity, leadership, strategy, resistance, aspiration and language, that Chartist poetry performed core political activities within the movement. In his analysis of the representation of political agency in Chartist verse, Randall focuses on

---

[101] O. Ashton, R. Fyson and S. Roberts (eds.), *The Chartist Legacy* (Rendlesham: Merlin, 1999). The two essays in question are: K. J. Mays, 'Subjectivity, Community and the Nature of Truth-telling in Two Chartist Autobiographies', 196–231: and T. Randall, 'Chartist Poetry and Song', 171–95. Randall's contribution is a distillation of his PhD Thesis, *Towards A Cultural Democracy: Chartist Literature, 1837–1860* (University of Sussex, 1994).
[102] T. Randall, 'Chartist Poetry and Song', 172.   [103] *Ibid.*, 173–5.   [104] *Ibid.*, 172.

the role of 'images of nature as an analogy or symbol for revolutionary change', and notes that Maidment regards such images as an attempt to legitimise revolution, whilst Ashraf sees them as providing Chartists with an image of irresistible power. However, in a reading which literalises these natural metaphors (and thus discounts their operation as a figure for, rather than an analogue of, the desired political change), Randall insists on their problematic aspect, arguing that they are frequently deployed in contradictory ways and, as a result, produce 'a mixed political message'. On the one hand, argues Randall, Nature's cyclical nature encodes, at best, only a temporary victory – 'if freedom arrives with spring, tyranny will return with winter'. On the other hand, 'in stressing the natural inevitability of liberty's conquest of tyranny, such images appear to fore-close on the need for human action'.[105]

Randall identifies a similar weakness in Chartist poetry's representa-tion of the revolution as occurring 'in a single instant of time, usually conceived as "the day" or "the hour" '.[106] He also suggests that Chartist poetry's reliance on 'abstract binary oppositions, such as "freedom" and "oppression"' left it vulnerable to ideological capture during the Crimean War when the freedom/tyranny binary became reoriented around nation rather than class such that British freedom confronted Russian tyranny.[107]

The new millennium has seen something of a resurgence of interest in Chartist poetry. Three Chartist poets (Thomas Cooper, Ernest Jones and Gerald Massey) were included in Valentine Cunningham's *The Victorians: An Anthology of Poetry and Poetics* (2000) and Gerald Massey was also included in T. J. Collins and V. J. Rundle's *The Broadview Anthology of Victorian Poetry and Poetic Theory* (2000).[108] The increasing academic visibility of Chartist poetry was confirmed by the appearance of a special issue of *Victorian Poetry* dedicated to 'The Poetics of the Working Classes' and containing four essays devoted to Chartist poetry. Two of these, Stephanie Kuduk's 'Sedition, Criticism and Epic Poetry in Thomas Cooper's *The Purgatory of Suicides*', and Ronald Paul's 'In Louring Hindostan: Chartism and Empire in Ernest Jones's *The New World*', as their titles suggest, offered detailed readings of an individual work by a labour laureate. Of the other two essays, Kelly J. Mays' 'Slaves in Heaven, Laborers in Hell: Chartist Poets' Ambivalent Identification

---

[105] *Ibid.*, 177–9.   [106] *Ibid.*, 179.   [107] *Ibid.*, 190.
[108] V. Cunningham (ed.), *The Victorians: An Anthology of Poetry and Poetics* (Oxford: Blackwell, 2000); T. J. Collins and V. J. Rundle (eds.), *The Broadview Anthology of Victorian Poetry and Poetic Theory* (Peterborough, Ontario: Broadview, 2000).

with the (Black) Slave', examines the 'multiple, intersecting, sometimes contradictory uses and definitions of slavery' in Chartist poetry, whilst my own 'Poetic Agency: Metonymy and Metaphor in Chartist Poetry 1838–1852' examined the relationship between changing representations of agency in Chartist poetry and debates over political strategy in the wider movement.[109]

In 2003, the appearance of the first full-length biography of Ernest Jones, Miles Taylor's *Ernest Jones, Chartism and the Romance of Politics 1819–1869*, demonstrates that historians are beginning to heed Schwab's call regarding the evidential validity of poetry. Not only does Taylor argue that Jones' poetry is central to an understanding of his 'almost instant success within the Chartist movement', he also uses his poetry to track Jones' political and ideological development, or rather to demonstrate the continuities between his pre-Chartist and Chartist attitudes.[110] However, Taylor generally treats Jones' poetry as consisting entirely of content and is largely uninterested in both the polysemic aspects of literary language and the interplay between form and content in the generation of meaning. One result of this is that Taylor's Jones remains intellectually static, particularly in respect of his religious attitudes before and after his imprisonment, whereas Roy Vickers argues that Jones' use of 'Christian motifs, rites and language' in his poetry 'differ[s] markedly' between the appearance of *Chartist Poems and Fugitive Pieces* (1846) and his prison poems published in *Notes to the People* (1851–52).[111]

2006 saw the publication, under the general editorship of John Goodridge, of the three-volume series *Nineteenth-Century English Labouring-Class Poets 1800–1900*. The second volume deals with the period from 1830 to 1860, and its editor Kaye Kossick comments on 'the extraordinary efflorescence of literature, poetry and song that [Chartism] inspired', and includes poetry from Thomas Cooper, Gerald Massey and Robert Peddie

---

[109] *Victorian Poetry*, 39: 2 (Summer 2001). The four essays in question are: S. Kuduk, 'Sedition, Criticism and Epic Poetry in Thomas Cooper's *The Purgatory of Suicides*', 165–86: R. Paul, 'In Louring Hindostan: Chartism and Empire in Ernest Jones's *The New World*', 189–204: K. J. Mays, 'Slaves in Heaven, Laborers in Hell: Chartist Poets' Ambivalent Identification with the (Black) Slave', 137–63: M. Sanders, 'Poetic Agency: Metonymy and Metaphor in Chartist Poetry 1838–1852', 111–35.

[110] M. Taylor, *Ernest Jones, Chartism and the Romance of Politics 1819–1869* (Oxford University Press, 2003), 78, 67–8, 85–8.

[111] R. Vickers, 'Christian Election, Holy Communion and Psalmic Language in Ernest Jones's Chartist Poetry', *Journal of Victorian Culture*, 11: 1 (2006), 59–83. This article draws on Vickers' PhD Thesis, *The Gospel of Social Discontent. Religious Language and the Narrative of Christian Election in the Chartist Poetry of Cooper, Jones and Linton* (Liverpool John Moores University, 2005).

as representative of Chartist poetry.[112] Arguably, Chartist poetry now has a higher academic profile than at any time in the past half-century: monographs, a journal special issue, scholarly articles and conferences papers, its reappearance in anthologies of Victorian poetry and even on the undergraduate syllabus in some institutions, are testimony to this welcome development.

However, this emergent acceptance of the importance of Chartist poetry remains doubly vulnerable. It rests on a narrow empirical foundation which is itself the product of a limited theorisation of the object of analysis. Most existing scholarship on Chartist poetry has tended to concentrate on the handful of 'Labour Laureates' (Cooper, Jones, Massey) and on poetry of an obvious and immediate political nature. In short, it has operated with what might be described as a 'self-evident' definition of its object of study, constructing Chartist poetry as an 'ideal type' consisting of poems on a recognisably Chartist theme written by self-identified Chartist poets. However, this ignores the atypicality of the Labour Laureates. The overwhelming majority of Chartist poets did not achieve widespread recognition in their lifetimes, nor did they publish volumes of their work. Instead, the typical Chartist poet enjoyed a limited, local reputation and published their work in the periodical press. Hence, the need to construct the poetry column itself as the object of study.

An examination of a representative sample of the *Northern Star*'s poetry column serves to illustrate these points. The following list gives the date of publication, title, author, and a brief indication of the contents of the first thirteen poems to be published in the poetry column in 1838.

> 6 January 1838: 'Working Men's Rhymes – No. 1', John Smithson (poem inculcating core Chartist principles and explaining the need for male suffrage, short Parliaments and the ballot).
>
> 13 January 1838: 'The Tear of Beauty', T. B. Smith (sentimental poem celebrating the beauty of a weeping woman).
>
> 20 January 1838: 'Plaint of the Wandering Irish Peasant', J. B. Walker (self-explanatory title, poem also calls on 'Albion' not to forget 'Erin').
>
> 3 February 1838: 'Answer to Beauty's Tear', B. T. (offers a sharp critique of 'The Tear of Beauty' for ignoring the suffering, often male-authored, which is the usual cause of beauty's tears).

---

[112] K. Kossick (ed.), *Nineteenth-Century English Labouring-Class Poets 1800–1900. Volume II 1830–1860* (Pickering & Chatto, 2006), xxvii.

3 February 1828: 'Lines on the Conviction of the Glasgow Cotton Spinners', T. B. Smith (a poem arguing that the conviction of the Glasgow cotton spinners is a further sign of labour's enslaved position).

17 February 1838: 'The Slaves' Address to British Females', A. L. (a poem advocating abolition).

17 February 1838: '[2] Sonnets Addressed to a Certain Lord', L. (the first sonnet warns an aristocratic minister against planning the military repression of Chartism; the second implicitly claims Christianity's moral authority for Chartism).

3 March 1838: 'The Smile of Beauty (A Counterpart to the Tear of Beauty)', T. B. Smith (a sentimental counterpart to 'The Tear of Beauty' rather than a response to 'Answer to Beauty's Tear' which celebrates the moral and spiritual influence of the smiling woman).

3 March 1838: 'The Portrait of Arthur O'Connor', J. B. Walker (self-explanatory title, poem emphasises the manly heroism of its subject, one of the leaders of the United Irishmen).

24 March 1838: 'New Poor Law Rhymes: The Wanderer', J. Gower (a poem contrasting the compassion and freedom of nature with the cruelty and oppression practised by society).

24 March 1848: 'Lines on Factories', L. S. (a poem criticising factory conditions).

31 March 1838: 'The Victim of the Lash': Robert Dibb (a poem opposing the use of flogging as a punishment within the army).

None of these poems is the work of a 'labour laureate'. Indeed, only T. B. Smith and Robert Dibb subsequently appear in the Poetry column.[113] Four of the nine poets are practically anonymous (B. T., A. L., L., and L. S.) including, probably, the only woman writer in the group (B. T.). Formally, these poems range from rhyming couplets through quatrains, sestets and nine-line stanzas, to the sonnet. However, it is the quatrain which dominates, providing the form for six of the thirteen poems. Three of the poems (the 'Beauty' series) are best described as sentimental and only two ('Working Men's Rhymes' and the first of the sonnets) take Chartism itself as their subject. The eight remaining poems are all, broadly speaking, 'political' and cover a wide range of issues. Some of these, such as factory reform, trade unionism and the campaign against the New Poor Law, are closely connected with Chartism, whilst others belong to

[113] T. B. Smith published eleven poems in total: six in 1838, four in 1839 and one in 1843. Robert Dibb published eight poems: seven in 1838 and one in 1839.

the broader spectrum of radical politics (Ireland, abolition, and military reform).

If we adhere to the definition of Chartist poetry as 'political' poetry, then between half and three-quarters of these poems qualify (depending on what constitutes an appropriate degree of political relevance). However, even the most generous definition of what constitutes a political poem would exclude a quarter of the Poetry column's contents. Is such an exclusion warranted? It would be a questionable methodological assumption which considers that the editor of the poetry column knew exactly what he was doing when he decided to publish, for example, 'Working Men's Rhymes – No. 1' but which views the inclusion of 'Answer to Beauty's Tear' as an aberrant editorial decision. Similarly, on what grounds would it be appropriate to decide that 'Lines on the Conviction of the Glasgow Cotton Spinners' is a Chartist poem, whilst the two 'Beauty' poems by the same author are not, especially when 'The Tear of Beauty' elicits a response from a fellow reader of the *Northern Star*? This study assumes that both the contributors to, and the editors of, the poetry column were engaged in Chartist activity, and therefore that all the poems published therein can be defined as Chartist poetry.

The focus on the poetry column, on individual poems already situated in their immediate political and historical context, and where anonymity, pseudonymity and simple historical obscurity foreclose any attempt at authorial explanation, opens up the possibility of writing a literary history which is something other than a form of historicised biography. It also alerts us to the dialogic nature of these poems – as part of a regular column, individual poems were necessarily part of an ongoing conversation (sometimes self-consciously so in the case of poems explicitly written in response to an earlier contribution). Furthermore, as part of a newspaper, the poetry column needs to be read 'horizontally' as well as 'vertically' (to use Ian Haywood's terms), that is in terms of the links and connections it establishes with other elements in the newspaper.[114] Finally, by paying close attention to what was actually published in the poetry column, we can avoid a reductive and anachronistic definition of Chartist poetry in which only poems about Chartism (or what is considered to be an appropriate political theme) qualify.

---

[114] I. Haywood, *The Revolution in Popular Literature: Print, Politics and the People, 1790–1860* (Cambridge University Press, 2005), 187–9.

CHAPTER 3

'A jackass load of poetry': the Northern Star's poetry column 1838–1852

The recovery of nineteenth-century working-class reading practices has proceeded apace in recent years. Paul Murphy's *Towards a Working-Class Canon* tracks the changing attitudes towards literature expressed in radical journals between 1816 and 1858, whilst Jonathan Rose's *The Intellectual Life of the British Working Classes* demonstrates the deep and persistent drive to cultural literacy within the working-class movement.[1] Most recently, Ian Haywood in *The Revolution in Popular Literature* has traced the British state's responses to the emergence of the 'common reader' in the 1790s, demonstrating that policies of direct repression of the radical press were also accompanied by attempts to provide alternative reading material, thereby making the periodical press one of the most significant sites of political struggle between 1790 and 1860.[2]

Despite acknowledging the importance of the Chartist press, historians have been reluctant to grant literary production the same significance and agency which they so readily accord to literacy. For example, whilst Dorothy Thompson in *The Early Chartists* insists on 'a definition of Chartism . . . as the response of a literate and sophisticated working class', her selection of representative Chartist documents contains not a single poem.[3] Similarly, Edward Royle's *Chartism* discusses the careers of Thomas Cooper and Ernest Jones without once mentioning their poetry, whilst a chapter entitled 'Chartist Culture' makes no reference to Chartist poetry. As the previous chapter has shown, more recently historians have begun to treat Chartist poetry as a central rather than an incidental

---

[1] P. T. Murphy, *Towards A Working-Class Canon: Literary Criticism in British Working-Class Periodicals 1816–1858* (Ohio State University Press, 1994); Jonathan Rose, *The Intellectual Life of the British Working Classes* (New Haven: Yale University Press, 2001).

[2] I. Haywood, *The Revolution in Popular Literature: Print, Politics and the People, 1790–1860* (Cambridge University Press, 2005).

[3] D. Thompson, *The Early Chartists* (Macmillan, 1971), 13.

aspect of the movement.[4] However, it remains the case that the increased attention paid to working-class literary consumption has not yet extended into the sphere of working-class literary *production*.

This chapter aims to augment our understanding of the latter through a detailed analysis of one of the richest archives of nineteenth-century working-class writing, namely the poetry column of the leading Chartist newspaper, the *Northern Star*.[5] During its lifetime, this column published almost 1,500 poems (or excerpts from poems). These poems were the work of at least 390 Chartist poets, the vast majority of whom were working men. This chapter provides, for the first time, a full survey of the *Northern Star*'s poetry column, quantifying the number of poems and poets published on an annual basis, as well as the ratio of 'Chartist produced' to 'non-Chartist produced' poems (see Table 3.1 for full details).[6] In so doing, it provides a much firmer empirical base than has previously existed from which to view the relationship between Chartist poetry and the wider Chartist movement. For the purposes of gauging the extent and rate of poetry production from *within* the Chartist movement, this chapter distinguishes between 'Chartist produced' and 'non-Chartist produced' poetry. The latter category includes poetry reprinted from non-Chartist journals, poetry by 'canonical' poets such as Shelley, Byron, and Shakespeare, and poetry by contemporary poets who were not expressly affiliated with Chartism such as Charles Mackay and Beranger. All other contributions to the poetry column are assumed to be the work of Chartists and thus are designated as Chartist produced poetry.[7]

---

[4] Edward Royle, *Chartism* (Longman, 1986). It should be noted that Royle does include 'The Lion of Freedom' (tentatively attributed to Thomas Cooper) and an extract from Ernest Jones' 'The New World' in the 'Documents' section of his book. However, Miles Taylor's recent study, *Ernest Jones, Chartism and the Romance of Politics 1819–1869*, for example, argues for the inseparability of Jones' poetry and his politics.

[5] The average weekly circulation figures for the *Northern Star* are: 1839 : 36,000 copies; 1840 : 18,700; 1842 : 12,500; 1843–1847 : 8,700 maximum; 1848 : 12,000. Murphy, *Towards A Working-Class Canon*, 10. At its peak in 1839 the *Northern Star* enjoyed a weekly circulation of 50,000. It is generally assumed that a reasonable estimate of a working-class journal's readership in this period may be obtained by multiplying the circulation figures by a factor of between twenty and thirty.

[6] Although many scholars have noted in passing that, for the greater part of its existence, the *Northern Star* published a weekly poetry column, very little has been established beyond this salient fact. Stephen Roberts' essay, 'Who Wrote to the *Northern Star*?', only provides an alphabetical list of contributors to the *Northern Star*'s poetry column between 1838 and 1842. Stephen Roberts, 'Who Wrote to the *Northern Star*?', in Owen Ashton *et al.*, (eds.), *The Duty of Discontent: Essays for Dorothy Thompson* (New York: Mansell, 1995).

[7] This division is not entirely secure and probably overstates the absolute number of poems produced *within* the Chartist movement. However, the number of poems misattributed by this classification system is very small (at most 30 poems/extracts out of a total of 1,500, or some 2 per cent of the total).

Table 3.1. *The Poetry Column of the* Northern Star *1838–1852*

Year of publication	Number of poems published	Minimum number of rejected poems	Number of non-Chartist-produced poems and/or poems published elsewhere	Maximum number of Chartist-produced poems	Maximum number of Chartist poets
1838	61	23	6 (10%)	55 (90%)	34 – 42
1839	77	31	25 (32%)	52 (68%)	31 – 44
1840	146	85	12 (8%)	134 (92%)	55 – 74
1841	133	125	4 (3%)	129 (97%)	57 – 75
1842	95	10	3 (3%)	92 (97%)	38 – 51
1843	85	31	26 (31%)	59 (69%)	32 – 40
1844	131	58	47 (36%)	84 (64%)	40 – 59
1845	115	21	66 (57%)	49 (43%)	28 – 37
1846	143	21	60 (42%)	83 (58%)	37 – 46
1847	120	15	59 (49%)	61 (51%)	28 – 35
1848	118	19	64 (54%)	54 (46%)	32 – 40
1849	91	1	45 (49%)	46 (51%)	29 – 39
1850	73	5	15 (21%)	58 (79%)	29 – 43
1851	59	3	26 (44%)	33 (56%)	18 – 27
1852	35	2	14 (40%)	21 (60%)	9 – 16

A detailed analysis of the *Northern Star* reveals the dialectical interplay between readership and editor in the creation of the poetry column's editorial policy. Initially, the sheer volume of poetry produced by rank and file Chartists literally forced the poetry column from the margins to the centre of the paper. Once established as an important Chartist activity in its own right, Chartist poetic production becomes the subject of a number of editorial interventions. This chapter seeks to reconstruct the editorial policy of the poetry column, thereby demonstrating the import-ance accorded aesthetic value throughout its existence. In particular, it argues that from 1844 onwards the editor of the column adopted a number of strategies in an attempt to enhance the quality of Chartist poetic production. Furthermore, it argues that raising the standard of Chartist poetry was seen as an important aspect of the movement's strategy.

For the first two years of its existence, the poetry column appeared on the inside back page (page 7) of the *Northern Star*. Although this position suggests it might have begun as something of an editorial afterthought, the paper's readers (as writers) quickly signalled their commitment to its institution by inundating the editor with original poetry. The

'To Readers and Correspondents' column (which records the rejection of poems deemed insufficiently accomplished to merit publication) provides evidence which suggests a dramatic increase in Chartist literary production in the period from 1838 to 1841. In 1838 at least 23 poems were rejected individually by the poetry column's editor, rising to a minimum of 31 in 1839, 85 in 1840 and a staggering 125 in 1841.[8]

The rate of collective rejections published in the same column provides further evidence of increasing Chartist poetic production. On three separate occasions in March 1838, the editor refers to the 'large number of poetical favours' received, and by the end of the same month there is more than a hint of tetchiness in his remark: 'We have received as much poetry as a donkey could draw; we shall select from it as occasion offers, so let none be jealous, or we will take it by lot' (*NS*, 31 March 1838). There appears to have been little respite for the editor who issues further collective rejections in May, June and August. By late December, one senses that the editor has finally lost patience, as a note addressed to 'The Poets' reads: 'We get Rhymes of a most rubbishly description by the score. We cannot pretend to enumerate them. We shall select, from time to time, such as we think worth publishing, and burn the rest' (*NS*, 22 December 1838).

1839 appears to have been a far less demanding year in this respect with only one collective refusal issued by the editor. 1840 begins equally quietly with no collective rejection until the middle of July, when 'A host of poetical favours [are] declined' (*NS*, 18 July 1840). At this point, however, the floodgates appear to have opened. Collective rejections are delivered in August and September, whilst in October the editor claims first to be 'glutted with poetry', and then to have 'almost a jackass load of what claims to be original poetry waiting for insertion' (*NS*, 17 October 1840). By November 1840 the editor is begging for mercy. 'The Poets must really give us a little breathing time. We have heaps upon heaps accumulating which we cannot find room for' (*NS*, 7 November 1840). The following week an apparently exhausted editor can only write, 'We must refer some dozen or two of Poets to the notice in our last' (*NS*, 14 November 1840). The collective rejections for 1841 follow an almost identical pattern.[9]

---

[8] The actual numbers of rejected poems cannot be calculated with absolute precision, for the simple reason that the 'Notes to Readers' column sometimes issues non-specific, but decidedly multiple, rejections. For example, in September 1841 'fifty other poets' are rejected and in October of the same year 'a dozen poetical contributions are declined'. We have no way of knowing whether such statements are a record of literal or poetic truth.

[9] The first six months of 1841 see no collective rejections at all. July marks the start of editorial complaints about the volume of poetry received with collective rejections issued for the weeks of the 3rd, 17th, 24th and 31st July. August, September and October witness four further collective

Between 1838 and 1841, the poetry column itself appears with increasing frequency (42 weeks in 1838, 47 in 1839, and 48 in both 1840 and 1841), whilst the number of poems published more than doubles over the same period (from 61 to 133). The evidence also indicates growing numbers of published Chartist poets (and would-be poets) in this period. The maximum number of published Chartist poets for 1838 and 1839 is somewhere in the range of 31–44. In contrast, for 1840 and 1841, the range is 55–75.[10] While the increase in the volume of poetry between 1838 and 1839 is explicable in terms of an increase in the number of poems borrowed from other literary sources, similar increases in 1840 and 1841 are accompanied by a decline in the numbers of such borrowings (both absolute and relative in comparison to 1839).

During this period the location of the poetry column also changes. Between June and September 1840 it becomes more mobile, appearing variously on pages three and six, as well as its original location on page seven. Then, from 26 September 1840, it takes up a permanent position on page three, the page preceding the *Northern Star*'s editorial columns on page five. In little more than two years the poetry column moves, both literally and symbolically, from the margins to the ideological centre of the *Northern Star*.[11] The available evidence points unmistakably towards the increasing presence and importance of poetry within the Chartist movement in this period. It is also possible that it was the amount of poetry produced by the *Northern Star*'s own readers which first established the prestige and importance of the poetry column.

By the close of 1841, the volume of unsolicited poetic manuscripts threatened to overwhelm the *Northern Star*'s editor, prompting a change

---

rejections. November sees the editor issue two collective rejections on 13th and 20th, before finally pleading for mercy – 'The Poets must really give us a little respite; we have loads of their obliging communications unlooked at', *NS*, 27 November 1841, 4. 'The Poets' evidently took little heed as December sees the editor issue three further collective rejections culminating with the terse notice, 'Fifty Poets must wait their turns', *NS*, 18 December 1841, 5.

[10] The minimum figure is generated by assuming that all anonymously published poems were the work of the same poet (an extremely unlikely hypothesis). The maximum figure assumes that all anonymously published poems were the work of separate poets (a rather more probable scenario). The true figure falls somewhere between these two points but, I would suggest, closer to the top rather than the middle of the range. The category of 'non-Chartist' poetry includes poetry reprinted from non-Chartist journals, poetry by canonical poets (e.g. Shelley, Byron, Shakespeare), and poetry by contemporary 'minor' poets who were not expressly affiliated with Chartism (e.g. Charles Mackay).

[11] Given the probability that the typesetting of the *Northern Star* followed the same practice as many other weekly periodicals – i.e. that the process began with setting page one first and then filled each page in sequence as the week progressed – the presence of the poetry column on page three makes it far more difficult to view this item as a mere 'filler'.

of editorial policy which was announced to readers in the first edition for 1842:

The Poets. – Our poetical friends have been as usual exceedingly bounteous: we have so large a stock of poetry and apologies for poetry on hand, and our friends supply us constantly so liberally, that we shall not henceforth particularly notice this department in our 'Notices to Correspondents'. We shall select from the mass sent us as much as we have room for, with as much impartiality as possible. Accepted pieces will, therefore, be known by their appearance in the paper; and authors whose communications do not appear will not, therefore, conclude that they are rejected because of demerit, as it would be impossible for us find room for half of even the readable poetry that comes to us.[12]

In the immediate aftermath of this announcement, however, glut quickly became dearth as 1842 and 1843 proved to be lean years for the *Star*'s poetry column.

In 1842, fewer than a hundred poems were published and this decline was matched by a corresponding decline in the numbers of individual Chartist poets published. Even on the most generous calculation possible, the *maximum* number of Chartist poets publishing in 1842 falls some way short of the *minimum* number publishing in each of the two previous years. 1843 witnessed a further decline. Only eighty-five poems were published and of these almost a third were taken either from other (non-Chartist) periodicals or from the works of established 'canonical' poets. This represented a return to the publishing pattern of 1839 – the only previous year to see a similar degree of 'non-Chartist produced' verse appear in the poetry column. This serious decline in Chartist produced poetry underlines both the fracturing of the Chartist movement by the emergence of 'educational', 'temperance' and 'religious' wings of Chartism and the defeat of the mass strikes of 1842.[13]

Any attempt to reconstruct the editorial policy of the *Northern Star*'s poetry column faces a number of serious difficulties. So little is known about the quotidian operation of the *Northern Star*, that it is impossible to answer definitively even such a simple question as who was in overall charge of the poetry column. This chapter assumes that the column was under the immediate control of William Hill until July 1843 and then G. J. Harney until August 1850 (possibly in conjunction with Ernest Jones

---

[12] *Northern Star*, 1 January 1842, 5. In fact, the practice of acknowledging individual contributions resumes from June 1842.

[13] For further details see, for example, Royle, *Chartism*, 29–39. For a complete account of the mass strikes of 1842 see Mick Jenkins, *The General Strike of 1842* (Lawrence & Wishart, 1980).

from 1847–8). Following Harney's departure the only certainty is the appointment of Gerald Massey as the literary editor of the *Northern Star*'s successor, the *Star of Freedom*.[14]

In the absence of a detailed first-hand account of the workings of the *Northern Star*, the main clues to the editorial policy of the poetry column are provided by the column itself and the 'To Readers and Correspondents' section. The latter is of particular importance, insofar as the editor often gives reasons for rejecting individual poems. During the period of Hill's editorship his rejections are characterised by an uncompromising, and often brutally expressed, commitment to literary quality and aesthetic value:

W. M., A Worsbro' Common Weaver, desires us to alter any word we think proper, or put in any new words that may be needed in his verses. The best thing we cant [sic] suggest to him is, to alter all the words, or, what might be still better, take them all away, and leave the paper blank. (*NS*, 15 December 1838)

R. M. – The quality of the poetry compels us to reject the 'Lines on the National Convention'. (*NS*, 20 July 1839)

Margaret Duffey. – The lines written by her husband in Northallerton hell-hole are well calculated to be interesting to her; but they have not literary merit to make them bear the test of criticism. (*NS*, 21 November 1840)

The willingness of Chartist writers to brave such fierce criticism in such numbers is a further indication of the prestige that attached to publication in the poetry column. Although none of Hill's successors would display the same brutality, the desire to improve the aesthetic standard of Chartist poetry actually intensified following his departure as editor of the *Northern Star*.

In July 1843, Joshua Hobson replaced William Hill as editor of the *Northern Star*, and shortly afterwards, George Julian Harney was appointed to the post of assistant editor. Harney was an enthusiastic champion of poetry in general and of Byron in particular and it is noticeable that following his appointment, individual and collective rejection notices begin to reappear in the 'To Readers and Correspondents' column. In

---

[14] William Hill was the editor of the *Northern Star* until July 1843. Joshua Hobson then became editor until October 1845. G. J. Harney, who had been appointed sub-editor in October 1843, succeeded Hobson as editor and continued in this post until August 1850. Massey became literary editor of the *Star of Freedom* in 1852. Harney is almost certainly the most important figure as regards the development of a coherent editorial policy and it is no accident that such major innovations in the poetry column such as the 'Beauties of Byron' and 'Feast of the Poets' series coincided with his time in the editorial chair.

addition, from 1844 onwards, Harney initiates a number of new editorial strategies which significantly alter the nature of the *Star*'s poetry column.

The first four months of 1844 see a resurgence of Chartist poetic activity. In this period the poetry column publishes forty-nine poems (almost twice the number published in the corresponding period the previous year) and the overwhelming majority of these (thirty-four poems) are Chartist produced. Over the entire year the poetry column publishes 131 poems (almost matching the numbers published in 1840 and 1841) and there is a sizeable increase in the number of Chartist poets publishing in the *Northern Star* compared with the previous year.

However, 1844 should not be seen as simply repeating the pattern of 1840 and 1841. For under Harney's control there is a discernible shift in the editorial strategy of the poetry column, as evidenced by the 'To Readers and Correspondents' column of 11 May 1844.

Poetry. – We have had such a sickner [sic] this week of 'prose run mad,' that we are compelled to cry 'hold, enough,' and to entreat our rhyming friends to desist from their 'shocking bad' labours for a season. We do not say that all is 'dross' excluded from our columns; more than one piece rejected containing germs of poesy, which, by labour on the part of the writers, may yet be quickened into life and bring forth good fruit. But let our friends be in no hurry to publish; many a gifted man has wrote good poetry years before he wanted to exhibit it in the light of day: and our poetic friends would do well to follow this good example and strive to improve in their vocation ere they venture the terrible risk of being 'damned to everlasting fame.' For ourselves, we have 'registered a vow' never (knowingly and wilfully) to give publicity to any more trash, feeling assured that we shall best gratify our readers in general, and instruct our poetic friends in particular, by calling from the deathless pages of Byron, Shelley, Burns, Nichol, &c., &c., rather than by giving insertion to outpourings which can lay no claim to the title of 'immortal verse.' Of course all that may cross our path, original and really poetic, will find with us ready insertion. We shall only go back to the past when the (too-oft) degenerate present fails to reach, or at any rate fails to approach, our standard of excellence. (*NS*, 11 May 1844)

Underpinning this statement is a clear belief that it is not necessary to encourage Chartist poetic production *per se*, but rather to improve its overall quality. The new policy affirms, in the strongest possible terms, the primacy of aesthetic value. It identifies a canon of exemplary writers and declares its intention to publish work from such writers in preference to 'trash' from the pens of Chartists. In short, this statement declares that the key problem confronting the Chartist poetic project is that of transforming quantity into quality. Implicit in this policy is a belief that there is a vital relation between the poetical and political condition of the

Chartist movement. Put simply, Chartists argued that the capacity of the working classes both to recognise and produce good poetry demonstrated their fitness for the franchise. Following the publication of Thomas Cooper's *The Purgatory of Suicides* (1845) this 'argument from culture' is made with increasing frequency and confidence. For example, the *Northern Star* reported Thomas Wakley MP telling a meeting held in honour of Thomas Cooper, '[that in] thus selecting intellect, feeling and moral qualities of the highest order to do homage to, they were most effectually showing their right and their fitness to participate in political privileges' (*NS*, 9 May 1846).

The pursuit of this strategic objective alters the nature of the poetry column. For example, 1844 sees the highest amount of 'non-Chartist produced' poetry (in both absolute and relative terms) since the column's inception. Some 47 poems (from a total of 131) fall into this category, and the overwhelming majority of these (35 poems) are published in the aftermath of the May proclamation. The *Northern Star* also begins to review more poetry and to carry considerably more articles on individual poets, including non-Chartist poets.[15]

The publication figures for 1845 appear to confirm this sense of the increasing 'professionalisation' of poetry within the Chartist movement. Almost 60 per cent of that year's poetry column (66 out of 115 poems published) is non-Chartist produced. The percentage of Chartist produced poems represents the lowest such figure in the entire history of the *Northern Star* whilst the raw number of such poems at forty-nine (maximum) is the lowest figure to date. Similarly, the number of Chartist poets, given by the range 28–37 (or half the number publishing in 1840 and 1841), represents both the lowest minimum and maximum figures to date.

These figures are largely the result of the introduction, almost certainly by Harney, of two editorial innovations: the 'Beauties of Byron' and 'The Feast of the Poets'. The first of these underlined the new importance accorded to the editor's own 'standard of excellence'. From 12 July 1845 the poetry column offered its readers a new series entitled 'Beauties of Byron', which ran on a near-weekly basis until November 1846 (reaching its final, forty-fourth, number on 11 November).[16] In 1845 over a fifth

---

[15] See, for example, the following articles; 'Burns, the Poor Man's Poet', *NS*, 24 August 1844, 31 August 1844, and 7 September 1844; 'John Clare, the Peasant Poet', *NS*, 5 October 1844; 'Frances Brown, the Blind Poetess', *NS*, 30 November 1844.

[16] The first 'Beauties of Byron' series was dominated by extracts from *Childe Harold*, which featured for seventeen weeks between 30 August 1845 and 1 January 1846; *English Bards and Scotch*

of the poetry column's output was given over to Byron, whose work accounted for nearly *seven times* as many poems within the pages of the *Northern Star* as those from even the most frequently published Chartist poets, Thomas Doubleday and James McKowen (who only published four poems each). In 1846, Byron's poetry provided more than a tenth of the poetry column's output and only Ernest Jones – who contributed eighteen poems – came close to matching Byron's total of twenty poems.

'The Feast of the Poets' was announced to readers on 1 March 1845:

> Notice. Finding that our poetical scraps, both original and selected, accumulate much more rapidly than we can dispose of them by the ordinary channel, we have been induced to propose to ourselves and contributors the following arrangement – viz., to give quarterly, in our columns, a selection of poetical pieces, such selection to be entitled

> 'THE FEAST OF THE POETS'
> The first selection will appear this month (March), the next in June, the next in September, and so on. The first of the 'Feasts' will 'come off' in the *Star* of March 22. (*NS*, 1 March 1845)

The very title, 'The Feast of the Poets', implies abundance, and throughout its lifetime the 'Feast' usually occupied almost an entire page of the newspaper.[17] The inaugural 'Feast', for example, contained seven poems. That each one came from the pen of a different poet suggests that the 'Feasts' were intended to showcase and thus encourage emerging Chartist literary talent at a time when the poetry column itself was dominated by the 'Beauties of Byron' series. However, the fact that the 'Feast' also offered advice to aspiring writers indicates Harney's continuing desire to raise the literary standard of Chartist poetic production. Indeed, the editorial preface to the first 'Feast' of 1846 contains an explicit statement of his disappointment at the generally low aesthetic standard of the poetry sent to him:

> We cannot say much for most of the original contributions we have received, nevertheless, taking the will for the deed, we are disposed to make large allowances. The following pieces are the best furnished by our contributors. (*NS*, 11 April 1846)

Reviewers, *The Giaour* and *The Vision of Judgement* were the next most featured works, appearing for three weeks each. A 'second series' began on 6 January 1849 but only lasted for five numbers, coming to an end on 3 February 1849.

[17] The first 'Feast' was postponed until 19 April and the second was published the following week. Subsequent 'Feasts' in 1845 followed this fortnightly format occurring on the last week of June and the first week of July, and on 22 and 29 September. The 'Feast' continued beyond 1845, occurring five times in 1846, six times in 1847, and once in 1849.

The subsequent week's 'Feast' announced its 'intention to devote the second part of each of our quarterly poetical "feasts" to an examination of the works of some one of the master-spirits of poetry, living or dead, whose writings have been devoted to the cause of human progress' (*NS*, 18 April 1846). Taken together these two editorial statements effectively repeat the main themes of 11 May 1844: a lament at the dearth of original Chartist poetic talent and the accompanying need for aspiring Chartist poets to study and learn from (and, perhaps, even imitate) the models provided by more established poets.

Somewhat ironically, Harney's disappointment is exacerbated by the fact that in 1845 Chartist poetry was celebrating its first major success, in the form of Thomas Cooper's 'Chartist epic', *The Purgatory of Suicides*. Beginning on 6 September 1845 the *Northern Star* began a review of *The Purgatory of Suicides* which combined extensive extracts with commentary. This practice continued until 13 December 1845. The coverage given to this work indicates the pride with which the movement as a whole greeted the poem.[18] In the 'Feast of the Poets' for September 1845, it is hailed as a model for Chartist poetry and would-be poets are advised to:

read THOMAS COOPER'S *Purgatory of Suicides*, and take courage by his example. He is the first who has really given to the world Chartist poetry, worthy of the name; we trust, however, that he will not stand alone. (*NS*, 27 September 1845)

For Chartist reviewers it is the combination of literary and intellectual ambition which makes *The Purgatory of Suicide*s a model for emulation by other Chartist poets. The poem's formal sophistication (an epic in ten books written in Spenserian stanzas) and literary allusiveness, was matched by the depth of its historical and philosophical knowledge. Furthermore, the fact of its publication by a non-Chartist publisher, Jeremiah How, and the attention it attracted beyond the Chartist press constituted a real breakthrough for Chartist poetry. To borrow Ian Haywood's formulation, *The Purgatory of Suicides* represented a real victory in 'the realm of symbolic representation' and as Stephanie Kuduk has shown, the significance of this victory was not lost on the poem's Chartist readers.[19]

---

[18] In total, the extended review of *The Purgatory of Suicides* spanned fourteen issues of the *Northern Star* and occupied somewhere in the region of eighteen full columns.

[19] Thomas Cooper's autobiography gives details of the publication of, and critical response to, the first edition of *The Purgatory of Suicides*, see T. Cooper, *The Life of Thomas Cooper* (Leicester University Press, 1971), 271–84. I. Haywood, *Chartist Fiction* (Aldershot: Ashgate, 1998), ix; Stephanie Kuduk, 'Sedition, Criticism and Epic Poetry in Thomas Cooper's *The Purgatory of Suicides*', *Victorian Poetry* 39 (2001): 183.

Yet another editorial innovation was announced in January 1846 in the form of a series entitled 'Songs for the People'. The rationale for this series was given as a desire to inject more variety into the poetry column.

> For many months past our poet's column has been exclusively occupied with extracts from the writings of BYRON. Desirous, however, of infusing more variety into this column, we have for some time past intended to give weekly, in addition to the 'Beauties [of Byron]', a good song, original or select. (*NS*, 1 January 1846)

'Songs for the People' ran for thirty-seven numbers over thirty-three weeks. Its first three offerings were 'select' rather than 'original' and consisted of Thomas Spence's 'The Land', Shelley's 'To the Men of England', and the 'Marseillaise'. Thereafter, original Chartist songs were predominant and provided twenty-eight of the next thirty-four published songs.

In 1846 the *Northern Star*'s poetry column reaches its highest point of editorial diversity, offering its readers, 'The Beauties of Byron', 'Songs for the People' and the 'Feast of the Poets' series, whilst continuing to print original Chartist produced poetry as well as a considerable amount of non-Chartist produced poetry. The evidence suggests that these editorial distinctions are hierarchical as well as functional, with the two 'named series' indicating greater poetic value. The majority of the poems published in the 'Songs for the People' series come from the pens of more established writers, whilst first-time (and once-only) time contributors provide a mere eight of the thirty-seven poems published in this series. The publication record for the entire column corroborates this sense of an increasing internal differentiation of Chartist poetic production, with the emergence of a handful of recognised 'labour laureates' (pre-eminently Thomas Cooper and Ernest Jones, but also John Arnott, Alfred Fennell, Edwin Gill, James McKowen, T. R. Smart and J. Harkness) squeezing out the occasional contributors.

The installation of Ernest Jones as the movement's leading poet not only confirms the increasing specialisation of Chartist poetic production but also attests to the important role it played in the internal politics of Chartism. As Anne Janowitz has shown, the speed with which Jones becomes the movement's laureate owes much to the spectacular falling out between Cooper and O'Connor.[20] Jones' poetry is published in the poetry column on eight out of the nine weeks in which the Cooper

---

[20] A. Janowitz, *Lyric and Labor in the Romantic Tradition* (Cambridge University Press, 1998), 160–92.

controversy rages in the columns of the *Northern Star*. The implicit contrast between Chartism's older, rebellious and ungrateful bard, and its newer, obedient poetic son, could hardly be greater, particularly as a number of Jones' poems emphasise his commitment to the movement, exemplified in titles such as 'A Chartist March', 'Our Destiny', 'Our Warning' and 'Our Cheer' (*NS*, 11 June 1846; 11 July 1846; 1 August 1846; 8 August 1846).

The moment of Cooper's expulsion from the Chartist movement (on the motion of Ernest Jones) may be said to mark the beginning of the end of the Chartist poetic project. In 1847, the poetry column is characterised by a sense of declining or, at the very least, dissipating energy. It publishes fewer poems in total than the previous year, fewer Chartist poems within this reduced total, and the number of published Chartist poets falls by a quarter compared with 1846. The 'Songs for the People' series makes no appearance and the 'Beauties of Byron' appears only twice. The 'Feast of the Poets' no longer serves as a showcase for original Chartist poetry.[21] A weary-sounding editor introduces the first 'Feast' of 1847 thus:

After long delay and repeated postponements, we this week make 'a desperate attempt' to clear off a mass of manuscript bearing the 'outward and visible form' of 'Poetry;' but, for the most part, we regret to say, containing but little of its 'inward and spiritual' essence. 'We cull the choicest'. (*NS*, 24 April 1847)

This loss of vitality is reflected in the 'To Readers and Correspondents' column which rejects a mere fifteen separately identifiable poets/poems (the lowest such total since 1842) and issues only a single collective rejection all year.

The poetry column for the first half of 1848 confirms the connection which existed between song and militancy in the Chartist imagination. In April 1848, 'A Republican' wrote to the *Northern Star* lamenting the lack of an English 'Marseillaise':

I have been thinking that the Democrats of England are much behind those of France and other nations, in not having their national democratic anthems. Why have we not our 'Democratic Hymn' as our French brethren have their 'Hymn of the Girondins', and the 'Marseillaise!' I think that if the Chartist Executive

---

[21] The following week's 'Feast' contained only one original poem by Ernest Jones with the bulk of the column provided by selections from already-published volumes (1 May 1847, 3). The next instalment of the 'Feast' introduced at most two previously unpublished Chartist poets (8 May 1847, 3). In similar fashion, the first of the summer's 'Feasts' contained only one poem by a previously unpublished poet, whilst the next two were dedicated to poetry from America (26 June 1847, 3; 3 July 1847, 3; 10 July 1847, 3). Thereafter the 'Feast' effectively disappears from the *Northern Star*, appearing on one further occasion only (23 June 1849).

Council would take up the matter, and offer a small prize for the best lyric that could be produced, embodying the sentiments of the people, there are many poets in England who would 'string their lyre' to such a theme. What do you think of the suggestion? (*NS*, 8 April 1848)

Harney commended the suggestion and although the Chartist Executive did not 'take up the matter', Chartist poets did. Three versions of the 'Marseillaise' and two of the 'Chorus of the Girondists' appear in the poetry column in this year. Indeed, almost half of the poetry column's output to May 1848 was designated as 'song', suggesting that at times of intensified political activity Chartist poets responded with poetry deliberately designed to mobilise the movement.[22]

The second half of 1848 was marked by the ferocity of the state's repression of the Chartist movement.[23] Unsurprisingly, Chartism's forced disintegration accelerated the decline of its poetic project. In the second half of 1848 the poetry column is dominated by poems taken from other journals or from the work of established non-Chartist poets. Tellingly, there is no 'Feast of the Poets' in 1848.

Neither the movement nor its poetic project proved capable of recovering from the defeat of 1848. The poetry column for 1849 begins by resurrecting the 'Beauties of Byron', but this second series only lasts for five numbers. In the final week of January the poetry column reprints two radical poems both of which are over fifty years old, and in the final week of February it reprints Ernest Jones' translations of the 'Marseillaise' and 'Chorus of the Girondists' which had first appeared the previous April. It is difficult to see these recyclings and attempted resurrections as anything other than symptoms of an ineluctable decline. Even the reappearance of the 'Feast of the Poets' on 23 June 1849, rather than heralding a resurgence of the *Northern Star*'s poetry column, instead marks its creative exhaustion.

Yet this decline is not one of Chartist poetic production as such. The final paragraph of the very last 'Feast of the Poets' issues a refrain which is almost a decade old:

Within the last few months we have received a heap of 'poetical' contributions, almost all of which, we are sorry to say, were not worth publication. 'A word to the wise sufficeth.' Those whose 'poetical' favours we have not noticed, will understand why (*NS*, 23 June 1849)

---

[22] Twenty-eight poems were styled 'songs'; ten of which specified the tune to which they could be sung. Sixteen of the twenty-eight poems were published before May 1848.

[23] John Saville emphasises 'the physical destruction by imprisonment of the Chartist leadership in [the] summer months of 1848.' John Saville, *1848. The British State and the Chartist Movement* (Cambridge University Press, 1990), 162.

The perennial problem of increasing the quality rather than the quantity of Chartist poetry is compounded by a dual shift in the movement's literary 'centre of gravity'. The first of these is that the *Northern Star* no longer enjoys a position of predominance and is therefore no longer the undisputed centre of Chartist literary energies. Instead, in 1849, the most significant creative upsurge is to be found in other radical periodicals, most noticeably the *Uxbridge Spirit of Freedom* and the *Democratic Review* (edited by Harney).

Paradoxically, it might be argued that it is the very success of the Chartist poetic project which produces the appearance of decline. A noticeable feature of the poetry column from 1847 to 1849 is the number of poems imported, initially from 'sympathetic' publications such as *Howitt's Journal*, and thereafter from other Chartist journals. In 1848 the proportion of poems 'imported' from outside sources (including periodicals and non-Chartist produced poetry) rises to over 50 per cent of the poetry column's output for only the second time in the history of the *Northern Star*. The poetry column for 1849 attests to the increasingly diffuse nature of both the Chartist movement and Chartist poetic production. The column is heavily dependent on other Chartist and radical working-class journals such as the *Democratic Review*, *The Reasoner* and in particular the *Uxbridge Spirit of Freedom*, co-edited by the most important, and in many ways the most remarkable, poet of late Chartism – Gerald Massey.[24]

The second, and far more important, long-term shift finds symbolic expression in the *Northern Star* for 31 March with the first instalment of Thomas Martin Wheeler's Chartist novel *Sunshine and Shadow*. Although Wheeler's novel feels the need to harness poetry's cultural capital through the use of poetic epigraphs, its emergence alongside periodicals such as *Reynolds's Political Instructor* marks the growing importance of prose narratives in cultural 'fact' if not yet in cultural 'theory'.[25]

---

[24] Following Ernest Jones' imprisonment, Massey emerges as the most influential and distinctive poetic voice of Chartism. From 1849 to 1852 inclusive, Massey is the most published poet in the *Northern Star*'s poetry column. He also becomes the *Star*'s literary editor in its final months. For further details of Massey's life see David Shaw, *Gerald Massey: Chartist, Poet, Radical and Free-thinker* (Buckland, 1995).

[25] It is interesting to note that this change in the Chartist movement's literary 'centre of gravity' coincides with a similar shift in bourgeois literary culture. Moreover, the same disjuncture between cultural theory and fact is observable in bourgeois literary culture with poetry theoretically privileged as the more important art form and fiction practically recognised as the public's favoured reading matter. The implications of this for working-class poets have yet to be fully addressed. Were they conscious of the fact that they were working in a subordinate genre? Did the decreasing cultural importance/influence of poetry hamper or assist their chances of publication?

The fate of the *Northern Star*'s poetry column from 1850 onwards confirms the waning importance of poetry within the movement. There is a further decline in the number of poems published, which falls by over a fifth to seventy-three from the previous year's total of ninety-one (and is almost half the total for 1846). Not even Ernest Jones' release from prison in July 1850 is able to galvanise the *Northern Star*'s poetry column. The *Northern Star* only publishes a single poem by Jones in 1850 ('Easter Hymn') and that in the context of a review of the *Red Republican* rather than in the poetry column proper (*NS*, 10 August 1850). Moreover, in an advert for a series of forthcoming poetical works Jones makes the startling announcement that he is abandoning poetry:

These will, probably, be among the last of my poetical works, for harder and sterner toils now call me to the field. The age has passed, when nations can be SUNG into liberty: perhaps it is well – for enthusiasm is the child of an hour – conviction is the father of centuries. (*NS*, 3 August 1850)

Jones here not only questions the political agency of poetry, he also subordinates poetry to prose, albeit in this case the prose of political analysis and theory rather than that of fiction.

In 1851, the number of poems published falls to fifty-nine, barely more than one per week, and the reduced physical size of the poetry column symbolises its decreasing status within the movement. The number of Chartist poets falls to between eighteen and twenty-seven. Further evidence of the collapse of Chartist poetic production is suggested by the increased presence of contemporary, non-Chartist poets in the poetry column, most notably, Barrett Browning, Meredith, Kingsley, Landor and Tennyson.

In 1852 the poetry column publishes only thirty-five poems and runs for twenty-three weeks until, on 4 September, it is replaced by a section entitled 'Waifs and Strays'. This meagre total is greatly augmented by the 'May Garland' which contains ten poems (*NS*, 8 May 1852). At sixteen, the *maximum* number of Chartist poets is lower than any previous *minimum* number. The poetry column shares the same ignominious end as its parent publication. Not even the return of Harney as editor, the appointment of Massey as literary editor and a change of name to the *Star of Freedom* could save either the publication or its poetry column.

Beyond the ranks of labour historians and those literary scholars interested in the 'hungry forties', the history of Chartism is frequently reduced to one or at most two moments of drama: the Newport rising in 1839 and the Kennington Common demonstration in 1848. Historians of the Chartist movement have generally organised their chronologies around what Edward Royle in *Revolutionary Britannia?* terms the three Chartist crises of 1839/40, 1842 and 1848.[26] These nodal points usually form the basis of a tripartite history, such as that offered by Royle's *Chartism*, which identifies the following stages; 1836–1840 ('The years of promise unfulfilled'), 1840–1847 ('New moves and new hopes') and 1848–1858 ('Reconciliation to defeat').[27]

In contrast, literary scholars have tended to posit a homogeneous Chartist literary history which is curiously, and unconvincingly, de-coupled from the actual history of the wider movement. The critic most attuned to the historical nuances of Chartist poetic production, Anne Janowitz, divides Chartist literary history into three phases. Between 1838 and 1842, she argues that 'Chartist poetry was chiefly engaged in trying to formulate an independent poetic project'.[28] Post-1842, Chartist poetry becomes 'less militant and analytical', whilst the post-1851 period is marked by 'a newly complex poetry of defeat and hope'.[29] The evidence of the *Northern Star*'s poetry column suggests an even more complex relationship between Chartism's political and poetic fortunes. There is indeed an initial period of remarkable growth in Chartist poetic production between 1838 and 1841. The fact that this phase extends into 1841 suggests that the movement's poetic energies did not immediately decline after the failed Newport and Yorkshire insurrections in the winter of 1839/40.

The subsequent phase is one of declining poetic production during a significant upsurge in Chartist activity, the mass strikes of 1842, which is followed by a downturn in Chartist energies in the aftermath of the strikes' failure. The third period is, from the literary point of view, the most remarkable. From 1844 to 1846 there is a sustained attempt on the part of the editor of the poetry column to improve the quality of poetic production. This editorial policy reflects a widely held conviction that the poetic and political conditions of the movement were vitally connected. In the interval between the rejection of the second petition and the emergence of the Land Plan, it can be argued that Chartism's primary strategy was to use poetry both to demonstrate the working classes' fitness for the franchise (the 'argument from culture') and to lay the groundwork for democracy. The publication of Cooper's *The Purgatory of Suicides* seems to validate this strategy. However, it was comprehensively

[26] E. Royle, *Revolutionary Britannia?* (Manchester University Press, 2000), 92–135.
[27] E. Royle, *Chartism* (Longman, 1986).   [28] Janowitz, *Lyric and Labor*, 135.
[29] *Ibid.*, 136, 151.

derailed following Cooper's expulsion from the movement and Ernest Jones' installation as Chartism's laureate.

The final phase of Chartist literary history is one of occasional upturns within a context of ineluctable decline. Between 1847 and 1850, the indices of the movement's poetic health are mixed. The steady decline in the numbers of poems published is sometimes accompanied by a small rise in the number of Chartist poets (1848, 1850) or a rise in the percentage of Chartist produced poems (1849, 1850). Similarly, across the wider movement, the increased publishing opportunities for Chartist poets in a variety of journals needs to be set against the increasing use of fiction to propagate Chartist ideas and Jones' disavowal of poetry in August 1850.[30] However, by 1851 it is clear that any sense of a Chartist poetic project has collapsed with the implosion of the wider movement. At this terminus, the previously staggered continuities between Chartism's political and literary histories fatally coincide. The historical logic which reads Chartism's literary decline as an effect of its political demise is irrefutable, yet there is a compelling cultural logic which suggests that the movement's literary decline also played a causal role in its political collapse.

---

[30] For details of the role of fiction in the Chartist movement see Ian Haywood's study, *The Revolution in Popular Literature* as well as his anthologies: *The Literature of Struggle* (Aldershot: Scolar Press, 1995); *Chartist Fiction* (Aldershot: Ashgate, 1998); *Chartist Fiction Vol. 2: Ernest Jones, Women's Wrongs* (Aldershot: Ashgate, 2001).

CHAPTER 4

Insurrectionary sonnets: the ideological afterlife of the Newport uprising

There has recently been in this county an armed insurrection; there
has been an attempt to take forcible possession of the town of
Newport; there has been a conflict between the insurgents and the
Queen's troops; there has been bloodshed; the loss of many lives.
The intelligence of these outrages has caused alarm and dismay
throughout the Kingdom.

> The Attorney-General's Opening Address at the Monmouth Special
> Commission[1]

On the night of 3 November 1839, John Frost, Zephaniah Williams and
William Jones (the leaders of South Wales Chartism) assembled a force
of some 7,000 armed colliers and ironworkers. After a night march, this
force arrived in Newport early the next morning where, following a short
but fierce battle with a small detachment of regular troops in the Westgate Hotel, they were dispersed leaving at least twenty-four people dead
and a further fifty wounded. In the aftermath of these events twenty-one
men, including Frost, Williams and Jones, were charged with high
treason before a Special Commission held in Monmouth.[2]

Faced with uncertainties regarding both the exact sequence of events at
Newport and the aims and intentions of the insurgents, historians have
concentrated on tracing the origins of the Newport uprising, identifying
the aims of the insurgents, establishing what happened at Newport and
assessing the potential threat posed by this insurrection.[3] Comparatively
little attention has been given to what might be termed the 'ideological
afterlife' of Newport within the Chartist movement and which is the
main focus of this chapter. It begins by tracing the response to Newport

---

[1] *Trial of John Frost for High Treason* (2 Vols) (New York: Garland Publishing, 1986 [1840]), 58.
[2] Edward Royle, *Revolutionary Britannia?* (Manchester University Press, 2000), 106–7.
[3] Major studies of the Newport insurrection include: David Williams, *John Frost A Study in Chartism* (Evelyn, Adams & Mackay, 1969); Ivor Wilks, *South Wales and the Rising of 1839* (Beckenham: Croom Helm, 1984); David J. V. Jones, *The Last Rising: The Newport Insurrection of 1839* (Oxford University Press, 1985). Wilks' study contains a detailed account of the historiography of Newport, 246–51.

in the pages of the *Northern Star*, from the first reports of the insurrection to the transportation of Frost and his fellow prisoners. Particular attention is given to four aspects of the Chartist response; the changing rhetorical and political significance accorded violence, the construction of a narrative of the events at Newport, the interplay between law and history in the Special Commission, and the significance of discourses of family and gender in the campaign to save Frost from hanging.

The second half of the chapter focuses on the apparently belated response of the *Northern Star*'s poetry column to Newport. It demonstrates that an initial phase of silence or, at most, oblique commentary is followed by a period of sustained poetic engagement following Frost's transportation. It examines the ideological work performed by Chartist poetry in relation to the four areas identified above. However, in order to avoid reducing the poetry to a simple repetition or reiteration of a prior editorial discourse, attention will be given to the differences (as well as the similarities) between the 'poetic' and 'editorial' discourses of Newport. Particular attention will be given to the poetry's efforts to locate Newport within British radical historiography and the ways in which the themes of exile and return are deployed to create a specific form of Chartist agency in the post-Newport period.

From Gammage onwards, the historiography of Chartism has often been constructed around the perceived opposition between 'physical force' and 'moral force' Chartism.[4] As many historians, including Edward Royle, have noted, whilst 'Gammage's crude division remains [analytically] appropriate' it offers an overly simplified account of the attitudes towards political violence which existed within the Chartist movement.[5] Historians have generally analysed these attitudes with reference to their credibility as political strategy or to the internal politics of Chartism.[6] However, my interest lies in the ways in which Chartism imagines violence and, in particular, the structuring role played by three 'myths of violence' (using 'myth' in its Barthesian sense). The first of these myths – the myth of 'Peterloo' – articulated the people's readiness (and right) to resist armed oppression. The second myth of '1832' – the Reform Bill crisis – encoded the strategic use of the threat of violence to achieve political reform, while the third – the French Revolution – represented proactive insurrectionary violence on the part of the people. These myths enjoyed differing levels of popularity within the movement; the first and second commanding

[4] R. C. Gammage, *History of the Chartist Movement 1837–1854* (Merlin, 1969), 16–18.
[5] Edward Royle, *Chartism* (Longman, 1986), 54.   [6] *Ibid.*, 54–65.

widespread support while the third constituted a minority current within Chartism.[7]

Barthes describes myth as 'a peculiar system' owing to its constitution as 'a second-order semiological system'.[8] Two aspects of this system are particularly important to an understanding of the role of myths of violence in the Chartist imaginary. Firstly, argues Barthes, at the level of the mythic signifier ('form') 'meaning is already complete, [the form] postulates a kind of knowledge, a past, a memory, a comparative order of facts, ideas, decisions'. However, as form 'the meaning leaves its contingency behind', thereby transforming 'history into nature' and 'motive [into] reason'.[9] Simultaneously, however, the apparent fullness of myth is accompanied by epistemological indeterminacy, 'the knowledge contained in a mythical concept is confused, made of yielding, shapeless associations' and it is precisely this openness and flexibility which gives myth its historical efficacy.[10]

For Barthes, 'myth acts economically ... it establishes a blissful clarity: things appear to mean something by themselves'.[11] Thus the myth of 'Peterloo' comes to have a fixed meaning in the Chartist imaginary (popular triumph over tyrannical repression), and encodes knowledge (legitimate popular demands are ultimately irresistible). However, this knowledge is apparent rather than absolute; it offers an interpretation of a historical event rather than an analysis of the historical process. In short, its knowledge is 'functional' (in Barthes' sense), intended to allow a political desire to (mis)recognise itself as a political fact. It promises the Chartists that as custodians of the popular will (and thus inheritors of Peterloo) they too will ultimately triumph in spite of forcible repression (as did their forebears at Peterloo). The myth of '1832' operates in broadly similar fashion, although the threat of popular violence introduces a greater degree of ambiguity (is the threat of violence symbolic or actual?). Finally, the myth of the French Revolution can be seen either as the negative counterpart of 'Peterloo' (in which violence becomes necessary) or as encoding a belief in the restorative effects of political violence.

Concrete examples of Chartist thinking about violence can be marked by the simultaneous presence of all three structuring myths. Gammage,

---

[7] Gammage, for example, notes that many delegates to the first Chartist Convention 'expressed their indignation' at those Chartists (particularly George Julian Harney) 'who were injuring the cause by making use of French terms and wearing French emblems', *History of the Chartist Movement*, 107.
[8] Roland Barthes, *Mythologies* (Paladin, 1973), 123.   [9] *Ibid.*, 127 and 140.
[10] *Ibid.*, 129–30.   [11] *Ibid.*, 156.

for example, recalls a young Trowbridge chemist called Potts 'decorat[ing] his window with a formidable array of bullets, which he had sufficient boldness to label as "tory pills"!'[12] Potts' visual and verbal pun not only represents political violence as possessing a restorative, medicinal function (the positive insurrectionary myth) and carrying a clear threat of violence ('1832'), but also alludes to the 'steel lozenges' of Peterloo.[13] Furthermore, for all its audacity, Potts' joke indicates the extent to which the Chartist movement was far more comfortable with the idea rather than the reality of physical force. In this case, whilst the reality of violence is encoded in the content of the pun (the bullets), the joke form itself provides partial insulation against that reality.

The ambivalences, uncertainties and disavowals which structure Potts' joke are equally present in the more serious invocations of violence made at the Chartist National Convention of 1839. The resolution passed by the National Convention on 17 May 1839 affirmed the right of self-defence while calling on Chartists to attend meetings unarmed. Shortly afterwards, addressing the great West Riding meeting at Peep Green, O'Connor declared 'I am for repelling attack by attack' whilst O'Brien warned against 'premature and partial outbreaks'.[14] Yet less than a month later, on the floor of the Convention, O'Connor declared that the people were now in a position to take universal suffrage by force if necessary.[15] A similar ambivalence is found in the *Northern Star*'s poetry column for 9 November 1839, which contains two poems: the anonymous 'The Right Divine' and 'The Winds' from the US poet William Cullen Bryant. Torn, like the wider movement, between the competing claims of 'moral' and 'physical' force these poems encode the tension between a desire for peaceful social change and a historical consciousness of the likelihood of violent confrontation. 'The Right Divine' ends with a warning that 'The *hour* of retribution's nigh', whilst 'The Winds' prophesies that the

> . . . wronged spirit of our race
>   Shall break, as soon he must, his long-worn chains,
>   And leap, in freedom, from his prison-place,

---

[12] Gammage, *History of the Chartist Movement*, 80.

[13] In the aftermath of Peterloo a cartoon was issued depicting soldiers 'curing' protests by thrusting 'steel lozenges' (their bayonets) into the mouths of the people.

[14] Gammage, *History of the Chartist Movement*, 112–14.

[15] *Ibid.*, 125. Following the authorities' decision to use the metropolitan police against a Chartist meeting in Birmingham's Bull Ring, attitudes appear to have hardened as many Chartist leaders became convinced that the Whigs would resort to brute force to repel the people's demands, *ibid.*, 133–7.

To their original readers, both poems must have seemed uncannily prescient, appearing as they did in the edition of the *Northern Star* which carried the first reports of the Newport uprising.

In the immediate aftermath of Newport, O'Connor swiftly distanced himself from the insurrectionary myth. At a meeting in Oldham he declared, 'in whatever way I gain the victory, it shall be a bloodless one' and insisted that he had always opposed 'physical revolution' on the grounds that it 'always failed to produce any good effect for the working classes!'[16] In a passage that simultaneously affirms his own physical courage and willingness to sacrifice himself for the cause, whilst presenting further arguments against physical force, O'Connor declares:

When any danger is to be run, I would rather run it myself, than suffer the people to do it. (Applause) My proper place is with the people, to remain with them; at the same time I should be guilty of high treason to them, if I were to present an unarmed, undisciplined mass of men, to an armed and disciplined army.[17]

This belated recognition of the realities of an armed collision with the organised forces of state power prompts a careful recasting of physical force arguments in which the myth of Peterloo becomes increasingly dominant. Whilst neither O'Connor nor the *Northern Star* ever renounced the people's right to arm in self-defence, it is possible to trace significant changes in both rhetoric and analysis from November 1839 onwards.[18] Addressing meetings in Sunderland and Manchester, O'Connor drew on the myth of Peterloo by framing his argument in terms of the necessity of dying (as opposed to fighting) for the cause, thereby emphasising the sacrificial nature of a commitment to physical force.[19] The echoes of Peterloo are reinforced at the Manchester meeting when O'Connor quotes Henry Hunt's warnings regarding the activities of spies within the radical movement.[20] The thrust of this warning, that those who are urging the movement on to violent confrontation are likely to be *agents provocateurs*,

---

[16] *Northern Star*, 9 November 1839, 'Mr O'Connor's Visit to Oldham', 1. In an intriguing echo of Carlyle's assessment of the *sans-culottes* in the French Revolution, O'Connor attributes this to the fact that the 'excitement' and 'energy' unleashed in such situations are destructive rather than constructive.

[17] *Ibid.* Subsequently, an editorial column argues that 'to oppose an unarmed, or ill armed and undisciplined multitude to organised and disciplined troops is to murder them', *Northern Star*, 11 January 1840, 4.

[18] The right to arm in self-defence is affirmed in the *Northern Star* for 28 December 1839 and again on 11 January 1840.

[19] *Northern Star*, 30 November 1839, 6; and 7 December 1839, 1.

[20] *Northern Star*, 7 December 1839, 1.

is repeated in editorials throughout December and January.[21] In response to the attempted rising in Sheffield, for example, the *Northern Star* comments:

With most inexpressible pain, we chronicle in another part of our paper, the stark-staring mad proceedings of a small knot of fools at Sheffield!

What are the people about? Are they entirely demented?! Do they not know that they are betrayed? that blood hounds are laid on the scent! Have they forgotten CASTLES, OLIVER, and POPAY? Have we not been cautioning them, week after week, about the movements of stealthy, but violent and extreme parties?[22]

As the *Northern Star* seeks to distance itself from these later failed insurrections, it increasingly attributes responsibility for the violence to the government. It argues both that popular violence is an inevitable result of tyrannical oppression and that it is deliberately instigated by the government through its network of spies and *agents provocateurs*. The *Northern Star*'s counsel to the Chartist movement in contrast takes on a decidedly 'moral force' aspect. A December editorial identifies education and sobriety as the two surest ways of 'accelerat[ing] the triumph of the people's cause'.[23] Similarly, the editorial for 25 January 1840 analyses the current political situation and appraises Chartist strategy, firmly rejecting violence and clearly identifying 'moral force' as the route to power:

We do most earnestly beg of the madmen, who have been so reckless and insane as to conceive and try to execute deeds of violence, to pause and reflect calmly on their position. We implore them not by their own act to ruin a cause for which both we and they have suffered and endured so much.

. . .

The people of this country are irresistible in their *moral* strength. We call upon them to exert it.[24]

The first reports of the Newport uprising to appear in the *Northern Star* were taken from the *Sun* and *Morning Herald*. The report from the *Sun* was prefaced by the *Northern Star*'s own remarks concerning the 'seemingly mad and ill-concerted hostile movements in Wales'.[25] In its first editorial on the subject, 'The Insurrection and its Causes', the *Northern*

---

[21] *Northern Star*, 7 December 1839, 28 December 1839, 11 January 1840, 18 January 1840, 25 January 1840.

[22] *Northern Star*, 18 January 1840, 4. The attempted insurrections at Bethnal Green and Bradford draw similar comments. The following week the *Northern Star* contains an even stronger condemnation and argues that outbreaks of violence will only secure the execution of the Newport prisoners, *Northern Star*, 25 January 1840.

[23] *Northern Star*, 28 December 1839, 4.   [24] *Northern Star*, 25 January 1840, 4.

[25] *Northern Star*, 9 November 1839, 8.

Star characterised Newport as the 'fierce yell of men rendered desperate by tyranny' and argued that it was the government's policy of effectively criminalising Chartist activity that had provoked a violent response:

Will they [the Government] take warning; or will they still set themselves against the voice of the whole people! Will they dare the sleeping ire, and rouse the latent vengeance of a people who begin to think they have been patient overmuch! Will they court the firebrand and the steel, in the insane hope that their names may descend to posterity with the infamous celebrity of having goaded a virtuous people to distraction, and afterwards Dragooned them into quiescence?[26]

Addressing a meeting at Stockport, O'Connor sounded a similar note, claiming that a lack of legal protection had forced the people to take 'the law into their own hands'. Comparing the current situation with Ireland in 1798, where he argues that the government deliberately fomented rebellion, O'Connor warns his audience that:

The same policy is now pursued in England: it is sought to incite a rebellion in England, as a pretext for converting the Government of the country into a military despotism.[27]

However, the following week the *Northern Star* announces that its initial assessment of the insurrection was incorrect:

Having no grounds whereon to form a judgement of the insurrection in Wales, than the reports of a press which we were justified in using sceptically, we inclined last week, to view the recent outbreak, as the madness of a few, heightened by the colouring of the Government artists, but from the evidence of some of the witnesses, we are now justified in giving the whole proceedings the stamp of reality. That it was a mountain torrent long pent up until continued oppression, and multiplied insult, prematurely burst the dams, we now believe. That other and nobler motives than plunder, devastation, or merely the supply of immediate want, urged the assailants to the attack is manifest from the fact that many are sworn to be in good and constant employment.[28]

Far from being a 'mad' outbreak, the *Northern Star* insists that insurrection was nobly motivated by a people's desire to resist slavery. Indeed, resistance to slavery provides the major theme of the editorial which is prefaced by the 'noble sentiments' of the anti-slavery speech from Sheridan Knowles' *Huon*.[29] The *Northern Star* connects economic degradation

---

[26] *Ibid.*, 5.   [27] *Ibid.*, 1.   [28] *Northern Star*, 16 November 1839, 4.

[29] *Ibid.*, 4. For a discussion of the trope of slavery within Chartist poetry see Kelly J. Mays, 'Slaves in Heaven, Laborers in Hell: Chartist Poets' Ambivalent Identification with the (Black) Slave', *Victorian Poetry* 39:2 (2001), 137–63. However, Mays overstates the extent to which slavery functions as an 'abstract' trope or metaphor within Chartist discourse. In describing the British

with political oppression, arguing that the 'middle classes, who have now by the operation of machinery, turned man into a beast of burden ... hope to hold power and increase oppression by the bayonet'. In a telling appropriation of industrial imagery, it accuses the middle classes of having 'closed the safety valve, which alone prevented the boiler from long since exploding', and proffers Newport as 'a practical instance of what is sure to follow the putting down of the free expression of opinion'.[30] In the next two numbers of the *Northern Star*, resistance to oppression is defined as a national-religious characteristic of the Welsh with O'Connor praising the 'Welsh religious detestation of oppression'.[31] In short, Newport needed to be cast as a *response* to tyranny before the *Northern Star* felt comfortable defending it.

The representation of Newport as reactive rather than proactive continues with O'Connor's repetition of his accusation that the violence at Newport was deliberately provoked by the Whigs.[32] The *Northern Star* voices its 'conviction ... that a wholesale plan of ridding out the population had been unscrupulously determined on' and in the space of a few paragraphs describes the events at Newport as a 'horrible, cold-blooded atrocity', 'totally unnecessary slaughter' and 'military butcher[y]'.[33] Thus, the *Northern Star*'s interpretation of Newport evolves in tandem with its general attitude towards political violence in placing increasing responsibility for the violence on the government.

The ideologically over-determined nature of Chartist interpretations of Newport is made clear in O'Connor's speech to a public meeting in Stockport:

[O'Connor] did not think there was a single man who could kill another in cold blood for the sake of the Charter; nor did they ever take an active part only until roused in self-defence. It was proved before the magistrates at Newport that

labourer as a 'slave', Chartists were drawing attention to the fact that the labourer was denied both political and economic rights. David J. V. Jones, for example, comments that in the South Wales industrial belt, 'Employers and agents had an extraordinary degree of control over the lives of working people', Jones, *The Last Rising*, 34. In such situations, I would argue, 'slavery' is not an abstract trope but an attempt to figure the connections between economic exploitation and political oppression. This is not to deny the especial horrors of (black) chattel slavery in the USA.
[30] *Northern Star*, 16 November 1839, 4. A few weeks later, O'Connor offers an even more exact version of this trope warning the 'Attorney-General [who] might think, as he had lately boasted, that he had put down public meetings, [but] let him recollect that there was such a thing as condensation of power – that there was such a thing as condensation of steam – that there was such a thing as producing more by one machine than a thousand hands. (Applause)' *Northern Star*, 7 December 1839, 1.
[31] *Northern Star*, 23 November 1839, 5, and 30 November 1839, 3.
[32] *Northern Star*, 30 November 1839, 6.   [33] *Ibid.*, 4.

the people were led on by a deserter from the regiment, who fired the first shot; and that the people had been deluded. The soldiers fired upon them, and although the people retreated, they kept firing upon them – in fact, they were butchered as they fled. The whole business was a Whig trick.[34]

The attribution of culpability to a deserter reads rather like a Chartist version of the Tory myth of the outside agitator and seems all too obviously to serve an ideological need.[35] Here the 'deserter' is the scapegoat whose expulsion removes the source of the pollution from the community. Similarly, the structural effects of the 'myth of Peterloo' are readily observable in O'Connor's account of the military firing upon fleeing civilians.[36] It appears to have become literally unthinkable that a Chartist might have initiated the violence.

By the start of 1840 we see various aspects of previous drafts of the narrative of Newport coalesce into a definitive Chartist version, which is offered to readers of the *Northern Star* in an editorial entitled 'Frost and the Trials'. This editorial contains extracts from what it claims is a suppressed government report which says that the original 'object' of the Welsh Chartists was 'that of making a great demonstration of their moral power'.[37] However, on hearing that a number of local Chartists had been arrested and imprisoned by the Newport authorities a decision was made to march on the Westgate Hotel with a view to obtaining their release. On the steps of the hotel, a scuffle broke out between the Chartists and

---

[34] *Northern Star*, 7 December 1839, 6.

[35] Marilyn Butler, *Romantics, Rebels and Reactionaries* (Oxford University Press, 1981).

[36] It should be noted that David Williams in *John Frost A Study In Chartism* observes that not only was the question of who fired the first shot never satisfactorily answered, but also James Hodge gave evidence at the trial that a deserter was involved in co-ordinating the march on Newport. Williams also notes that 'one of the killed was believed to be a deserter' although others maintained that 'one of the killed was an *agent provocateur* who had claimed he was a deserter', 228 and 222. This latter claim was made by William Cardo who also advanced the most outlandish interpretation of the Newport uprising, claiming that it was 'the result of a Russian agency' and accusing Palmerston of 'treason' for 'direct[ing] attention to Newport' whilst the Russian Navy gathered 'within twenty miles' of the British shore, *Northern Star*, 7 December 1839. Whilst Cardo was cheered by his audience, his accusations were not repeated by the Chartist movement and Williams attributes them to Cardo's having come under the influence of the arch-Russophobe, David Urquhart, D. Williams, *John Frost A Study In Chartism*, 246–9. Further evidence of Chartist susceptibility to Urquhart's analysis is provided by Robert Peter's poem, 'Britannia's Lament', which comments 'The Northern Bear spreads out his paws', *Northern Star*, 30 May 1840, 7. In addition, it should be noted that in his autobiography Thomas Frost offers an even more elaborate version of the Russian plot theory, the details of which he says were told to him by the Abbe Defourny, T. Frost, *Forty Years' Recollections: Literary and Political* (Sampson Low, Marston, Searle & Rivington, 1880), 103–11.

[37] *Northern Star*, 4 January 1840, 4.

the Special Constables. An unnamed government agent gives the following account of what happened next:

Unfortunately a young boy, whether by accident or otherwise is as yet unrevealed, let fly a small fowling piece. The 300 Chartists, imagining that they had been fired upon, discharged a few guns, when the military, who all this time were ensconced in a darkened room, commenced a most deadly fire upon them ... This murderous fire they did not discontinue until their ammunition was all but exhausted.[38]

The *Northern Star* insists that this evidence discredits those interpretations of Newport offered by the non-Chartist press, offering instead a version in which Newport 'seems to have been a proper, a reasonable, and a perfectly warrantable proceeding on the part of the people, foolishly or maliciously converted by the magistrates into a riot, for the insane purpose of laying the spirit of Chartism in a sea of blood'.[39] In this account, Newport is assimilated into the myth of Peterloo, becoming a moral force demonstration against tyranny in which Chartists are the victims rather than the perpetrators of violence, and the local magistracy bear the heaviest responsibility for the deaths which ensued.

The editorial's emphasis on the 'accidental' aspects of Newport appear designed to give the government room for manoeuvre as regards the eventual sentencing of Frost. (Interestingly, the *Northern Star* is in no doubt that the government 'will contrive' Frost's conviction, but does not believe they intend to execute him.) The *Northern Star* predicts that the government will look for the means 'to assume the attitude of mercy' and calls on 'the people' not to jeopardise this possibility 'by any violence of act or language'. This editorial ends by reversing the conventional relationship between moral and physical force by arguing that if the people possess insufficient moral force to achieve their object, then physical force will be of no avail:

There is enough of power in the people's hands to attain for them all they ask for, if they have but honesty and virtue to make use of it; and if they have not strength of mind to use their moral force with unanimity and courage, that of itself is proof that they have not the power of effecting anything by force.[40]

In the aftermath of Newport, Chartism was clearly more comfortable discussing the legal proceedings against Frost and his co-defendants Jones and Williams than it was discussing 'Newport' itself. From the outset two

---

[38] *Ibid.*   [39] *Ibid.*   [40] *Ibid.*

themes dominated; the importance of saving Frost and the perceived illegitimacy of the processes by which Frost was accused, tried and convicted. Both themes are present in Feargus O'Connor's first letter on the matter which appears in the *Northern Star* for 16 November. O'Connor argues that the government is unlikely to sanction a Special Commission before Christmas ('as the conviction of Mr FROST . . . would not be the most palatable Christmas box, with which to amuse the half-fed working people') and calls on the Chartist movement to use this time to mobilise on Frost's behalf:

What then becomes our duty? Again I say to strain every point for the liberation of Frost.[41]

O'Connor also argues that one of the reasons why a Special Commission would be an 'injustice' is precisely because of the expense it imposes on the defence.[42] Indeed, the financial cost of Frost's defence becomes a regular refrain in the *Northern Star*. An editorial entitled 'O'Connell and Frost' calls on all Chartists from 16 December to 'leave off drinking till the end of the year,' and to give all the money saved by this measure to the Defence Fund. In an appeal which fuses personal responsibility, political solidarity and domestic paternalism the *Northern Star* addresses an imagined reader, 'Let him, every time he thinks about a pint of ale, and is about to call for it, say to himself – "I am the better without it, and poor FROST may leave a widow and seven fatherless children, if I leave him without the price of it.".'[43]

In addition to highlighting its cost, the *Northern Star* argued from the outset that the trial itself was prejudiced, commenting acerbically in its editorial, 'Mr Henry Frost, Son of the Welsh Patriot':

If . . . the nomination of Judges, appointment of jurors, selection of time, secret service money to bribe, professional gentlemen to mystify, and a Whig Government to execute, be not enough to constitute and bring home a charge of treason, the Devil is in the dice.[44]

---

[41] *Northern Star*, 16 November 1839, 4.
[42] At a meeting in Stockport O'Connor claimed that the 'prosecution would soon cost upwards of £30,000; and surely the working classes could find £1000 for the defence.' The difficulty of raising such a sum is suggested by the fact that this meeting raised £2 9s 1d towards the defence of Frost. The following week an editorial, entitled 'O'Connell and Frost', announced that Sir Frederick Pollock and Mr Fitzroy Kelly had been hired for the defence at a cost of 300 guineas each (as a special retainer), 4s 6d each per mile to Monmouth and back, 25 guineas per clerk plus a 'heavy fee with brief [and] all expenses paid'. *Northern Star*, 7 December 1839, 6.
[43] *Northern Star*, 14 December 1839, 4.   [44] *Northern Star*, 23 November 1839, 4.

The following week the *Northern Star* reprints a letter from Feargus O'Connor to the Marquis of Normanby (the Home Secretary) calling for a postponement of the trial, citing 'the excitement and prejudice created by the *Times*, the applause so lately bestowed upon the military, the emulation likely to be produced by the honours bestowed upon the mayor', as factors preventing a fair trial.[45] The timing and the location of the Special Commission were also matters of particular concern to Frost's solicitor who wrote to Normanby asking him to postpone the trial, citing the recent case of Archibald Bolam ('found deluged in the gore of his unoffending victim') whose trial was postponed precisely because the strength of local feeling against him rendered a fair trial impossible.[46]

In the weeks leading up to the trial, the *Northern Star* also concentrated its fire on the concept of treason itself. In an editorial entitled 'Treason' it argues that treason is defined by power rather than law, 'that deed, which, if it succeeded, would be called a glorious instance of patriotism, when it fails, is mostly denominated a seditious and treasonable attempt'. In addition, it argues that definitions of treason are subject to wide historical variations, 'its nature and qualities have changed as often as the phases of the moon'.[47] An accompanying series of articles on state trials covering 500 years of English history (from the reign of Henry II to that of Charles I) is used by the *Northern Star* to demonstrate that treason trials invariably abandon legal norms and are symptomatic of a crisis of political legitimacy.[48]

The nature of the sermon preached before the judges on the opening day of the Special Commission must have confirmed Chartist fears concerning the impartiality of the trial. The text for the sermon was II Peter 2:19, 'While they promise them liberty, they themselves are the servants of corruption'. In an unmistakable allusion to Chartism, the preacher glossed his chosen text, 'but we have our Apostles of liberty now, preachers of the will of men, setting themselves and their victim followers

[45] *Northern Star*, 30 November 1839, 3.
[46] The *Northern Star* was not alone in criticising the treatment of the accused Chartists. The *Weekly Dispatch*, whilst condemning Newport as 'an enormous folly and as great a crime', nonetheless argues that the decision to hold the Special Commission in Monmouth 'is an offensive insult upon justice' which threatens to bring the law itself into disrepute. Furthermore, it describes the existing law of treason as 'abominably stupid' and as 'trash' and also criticises the judge's initial address to the jury. Unsurprisingly, the *Northern Star* reprints this article on its front page, 21 December 1839, 1. David Williams notes that the *Edinburgh Review* also opposed the holding of the Special Commission in Newport, *John Frost A Study In Chartism*, 258.
[47] *Northern Star*, 23 November 1839, 4.
[48] This series runs from 30 November 1839 to 25 January 1840.

against all that is holy and all that is true'. He continued by attributing 'the late heart-rending convulsion' to the growth of 'national infidelity' and traced the causes of the outbreak to the neglect of the spiritual needs of the populace.[49]

When the trial itself opened, its first two days were occupied with procedural arguments.[50] Although some of these, such as the debate as to whether a juryman could be challenged after the oath had begun to be administered (which takes up a full ten pages in the trial transcripts), may strike modern eyes as bordering on the parodic they nonetheless played a doubly important role. The mere fact of their existence was enough for the *Northern Star* to pronounce that the trial was procedurally flawed as well as prejudiced, and hence to declare after the 'guilty' verdict that 'Frost has been tried without law; convicted without evidence; and if executed, will be murdered.'[51] Even more importantly for Frost and his co-accused, these technical objections were heard before the court of the Exchequer and although the defence lost their case (on a 9–6 majority decision), the fortnight it had taken to hear the case was sufficient, as David Williams has shown, to save the lives of the prisoners.[52]

By the end of the trial the *Northern Star* was not only adamant that the case against Frost had not been proved, it was also suggesting that Frost himself had been 'the victim of a black conspiracy'. It argued that the 'evidence' of Frost's guilt presented by the prosecution came from untrustworthy, sometimes perjured, witnesses.[53] As soon as the guilty

---

[49] *Northern Star*, 28 December 1839, 2.

[50] For a detailed account of these procedural disputes concerning the calling of the jury, challenges to individual jurymen, and a prolonged debate over the delivery of the jury list and witness list and the timing of the defence's objections to the same, see D. Williams, *John Frost A Study In Chartism*, 269–74.

[51] *Northern Star*, 18 January 1840, 4.

[52] D. Williams, *John Frost A Study In Chartism*, 286–94.

[53] In an editorial entitled 'Frost and his Trial', the *Northern Star* commented:

We find every one of the material witnesses to be accomplices and traitors, and we find them, with these two brands, taken into the employ and favour of the partisans of Government; men who would have seen them starving for want of bread rather than have engaged them at any price, had it not been for their willingness to swear against Mr Frost. The boys Rees and Coles, who swore to the principal overt act, were perjured beyond all doubt, as ably proved by Sir Frederick Pollock from their own mouths. Hodge perjured himself, and he was an accomplice (*Northern Star*, 18 January 1840, 4).

This view of the case was not without foundation; as David Williams argues, under Pollock's cross-examination 'several [witnesses] had not proved very satisfactory' and the 'case for the Crown was thus badly shaken'. More importantly, the Lord Chief Justice appears to have been unpersuaded by the prosecution case and, in the words of the Attorney-General, to have 'summed up for an acquittal' (D. Williams, *John Frost A Study In Chartism*, 277–9 and 283).

verdict was announced, the *Northern Star* called on its readers to mobilise on behalf of Frost.

Let strong memorials, firmly, but respectfully, worded, pour into the Home Office, from all quarters, like hail. Let every effort that can be made be made instantly; BUT LET ALL BE DONE PEACABLY; NOTHING WILL BE GOT BY VIOLENCE.[54]

The campaign to save Frost's life was multi-faceted. It included the legal-procedural challenge discussed above, but in terms of Chartist mobili-sation this was overshadowed by a campaign which focused on the respective characters and domestic situations of Frost and Queen Victoria.

  The character of Frost played an important role in the debate over Newport, with the *Northern Star* both noting and refuting the *Times*' attacks on him. O'Connor's letter for 16 November argues that rather than being the 'bloodthirsty and overbearing tyrant' of the non-Chartist press's imagination, Frost has been 'pounced upon' precisely because he has always 'sympathized with the poor and oppressed'.[55] From the outset, the Chartists sought to portray Frost as a 'noble-minded and patriotic man'.[56] During the trial, his defence team argued that his feelings for, and sense of responsibility to, his wife and daughters, provided sufficient guarantee of his peaceable intentions. The defence advocate Sir Frederick Pollock in his closing address to the jury, reminded them of their own 'feelings as men, as fathers, and as husbands' and asked:

can you believe that Mr Frost on that day contemplated, in the town of New-port, from which he had not removed those members of his family, to whom he is dearly attached – a scene of bloodshed and revolution.[57]

---

[54] *Northern Star*, 11 January 1840, 4.   [55] *Northern Star*, 16 November 1839, 4.
[56] *Northern Star*, 23 November 1839, 7. A measure of Frost's significance is perhaps given by O'Connor's increasing attempts to align himself with Frost. At a Huddersfield meeting in November, O'Connor announces that 'he would sell his coat from his back, and go in his shirt sleeves, rather than that his friend Frost should be undefended. (Great cheering)' (*Northern Star*, 30 November 1839, 1). The following week, O'Connor emphasises his exertions on Frost's behalf and declares his readiness to share Frost's fate (*Northern Star*, 7 December 1839, 6). O'Connor also announces that the 'whole of the profit' from the *Northern Star* for 21 December 1839 will be given to Frost's defence fund and the following week, the editor of the *Northern Star* praises the 'almost supernatural exertions' of its proprietor on Frost's behalf (*Northern Star*, 21 December 1839, 4 and 28 November 1839, 4).
[57] *Trial of John Frost*, 477. Mr Kelly also referred to Frost's domestic affections and responsibilities in his closing address to the jury, 'Gentlemen, recollect that at this very time, when Mr Frost is supposed to have meditated, ay, and actually to have attempted to attack and overpower the military, and so to turn Newport into a scene of rebellion and of bloodshed, he had his own wife and five helpless female children in his house, and defenceless. Just make the case your own. I hope

In his reply, the Solicitor-General argued that Frost's disappearance immediately after the shooting rather undermined the defence's portrait of him as a dutiful and caring husband and father.[58]

The campaign to save Frost from execution coincided with the preparations for the marriage of Queen Victoria; and this temporal coincidence quickly became invested with symbolic significance. The meaning of the two 'events' became intertwined and the contrast between the threatened dissolution of Frost's family and the queen's marriage became an increasingly important trope within this campaign. The *Northern Star* quickly followed the lead of the *Weekly Dispatch* in arguing that the royal marriage provided an appropriate occasion for 'showing mercy' to Frost and his co-accused.[59] It prints 'Memorials' to the Queen that had been adopted at public meetings at Huddersfield and Dewsbury. These sought, in noticeably respectful tones, to 'remind your Majesty that the brightest gem in the British Crown is the attribute of mercy'.[60] The decision to commute Frost's sentence to that of transportation was, mistakenly, interpreted by many Chartists as a sign of the Queen's sympathy.[61] An Address adopted at the Manchester Delegate meeting (called to procure a free pardon for Frost, Jones and Williams) begins by observing that 'Our most gracious Sovereign has closed her ears against an appeal made by a faction for blood', whilst a Memorial adopted at the same meeting concludes:

we most humbly implore your Majesty to exercise your brightest prerogative, that which becomes the Throned Monarch better than this Crown, and to restore the unhappy prisoners to the bosoms of their supplicating families, and according to the request of a grateful and delighted nation. By these means you will render your approaching nuptials truly happy amid the exultations of a grateful people pouring blessings on your head, and thereby prevent your name from descending to posterity with that appellation attached to it, which the page of history has indelibly stamped upon the name of your female predecessors in royalty.[62]

However, as the allusion to 'bloody Mary' suggests, the Chartist attitude towards the monarch was not always respectful, and a much more critical and confrontational tone can also be found in the columns of the *Northern Star*. In its editorial of 25 January 1840 it castigates the Queen's Speech to Parliament as both 'insolent and heartless' for concentrating on

I am addressing some fathers and husbands. If you in an evil hour were to be stimulated by bad passions to embroil your country in civil commotion and bloodshed, and you were to seek to carry your objects in a town in which your wife and five or six helpless children were dwelling, would not your first act be to give warning to them?' (*ibid.*, 590).
[58] *Ibid.*, 633.   [59] *Northern Star*, 21 December 1839, 1.   [60] *Northern Star*, 1 February 1840, 1.
[61] D. Jones, *The Last Rising*, 197.   [62] *Northern Star*, 8 February 1840, 1.

her own forthcoming marriage rather than the 'people's sufferings'. It glosses her speech as: '**Your young Queen is to be married; and some few thousands of you may perish, to feed the Royal Bridegroom!**' (original emphasis). However, it continues by distinguishing Victoria from both her office and her advisers. The latter are held responsible for Victoria's speech – 'from *your* heartlessness, not *hers*, proceeds this vile and inhuman avowal' – and condemns the Cabinet in particular for failing to protect the young woman in its care – 'is your conduct gentlemanly, is it manly, is it decent, – thus to expose a woman to such fearful conflict?' The Cabinet is shown to have offended against caste, masculine virtue and basic decency, and this threefold failure clearly delegitimises their authority. The *Northern Star* detects something similar in the government's treatment of the working classes:

Is it *gallant* or *gentlemanly* to rob and insult the wives and children of mechanics and peasants? To hang and quarter the husband and father who dares to resist oppression?[63]

Throughout the editorial this crisis of patriarchal and paternalist norms and values is understood to be intimately connected with the political crisis which has engulfed the nation. It opens on an apocalyptic note – 'We are at the mouth of a volcano . . . on the eve of a great national crisis' – and argues that the country will shortly witness a decisive 'struggle' between 'despotism' and 'freedom'. The source of this crisis is to be found in the absence of any 'principle of [social] coherence or consistency'. The social order is about to tear itself to pieces as the forces of Mammonism confront those of patriotism and domesticity, in a conflict which the *Northern Star* declares to be historically unprecedented.

The only ruling power is intense and grasping selfishness; the only acknowledged duty is the idol Mammon, seated on a throne of blood. The land of our fathers, that land which is hallowed to our heart's best affections, by every tender recollection, and every endearing association – that sacred spot, in which are concentrated all the blandishments of affection, all the sweets of friendship, and all the softening and ennobling charities of home, is threatened with a severe and iron rule, which, if once allowed to be established, may require ages of exertion, and oceans of blood, to uproot and destroy it.[64]

---

[63] *Northern Star*, 25 January 1840, 4.
[64] This conflict between money and human affection is simultaneously represented by the *Northern Star* as a class conflict in which an aristocracy 'unacquaint[ed] with the simplest and most common springs of human feeling; [and] a middle class of money-mongers and capitalists' who care nothing for their workforce, stand opposed to 'a people . . . goaded by wrong and misery to despair on the one hand, and to distraction on the other' (*Ibid*).

Although the *Northern Star* protested its affection for 'the poor young girl, whom we sincerely pity, and as sincerely love,' elsewhere some Chartists showed hostility towards this 'subversion' of proper patriarchal values.[65] At a Huddersfield meeting, for example, a Mr Cunningham declared:

what a bad state of society that must be, which put at the disposal of a young woman of twenty-one the life of a man old enough to be her father, and who was, indeed, the father of a numerous family.[66]

This reaffirmation of patriarchal values is accompanied by the projection of the requisite feminine virtues onto Queen Victoria. In an editorial entitled 'The Queen and Mrs Frost', the *Northern Star* combines two potent myths; the personal meeting between monarch and subject and the unfailing appeal to shared womanly and domestic sympathies:

Our Monarch is called gracious; is a female imbued with all the soft and kindly feelings of her sex; and could she, upon the day after her marriage, refuse the application of Mrs Frost and her lovely daughters, when imploring pardon for husbands and fathers?[67]

Domestic sympathies of a manly nature provide the basis for condemning the actual transportation of Frost and his fellow prisoners in the following week's *Northern Star*. In an editorial entitled 'The Body Snatchers', the paper protests against the 'cowardly and disgusting . . . removal of the Monmouth prisoners at dead of night'. If the previous week's editorial used the narrative of domestic sentiment, then 'The Body Snatchers' borrows from the Gothic (and its near relation the melodramatic) with its themes of imprisonment, exile, and bodily and mental suffering.

They are first awoke, and then aroused to sorrowful reflection, by the clanking of their manacles. They have been partially prepared for death, and are relieved from the anticipation of the one sudden shock and conclusive struggle, by the announcement that life is to be spent in perpetual torture, not only of bodily suffering, but of mental anguish and despair. The wife of the bosom, the offspring of the loins, the associations of youth, the anticipations of old age, all to be bade adieu to and for ever. The delight of home, the society of the partner wife, the prattle of innocent children, flash across the victim's mind, and he becomes unmanned.[68]

---

[65] *Ibid.*   [66] *Northern Star*, 1 February 1840, 1.
[67] *Northern Star*, 8 February 1840, 4.   [68] *Northern Star*, 15 February 1840, 4.

The Chartist movement barely had time to assimilate the fact of Frost's transportation before it had to deal with a further onslaught from the government. As Royle notes, the repressive state apparatus was particularly active throughout February and March 1840, when '[m]ost of the national leaders, scores of local leaders, and hundreds of followers were tried and imprisoned'.[69] By the summer of 1840 Chartism, in organisational terms, was at a low ebb. Yet the poetry column's most sustained engagement with the Newport uprising also occurs during this period. The second half of this chapter examines the poetic response to Newport focusing on four key areas; the initial period of silence, the quest for appropriate historical analogues, attempts to explain and interpret Newport, and finally, poems of exile and return.

Somewhat paradoxically, it is necessary to begin by considering the apparent non-response of Chartist poetry to Newport. The first poetry column to be published after Newport offers its readers a decidedly apolitical poem. 'Philosophical Links' by A. Park is an uncontroversial collection of moral and existential musings.[70] The ideas and sentiments expressed in this poem are entirely conventional and unremarkable in themselves. What is striking about it, however, is its formal complexity which is visibly apparent in its diamond-shaped nine-line stanzas with their symmetrical metrical scheme.

It is difficult to see the intricacy and formal sophistication of 'Philosophical Links' as anything other than a form of displacement. In effect, the overly 'poetical' nature of the poem is overdetermined by the inability of the poetry column itself to provide an appropriate political response to Newport. Immediately to the right of the poetry column there is an extract from *The Educator* (headed 'Benefits of a Taste for Poetry') which discusses the importance of introducing the working classes to 'the richest portion of their birthright'. It argues that the working classes stand most in need of the morally improving influence of poetry:

The harshness of the realities about them requires its softening and soothing influence. It is a good which they may have with no evil attendant. Its purifying excitement may displace stimulants which brutalize and degrade them.[71]

---

[69] Royle, *Chartism*, 28.
[70] For example, the first three stanzas comment on the transience of life's joys; the flower, beauty and the maiden are respectively warned that their beauty, purity and happiness will be short-lived. The poem then calls for the unrestrained embrace of life, advising its readers to 'Sing' (v.4) and 'Love' (v.5) precisely because 'Death' (v.8) and the 'Grave' (v.9) await us all. A. Park, 'Philosophical Musings', *Northern Star*, 20 November 1839, 7.
[71] *Northern Star*, 23 November 1839, 7.

For the remainder of 1839 the poetry column consists of comic poems borrowed from other periodicals.[72] Many of these are taken from the Tory periodical *John Bull* including 'Lord Tomnoddy; or, The Execution. A Sporting Anecdote'; a poem about a bored aristocrat who decides to attend a hanging for its novelty value:

> But to see a man swing
> At the end of a string,
> With his neck in a noose will be quite a new thing.[73]

Aristocratic callousness pervades the poem; in the course of his drive to the execution site, Lord Tomnoddy spatters the general public and knocks down an old woman and a stall. He installs himself in a gin-shop in front of the jail and proceeds to eat and drink to pass the time before the 'sport' begins. His over-exertion in the field, however, causes him to fall asleep and miss the event. *John Bull*'s Tory readership undoubtedly derived pleasure from this satire at the Whigs' expense. However, for readers of the *Northern Star*, the delight in Whig discomfort must have been undercut by thoughts of Frost's impending trial and in this context the poem's jingle seems macabre rather than comic.

At first sight this silence appears to indicate a collective inability on the part of Chartist poets to find an appropriate poetical response to Newport. However, a tantalising note in the 'To Readers and Correspondents' section for 21 December 1839 reads:

W. S. – We do not think the verses would serve Frost at all; but we do not see why he should therefore 'burn the pen that wrote 'em.' The pen may be useful in the performance of other and better service.[74]

Unfortunately, this reply gives no indication of the nature of W. S.'s verses but it does provide evidence that the *Northern Star* was giving careful thought to the contents of its poetry column. The presence of philosophical, comic and satirical poems (taken from non-Chartist periodicals and therefore in a sense already 'authorised') can be seen as a policy of avoiding poetry which might in any way be harmful to Frost and the other prisoners.

---

[72] These poems include; Anon., 'Crumbs of Comfort for the Single Ladies of Anywhere Affectionately Presented to them by the Married Ladies of Somewhere' (described as being 'reprinted from an Old Newspaper'), *Northern Star*, 30 November 1839, 7; Anon., 'Prospects, Present and Future' (taken from *John Bull*), *Northern Star*, 7 December 1839, 7; Anon., 'Advertisement and Sale Extraordinary' (taken from *John Bull*), *Northern Star*, 21 December 1839, 7.

[73] *Northern Star*, 14 December 1839, 7.   [74] *Northern Star*, 21 December 1839, 4.

In the period surrounding Frost's trial, the poetry column published a mixture of cautiously political poems (such as John Goodwin Barmby's 'The Irish Fatherland' and 'The Mechanics of Young England – A Berangeism'[75]) and conventional pieces such as 'Sonnet to Fame' by Edward Thomas and 'Sonnet – The Poet's Solitude' by G. M.[76] Although none of these poems refers directly to Newport it is possible to read the political poems as offering a form of oblique commentary. For example, 'The Irish Fatherland' seeks to arouse Irish patriotism; its third stanza invokes the past heroes of Erin, 'Emmet, Gratton, and O'Connor' and its final couplet carries an ambiguously figured undertone of violence, 'Grow shillelaghs to each hand, / As swears our Irish Fatherland?' The conjunction of heroic leadership allied to the threat of physical force carries echoes of Newport and Frost, yet the Irish context also enables its disavowal if necessary.

'The Mechanics of Young England – A Berangeism' ends on a similarly ambivalent note regarding the threat or use of violence:

> Our arms they are, they are our hands,
>   In city or in town,
> May they possess the rights of man,
>   Without the despot's frown.

The punning ambiguity of 'arms' as both limbs and weapons encodes two alternatives in the poem's penultimate line – 'May they possess the rights of man'. Here possession can be either a case of holding on to (arms as limbs) or of forcibly seizing (arms as weapons). Intriguingly, this studied ambiguity attracts no editorial comment, unlike the celebration of the passing of the tankard. An editorial note condemns the practice as one of the ways in which working-class slavery is perpetuated and urges the mechanics to throw the tankard away.

At first sight neither 'Sonnet to Fame' nor 'Sonnet – The Poet's Solitude' appears to speak, even obliquely, of Newport. However, their appearance in the first poetry column to be printed after Frost's trial provides an additional interpretative field. One wonders, in the case of 'Sonnet to Fame', how Chartist readers responded to phrases such as 'empty glories' or 'The world's acclaim / Or bitter censure, I will heed no more' as well as the presence of those images of natural power which so often provided Chartist poetry with its metaphors of agency?[77] Similarly, the opening

---

[75] *Northern Star*, 4 January 1840, 7.   [76] *Northern Star*, 25 January 1840, 7.
[77] For a discussion of the relationship between images of natural power and ideas of political agency, see M. Sanders, 'Poetic Agency: Metonymy and Metaphor in Chartist Poetry 1838–1852', *Victorian Poetry*, 39:2 (2001), 111–35.

quatrain of 'Sonnet – The Poet's Solitude' could well be read with reference to Frost's plight:

> Nay, pity not his solitary doom;
>   He does not ask the world to sympathise;
>   His realm and intellectual kingdom lies
> Within the limits of that narrow room.

The first explicit poetic invocation of Frost is an acrostic from P. W. B. which appears in the poetry column for 1 February 1840 and takes the form of a prayer for merciful intercession.

> JEHOVAH, Lord, I humbly thee address,
> On thine eternal throne of righteousness;
> Hear, and relieve the groanings of distress,
> Now in this land flowing with plenteousness.
> Fell tyrant lordlings, who thy laws transgress,
> Repudiate, and their thirst for blood suppress;
> Old England's rights restore, her wrongs redress:
> Save, save my country from all that oppress,
> Then let thy servant, Lord, depart in peace![78]

Perhaps the most striking feature of this poem (aside from its monotonous rhyme scheme) is the complete absence of human agency from its lines. The 'Fell tyrant lordlings', whose 'thirst for blood' presumably encompasses that of John Frost, are to be repudiated and suppressed by God rather than resisted by the Chartist movement.

Following the commuting of Frost's death sentence into that of transportation for life, Chartist poetry turned its attention towards interpreting the significance of Newport. In the following months a further twenty-one poems on the subject of Newport and its aftermath appeared in the poetry column of the *Northern Star*. The vast majority of these (sixteen of the twenty-two) appear between May and August, a respectable distance in time from Frost's transportation which occurred at the end of February. Many of these poems are dated from Newport, suggesting a direct correlation between geographical proximity and poetic authority.

Earlier this chapter traced the process whereby over the course of a number of editorial articles 'Newport' was increasingly assimilated into the myth of Peterloo. A related process can be observed in the poetry column, although here the initial task addressed by the poets is that of finding an appropriate historical analogue for Newport. Philip Bevan's

---

[78] *Northern Star*, 1 February 1840, 8.

poem 'The Covenanters', for example, develops the practice of indirect comment first encountered in Barmby's 'The Irish Fatherland'. Its opening, which describes a gathering of the Covenanters, would serve equally well as an account of a Chartist 'monster' meeting:

> They rais'd the prayer, they sang the hymn,
> Within nor fane, nor hall,
> 'Twas by the mountain's lonely stream,
> Beneath the forest tall.[79]

The identification of Chartism with the Covenanters had already been made by Feargus O'Connor at a public meeting held on behalf of Frost in Sunderland in November 1839.[80] Bevan's poem represents the Covenanters in unmistakably phallic terms as men who have gathered in defence of their freedom:

> And trusty weapons arm'd each thigh,
> And firm the steps they trod,
> As men prepared to stand or die,
> Erect before their God.

The conjunction of armed resistance, civil freedom and 'authentic' masculinity in this poem, such that each is seen as both precondition and expression of the other terms, suggests the imaginary power exerted by the idea of 'physical force' and helps to explain the persistence of martial rhetoric, as noted by Armstrong, within Chartist poetry.[81]

Yet despite the powerful cathexis effected by the notion of 'physical force', the poem is unable to imagine its first use by the Covenanters themselves. In the verse quoted above they are ready 'to stand or die' rather than 'to fight or die'. Again, this recalls O'Connor's Sunderland speech which emphasised a readiness to die (rather than fight) for the cause.[82] In the final two stanzas the Covenanters are represented as 'martyrs'; they are the attacked rather than the attackers (a further indication of the pressure exerted by the myth of Peterloo).

Thereafter, the quest for historical analogy is largely conducted through the 'Chartism from Shakespeare' series (which runs from 25 April to 23 May 1840). The final number in the series, number four, is actually titled 'Frost and Physical Force' and consists of two extended extracts

---

[79] *Northern Star*, 22 February 1840, 7.   [80] *Northern Star*, 30 November 1839, 6.
[81] Isobel Armstrong, *Victorian Poetry. Poetry, Poetics and Politics* (Routledge, 1996), 191–3.
[82] *Northern Star*, 30 November 1839, 6.

(totalling 153 lines) from *Henry IV, Part Two* (a rebellion, incidentally, which was referred to during Frost's trial).[83] In the first extract, Mowbray, Hastings, Bardolph and the Archbishop discuss the prospects of their intended rebellion. Bardolph counsels caution and in particular advises against over-optimistic assessments of either their own strengths or the King's weaknesses. Hastings, by contrast, is confident of victory. Bardolph's caution would seem to echo those sounded by the *Northern Star* against 'the movements of stealthy, but violent and extreme parties'.[84] In the second extract, the Archbishop, called on to explain his involvement in the rebellion, refers to the general suffering of 'the commonwealth' and the King's refusal to listen to petitioners. In particular, the Archbishop's complaint to Westmoreland,

> . . . I sent your Grace
> The parcels and particulars of our grief;
> The which hath been with scorn shoved from the court,

must have resonated with a Chartist readership aware of how their own petition had been received by Parliament, as would his insistence that the ultimate responsibility for the current unrest resides with the government rather than the rebels. Similarly, Hastings' defiant prediction that resistance will continue for as long as injustice persists is surely intended as a statement of Chartist resolve:

> And though we here fall down,
> We have supplies to second our attempt;
> If they miscarry, theirs shall second them;
> And so success of mischief shall be born;
> And heir from heir shall hold this quarrel up,
> Whiles England shall have generation.

Elsewhere, the interpretation of Newport through historical analogy is augmented by the use of allegory and biblical allusion. Both of these interpretative frames are in evidence in a poem which shares the column with Bevan's 'The Covenanters', McDouall's 'Now Wide and Far the Tyrant's Power Prevails'.[85] This poem is framed by an epigraph drawn from Psalm 37 (Scotch Version), 'I saw the wicked great in power, / Spread like a green bay tree', yet its opening stanza involves the allegorical figure of 'meek-eyed mercy' who languishes ''neath the scorching

---

[83] *Trial of John Frost*, 554–6.   [84] *Northern Star*, 18 January 1840, 4.
[85] *Northern Star*, 22 February 1840, 7.

glare / Of the destroying daemon'. The second stanza fuses the biblical and allegorical by likening tyranny to 'a vast upas tree of death' which 'sheds / Its with'ring influence o'er our luckless land'. Allegory's capacity to encode contemporary experience is attested to by the careful combination of symbols of economic devastation (the blighted land surrounding the upas tree) and political repression (the tyrant's 'victims share the shameless felon's lot'). Much of the poem seems sunk in despair as the emphasis on tyranny's 'with'ring influence' and spreading shadows suggests its apparent invincibility. Yet the final four lines of the poem engender optimism by means of an astute pun which closes the distance between allegory and event:

> But it shall fade and fall, its doom's at hand,
>   A power's at work to set the country free;
> A *Frost* they cannot *banish*, nor command
>   Shall *nip* the *growth* of this destroying tree.

Following Frost's transportation, the poetry column begins to advance cautiously towards an increasingly direct and extensive engagement with Newport. This process begins in the *Northern Star* for 7 March 1840 with the poems 'Frost' by Philip Bevan and 'The Vision of Liberty' by J. L. (almost certainly Jonathan Lefevre). Bevan's poem continues the strategy, identified earlier, of emphasising the nobility of Frost's character; its opening stanza depicts Frost as a heroic individual who stands firm against a sea of oppressors: 'Who lifts his head against a host / Of foes malign? undaunted Frost!' The poem emphasises and connects both his courage and emotional self-control: 'He heard his doom, a gory grave, / But no faint sigh the patriot gave.' Frost's heroism is contrasted with the moral bankruptcy of his accusers who are depicted as 'the brood / Of knaves, corrupt, that seeks his blood'. Tellingly, this poem attributes responsibility for the violence of Newport to Chartism's opponents. These are characterised as 'bloodhounds' who set 'toils' and 'snares' to entrap Frost, and who are responsible for the 'murd'rous fire' at the Westgate Hotel (thereby echoing the *Northern Star*'s warnings against *agents provocateurs* given on 7 December 1839). This poem, perhaps taking its cue from the campaign to procure Victoria's intercession on Frost's behalf, posits 'mercy' as the countervailing force available to Chartism. It is mercy that 'tears [Frost's] chains away!' and the penultimate stanza asks 'shall soft mercy's voice be drown'd / By foeman's malice mutt'ring round?' The final stanza answers this question by calling on the Chartist movement to realise mercy's power by securing Frost's release.

> Forbid it, Heaven! forbid it all
> Who answer to stern freedom's call;
> With all our voices, all our prayers;
> And tear the patriots from the snares.[86]

If the myth of Peterloo made it difficult for the *Northern Star* to defend the first use of violence then this difficulty was compounded for Chartist poets by the influence of Shelley's *The Mask of Anarchy*. This poem offered a powerful rendering of the myth of Peterloo and the *Northern Star*'s poetry column for 13 April 1839 reprinted twenty stanzas from the poem under the title 'To the People'.[87] From Martha Vicinus's *The Industrial Muse* onwards, the idea of Shelley's influence on Chartist poets has become a critical commonplace.[88] In these discussions the focus has fallen exclusively on Shelley as an enabling force. Far less attention has been given to the question of those areas where the Shelleyan legacy (particularly his pacifism) might constitute an obstacle to be negotiated rather than a model to be embraced. Two poems by Jonathan Lefevre, 'The Vision of Liberty' and 'The Enslaved', exemplify this problem; both poems approach, albeit cautiously, an endorsement of proactive violence which necessitates an engagement with Shelley's *The Mask of Anarchy*.[89]

'The Vision of Liberty' (dated Bristol, 21 February 1840) which appeared in the *Northern Star*'s poetry column for 7 March 1840, is an unusually bloody poem by Chartist standards. It presents itself, like *The Mask of Anarchy*, as a dream vision in which the forces of Anarchy confront those of Liberty. More than half the poem (five stanzas out of nine) is given over to a 'gory' account of this 'crash of meeting foes':

> His long arm swept a gory blade
> Which he whirl'd in fury o'er his head; (v.4)
> . . .
> The snorting steeds before them fled
> As they strode over heaps of gory dead. (v.5)
> . . .
> The corpses around fell thick and fast,

---

[86] *Northern Star*, 7 March 1840, 3.
[87] The *Northern Star* reprints verses 37–47, 65–69, 72–74 and 91.
[88] See Chapter 1 for a summary of Vicinus's account of Shelley's influence on Chartist poetry.
[89] J. L., 'The Vision of Liberty', *Northern Star*, 7 March 1840, 3; Jonathan Lefevre, 'The Enslaved', *Northern Star*, 28 March 1840, 7. My assumption that J. L. is Jonathan Lefevre is based on the stylistic and thematic similarities between the two poems and the fact that both are dated from Bristol.

> As withered leaves at chill winter's blast;
> And fiercely the steeds plashed on in blood,
> And the ground was drenched with the crimson flood; (v.7)[90]

Precisely because the poem depicts the battle as already in progress, there is no original moment of violence which provokes retaliation, only simultaneous violence on both sides. This is, in part, a disavowal of *The Mask of Anarchy* which recommends 'folded arms' in response to tyranny's violence, as well as a step towards open acknowledgement of the Chartist violence at Newport. In a further departure from Shelley, 'The Vision of Liberty' emphasises an uncanny absence of sound in its depiction of the battle. Whereas in *The Mask of Anarchy* 'the dead air seemed alive / With the clash of clanging wheels' (v.76), in 'The Vision of Liberty' 'a deadly warfare seemed waging there / In silence' (v.3). Shelley's poem is constructed around a series of oppositions – aggressive/passive, noise/silence, tyranny/liberty – Lefevre resists these binaries, offering instead aggression and silence on both sides. This makes 'The Vision of Liberty' a far less ideologically comfortable poem as the reader is never certain with whom s/he is identifying (or meant to be identifying) and this discomfort is exacerbated by the emphasis on silence which invests the whole poem with a strong sense of the uncanny.

However, despite recognising the likelihood (and hence necessity) of violence, the poem falls short of advocating insurrection. Indeed, by the seventh stanza both armies have fought themselves to the point of mutual extinction, 'the host was dwindled and weak and few, / . . . And strength was decaying and valour expiring'. This deadly impasse is transformed in the poem's penultimate stanza by the appearance of 'a meteor' which:

> . . . shot from its lofty place on high,
> And burst 'mid this gory anarchy.
> It fell on the earth and exploded loud,
> As a thunder vast amid the crowd.
> The horse and his rider and all things blended,
> Dissolving in light, and my dream was ended.

The poem's final stanza records the triumph of Wisdom and Liberty, presumably as a result of this apocalyptic transformation, though the poem's closing couplet also alludes (albeit rather bathetically) to the role of violent resistance:

[90] *Northern Star*, 7 March 1840, 3.

> For the worm had turned on the foot that crushed it,
> But Anarchy slept, for Peace had hushed it.

These final two stanzas would appear to revisit and revise stanzas 25–38 of *The Mask of Anarchy* which also depict an apocalyptic intervention (accompanied by thunder) which prevents disaster, and where the death of Anarchy and the flight of his horse herald the emergence of a new order.

The next poem by Lefevre to appear in the *Northern Star*'s poetry column, 'The Enslaved', approaches even nearer to the open avowal of violence. It opens with a rallying call, 'Up, Britons, up! ye trampled slaves, be free!' and its second stanza not only repeats the call to rise but also enjoins its readers to arm, 'Flash from each thigh a weapon'. Similarly the third stanza calls upon 'Justice . . . [to] / Nerve the weak arm with strength!' This sequence of increasingly insurrectionary calls is interrupted by three verses in which a slave and another unspecified figure debate slavery.[91] The purpose of this discussion is to establish that a form of 'masked' slavery does exist in Britain, which in turn would appear to legitimise violent resistance on the part of the British 'slaves'. The final stanza depicts such violence with a studied ambiguity:

> Ye who are left, last of the garrison
> Which right defended, quit yourselves like men.
> The dwelling fired, and murder, are not yours:
> The steady eye, the unflinching hand, insures
> The fall of despotism – the tyrants' flight;
> Then sheathed the sword, and ended thus the fight,
> Britain is free![92]

Although this stanza still casts violence in defensive terms and is careful to redistribute responsibility for violence away from Chartism there is nonetheless an unapologetic affirmation of the necessity of violence, 'The steady eye, the unflinching hand, *insures* / The fall of despotism' (my emphasis), which is rare in Chartist poetry and which also revises Shelley's pacific injunction, 'With folded arms and steady eyes . . . / Look upon them as they slay' (v.85).

Further evidence of the difficulties which Newport created for the Chartist poets can be found in the work of the single most important poetic commentator on Newport – Iota – who produced a sequence of nine sonnets under the heading 'Sonnets Devoted to Chartism' and two

---

[91] For a discussion of the treatment of slavery within this poem see Mays, 'Slaves in Heaven', 148–51.
[92] *Northern Star*, 28 March 1840.

other poems 'Stanzas Addressed to the Patriot's Wife – Mrs Frost' and 'The Mountain Minstrel's Appeal', all of which appeared in the *Northern Star*'s poetry column between 9 May and 15 August 1840. Iota's poems are all dated from Newport and all appear to have been composed before the end of May 1840.

In 'Stanzas Addressed to the Patriot's Wife – Mrs Frost', Iota repeats the *Northern Star*'s claim, noted earlier, that Newport was a response to tyranny. The poem offers a version of the Peterloo myth arguing that a prolonged period of oppression 'roused him [Frost] to withstand / In arms – the freeman's just though last appeal' (*NS*, 16 May 1840). However, 'The Mountain Minstrel's Appeal', modifies this position somewhat by representing Newport as an uncontrollable emotional response to the oppression of the poor, whilst simultaneously hinting at the machinations of tyranny:

> They saw how the poor by their lordlings were spurn'd –
> They beheld the whole country oppres'd;
> And the fire of their youth to their bosoms return'd
> To aid and relieve the distress'd.
>
> With a generous ardour, for *prudence* too strong,
> And regardless, though dangers oppose;
> In an ill-fated hour, they were hurried along.
> And were caught in the toils of their foes.[93]

In these stanzas Newport is explained rather than defended. It is seen as an understandable response to an intolerable situation, but there is little sense here of even that qualified defence of physical force offered in the earlier poem.

However, it is Iota's series of 'Sonnets Devoted to Chartism' which constitutes the most significant poetic assessment of Newport. In the first of these, the various responses to the uprising are characterised as emotional states:

> . . . The gay
> Have laughed – the sober heaved a heart-felt sigh
> When Newport hath been named. The tearful eye
> Hath been its tribute o'er the grave to pay

The poem's closing lines capture the ambivalence of the Chartist response to Newport; unwilling to denigrate the sacrifice yet unable to endorse the use of violence.

---

[93] *Northern Star*, 6 June 1840.

> The fallen brave! – fall'n in a glorious cause,
> Howe'er mistaken in their way; – to gain
> Their country's liberty they strove; though slain,
>   Not fruitless was their fight, but worthy our applause.[94]

The patriot martyr provides the theme for Iota's next sonnet which commemorates one of the Chartists killed at Newport, George Shell. The shift in focus to the patriot martyr (a familiar and important trope within radical historiography) appears to have emboldened Iota, as this poem sounds a much more confident note than its predecessor. Iota castigates the government, declaring that Shell's death 'reflects upon thy foes a shame / Which ages shall not wipe away.' Furthermore, he predicts that the 'slaves' will shortly make a 'glorious stand / . . . For Labour – Virtue – Honour – Freedom's sake!' (*NS*, 27 June 1840).

The sonnet to Shell is accompanied by another which revisits (both literally and thematically) the place and subject of Iota's first sonnet. The poem opens with Iota remembering Frost by re-tracing one of his favourite walks. Initially, Frost is unambiguously acclaimed as 'One of the noblest patriots of the age', yet the consequences of this identity register the political divisions in the country as Frost is simultaneously 'that friend / Of man – and victim of the tyrant's rage.' The immediate relationship between poet and subject is transformed by the daring use of enjambement which connects the intimate ('friend') with the political ('of man'). The connection between the peripatetic and the political is reinforced as the poet recalls how Frost himself,

> . . . wandered o'er this pleasant way,
>   With heart-felt ardour for his country's weal,
> And fond anticipations of the day
>   When England's glory – FREEDOM, should be real.[95]

Once more, Iota emphasises the emotional dimension of Frost's politics, 'heart-felt ardour' and 'fond anticipations' inform his actions. Frost's objectives are couched in political terms, 'FREEDOM' and 'rights' but their political consequences are unmistakably economic. Freedom is understood as a state which reverses the abuses most closely associated with the factory system (which, even in South Wales with its foundries and mines, serves as the symbol of capitalist oppression):

> When men no more should be the slaves of gain,
>   Nor infants die to fill the Moloch maw

---

[94] *Northern Star*, 9 May 1840.   [95] *Northern Star*, 27 June 1840.

> Of despot lordlings – tyrants of the loom,
> Who yearly hurl their thousands to th' untimely tomb.

The *Northern Star* publishes no further poems from Iota until the poetry column for 1 August 1840, which publishes four more sonnets in the sequence (erroneously numbered III to VI, when they should read IV to VII). The fourth and fifth sonnets in the sequence offer the most detailed interpretation of Newport. The crucial question is posed by the opening lines of Sonnet IV:

> What fury maddened yonder mountain race,
> And unto desperation drove their chiefs?

In answer to this question (what prompted Newport?) the poem suggests three possible answers; oppression and want, 'wanton mischief' and the prospect of plunder. The initial question assumes that Newport must be the product of intense emotions ('fury maddened', 'desperation') and only the 'severe heart-rending griefs' occasioned by oppression seem capable of evoking such a response. In short, this sonnet repeats the *Northern Star*'s initial assessment of Newport as the 'fierce yell of men rendered desperate by tyranny'.

As was noted earlier in this chapter, the *Northern Star* quickly abandoned this interpretation of Newport. Iota, similarly, rejects this explanation in his next sonnet, in particular, taking issue with the use of the word 'desperate'. Iota refutes this explanation of Newport precisely because it is predicated on the loss of emotional control and subsequent surrender to irrational forces:

> Think not the PATRIOT formed so wild a plan;
> Or that his mind had grown so desperate;

Rather, deploying a line of argument used during the Monmouth trials, Iota insists on Frost's emotional propriety, arguing that his domestic affections prevented any such loss of control:

> He loved his wife too well to step one span
> Aside from virtue's path,

Instead, Iota proposes another and politically far more radical explanation for Newport; namely, that it was the result of virtue.

> . . . But virtue can
> Herself conceive, determine, execute,
> The ridding of the world of tyranny,

Of the three key words which are repeated in this sonnet, 'virtue', 'cause' and 'murder', virtue is by far the most complex. It carries connotations of moral probity, of 'manly qualities' of courage and valour, and also suggests divine sanction. Iota uses it to suggest that Frost felt compelled to act not as a result of uncontrollable emotion, but rather in conformity with the logical conclusions drawn by his moral intelligence. Iota's account of this conclusion reads like a radicalised version of utilitarianism's central dictum, as Frost's action is undertaken 'To minimise the sum of misery / Endured by man.'

However, Iota introduces yet another hermeneutic twist in the next sonnet (Sonnet VI) which begins by distinguishing between the tyrant and tyranny. Frost, Iota argues, 'contemplated' the end of tyranny and not the destruction of the tyrant. The nicety of this analysis marks both a sophisticated political understanding and a retreat from the qualified defence of violence offered in the previous sonnet. The implication of these lines is that Newport was intended as a peaceful demonstration (the core of Frost's defence at his trial) 'which might have led / To bloodless freedom from despotic thrall' (*NS*, 1 August 1840). Once more following the pattern established by the *Northern Star*'s own editorials, Iota finds a scapegoat for the initial violence at Newport in the form of an unknown member of the crowd (rather than a deserter or a young boy). The actions of this individual were not sanctioned by Frost who, in the poem, laments, 'That mad, rash firing, unexpected all / By me'. In a somewhat overdetermined attempt to exculpate Frost, the sonnet's final line represents the first shot as an act of 'drunk insanity'.

Sonnet VII is the only properly Petrarchan sonnet in the sequence. Its octave resumes the interrogative style of Sonnet IV and in a series of four questions asks, how long will tyranny endure? Each question occupies two lines and is organised around the contrast between the well-being unfairly enjoyed by tyranny and the equally unfair suffering undergone by its victims. The poem's opening lines provide a representative example:

> Shall tyranny have rest whilst patriots roam
>   In foreign lands far from their native climes?

The sense of defeated resignation which informs the octave is countered by the sestet which reassures its readers that:

> Justice is retributive; soon or late,
>   Reward will follow the oppressor's wrong.

In an equally optimistic vein, the poem ends with the declaration:

> Th'eternal principles of truth and right;
>   And equity shall overcome the tyrant's might.

It is striking, however, that these affirmations of eventual victory are unaccompanied by any sense of concrete agency beyond the moral abstractions of 'truth and right'. Furthermore, whilst victory is both morally sure and formally assured by the rhyming of 'soon or late' with 'inevitable fate', it remains temporally uncertain.

The final two sonnets in the sequence appear (once again incorrectly numbered) a fortnight later in the poetry column for 15 August 1840. Sonnet VIII returns to the countryside of Sonnets I and III, now figured as pleasures denied to the exiled 'patriot THREE' who, for example, 'No more inhale this sweet salubrious air'. Iota recalls Frost in this landscape contemplating his desired future:

> Beneath the lofty oak where branches shield
> Alike from sun or storm, the PATRIOT stood
>   Contemplating the *future*, when the rights
>   Of man would be secured to all their sons
>   Of toil – when all their moral, mental fights,
>   Free from the trenchant swords or thund'ring guns,
> Should end in triumph innocent of blood.

Note the tripling of effects here; Frost 'the PATRIOT' stands beneath 'the lofty oak' and engages in patriotic thoughts. In similar fashion, the poem offers an interesting temporal cathexis in which the present poet remembers a past moment which had the future as its object of contemplation. Frost's vision is one in which the working classes, 'the sons / Of toil', obtain their political rights by the peaceful means of 'moral, mental fights'.

The final sonnet offers a more detailed account of Frost's ideal future society. Its most important characteristics are social and domestic harmony and economic abundance, 'Peace, plenty, and content' (*NS*, 15 August 1840). Significantly, Frost is not seen to imagine a classless society. The benefits of 'Peace, plenty, and content' are intended for 'the palace', the 'peasant's cot' and the 'closely-huddled houses of the poor' (images which acknowledge the existence of both an urban and a rural working class). This utopia envisages the abolition of class hostility rather than class differences which will be achieved through the impartial administration of the law by magistrates committed to 'Virtue's stern career'. Interestingly, these virtuous magistrates are represented in the poem as immune to public opinion, moved by neither 'applause / Nor scorn' in the execution of their duties. This is significant because it accords ultimate legitimacy not to public opinion but rather to a moral absolute, 'Virtue'. The foundational belief underpinning this vision might be summarised as follows: the virtuous society must necessarily be a socially just society (where social justice is understood in terms of a thoroughly impartial legal system – both with regard to the development and the implementation of the law) and such a society must also necessarily be one which generates economic security ('plenty') for all its members.

Unsurprisingly, many poems deal with Frost's exile; the first such poem entitled 'Frost' and attributed to J. H. appears in the *Northern Star* for 2 May 1840. An editorial note explains the poem's occasion and its origins.

Poor John Frost is now many a mile from us. The following Lines were suggested to me from reading Moore's lines – 'She is far from the land'.

The original poem (one of Thomas Moore's *Irish Melodies*) describes an exiled Irish woman who is lamenting the death of her 'young hero' in the struggle for Irish freedom.[96] In J. H.'s version she is replaced by the figure of Frost, who laments his exile from his homeland and family. Aside from the gender of the relevant pronouns, much of the poem remains substantially unaltered, with the exception of two more significant changes to the poem's closing stanzas. Moore's poem ends on a melancholy note, anticipating the imminent death of the subject of the poem.

> He had lived for his love, for his country he died,
>   They were all that to life entwined him;
> Nor soon shall the tears of his country be dried,
>   Nor long will his love stay behind him.
>
> Oh! make her a grave where the sunbeams rest
>   When they promise a glorious morrow;
> They'll shine o'er her sleep, like a smile from the West,
>   From her own lovèd island of sorrow.

J. H. strives to avoid a fatalistic ending by emphasising the renewal of political resistance in the penultimate verse and providing Frost with a saintly halo in the final stanza.

> He lived for his country, for freedom he tried
>   To raise up the wretched he wish'd;
> Nor soon shall the tears of his country be dried,
>   Nor for long shall its efforts desist.
>
> Oh! he turns to a spot where the sunbeams rest,
>   When they promise a gloomy morrow;
> They shine o'er his form like a smile from the west,
>   From his own lov'd island of sorrow.

---

[96] Thomas Moore, *Poetical Works* (Frederick Warne, no date), 219.

The opening stanzas find Frost weeping at the thought of the home and family he has been forced to leave:

> He recalls the scenes of his dear native land,
>> The hearts who to life had entwined him;
> And the tears fall uncheck'd by one friendly hand
>> For the joys he has left behind him.

Frost's emotional suffering confirms his credentials as a sincere patriot and a good family man (and remind us of the importance of national and domestic discourses in the construction of Chartist claims to legitimacy). In the third stanza, Frost's tears are mirrored by those of his country, thereby setting up a correspondence between the patriot's body and the homeland. Frost's exile from Wales, therefore, is also Wales's (and Britain's) condition of self-estrangement. The poem ends on a note of promise. The 'tears' which signified exile and loss are replaced by 'sunbeams' which shine on Frost 'like a smile'. The substitution of a smile for tears suggests the repair of the harm caused by exile whilst the aura of natural light surrounding Frost suggests heavenly approval.

The poetry column for the final week of July contains two further poems (both anonymous) on the theme of Frost's exile, 'The Lament of our Beloved Captive, John Frost, Esq.' and 'The Captive's Dream'. The first of these, written in eight alternately rhyming quatrains, ventriloquises the exiled Chartist leader as he recalls his homeland. This emphasis on a remembered landscape replete with personal and political associations recalls the first and third sonnets from Iota's sequence and J. H.'s re-write of Moore. Frost's emotional and psychological suffering as well as his continued loyalty to the Chartist cause are all foregrounded in the early stages of the poem, although Chartist agency within the poem is restricted to 'prayers' (verse three) and collective radical memory in verse seven:

> But no! the fond record the people have borne me
> Shall survive the frail form that must moulder in dust,
> And a thousand brave spirits shall live but to mourn me,
> When the voice that hath cheer'd them forever is hush'd.[97]

The consolation provided by the anticipation of Frost's posthumous reputation sounds an ambivalent note here as it suggests both the tenacious perseverance of the movement but also Frost's own personal (and their collective) defeat. Indeed, it is difficult to assess the tenor of the

---

[97] *Northern Star*, 25 July 1840.

poem's closing three stanzas. The fifth verse describes Frost's desire to return home, however, the following stanza dismisses this desire as 'vain . . . and hopeless' and anticipates instead his imminent death. The seventh stanza, as we have seen, deals with the consolation of posthumous reputation and may, perhaps, be read as a rebuttal of the previous stanza's despair. The final stanza strikes a valedictory note:

> 'Farewell! Then my country! – my beautiful home!
> Deep, deep in this breast doth your memory dwell;
> Though ne'er o'er its green hills my footsteps may roam,
> My heart is my country's – farewell!! Oh farewell!!'

Although the final line affirms Frost's continued commitment to the cause ('country' here as elsewhere signifies both landscape and people), the absence of an imagined return suggests at best a resigned acceptance of current defeat which is barely offset by the prospect of future vindication.

'The Captive's Dream', the poem which follows 'The Lament', provides both political analysis and programme through a skilful manipulation of the reader's emotional responses. Although Frost is the narrated, rather than the narrating, subject of the poem; it too emphasises his fierce attachment to those native landscapes from which he is now exiled. These local landscapes are closely associated with memories of his youth and the overall effect is suggestive of a kind of plenitude:

> And he dream'd that he saw, from their sunny Height,
> The smiling scenes of his youth's delight.
> . . .
> One moment the captive paused to gaze
> O'er the hallow'd spot of his brightest days;
> And a gush of remembrance thrill'd him through.[98]

In this poem, the exiled Frost dreams of an actual return to his home. On returning, he finds the land gripped by carnivalesque freedom, figured here as an excess of pleasurable sensation and emotions:

> 'Give way', he exclaimed, 'to my heart's delight;
> 'Tis swimming in raptures fresh and bright
> I am lighted up with its burning sway;
> 'Tis the heart's rapture, – Give way, give way.'

Initially, the poem offers direct access to Frost's emotional state and is, in effect, inviting the reader to share his dream. At this point of heightened emotional satisfaction the poem breaks the illusion by reminding the reader that they are witnessing a dream state. The reader is, therefore, 'awakened' before Frost and thus distanced from his waking emotions. Whereas, in the dream, the reader had direct access to Frost's emotions, in the waking world s/he has access only to the exterior signs of his emotions, 'The frown of madness is on his brow; / And his eye is rolling in wildness there.' In the waking state, Frost becomes a prisoner once more and is constructed as the object of the reader's contemplation:

> And there was the dungeon, and there was the chain,
> And there was the prisoner in bondage again,
> The wide world of gladness forever clos'd o'er him.

In the poem Frost's dream of freedom is thwarted by the intervention of the British State. In similar fashion, the reader's pleasurable identification with Frost is checked when the latter is objectified as prisoner and victim. The reason for this disrupted identification is made clear in the final section which calls on the reader to restore the poem's initial emotional state by securing Frost's freedom.

> Make him happy, as he in his fancy seem'd.
> Blest! As he in his slumbers fondly dream'd,
> Send his pardon;

The agency possessed by the poem's readership stands in contrast to Frost's powerlessness as a prisoner, hence the need to disrupt the reader's identification with Frost midway through the poem. Their emotional experiences are analogous but neither synchronous nor identical; the reader must experience Frost's joy in order to want to recapture it, but at the same time, in order to be able to restore his freedom, s/he must not experience his powerlessness. A final suture is achieved by the poem's identification of Frost's freedom and return as a victory for Chartism, thus the happiness reclaimed by and for Frost will be spread throughout the entire movement.[99]

---

[99] A further poem on the subject of Frost's exile, written by George Binns (himself a Chartist prisoner), entitled simply 'John Frost' initially emphasises the fact of Frost's exile and criticises those who passed such a sentence on him. The fourth stanza connects, with great poetic economy, the fact of Frost's exile, the political necessity of campaigning for his return and the likelihood of resistance to this campaign:

> He is gone, it is true, he is gone!
>   But perish the slaves of despair!
> And so perish that hard-hearted one,
>   Who laughs at and mocks at our prayer.

After the completion of Iota's sonnet sequence the poetry column published no further poems on Newport for a month. When it returned, Shell rather than Frost was its poetic subject. John Watkins' 'Lines on Shell, Killed at Newport' is, perhaps surprisingly, the only poem on this subject to be published in the *Northern Star*.[100] Unlike Iota, Watkins writes at a distance from the events at Newport and in place of personal recollection he attempts a very public poem which seeks to encapsulate Shell's history and his political significance in four sestets. The poem aims at a memorability coupled with a stark simplicity. Unfortunately Watkins' quest for simplicity only sounds a banal note as the contrived nature of the *aabccb* rhyme scheme dominates its pedagogic efforts, whilst the third line's use of internal rhyme imparts an almost comic tone which cuts across the seriousness of the events described.

> They shot him, shot the father's son –
> Too soon his honest race was run.
> The 'red-coat' fired – poor Shell expir'd
> Freedom! he cried.
> He spoke, and died.
> He gain'd the freedom, he required.[101]

Watkins, one of the most prolific and formally ambitious of the early Chartist poets, returns to the subject of Newport with a verse drama entitled 'John Frost, or the Insurrection at Newport'. The 'Prologue' to this drama is published in the poetry column for 5 December 1840. Written in rhyming couplets and spoken by a druid, it traces the historic displacement of the Ancient Britons by the Picts, Scots, and Saxons, and their final enslavement under the Norman Yoke. Post-conquest history is figured as a dual history of continuous tyranny and unbroken resistance represented by the opposition of imprisoned bodies and free minds: 'Aye, they may chain the body, but in mind / We are still free' (*NS*, 5

This stanza's second line combines straightforward commentary, Chartism's failure has caused 'the slaves' to despair, with prediction 'the slaves of despair' will perish, and exhortation ('the slaves of despair' deserve to perish). The poem's final stanza recalls 'The Captive's Dream' insofar as it imparts a near messianic tone to the idea of Frost's return, which, once again, is seen as a precondition for establishing social peace in Britain.

> He is gone! but ere Britain have rest,
> Ere her thunders of discord are done,
> Let the cry, 'he is gone,' be reversed
> To lo! he is come! he is come!

[100] For Shell's status as a Chartist martyr, see Gammage, *History of the Chartist Movement*, 162–3.
[101] *Northern Star*, 26 September 1840.

December 1840). The desire for freedom is seen as an innate instinct, 'Born with our life this love of liberty, / 'Tis nature instinct, and can never die'.[102] This tradition of resistance has culminated in the Newport uprising and the 'Prologue' ends with an unambiguous endorsement of Shell's example and an assertion of eventual victory.

> All foes are conquer'd when we conquer fear,
> As did bold Shell, who braved a bloody bier:
> To gain his rights, he took the manliest course,
> The plain straightforward argument of force!
> Vengeance! is now our cry; remember Shell!
> We'll live like him – at least we'll die as well.
> Cambria's young friend, whose faith the dungeon tries,
> Shall come and kindle hope in beaming eyes.
> Silurian Frosts again shall lead us on,
> And Freedom's baffled battle yet be won!

It is rare to find such an unambiguous defence of Newport in Chartist poetry. Indeed, Malcolm Chase notes that such passages in the play 'came as close to openly espousing revolution as any Chartist in print at this time' and suggests that the 'tone of [the play's] language perhaps provides one clue as to why the author's fellow Chartists were reluctant to venture on performance and similarly why London's leading radical publishers declined to publish it'.[103]

Another extract from this play appears in the first poetry column for 1841 under the title 'Extracts from the Play of John Frost' (*NS*, 2 January 1841). The scene opens with Frost reading from the Sermon on the Mount. His chosen text, 'Blessed are the merciful: for they shall obtain mercy'

---

[102] Watkins' 'Prologue' recalls an earlier poem called 'Cambria' by Aneurim, *Northern Star*, 20 June 1840, 6. 'Cambria' also begins by invoking Wales's long history of resistance to foreign domination, beginning with its opposition to the invading Romans:

> . . . from thy breezy mountains came
> The Britons of undying name;
> Who stemm'd the might of Roman pow'r

Aneurim identifies this 'spirit' of liberty as a national characteristic of the Welsh, 'Cambrians! our sires that spirit drew, / Unbounded, and bequeathed to you'. In similar fashion, this spirit infused the bardic songs and Aneurim represents the movement towards freedom through bardic images. For example, the Welsh are shown to respond to freedom as the lyre responds to the bard's hands and the final image of liberty represents it as 'a voice with songs sublime; / . . . a form of giant force'. Whilst 'Cambria' is an unmistakably nationalistic poem it is not chauvinistic. The Welsh will respond to and assist any attempt for freedom made by the English, Scottish or the Irish, although Aneurim hopes that the Welsh will be at the vanguard of any such movement.

[103] I am grateful to Malcolm Chase for providing me with this information.

(Matthew 5:7) allows Frost to critique his treatment at the hands of his supposedly Christian jailers. His conclusion, 'I sought for mercy for the suff'ring poor, / And am condemn'd for't', lays claim to Christian authority for his actions. Indeed, Frost's self-representation here contains multiple allusions to Christ. Frost not only offers himself as a redemptive sacrifice, 'Oh, God! if 'tis expedient one man perish / For thy poor people's sake, I'll be that man', but his account of his trial, 'I was betray'd by my own counsellors, / And men, I saved, witness'd against me falsely', also contains clear Christian parallels. Finally, Frost's anticipation of the horrors that await him in the penal colony alludes to the scourging of Christ, 'To have the whip scourge off my blistered skin'.

Throughout the scene the Christian register operates in tandem with graphic accounts of physical suffering which would not be out of place in a 'penny dreadful' and which might be described as Gothic. In Frost's contemplation of his execution, the emphasis falls on the dismembering of his body and the disposal of his limbs:

> I'm sentenc'd to be hang'd, be drawn, and quarter'd –
> My sever'd limbs to be disposed of – how?
> Sold, strewn, or cook'd, as pleases our good Queen!

Following the announcement that the death sentence has been commuted to that of transportation, Frost lists at some length the varieties of suffering (both physical and mental) which he expects to undergo, 'In such an irresponsive wilderness, / Where man is authoriz'd to torture man'. Both the Gothic and Christian registers support the simple moral schema in the text, which sees a world polarised between good and evil. Frost contrasts his own reward with that of his local rival, Mayor Phillips (knighted in the aftermath of Newport) and avers, 'To pity poor men's woes is treason now. / The loyal laugh at them, are thank'd and knighted'. Frost detects a similar inversion of moral and political categories in the official designation of the commutation of his sentence as 'mercy'. Playing on the multiple meanings of 'transport' he remarks:

> Oh, 'tis sardonic! transport! aye, indeed!
> Transport in penal flames! – transported, ha!
> They'll next call hell, – heaven – devils, too,
> They'll christen angels –

and concludes, 'Vice reigns on earth and virtue is her victim.' The importance of this moral imagination is underlined by Frost's fears that he will become degraded in the environment of the penal colony, and the extract ends with his desire to be hanged immediately rather than undergo such a process.

> I shall go mad, or worse, become a fiend –
> And this they call their mercy – royal mercy!
> Be merciful, indeed, and give me death –
> Oh, let me die while yet I am a man –
> Give me some chance of leaving earth for heaven.

The belatedness of the Chartist poetic response to Newport allied to its willingness to remain within the ideological borders established by the *Northern Star*'s editorial columns, at first suggests that Chartist poetry functioned as a passive reflection or record of that earlier editorial commentary. As the poems by Philip Bevan and Iota show, Chartist poets did at times rework editorial material taken from the *Northern Star*. Indeed, as was shown earlier, Iota's Sonnets IV–VI not only include material from, but also repeat the narrative sequence of, that series of editorials which established the Chartist narrative of Newport. However, I want to argue that even those poems which can be traced to 'sources' in the *Northern Star* complement rather than repeat this prior ideological work. The Chartist poetic response to Newport plays a crucial role in establishing the Chartist memory or, more accurately, 'remembrance' of Newport.

'Remembrance' is used here in its Benjaminian sense to indicate 'a nonsubjective memory, emanating from a realm other than personal cognition or chronological narrations of past events'.[104] On a very basic level the poetry begins this process of remembrance by recalling 'Newport' to Chartist consciousness as the events themselves recede into the past. However, the poetry acts as more than a simple reminder. As I have shown in the preceding paragraphs, many of these poems perform complex cathexes ('The Covenanters'), engage in detailed political analysis (Iota's 'Sonnets') and seek to engender particular forms of sub-jective agency ('The Captive's Dream'). In short, the combined effect of this poetry is to produce that form of Benjaminian remembrance which enables a collective political subject to construct a sufficiently coherent narrative of its past actions to enable it to engage in future activity.[105] For Richard Wolin, remembrance constitutes itself as accumulated experience

---

[104] Susan A. Handelman, *Fragments of Redemption: Jewish Thought and Literary Theory in Benjamin, Scholem, and Levinas* (Indiana University Press, 1991), 150.

[105] Terry Eagleton, *Walter Benjamin or Towards a Revolutionary Criticism* (Verso, 1981), 73.

which is culturally transmissible.[106] To return to the theoretical paradigm of this chapter's opening paragraphs, it is clear that Barthesian myth and Benjaminian remembrance share a number of common features. Both depend on what might be called a 'logic of compression'; that is to say, selecting from the mass of incident and detail those elements necessary for its own purposes. These are then orchestrated into a narrative which encodes both knowledge and forms of agency which are transmissible and, therefore, capable of sustaining present and future action.

However, our understanding of the ideological work performed by Chartist poetry would be incomplete without a consideration of the role played by the 'political unconscious'. Barthesian myth and Benjaminian remembrance both derive their power from their ability to sustain particular narratives. Yet, as Jameson reminds us, narrative derives its force from its ability to provide a symbolic resolution to insoluble social contradictions. In short, for Jameson, it is the insoluble social contradiction which constitutes the kernel of the 'real' in all narrative.[107] Insofar as Chartist poetry, collectively, gives rise to narrative, it too must be organised around a fundamental contradiction. In the case of the poetry of Newport this contradiction assumes the form of the difference between the theoretical right of armed resistance and the defence of Newport as the practical assertion of that right. As has been shown in the preceding analysis, both desires can be readily identified and traced in the poetry of Newport. However, apart from the poetry of John Watkins, nowhere are these two desires conjoined. When the right of armed resistance is affirmed (for example, 'The Vision of Liberty', 'The Enslaved'), Newport is conspicuously absent; similarly, where Newport is explicitly defended (most notably in Iota's 'Sonnets'), it is not represented as an insurrection. Clearly, this contradiction speaks of two very different forms of agency, and within the poetry these are often personified by Frost and Shell. Poems which focus on the exiled Frost necessarily internalise the experience of defeat. In these poems Frost is frequently associated with tears (whether his own or his country's) and lamentation becomes the main form of agency – 'And a thousand brave spirits shall live but to *mourn* me' (emphasis added). In contrast, Shell is associated with blood and his perceived martyrdom issues in calls for retribution – 'Vengeance! is now our cry; remember Shell!' That the figure of Frost rather than Shell

---

[106] Richard Wolin, *Walter Benjamin. An Aesthetic of Redemption* (New York: Columbia University Press, 1982), 228.
[107] F. Jameson, *The Political Unconscious* (Routledge, 1989), 77.

predominated in Chartist poetry confirms the general preference within the movement for constitutional as opposed to insurrectionary agency. In the ideological aftermath of Newport the Chartist movement like the Frost of Iota's eighth sonnet continued to dream of:

> . . . the *future*, when the rights
> Of man would be secured to all their sons
> Of toil – when all their moral, mental fights,
> Free from the trenchant swords or thund'ring guns,
> Should end in triumph innocent of blood.

CHAPTER 5

'Merry England': memory and nostalgia in the year of the mass strike

Once thou wert 'Merry England', and thy fruitful soil was blest;
Thy daughters then knew happiness, and thy sons had food and rest
Anon, 'Merry England'[1]

In the aftermath of Newport, the government arrested and imprisoned nearly 500 Chartists including many of the movement's national leaders. William Lovett and John Collins were imprisoned in Warwick jail, Peter Murray McDouall and Bronterre O'Brien languished in the castles of Chester and Lancaster, respectively, whilst Feargus O'Connor was confined in York castle. The government proclaimed that it had extinguished 'the chimera of Chartism', and paid little attention to Thomas Carlyle's warning that its 'living essence' remained a potent force in the body politic.[2]

The accuracy of Carlyle's prediction was soon demonstrated. In July 1840 the National Charter Association (NCA) was founded at a conference held in Manchester.[3] The steady release of national leaders between July 1840 and August 1841 gave renewed impetus to the movement nationally as well as permitting great ceremonial displays of revived Chartist strength as localities organised elaborate demonstrations to hail the liberation of their leaders.[4] By October 1841 the NCA had begun to

---

[1] *Northern Star*, 25 June 1842.
[2] Thomas Carlyle, 'Chartism' in A. Shelston (ed.), *Thomas Carlyle: Selected Writings* (Harmondsworth: Penguin, 1971), 151.
[3] Edward Royle comments that the NCA 'was to constitute the backbone of Chartist organisation for the next dozen years', Edward Royle, *Chartism* (Longman, 1986), 29. The NCA represented the Chartist movement's most sustained attempt to construct what Eileen Yeo calls 'an adequate form of national organisation which was both democratic and legal'. Eileen Yeo suggests that the difficulty of framing a legal movement is a factor which is often overlooked in accounts of Chartism. Eileen Yeo, 'Some Practices and Problems of Chartist Democracy' in J. Epstein and D. Thompson (eds.), *The Chartist Experience* (Macmillan, 1982), 345–80.
[4] For example, see the description of the Birmingham demonstration to celebrate the release of Lovett and Collins in R. C. Gammage, *History of the Chartist Movement*, 185.

organise a second petition, and by May 1842 the collective efforts of some 400 localities and 50,000 individual members had collected 3,317,752 signatures. The petition was presented by T. S. Duncombe to the House of Commons on 2nd May and, after a debate, was rejected by 287 votes to 49.[5]

Although the movement was better organised than in 1839 (as shown by the number of localities and the increased number of signatories to the petition) it was not without its own internal difficulties and divisions. In particular, tactical and strategic disagreements continued to bedevil Chartism. Lovett's 'new move' or 'knowledge Chartism' proposed education as the key means of working-class advance. Henry Vincent and Robert Lowery argued for 'Teetotal Chartism' and a closer alliance with the middle classes, whilst Arthur O'Neil headed 'Christian Chartism' which was especially influential in Scotland and the Midlands. All of these were opposed by Feargus O'Connor who feared the dilution of Chartist energies as well as a threat to his position as the movement's chief.[6]

In addition, Chartism faced two external, middle-class led, competitors in the shape of the Complete Suffrage Union (CSU) and the Anti-Corn Law League (ACLL).[7] Indeed, the struggle with the ACLL provided one of the sub-plots in the narrative of the strike-wave which swept the British mainland in August and September 1842. For the first and only time in Chartism's history, its actions coincided (and were briefly, but not unproblematically, co-ordinated) with those of the trades unions – an aspect of the strike which caused particular alarm to the government. A period of sustained state repression followed the collapse of the strike-wave with over 1,500 strikers tried in north-west England alone.[8] The second half of 1842 also saw Feargus O'Connor consolidate his position as the undisputed leader of the Chartist movement (with the poetry column playing an important part in this campaign), a fact confirmed by his triumph at the Complete Suffrage Union conference held in Birmingham at the end of December.

In 1842, Chartism also found itself operating in a new political environment. In the preceding August the Conservatives, led by Sir Robert Peel,

---

[5] Royle, *Chartism*, 30.   [6] *Ibid.*, 34–5; Gammage, *History of the Chartist Movement*, 195–7.

[7] Both Royle and Gammage agree that the unintended result of the CSU's activities was to strengthen O'Connor's dominance within Chartism, Royle, *Chartism*, 38–9; Gammage, *History of the Chartist Movement*, 198–200.

[8] For accounts of the 1842 strike-wave see, F. C. Mather, *Public Order in the Age of the Chartists* (Manchester University Press, 1966), and M. Jenkins, *The General Strike of 1842* (Lawrence & Wishart, 1980).

had won their first General Election since the passage of the 1832 Reform Bill. The question of who to support in this General Election had also added to the divisions within Chartism, with O'Connor advocating a policy of punishing the Whigs by voting Tory, whilst Bronterre O'Brien argued that Chartists should only form local electoral pacts where the other party was prepared to endorse a Chartist candidate.[9] The second Chartist petition reflects this changed political context. The first petition had carefully sought to identify middle-class and working-class grievances as stemming from the same cause, namely the continued aristocratic monopoly of Parliament and was careful to couch its demands in respectful tones:

capital brings no profit, and labour no remuneration . . . The energies of a mighty Kingdom have been wasted in building up the power of selfish and ignorant men . . . We come before your Honourable House to tell you with all humility, that this state of things must not be permitted to continue.[10]

The second petition strikes a much more combative note. It challenges the legitimacy of the current Parliament and emphasises working-class grievances, focusing in particular on the New Poor Law, but also referring to factory conditions and the 'starvation wages of the agricultural labourer':

Your petitioners instance . . . that your honourable House has not been elected by the people [and] perceive with feelings of indignation, the determination of your honourable House to continue the Poor Law in operation, notwithstanding the many proofs . . . of its unchristian character and of the cruel and murderous effects produced upon the wages of working men and the lives of the subjects of this realm.[11]

The second petition is far less respectful, even going so far as to compare the daily incomes of the sovereign and her spouse with those enjoyed by her labouring subjects (£167 17s 10d and £104 2s to 2d – $3\frac{3}{4}$d, respectively). The petition also notes 'the many grievances borne by the people of Ireland' and calls for the repeal of the Legislative Union with Ireland. Gammage records that this widening of the petition's scope was not without controversy and notes that a 'portion of the Scottish Chartists were opposed to the introduction of any other subject into the petition than the Charter'.[12]

The increased political significance of Ireland within Chartism partly reflects, as Dorothy Thompson has shown, a long-established tradition of

[9] Gammage, *History of the Chartist Movement*, 192–3.
[10] Max Morris (ed.), *From Cobbett to the Chartists 1815–1848* (Lawrence & Wishart, 1948) 141–2.
[11] *Ibid.*, 171–3.   [12] *Ibid.*, Gammage, *History of the Chartist Movement*, 208.

working-class radical interest in and involvement with the 'Irish question' and the 'very considerable Irish presence in the Chartist movement'.[13] Moreover, as Donald Read and Eric Glasgow have demonstrated, an alliance between British radicals and Irish nationalists was a long-cherished ambition of Feargus O'Connor.[14] In addition to these strategic questions, Ireland came to play an important role in the Chartist imaginary because of the opportunity it gave to both the movement and O'Connor to consolidate their respective identities through a dialectic of similarity and difference. In the *Northern Star*'s poetry column, Ireland becomes a significant topic from 1840 onwards. In the last two years of the 1830s, Ireland barely features in the poetry column, with J. B. Walker's 'Plaint of the Wandering Irish Peasant' the only instance of a poem which has Ireland as its primary focus.[15] However, from 1840 onwards, poems about Ireland feature regularly in the poetry column. Twelve poems which have Irish matters as their major theme are published in 1840 and these fall into three categories; 'nationalist/patriotic' poems, poems on the subject of exile from Ireland and poems satirising Daniel O'Connell.

The anti-O'Connell poems clearly owe their origin to the rivalry between O'Connor and O'Connell as well as to the organisational 'turf-war' between Chartism and the Repealers. O'Connell was viewed with suspicion by many English working-class radicals as a result of his hostility to trades unions, and for what many considered to be his duplicitous attitude towards Chartism.[16] In Sylvan's 'Lines Suggested by Daniel O'Connell's Visit to the Anti-Corn Law Dinner at Manchester', O'Connell is represented as an opportunistic hypocrite who seeks to profit from Ireland's misery, her 'seeming friend' but 'certain foe' in Sylvan's words (*NS*, 4 April 1840). Similarly, Argus's 'Daniel O'Wheedle' criticises O'Connell for accepting ministerial office and reneging on his radical principles (*NS*, 5 September 1840). Feargus O'Connor himself even goes

---

[13] Dorothy Thompson, 'Ireland and the Irish in English Radicalism before 1850', in J. Epstein and D. Thompson (eds.), 120–2.

[14] D. Read and E. Glasgow, *Feargus O'Connor* (Edward Arnold, 1961), 73–5.

[15] *Northern Star*, 20 January 1838, 7. The only other poem with an Irish theme to be published prior to 1840 is Thomas Moore's 'Song. For the Poco-Curante Society', *Northern Star*, 4 May 1839.

[16] O'Connell had been a member of the committee (composed of MPs and the London Working Men's Association) which had drawn up the Six Points of the Charter, and his subsequent hostility to Chartism as well as his offer of 500,000 Irishmen to help suppress Chartism following the Newport insurrection had led many to share Gammage's view of him as an 'apostate', Gammage, *History of the Chartist Movement*, 165.

so far as to invent a 'poetic' dialogue between O'Connell and the Marquis of Normanby (the Home Secretary) in which 'N' tells 'D' that the Tories have even managed to find a way of sending 'Feargus' to jail so that O'Connell might consolidate his control over Irish opinion (*NS*, 11 July 1840). Finally, in the scabrous 'The Devil and Owen O'Connelly: or the New Irish Chancellor. A Romantic Ballad', the anonymous author not only has the devil assembling O'Connelly rather in the manner of Frankenstein's monster ('he stuffed the skull inside with the brains of a lawyer') before proceeding to direct his political career, but also features a scene in which the devil offers O'Connelly £10,000 per annum to pursue repeal. In response, O'Connelly makes a counter-offer to sell both 'Rent' and 'Repeal' to the devil for the Irish Chancellorship, and the poem ends with both parties 'Each resolving in his own mind / How he best might cheat the other' (*NS*, 19 December 1840). It is clear that this characterisation of O'Connell as an unscrupulous, opportunistic, self-interested politician who only poses as a patriot, serves as an anti-type to Feargus O'Connor.

O'Connell is also the target in two radical 'scraps' from L. T. Clancy, both of which contrast the sham radicalism of O'Connell with O'Connor's genuine commitment to the cause of Ireland. In the first squib, 'Song of the Irish Absentees' (*NS*, 2 July 1842), a group of Irish MPs lament the financial hardships they will have to undergo, or more accurately inflict on their tenants, as the result of Peel's new income tax. O'Connell is also given the final verse in which he makes clear that his priority remains the collection of the shilling 'rent' for the duration of what he hopes will be a long 'agitation'.[17] A month later Clancy returns to the attack with his 'Scraps For Radicals. No. XVI' (*NS*, 6 August 1842) in which he contrasts the willingness of 'brave Feargus' to speak in defence of 'Erin' with O'Connell's silence, 'Oh! where was the great Liberator, / The once mighty member for Clare?' Clancy also accuses O'Connell of helping to maintain Ireland's continued subjection and, therefore, of being her most lethal enemy:

> Then Erin, dread not the bold foeman,
>   But rather that final viper's breath,
> The base, who 'dare not be a Roman',
>   But counsel 'obedience to death'.

---

[17] In 1824 Daniel O'Connell started the 'Catholic rent' which conferred membership of the Catholic Association to anybody paying a shilling a year into its funds.

The personal rivalry between O'Connor and O'Connell is part of a wider campaign to establish an alliance between the Chartist and Irish causes both by identifying the similarities between the political and economic conditions of the labouring masses on both islands and by drawing the attention of the English to the long history of Irish resistance. Benjamin Gough's untitled poem, which appears in the first poetry column for 1842 under the heading 'Poetry for Ireland', exemplifies this strand (*NS*, 1 January 1842). The poem's opening stanza identifies callous rulers, negligent and absent aristocrats and priestcraft as the triple origin of 'Ireland's woes'. The evils of unchecked monarchy, aristocracy and priestly power would be all too familiar to English radicalism, which had long since formulated its own critique in these terms. If verse one identifies a common situation as the basis for alliance, the second stanza augments this by appealing to a complex of values which unite the Irish and the English. Gough commends the martial valour of the Irish and notes their willingness even 'For ingrate England [to] shed their dearest blood'. He continues by reminding his readers of Grattan and Curran as examples of Ireland's commitment to the cause of liberty before instancing her sense of honour, capacity for sympathy and poetic traditions as further examples of qualities which are revered by Irish and English alike. The stanza ends by conjoining martial and poetic prowess in opposition to oppression, 'Foremost in battle, loftiest on the lyre, / And yet oppression, damps her noblest fire!' Thus at a time when the alien nature of the Irish was being emphasised in the wider culture, Chartist poets were insisting not just on a common cause but on shared characteristics.[18]

A few months later another poem by L. T. Clancy 'The Land of Repeal and the Charter My Boys!' attempts the complementary action of convincing the Repealers that their cause is inseparable from that of the Charter. The poem seeks to identify Chartism with the spirit of Irish

---

[18] For representations of Irishness in the British culture, see L. Perry Curtis Jr., *Apes and Angels: The Irishman in Victorian Caricature* (Washington: Smithsonian Institute Press, 1997), and Michael de Nie, *The Eternal Paddy: Irish Identity in the British Press 1798–1882* (Madison: University of Wisconsin Press, 2004). The lines from Thomas Moore which precede Gough's poem increase this sense of kinship and affinity by making the mother country the object of a commitment which is simultaneously emotional and political (a cathexis which is frequently attempted in Chartist poetry):

> No! thy chains as they rankle thy blood as it runs,
> But makes thee more painfully dear to they sons;
> Whose hearts like the young of the desert-bird's nest,
> Drink love in each life-drop that flows from they breast!

history by invoking the memory of 'Brien Borouhe' (who united Ireland against the Danish invader) and, by means of its titular refrain, to link Repeal and the Charter. Clancy ends his poem by calling for unity amongst 'Britons' and grouping the three constituent nations into a symbolic republic represented metonymically by the tricolour of the poem's penultimate line:

> So come brothers, come Britons – unite – let us toast,
> For 'The fair that we love,' each true Irishman's boast,
> In the land of Repeal and the Charter my boys!
> To 'The rose of old England, in liberty's gem,'
> To 'the thistle of Scotland entwining its stem,'
> To 'the shamrock of Erin's bright emerald bloom,'
> To 'Our blossoming hope, to our tricolour'd plume,'
> In the land of Repeal and the Charter my boys![19]

However, the Chartist relationship to Ireland was not one of simple assimilation. The similarities between the situation of the labouring classes in both islands were important, but for a number of Chartist writers it was precisely the differences between the two traditions of resistance which needed to be understood. A common feature of Chartist poetry on Irish matters is the invocation of past Irish heroes, most notably Robert Emmet, one of the leaders of the United Irishmen who had been hanged and decapitated by the British government following the failed insurrection of 1803. The speech which Emmet made in his own defence was well-known to English radicals and, as Dorothy Thompson notes, '[p]erformances of the trial of Emmet were given throughout the British Isles by Chartist groups ... to rouse enthusiasm and raise funds'.[20] It is unsurprising, then, to find the anonymous 'Last Words of Emmet' in the poetry column for 15 January 1842. The poem records Emmet's confidence that his actions will be both understood and vindicated by a liberated future Ireland. In such an Ireland his grave will become 'a patriot's resting place' which will receive a 'tribute of ... tears' from his future countrymen. This image of the patriot-martyr's grave is one which becomes increasingly important in Chartist poetry, most noticeably in the work of the late Chartist poet Gerald Massey, its presence as a poetic trope indicating both a complex relationship to the historical past and ambivalence towards the role of violence in history.

---

[19] *Northern Star*, 23 April 1842.
[20] D. Thompson, 'Ireland and the Irish in English Radicalism before 1850', 137.

Emmet and the United Irish insurrections of 1798 and 1803 resonated in the Chartist imagination as both an inspirational and a cautionary tale. As Dorothy Thompson observes:

For those among the Chartists who believed that an armed rising was either desirable or unavoidable, the experience of the United Irish rising of 1798 was always in their consciousness, both as illustrating the possibility of a popular rising, and as illustrating the dangers of lack of preparation and the ruthlessness of British government action.[21]

The upsurge of poetic interest in Ireland after the failed Chartist uprisings indicates the extent to which 'Ireland' provided Chartist poets with a way of imagining insurrection. A noticeable feature of this poetry is the presence of blood-soaked images. In one of the earliest poems on Ireland to appear in the *Northern Star*, John Cook's 'Address to Erin' (*NS*, 16 June 1840) the poet predicts the emergence of heroes who will vanquish the tyrant 'Who stain'd thy rich vallies with gore'. Even in an ostensibly satirical squib such as L. T. Clancy's 'Scraps for Radicals. No. XVI' the blood runs freely; 'gore-crimson'd surge', 'bloody slaughter', 'blood-stained' and 'gore-crimson'd wreath' are used to describe recent Irish history.

However, ambivalences and uncertainties concerning the use of violence (except as a form of self-defence) are not absent from Chartist poetry on Ireland. In Benjamin Gough's poem, for example, the stanza celebrating Ireland's martial prowess is immediately followed by one in which 'the Almighty / . . . and his winnowing fan' will right Ireland's wrongs. The verse continues by denying England's claim to Ireland except by force of arms, and argues that unless this injustice is righted then 'retribution's blast' will surely follow. The appeal to divine authority in the face of a fundamental wrong and the assertion of a moral order which guarantees the ultimate overthrow of such injustice clearly resembles the arguments used by Chartist poets when writing in support of their own cause. The warning of retribution is also, albeit implicitly, a threat of violence, which is encoded in the familiar images of natural force which appear in the fourth and final stanza, where the poem warns the oppressors against provoking the 'nation's thunder' and its 'red volcanic fire'. John Cook's 'Address to Erin' strikes a similar note as he imagines the massing of heroes to free Ireland:

> . . . they shall come like a storm in the sky;
> And their voices like thunder shall roar;

---

[21] *Ibid.*, 145.

And revenge, like red lightning, shall dart from each eye;
And the tyrant shall fall, or the tyrant shall fly,
    Who stain'd thy rich vallies with gore.[22]

Yet L. T. Clancy's 'The Land of Repeal and the Charter My Boys!' tries to consign violence to Ireland's historical past. The second verse, which follows the celebration of Brien Borouhe's martial prowess, strikes a decidedly peaceable note, 'May each man be prudent, peace guiding his will'. The poem is clear that if violence is avoided by the people, 'then shall the foe, who dare challenge our right, / Feel the shameful defeat of a peaceable fight'. Thus, even though Ireland gave Chartist poets greater opportunity to contemplate insurrection, these imaginings were still attended by the same anxieties and ambivalences encountered in the previous chapter. These are registered poetically in those shifts of agent (from the nation to God), agency (from violence to peaceful methods), and temporality (heroic pasts, degraded presents and redeemed futures), and in the increasing popularity of the trope of the martyr's grave, which, by focusing attention on the victim of state violence, avoids those uncomfortable questions concerning its first use.

The increasing presence of Ireland in the *Northern Star*'s poetry column is paralleled by the increasing visibility of Chartism itself as an *object* of poetic representation. Like Ireland, Chartism had barely featured in the earliest years of the poetry column. In 1838 only Joseph Middleton's 'The Bonnie Green Banners' (*NS*, 14 April 1838) and Robert Dibb's 'The Gathering of the Great Northern Union' (*NS*, 2 June 1838) had taken the movement itself for their poetic theme. Similarly, in 1839 W. McDouall's 'Lines for the *Star*' (*NS*, 31 August 1839) and H. Drapier's 'Chartist's Appeal to the Queen' (*NS*, 31 August 1839) are the only poems to invoke the movement in their titles. However, after the failed uprisings of winter 1839/40 and the period of reprisal which ensued, Chartism itself became a dominant theme in the poetry column. In 1840, at least twenty-nine poems explicitly invoke an aspect of Chartism (whether the Charter itself or an individual leader), and this rises to thirty-six poems in 1841. As was shown in Chapter 3, 1840 and 1841 are the years which saw the highest number of Chartist poets and the maximum number of Chartist-produced poems in the entire history of the poetry column. Thus, in two of Chartism's hardest years (organisationally speaking) Chartist poetry plays a doubly significant political role. Firstly, as the numbers of poets show, it

---

[22] *Northern Star*, 13 June 1840.

becomes an important form of Chartist activity in its own right. Secondly, the number of poems about Chartism suggest that Chartist poetry performs a crucial role in maintaining and consolidating Chartist identity when other forms of affirmation, in particular the 'monster meeting', could not be practised.

Many of these poems celebrated Chartist leaders, prisoners and martyrs. In 1840, for example, individual poems are dedicated to O'Brien, White and Collins, Lovett and Collins and Shell.[23] However, these are overshadowed by the sheer volume of poetry dedicated to either John Frost or Feargus O'Connor. At least fifteen poems in 1840 deal directly with Frost while seven are dedicated to O'Connor.[24] However, from 1841 onwards O'Connor dominates the poetry column. In the weeks prior to his release from prison in August, the poetry column regularly reminded its readers of both O'Connor's captivity and his approaching liberation. Between 19th June and 28th August, six poems (out of twenty-five published) are explicitly dedicated to O'Connor, including Smart's 'Address of the Chartists of Leicester to Feargus O'Connor, Esq.' and Thomas M. Wheeler's 'The O'Connor Welcome'.[25] Nor did these poems stop with O'Connor's release, another seven poems followed his liberation, including 'The Lion of Freedom' which became O'Connor's signature song.[26] In contrast, other Chartist leaders are barely mentioned – Frost appears in the title of two poems and another poem celebrates the release of Williams and Binns from prison.

Throughout 1841 the poetry column assisted in the consolidation of O'Connor's position as Chartism's principal leader. For the first six months of 1842 this adulatory poetry ceases and there are no poems dedicated solely to O'Connor. However, the poetry column for 25 June contains F. G. Stourbridge's 'To Feargus O'Connor, Esq.' an acrostic whose first line – 'Fearless, firm, and faithful, too' – serves as a reliable guide to both tone and content. Thereafter, another six poems seek to reaffirm O'Connor's leadership credentials in the face of internal dissension within

[23] Dedicated poems appear on the following dates: 26 September 1840 (Shell); 26 September 1840 (O'Brien); 21 November 1840 (White and Collins); 12 December 1840 (Lovett and Collins). For details of these poems see Appendix B.

[24] For the poems dealing with John Frost see the previous chapter. Poems dedicated to O'Connor appeared on the following dates: 2 May 1840, 27 June 1840, 3 October 1840, 17 October 1840 (two), 24 October 1840, 7 November 1840. For details of these poems see Appendix B.

[25] See the following dates; 19 June 1841, 24 July 1841, 31 July 1841, 21 August 1841 (two), 28 August 1841. For details of these poems see Appendix B.

[26] See the following dates: 18 September 1841, 2 October 1841, 9 October 1841, 23 October 1841, 13 November 1841, 20 November 1841. For details of these poems see Appendix B.

Chartism, the rejection of the second petition, the mass strikes of August and September, and the external challenge posed by the CSU and the ACLL.[27]

These poems all cast O'Connor in the mode of the heroic leader. E. P. Mead's 'A New Chartist Song' (*NS*, 23 July 1842) refers to the 'Noble and dauntless O'Connor' and both F. G. Stourbridge and G. J. H. (possibly George Julian Harney) hail O'Connor as Chartism's 'chieftain'. Similarly, all the poems not only call for unity within the Chartist ranks but, more significantly, identify unity with unconditional support for O'Connor, as exemplified by G. J. H.'s exhortation to, 'Now a mighty phalanx form, / With the brave O'Connor join'. E. P. Mead's poems also attack O'Connor's rivals. In 'A New Chartist Song', for example, Mead castigates 'the new-moving land-lubbers' for opposing O'Connor's leadership, and later in the poem addresses the leaders of 'Knowledge', 'Teetotal' and 'Christian' Chartism directly:

> Lovett and Vincent, and Parson O'Neill,
> We cannot repose on YOUR honour;
> Tho' you profess such religion and zeal,
> We mean to stick fast to O'Connor!

Towards the end of the strike-wave, Mead attacks Bronterre O'Brien for criticising O'Connor in the *British Statesman*:

> Then cheer up, my hearties, and quit ye like men,
> And 'rally round Feargus, again and again,'
> In spite of the *Statesman* and heartless Bronterre,
> Who's as crazy, by Jove! as a very March hare;
> . . .
> I trust your contempt for O'Brien, like mine,
> Will only to Feargus your hearts more incline;[28]

Gammage alleges that Thomas Cooper had sought to enlist Mead's assistance in his campaign against O'Brien and it is possible that this poem is part of that campaign.[29]

The most emphatic statement of poetic support is provided by John Sixty's 'O'Connor's Demonstration' (*NS*, 30 July 1842 and 6 August 1842). At 201 lines published over 2 weeks this is a poem on a vast scale, both

---

[27] See the following dates: 25 June 1842, 9 July 1842, 23 July 1842, 30 July 1842, 6 August 1842, 17 September 1842, 15 October 1842, 12 November 1842. For details of these poems see Appendix B.

[28] *Northern Star*, 17 September 1842.

[29] Gammage, *History of the Chartist Movement*, 213. Gammage also reprints a letter from Thomas Cooper acknowledging (and lamenting the unfairness of) his hostility to O'Brien at this time, 404–10.

literally and in terms of its literary ambition. For Sixty offers his readers
a Chartist mini-epic replete with an opening invocation to the muse,
'Come, gentle goddess, wave thy heav'nly wing; / And touch the harp's
almost neglected string.' Sixty alludes to the *Iliad* to describe the Chartist
gathering, before insisting that the latter's importance exceeds that of its
classical forebear:

> And when old Priam from the Trojan wall
> Beheld thy radiance on each helmet fall;
> Not then, O! Sol, the day was half so great!
> That only weigh'd a captive woman's fate:
> While this, with great events, will proudly teem,
> And tyrants tremble at each glorious scene.

The gathered Chartists are likened to Agamemnon, 'And like Atrides
'mong the Grecian hosts, / Each son of freedom to his neighbour posts'.

The epic conceit, heightened poetic diction and use of heroic couplets
run the risk of becoming mock-heroic in the style of Pope. However,
'O'Connor's Demonstration' avoids this and the poem's artifice succeeds
in conveying the force and impact of a large Chartist meeting. The large
numbers embolden and give dignity to each individual Chartist, the
anticipated speech will strengthen loyalty to the cause and imbue its
audience with a sense of its own power:

> Each breast dilating at the glorious scene;
> And independence walks with manly mien.
> Now, near the spot where freedom's champion brave
> Shall warm the bosom of each *noble slave*;
> Illume his soul with love's pure heav'nly flame,
> The glorious impulse to immortal fame –
> To place each foot in union's conq'ring line
> . . .
> The mighty numbers bright with heav'nly light;
> Show how a people's all-sufficient might,
> Might so hurl down oppression's blood-built throne,

Thus the demonstration itself is shown to offer a brief foretaste of the very
freedom which is the aim of the agitation.

> Each soul illumin'd feels no loner pent;
> But floats supreme o'er slav'ry's grov'ling maze,
> And lives in freedom's bright refulgent blaze.

The poem, like the meeting it describes, is ready to manipulate the
readers' emotions by managing their expectations. The expectant crowd is

thrilled by the sight of a carriage which it believes to herald O'Connor's arrival only to discover that it 'bears some tyrant to his lordly home – ! / Some vile oppressor – some detested drone.' This enables the poet to fulminate against the aristocracy for some thirty-six lines and once more to build the audience's anticipation of O'Connor's arrival. Sixty uses the cheer which greets O'Connor's eventual arrival to emphasise the reciprocal relationship between orator and assembled crowd. The crowd's cheers both inspire O'Connor and call him into being as a leader:

> Again, its pealings reach the patriot's ear
> To press him onward in his great career!
> He hears the sound! his soul obeys the call,
> And bids defiance to oppressors all!

The crowd's cheers also mark the emergence of the working classes as an independent political force. Sixty makes the point that the drunken mob (in Chartist demonology always the tool of faction) has been replaced by a sober, disciplined body ready to struggle for its rights:

> Tremble, ye tyrants! tremble, as you hear
> The thrilling accents of that glorious cheer!
> . . .
> For know, these peals are not of drunken glee,
> But those of men determined to be free!

The poem's attention then turns to O'Connor's speech itself, concentrating on both its affect and effect on its hearers rather than its content. Its emotional rhythms are replayed for the reader, beginning sedately with an appeal to reason, 'he speaks to ev'ry mind / With reason, truth, and eloquence refin'd'. However, as the speech progresses, its emotional intensity increases as O'Connor thrills his audience with a sense of its collective power, prophesies eventual victory and appears to allude to his own martyrdom:

> He speaks! and lo, each tyrant trembling cowers,
> While conscious fear enthrals his flutt'ring pow'rs;
> He sees the tide impetuous rushing on,
> The banner smitten and the battle won;
> He sees, and feels his wretched bosom cleft
> Like the lorn maiden of her love bereft.

Next, the poem records the effect of this heady mixture of power and victimhood on the poet. Through the medium of O'Connor's speech, the poet transcends the present moment and, Moses-like, catches a glimpse of the promised land: a post-Charter future defined by agricultural plenty, romantic love and freedom:

> He speaks! and O! this grov'ling soul of mine
> Seems the vast hill of certainty to climb,
> From which she views all ranged in fair array
> The peaceful emblems of fair freedom's sway;
> . . .
> Sweet mellowing harvests deck the gen'rous soil,
> And plenty crowns the humble cotter's toil,
> . . .
> And gentle lovers, 'neath the shady grove,
> Enjoy the raptures of unsullied love.
> . . .
> Now, freedom comes, begirt with rays divine

The importance of O'Connor as a focus for Chartist identification should not be allowed to obscure the fact that throughout 1842 Chartist poetry frequently takes Chartism itself, rather than its leaders, as the subject of its poetic practice.[30] The challenge of representing the movement *as* a movement, of finding a poetic mode suited to the expression of political principles, should not be underestimated, and the success of Chartist poetry in this field deserves closer attention. One of the best poems in this respect is 'Presentation of the National Petition' by S. J. (*NS*, 4 June 1842). Published a month after its titular event, this poem offers an idealised self-representation of the movement which compresses the Chartist experience into a single, symbolically charged day. Its opening lines describe in a single sentence the 'organic' continuities which exist between Chartism, nature and British history:

> It was Nature's gay day,
> Bright smiling May day,
> Each heart was yearning our country to free;
> Thy banners were bringing,
> The people were singing
> Of the days of their fathers and sweet liberty.

Earlier, John Watkins in his 'Sonnet' (*NS*, 9 April 1842) had similarly identified 'liberty' as both the Chartist aim and the expression of native genius, ''Twas liberty inspir'd the British Bard' (exemplified, for Watkins,

---

[30] See the following dates: 9 April 1842, 4 June 1842, 18 June 1842, 9 July 1842 (three), 3 September 1842, 1 October 1842, 29 October 1842 (two), 5 November 1842 (two), 12 November 1842, 17 December 1842 (two). For details of these poems see Appendix B.

by Byron), whilst S. J. in another poem associates Chartism with the native radical tradition, 'Chartists in Paine and Cobbet read'.[31]

'Presentation of the National Petition' represents Chartism as a movement of controlled power, 'Thousands were marshall'd, / The throng forward marched'. The Chartist demonstration simultaneously enacts both strength and desire. S. J.'s hope is that the sight and sound of such disciplined numbers will overawe their opponents:

> With banners and band,
> The mighty assemblage of Chartists doth go,
> Their foes fill with wonder,
> As proudly they thunder
> Their shouts for their Charter, their hearts with hope fill'd.

However, the poem ends on a curiously anti-climactic note with the disappointment of Chartist expectations. The end of the day brings a close to the freedom temporarily obtained during the day of demonstration. Yet the denial of Chartist claims is not met with anger in the poem but with a thoughtful brooding – the problem of strategy identified in the previous chapter has still not been resolved. However, bluster is most definitely rejected by the poem whilst the 'brooding/foreboding' half-rhyme is perhaps more menacing for remaining indistinct:

> The evening descended,
> Their freedom was ended,
> The lads and the lasses walked thoughtfully away.
> Still the hope brooding,
> Of freedom foreboding,
> The enfranchised, their promises, yet would repay.

The movement from poems celebrating individual leaders to poems which seek to represent the movement in its entirety indicates Chartism's increasing political and ideological sophistication. Chartism had always been able to define itself in opposition to the Whigs and Tories. Now the presence of the ACLL and the CSU forced the movement to think carefully about its self-definition in relation to middle-class radicalism. This relationship could not be one of simple opposition, nor was it simply a disagreement concerning tactics and strategy, although such differences were important. Rather, by early 1842 Chartism knows itself to be both continuous with and distinct from the older forms of radicalism. Its apprehension of its own distinctiveness is as yet inchoate but its outlines

---

[31] S. J., 'Song of Freedom. Nine Cheers for the Charter', *Northern Star*, 29 October 1842.

are visible in the ambivalences (or antinomies) which structure its thinking and thus its poetry – such as the oscillation between the political and
the economic, between 'moral' and 'physical' force, as well as its attempts
to synthesise its political and economic critiques into an overarching
systemic 'moral' analysis. This is not to posit an ideal 'putative' consciousness towards which Chartism was moving, but rather to emphasise
the existence of multiple (but not infinite) possible developments in 1842,
only some of which were realised. The poem, which depends, in part, on
the polysemic nature of language (in which multiple meanings and the
possibility of alternative meanings are part of the condition of the meaning
'achieved' by the reader), is the form of cultural expression which comes
closest to recording this sense of multiple possibilities.

A sharper sense of the movement's identity developed in tandem with
the increasing sophistication of its economic and political critique of early
Victorian society. This was a reciprocal process in which a heightened
sense of identity sharpened the movement's analytical edge and a sharper
analysis strengthened the movement's self-definition. The question as to
the extent to which Chartism remained continuous with or represented
a decisive break from older forms of radicalism has been much debated
by labour historians. Key areas of debate include the question of how far
(if at all) Chartist economic theory had advanced beyond the idea of
a customary 'moral' economy, its ability to engage with classical political
economy and the extent to which it had assimilated the ideas of its critics
such as the Ricardian socialists. How did Chartism conceptualise the link
between the economic and the political? Did it theorise the working-class
condition as primarily one of oppression or exploitation? Did working-
class misery result from aristocratic control of the state ('old corruption'
as Cobbett called it), or was it caused by their loss of control over their
own labour-power ('proletarianisation' in Marx's terms)? Generally,
Chartism is considered to have leaned to the 'old' rather than the 'new' at
least until the emergence of an embryonic 'social-democratic' analysis in
the period after 1848.[32] However, by 1842 an emergent economic analysis,
struggling towards a theorisation of both exploitation and alienation (or
reification), is becoming visible alongside the more established older
analysis.

---

[32] For details of the 'old' and 'new' analyses and their dissemination see Patricia Hollis, *The Pauper
Press* (Oxford University Press, 1970). For the emergence of 'social-democratic' ideas, see Margot
Finn, *After Chartism: Class and Nation in English Radical Politics, 1848–1874* (Cambridge
University Press, 1993).

For most Chartists the origins of economic misery lay in the corruption of the country's political institutions. Political monopoly and economic mismanagement were synonymous, as Jesse Hammond's 'The Favoured Land' makes clear, 'For faction has crippled the loom and the plough' (*NS*, 2 April 1842). In this analysis only the restoration of 'lost' political rights would secure the economic well-being of the entire nation. Chartist thinking here shows the influence of William Cobbett who offered two contrasting definitions of national economic well-being: 'national wealth' and 'national prosperity'. National wealth, argued Cobbett, is the creation of the political economists and is defined as 'the products of the country over and above what was consumed, or used, by those whose labour had caused the products to be'. It is used to support the 'pensioners, placemen, gendarmerie, and in short, to whole millions, who did no work at all', and is measured by 'the number of chariots and fine-dressed people in and about the purlieus of the court'. Cobbett rejects this as a mystifying abstraction and prefers to talk of national prosperity:

[which] shows itself in very different ways: in the plentiful meal, the comfortable dwelling, the decent furniture and dress, the healthy and happy countenances, and the good morals of the labouring classes of the people. National wealth means, the Commonwealth, or Commonweal; and these mean, the general good, or happiness of the people, and the safety and honour of the state; and, these were not to be secured by robbing those who laboured, in order to support a large part of the community in idleness.[33]

This same contrast between wealth and prosperity (which is in some sense a conflict between quantitative and qualitative conceptions of value) informs two of John Watkins' poems, both entitled 'The Corn Laws and Emigration'. In both poems, the Corn Laws are shown to originate from the desire of the (aristocratic) landlords to inflate their own revenues at the expense of both the labouring classes and the farmers:

> . . . but a tax is laid on foreign grain,
> To make our home-grown corn its price maintain;
> And half-fed men may toil, and starve, and die,
> That idle lords may lift their heads on high.
> We might buy cheap, but landlords want great rents,
> To spend in keeping grand establishments.[34]

---

[33] W. Reitzel (ed.), *The Autobiography of William Cobbett* (Faber, 1967), 183–4.
[34] *Northern Star*, 1 January 1842.

> High rents rack'd farmers pay to swell the state
> Of little landlords whom we call the great;[35]

In addition, Watkins accuses the aristocracy of using its monopoly position to prevent land from being used for agricultural purposes, thereby 'wasting' the land (both literally and metaphorically):

> Our lords are locusts – 'men of wealth and pride
> Take up a space, that many poor supplied;
> Space for their lakes, their park's extended bounds,
> Space for their horses, equipage and hounds!'[36]

Watkins' charge clearly owes much to the distinction between 'productive' and 'unproductive' expenditure developed within political economy and similarly used to criticise the aristocracy.[37] Like the political economists, the Chartist poets are interested in the phenomenon of conspicuous consumption. However, unlike the political economists who only seek to indict the aristocracy, the Chartist writers use it to ground a systematic critique which is simultaneously moral and political as well as economic. Chartist poetry never deals with aristocratic consumption in isolation, rather it is always paired with working-class dearth as a way of illustrating the causal relationship between the two conditions. The inverted relationship between production and consumption is thus doubled; the productivity of the labourer enables aristocratic consumption, whilst the latter (which is always figured as unproductive) requires labouring-class deprivation as its corollary. Watkins, for example, cites 'Their feasts, their fancies, jewels, balls, and plays, / The poor man's nakedness and hunger pays', while Nussey writes in 'Happy Land', 'Thy proud pampered nobles indulge in each dainty; / Their concert-notes smother pale poverty's sigh'. In both poems the economic critique is simultaneously a moral one; aristocratic consumption is feckless, pride-filled and indulgent. The systematic critique is completed by the poem's awareness that it is only the aristocracy's control of Parliament which keeps the Corn Laws on the statute books. In this case the 'monopoly' of which so many Chartist writers complain is political as well as economic.[38]

---

[35] *Northern Star*, 8 January 1842.   [36] *Ibid.*

[37] For an overview of the debate surrounding 'productive' and 'unproductive' expenditure see E. Roll, *A History of Economic Thought* (Faber, 1973). For a more recent revisiting of the literary implications of this debate see Catherine Gallagher, *The Body Economic* (Princeton University Press, 2006).

[38] Monopoly is also criticised in the second of John Watkins' 'Corn Laws and Emigration' poems and in the anonymous 'The Old Year', both poems appear in the poetry column for 8 January 1842. Chartist writers seem to be using 'monopoly' in the Tudor sense of the granting of an exclusive trading privilege by the state.

The relationship between economic degradation and moral decline is readily apparent in these poems. The aristocracy is not only shown to violate the divine injunction which requires postlapsarian Man to labour (Genesis 3:19), but is also represented as exerting a corrosive moral force on the rest of the social order. Watkins instances the farmers as particularly affected, 'tenants ape their landlords' by hunting, shooting, drinking, gambling and generally living beyond their means and neglecting their duties:

> More on themselves they spend than on their land,
> Pastime obtains what labour should command;
> The soil grows poor for want of management.[39]

The shift from production to consumption is one which Watkins believes will be ultimately disastrous. Firstly, labour's wages are depressed to support 'high-living' farmers, secondly as the Exchequer becomes increasingly reliant on revenue generated from taxes on consumption, society becomes more vulnerable to general trade depressions. Indeed, the poem closes with a warning of general economic collapse:

> No work! no money! – when our trade is gone
> Work too must follow – buyers will be none.

The case against the Corn Laws is also underpinned by Chartism's belief in the abundance and benevolence of nature which finds its clearest expression in 'The Goodness of Nature Withheld from the Poor' (by J. R. of Leeds) which begins:

> O earth, the basis of our noble form,
> Foster'd with thy fruits where'er we roam,
> If we from pole to pole thy wonders trace,
> We find thee labouring to support our race;[40]

The lines which follow make it clear that nature provides the human race with sensual and aesthetic pleasures ('thy meadows sweet, / Bids us perambulate thy lovely scene') as well as physical sustenance. The intelligent application of human labour to nature should be enough to meet all human needs, 'Thy furrow'd fields, which all our wants supply', and by dint of their work, the labourers are entitled to a livelihood. Yet the simple act of framing these assumptions as questions alerts the readers to the disturbed nature of the existing social order.

---

[39] *Northern Star*, 8 January 1842.   [40] *Northern Star*, 22 January 1842.

> Ah! do these furrow'd fields supply the poor,
> Whose hungry cries for charity implore?
> Do they receive the share of nature's spoil?
> Do they receive the first fruits of the soil?

In this way the poet implicitly affirms the validity of his readers' ideological assumptions whilst directing their attention to their abuse. The poem continues by condemning the 'sordid wretches' who rob the poor of their rights and calls on God to 'reverse this shocking state' by restoring to the poor 'their honest rightful land'. Hunger clearly betokens the perversion of the world's immanent moral order and thus requires the inversion of the existing social order as remedy.

The denial of labour's fundamental right to a sufficiency is often cited as the reason for emigration in Chartist poetry. In G. Sheridan Nussey's 'The Emigrant Song' (*NS*, 9 April 1842), for example, the baleful economic consequences of political misrule transform emigration into a form of exile:

> Where we have plied our daily toil,
>   To raise the food of man,
> Monopoly usurps the soil,
>   Or blasts it with its ban:
> The Oligarchy deny us bread,
>   And vow that we rebel,
> If we but say, 'We would be fed.'
>   Old England, fare thee well.

Even though the poem's final stanza makes it clear that in leaving Britain the emigrants are exchanging slavery for freedom, nonetheless its closing lines make clear the depth of the speaker's emotional attachment to Britain – 'Yet our loved birth-land chained or free, / Within our hearts shall dwell'. Similar sentiments can be found in L. T. Clancy's 'Farewell to Cambria' (*NS*, 23 April 1842), whose exiled speaker laments 'Yes, I lov'd thee and thine, and for thee would have perish'd'. In Chartist poetry, both exile and emigrant insist on their identity as patriots.

Precisely because emigration was being advocated by non-Chartist commentators as a possible solution to the problems of 'surplus population' and economic crisis, its treatment in Chartist poetry illustrates the distinctiveness of the Chartist analysis. Non-Chartist commentators tend to emphasise the possibilities opened up by emigration. For example, Carlyle in *Chartism* instances a 'whole vacant Earth' calling for the entire over-population of Britain to 'Come and till me, come and reap me!'[41] Sir

---

[41] Carlyle, 'Chartism', 229.

Edward Bulwer strikes an even more triumphalist note in his 'The Song of the Emigrants' which envisages emigration as part of the imperial 'civilising' mission, as a way of spreading British freedom, labour, religion and law across the globe.

> Where is the Briton's Home?
> Where man's great Law can come,
> Where the great Truth can speak.
> Where the Slave's chain can break,
> Where the White's scourge can cease,
> Where the Black dwells in peace,
> . . .
> THERE is the Briton's Home![42]

Bulwer's celebration of emigration as part of his idealistic representation of the imperial project is undercut by the footnote which the editor of the *Northern Star* adds to his poem, 'We wish we could say all this of England'.

A more detailed riposte to Bulwer's poem comes in the form of 'Thomas MacQueen's Farewell to Britain' which appears in the poetry column for 13 August 1842. Over the course of ten Spenserian stanzas, MacQueen offers an accomplished and far-reaching poetic analysis of the costs, causes and consequences of emigration. MacQueen follows both Nussey and Clancy by emphasising the emotional attachments which both bind the emigrant to his native land and are the cause of great anguish to him. However, unlike his two predecessors, MacQueen does not separate the costs and causes of emigration into separate stanzas. Rather, through the image of fading light he forges a logical and an affective connection between his sense of emotional loss and the economic deprivation which forces his departure:

> Dear Isle! I dream'd not twenty years ago,
>   That I should wander on a stranger land;
> I dream'd not that the fond, fond filial gloom,
>   That bound my soul to thy bold rugged strand,
> Should dim and darken 'neath the withering wand
>   Of despot poverty,

The benign twilight ('fond . . . gloom') of his native isle is replaced by darkness brought about by 'the withering wand / Of despot poverty'. This latter image also connects economic loss with political misrule. The ruler's

---

[42] *Northern Star*, 23 July 1842.

wand brings dearth rather than plenty, poverty is both produced by the despot and acts with despotic force. Under such circumstances the economic migrant is banished as surely as the political rebel is sent into exile.

The use of darkness as a metaphor for political misrule continues in the second stanza. MacQueen recalls the 'Fresh pleasures' of his youth and laments that 'these bright things' are now all:

> . . . sunk in deathlike darkness; and anon
> The heart that loved them . . .
> . . . shiver'd forth a groan,
> And seemed to darken, too, as tho' it lived alone.

The following stanza traces Britain's decline to its rise as a colonial power. In opposition to Bulwer's vision of the imperial mission as one which exports freedom over the globe, MacQueen identifies a situation in which domestic and foreign slavery form an interlocking and mutually sustaining relationship:

> And thou wert hail'd 'Lord of the free and brave!'
> Thou breathest now of faction, feud and fraud –
> The heartless home of sycophant and slave!
> . . .
> [Now] bondsmen groan where'er that flag's unfurl'd,
> And thou art all wheres hail'd, 'The life-curse of the world!'

In the context of a capitalist market economy, labour is doubly degraded. Unlike the 'common beasts' which 'are fed, / And lodg'd and car'd for' by their owners, the labourer must 'First beg for work, then beg again for bread'. The fourth stanza concludes with the common contrast between 'famine-featur'd millions' and 'pamper'd luxury', making the familiar Chartist observation on the inverse relation between production and consumption. The fifth stanza shifts its focus from the economic to the political. Despite this misery, MacQueen explains:

> The tyrant trembles not: his men of blood,
> Poor trampled serfs, who murder for reward,
> Can give their friends cold sabre blades for food.

Here tyranny's response to starvation, 'cold sabre blades for food', recalls the 'Tory lozenges' of Peterloo. It also points to a fatal lack of solidarity amongst the poor caused by an inability to distinguish (class) friend from (class) enemy. MacQueen also traces this failure of solidarity to a failure of sympathy which is inculcated by the new economic relations:

> And the streams of sympathy, as if subdued
>> By one gold-grasping mania, stand still;
> And each one's soul, in selfish solitude,
>> Grows, like an anchorite, benumb'd and chill,
> Without one drop of balm to sweeten others' ill.

The essence of MacQueen's analysis here, the corrosive effects of economic individualism on human affections, reads like a striking anticipation of Dickens' *A Christmas Carol* (1843) as does the image of 'injur'd, and restless ghosts, still wandering' in the poem's final line.

The second half of this poem reprises and amplifies the key themes from the first five stanzas. The emotional cost of emigration is registered through images of dislocation and separation from the physical site of the writer's own past, 'The sacred sanctuary of all that's dear; / The haunts, the scenes which memory must revere' and his family history, 'I love thy very dust; in it are laid / The household friends, that led me on life's way'. The penultimate stanza acknowledges that he is writing within a distinct poetic tradition, 'many a harp has rung / This doleful note'. However, he insists that this poetry, including his own, remains inadequate for the task of expressing the exile's grief:

> But bards, in melody, like wizard's spell,
>> The mere dull sounds of sorrow may express;
> But ah! adieus and farewells cannot tell
>> The dark deep dismal horrors of distress –
>> The bosom-blighting pang – the parting bitterness!

In the final stanza the poem deploys the idea of distance to great effect, beginning with the gap which exists between poetic convention and feeling ('Farewell! I use, I must use fashion's forms; / The feeling lives to breathe itself in sighs') and closing with the existential split engendered by exile, 'While mem'ry seeks the past my thoughts must be / Like injur'd, restless ghosts, still wandering over thee!'

By figuring emigration as a form of exile, and by identifying its emotional causes (a failure of sympathy) and costs (a sense of dislocation and separation), Thomas MacQueen's poem demonstrates, without naming, the category of alienation. Even more significantly the poem offers alienation as a process which connects the economic and the political. 'Despot poverty' which causes emigration and its attendant emotional losses depends on a dual distortion of human feeling – the failure of sympathy on the part of the rich, and of solidarity on the part of the poor. The first is clearly identified as economic in origin, while the second is its political outgrowth. What we are witnessing here is the emergence of an analysis which recognises the internal/psychological as well as the external/physical dimensions of both exploitation and oppression.

Traditionally, Chartist poetry had represented economic exploitation through images of the loss of vital fluids, both literally as 'sweat' and metaphorically through the 'leech-like' vampirism of capital, as in A. W.'s poem 'To The Sons of Toil':

> How comes it that ye toil and sweat,
> . . .
> How comes, that man with tyrant heart
>   Is caused to rule another;
>   To rob, oppress, and, leech-like, suck
>   The life's blood of a brother?[43]

However, throughout 1842, Chartist poetry draws attention to the psychological consequences of both exploitation and oppression, and identifies both as part of a wider phenomenon – the denial of human dignity. Thus, 'Oppression' by D. C. emphasises the emotional degradation of the working class. It is their collective reduction to an abject servility which is *felt* more keenly than the economic and political circumstances which give rise to it, and which are only introduced in the poem's third verse. The poem itself concludes by answering these questions with an affirmation of the necessity of human dignity as both the agent as well as the desired outcome of the political process.

> Shall we for ever lick the dust
>   Or fear the tyrant's boding frown,
> And cringing, pander to the lust
>   Of pamper'd minions of a crown?
> Shall we for ever bear the scorn
>   Of heartless wealth and fancied power?
> Bequeath to ages yet unborn,
>   Our abjectness – a galling dower?
> Shall we for ever be the spoil
>   Of greedy avarice? and brood
> O'er festering wrongs and thankless toil
>   In calm and melancholy mood?
> . . .
> Forbid it God! the dignity
>   Of manhood must awaken'd be;
> Justice demands, and Liberty
>   Proclaims we must and shall be free![44]

[43] *Northern Star*, 3 April 1841.   [44] *Northern Star*, 3 September 1842.

D. C.'s poem is in one sense a companion piece to 'Thomas MacQueen's Farewell to his Country' insofar as it records the internalisation by the working classes of those emotionally and morally corrosive forces unleashed by the new economic individualism.

Chartist poetry also begins to register its opposition to the distortion and degradation of the human character by representing Chartism as a movement which preserves and affirms authentic, human feelings. Chartist poetry, therefore, anticipates what Kirstie Blair calls 'the discourse of the political heart' in the poetry of Elizabeth Barrett Browning, notably *Casa Guidi Windows*.[45] In another of S. J.'s poems, 'Nine Cheers for the Charter' (*NS*, 29 October 1842) Chartism is associated with 'ardour's true sigh' and 'the noblest joys [of] the heart'. Similarly, in Edwin Gill's 'The Charter For Ever Shall Weather the Storm' (which appears in the same poetry column) Chartism becomes the authentic expression of each individual Chartist's authentic self, 'each heart is with pure freedom burning'.

John Watkins offers a different articulation of this idea in his 'Chartist Song' (*NS*, 1 October 1842). A poem which anticipates many elements of Ernest Jones' 'The Better Hope'. Both poems record the poet's decision to abandon his (higher-class) home and family in order to join the Chartist movement. In Watkins' poem the father threatens to disown his son if he declares his Chartist sympathies, the son defies the paternal ban and leaves family, friends and his sweetheart 'for the sake of the cause'. However, the sense of sacrifice is offset by the poet's insistence on the emotional rewards offered by Chartism, 'There was never a tear, but a smile in my eye, / For I thought of the Charter and sweet liberty'. By means of political comradeship, Chartism offers genuine human contact across class boundaries which is figured by Watkins as an intense emotional sympathy, which carries a distinctly homosocial if not an homoerotic charge:

> I spoke to our lads, and I said 'come with me,
> You've been slaves long enough – 'tis time you were free.'
> Their eyes spark'd with fire, and it made my blood warm,
> So I cried out, at once – 'to arms, my lads – arm!'

Watkins' poem can be seen as an attempt to establish his credentials as a gentleman-leader of radicalism. He begins with the sacrifices which he

---

[45] For an extended analysis of the political significance of the heart, see Kirstie Blair, *Victorian Poetry and the Culture of the Heart* (Oxford University Press, 2006).

has made for the cause and which demonstrate the strength and sincerity of his commitment to Chartism, and thus validate his leadership aspirations. Although the poem offers authentic cross-class contact, it does not dissolve class boundaries. Within the poem, Watkins speaks both for and to the working classes who respond to his voice but are never given one of their own. Thus a fantasy regarding heroic leadership is encoded in this poem and, as both Lovett and Disraeli understood only too well, this fantasy could be subject to a conservative re-articulation.[46]

In this respect it is instructive to compare Watkins' 'Chartist Song' with Ernest Jones' 'The Better Hope' which also seeks to establish the credentials of a gentleman convert to Chartism. The importance of 'The Better Hope' is attested to by Jones' choice of it as the opening poem in his first Chartist collection entitled *Chartist Poems and other Fugitive Pieces* (1846).[47] Miles Taylor describes the poem as Jones' 'calling card' to the Chartist movement.[48] Like Watkins, Jones begins by describing his alienation from his home and family. However, unlike Watkins, Jones is not given an ultimatum by his father, rather he chooses to leave his home in search of real human fellowship. Taylor glosses this as a choice between the 'cold solemnity' and unnaturalness of the ancestral home and the 'broad, laughing world' beyond its walls.[49] However, this summary flattens out the poem's complexity. It is not the 'cold solemnity' of his father's home which troubles the poet but the emotional distortions, the frustrations of natural human impulses which attend the modern 'aristocracy':

> For the scutcheoned grace – of a titled race,
>   Is the armour the heart to hide.
>
> Oh! The eye sees but half, through a blazoned glass,
>   The smile of the sunshiny earth;
> And a laugh cannot pass – through a marbly mass,
>   But it loses the pulse of its mirth.

---

[46] William Lovett's 'Introduction' to his autobiography emphasises his belief in working-class independence and mistrust of external leadership, 'The Working Classes are still to a vast extent following blind guides, and trusting to leaders and orators outside their own ranks, to achieve that for them which their own efforts, self-sacrifices, and organization can alone effect.' *Life and Struggles of William Lovett* (MacGibbon & Kee, 1967 [1876]), xxxi. Benjamin Disraeli's *Sybil* offers numerous instances of the working classes responding to heroic leadership irrespective of its social origins or political affiliations.

[47] Ernest Jones, *Chartist Poems and other Fugitive Pieces* (MacGowan, 1846).

[48] Miles Taylor, *Ernest Jones, Chartism, and the Romance of Politics 1819–1869* (Oxford University Press, 2003), 85.

[49] *Ibid.*, 86.

> And I thought: there beyond in the broad, laughing world,
>   Men are happy in life's holiday!
> And I passed one and all – through each old-fashioned hall,
>   And wandered away and away!

Thus far, the emotional dynamic of Jones' poem resembles Watkins';
authentic human feeling is not possible in the repressive atmosphere of
the upper-class home and will only be achieved by recovering meaningful
contact with the broad mass of humankind. However, whilst Watkins'
poem accepts this formulation, Jones' problematises it. In the verse which
follows he discovers that 'the broad, laughing world' is a fantasy projection and that the real world is one where the 'giant' of industrialisation
terrorises the working classes.

> And fibre and flesh he bound down on a rack
>   Flame girt on a factory-floor;
> And the ghastly steel corse – plied its horrible force,
>   Still tearing the hearts of the poor.

At this point, the poet is almost overwhelmed by despair and contemplates returning to his former home, which at least offers material comforts
even if it means spiritual death. However, his soul revolts against this
conclusion and recalls him to his duty.

> Oh! then I looked back for my cold quiet home,
>   As the hell-hound looks back for the grave;
> But I heard my soul cry – who but cowards can fly,
>   While a tyrant yet tramples a slave?

'The Better Hope' ends with the poet's embrace of his duty, figured as
the decision to enlist as a footsoldier in the army of democracy.

> Then I bound on my armour to face the rough world,
>   And I'm going to march with the rest,
> Against tyrants to fight – for the sake of the right,
>   And, if baffled, to fall with the rest.

Jones eschews the fantasy of heroic leadership, breaking his established
rhyme scheme to give additional emphasis to his democratic commitment
by 'rhyming' 'rest' with 'rest' (at some point a 'rest/best' rhyme must surely
have suggested itself?). Watkins' poem with its unproblematic transfer of
allegiance from family to Charter, its assumption of heroic leadership and
its call to arms, lacks the maturity of Jones' poem with its recognition of
the discomforts of commitment, its rejection of heroic leadership and its
insistence on defensive rather than offensive armament.

The development of a more sophisticated and nuanced Chartist analysis is accompanied by a growing awareness of the fact that its intended addressees, the 'millions' or the 'people', were not an already existing entity but an imaginary formation which needed to be assembled from its constituent parts if Chartism were to become a real political force, This ideal category (the 'people') could only be realised through the operations of the imaginary: it had to be thought and felt by many in order to become real. In turn this demanded a more sophisticated mode of address, capable of acknowledging existing differences whilst also identifying those common characteristics which could underpin a shared identity.

'The People's Charter' by David Wright (*NS*, 9 July 1842) exemplifies this process by acknowledging the difference between the industrial and agricultural proletariats in its first two verses which identify 'the sons of industry' and the 'people of the common soil' respectively. The poem also insists that their shared economic and political situation (both groups are represented as exploited and oppressed) qualifies them for membership of a larger political entity, the 'millions', who by claiming the Charter will secure a new identity for themselves as 'Freedom's sons'. This movement towards the active construction of (rather than the assumption of a pre-given) economic and political unity amongst the component parts of the working class occurs in a number of Chartist poems. E. P. Mead's 'The Star' (which shares the poetry column with Wright's poem) describes the *Northern Star* 'shin[ing] o'er plough, loom, and mine' whilst George Lindsay's 'The Charter' calls on 'Reformers, then, of every grade, / Who toil at anvil, loom, or spade' to unite for the People's Charter (*NS*, 3 September 1842). Both Mead and Lindsay identify a tripartite division between agricultural labourers, textile workers and those involved in 'heavy industry' (mining and metallurgy), with each group figured metonymically through its tool or place of work; spade/plough, loom, and mine/anvil, respectively.

Chartism's greater awareness of its own internal complexity is matched by a similarly enlarged understanding of the political force which it confronted. In particular, a critique of the domestic repressive state apparatus and the wider imperial state emerges in Chartist poetry during 1842. In April, Benjamin Stott criticises the newly created police forces for being un-English instruments of tyranny, 'Thy *gens d'arme* – police force with despot formality / Now rules thee with rods like a nation of slaves' (*NS*, 16 April 1842). In May, F. identifies the standing army as a sign of the nation's oppression, in 'Old England' such an institution was simply unnecessary; 'No red coats had we then to threaten honest men' (*NS*, 7 May 1842). Two weeks later, F. turns a critical eye on the use of the standing army as an instrument of colonial tyranny and gives an early indication of Chartism's internationalism:

> The red blood of thy bravest sons
>   Is shed in foreign wars,
> To put down rising liberty
>   And aid the tyrants' cause.
>
> Where'er we turn, where'er we gaze,
>   Oppression still is plain,
> The Affghan and Canadian
>   Curse England's galling chain.[50]

In the period of intense legal reprisal which followed the end of the mass strikes the exact nature of the repressive state apparatus became brutally visible.[51] Benjamin Stott's 'The Britons May Boast' published shortly after the first trials had finished shows how the operations of informers, spies, police and courts constitute a system of oppression which is directed against Chartism:

> The patriot who dares to unbosom his mind,
>   . . .
>   Is humbled by perjurers, villains, and spies;
> And should he dare call for political right,
>   And tell to the world how humanity grieves,
> He is dragg'd from his bed in the dead of the night,
>   And cramm'd in a dungeon 'mid felons and thieves.
>
> In derision he next is arraign'd at the bar,
>   And Justice is dealt him with unsparing hand;
> He is sent from his country and kindred afar,
>   To pine and to die in a pestilent land.[52]

In view of the sentences of transportation which were then being handed down by the Chester and Liverpool Commissions (twenty-four men were sentenced to transportation ranging from three years to life),[53] such lines possess the immediacy of journalism and demonstrate just how swiftly the experience of the movement could be rendered into poetry. In a later poem published in the poetry column for 10 December 1842, Stott integrates

---

[50] *Northern Star*, 21 May 1842.   [51] See Jenkins, *The General Strike of 1842*, 219–38.
[52] *Northern Star*, 22 October 1842.   [53] Jenkins, *The General Strike of 1842*, 224.

the army into his analysis of systemic repression and offers a remarkably
succinct, quasi-Leninist, analysis of the state:

> We know that our tyrants will strive to subdue us,
> They have knaves to commit us, and soldiers to kill;
> They will deal out the justice of despots unto us,
> And the grave and the dungeon endeavour to fill.

However, these theoretical and analytical advances are not accompanied by a commensurate development in Chartist strategy. The events
of 1842 reiterated the lessons of the first petition, confirming the historical
exhaustion of two of radicalism's most cherished paradigms, voluntarism
('For a nation to be free, it is sufficient that she wills it') and the mass
platform (popular mobilisation supported by the threat of violence, which
was believed to have carried Reform in 1832). The Newport uprising had
already demonstrated the difficulties of insurrection, and whilst the British
working classes had developed a new strategy in the form of the 'mass
strike' accompanied by political action – as the months of August and
September had shown, very few of its leaders understood how to use this
weapon effectively, and a number were actively hostile to its use. The
apprehension of this changed historical conjuncture manifests itself in
two ways; in the appearance of a form of deferred agency in Chartist
poetry published prior to the strike-wave and in the reworking of
established Chartist poetic tropes in its aftermath.

'Address to the Starving Millions' by the Chartist lecturer E. P. Mead,
which appears in the *Northern Star* in the hiatus between the rejection of
the petition and the onset of the mass strikes, abounds with signs of crisis
and imminent disaster; 'the black'ning storm' (v.1), the impending wreck
of the ship of state (v.2) and the presence of 'starving millions' all indicate
that 'the hour is nigh' (v.4). Using rhetoric and imagery drawn from the
prophets of the Old Testament, Mead variously predicts, 'A day of
retribution's drawing near' (v.1), 'a fierce tornado will descend, / And
God will prove he is the poor man's friend' (v.7) and '[God's] thunders
wake! and lo! a moral war / Shall show to all his storm-careering car' (v.8).
Anger suffuses the whole poem, which is filled with images of destruction
and retribution, even as its expression is simultaneously accompanied by
calls to suspend action. This structure of arousal and deferral is exemplified in the poem's opening lines:

> My suffering fellow-countrymen, and women,
> A day of retribution's drawing near;

> *Yet wait awhile*; the black'ning storm is coming;
>
> The hand of justice will for you appear; [54] [my emphasis]

Retribution must be the inevitable outgrowth of God's plan for the world, it must not be undertaken or assisted by the oppressed themselves who are enjoined to remain passive throughout the poem. The somewhat paradoxical position of a Chartist lecturer calling for inaction has its syntactical counterpart in the clumsiness of the line 'The hand of justice will for you appear' in which the pronoun indicates the object rather than the subject of the verb. Political desire and political agency remain separated throughout the poem. Indeed in the final stanza Mead explicitly counsels patience and passivity:

> 'My brave companions! partners of my toil!'
>   Ye shall not long drag on white slavery's chain;
> Ye good distress'd bear up a little while,
>   Beneath your load of misery and pain;
> Your patient virtue shall not wait in vain,
> You must, ye shall, your glorious Charter gain.

This poem registers working-class anger at the injustice and suffering they endure as a result of aristocratic misgovernment and the machinations of priestcraft. However, the poem is also anxious that this emotion should not be allowed uncontrolled expression. In particular, the poem is concerned that working-class anger is easily manipulated by Chartism's opponents:

> Let no designing knave, of either faction,
>   Arouse your passions, or your souls inflame,
> Let peace, law, order, mark your every action,

The formal properties of the poem offer a revealing insight into the contradictions which the Chartist movement was seeking to negotiate. There is a clear belief that an unrepresentative system of government is the root cause of the people's suffering. This suffering generates an angry desire for a change to the political system. The desired change is in accordance with the divine will. However, the experience of Newport has left the movement fearful of any premature outbreak and, therefore, uneasy about the expression of anger. This leads in Mead's poem to the repeated refusal of a cathexis between protest at injustice, anger at misrule and remedial action; with divine intervention effectively serving to break

---

[54] *Northern Star*, 16 July 1842.

the circuit between the three. This imparts a curious sense of deferred agency to the whole poem – something must be done, something will be done, but not quite yet and not by us. Tellingly, the only stanza which recognises the efficacy of human agency occurs in verse six which predicts an impending alliance between the middle and working classes:

> The middle class, so long, alas! deluded,
> . . .
> Will join us heart and hand to get redress;
> Then the rich few oppressors must submit,
> And crouch, like beaten spaniels, at our feet.

A week later another poem from E. P. Mead, 'A New Chartist Song' (*NS*, 23 July 1842) reworks the trope of the shipwreck. Previously, Chartist poetry had used this trope in conjunction with the idea of the ship of state to suggest the political disaster awaiting the ruling classes unless they change political course.[55] In 1842, the Chartist movement itself becomes increasingly associated, and at times interchangeable, with the threatened vessel. E. P. Mead's 'A New Chartist Song' exemplifies this trend. Its opening lines – 'O, for a pilot to weather the storm, / For a thundering big 'un is brewing' – are not only prescient in light of the strike-wave that would sweep the country within a month of its publication, but identify the 'New middle-movers' (a conflation of Sturge's Complete Suffrage and the various 'new moves' within Chartism) as having 'ruin'd the noble old ship' to such an extent that Feargus must 'give her a thorough refit'.

Edwin Gill's 'The Charter For Ever Shall Weather the Storm' (*NS*, 29 October 1842) also reverses the conventional symbolic significance of ship and storm in Chartist poetry. In Gill's poem Chartism becomes the threatened ship and the images of natural power become associated with its enemies:

> Then huzza for the Charter, the good ship we sail in,
> Till the waves shall engulf us, no fears shall deform;
> . . .
> Though the quicksands of 'Humbug' are laid in our way,
> And 'Tyrannical ranks' oppose us in our course;
> Though 'Treacherous blasts' our tight bark are assailing,
> Triumphant she sails, nor shrink we from their force.

The poem registers the opposition which Chartism has already encountered and will have to overcome to achieve its aims. Unlike some earlier

---

[55] See, for example, the discussion of Charles Davlin's 'Questions From The Loom' in Chapter 1).

poems it does not underestimate the challenge Chartism faces, nor does it imagine Chartism's opponents being overpowered in a single instant. It emphasises, instead, through the perilous journey motif (with its echoes of *Pilgrim's Progress*) that political change must be conceived of as a process rather than an event. The reallocation of standard images of agency from Chartism to its opponents restates without resolving the perennial problem of agency.

One final aspect of the poetry column in 1842 which requires attention is the sudden appearance of a cluster of 'Merry England' poems in the period of uncertain paralysis between the rejection of the second petition and the beginnings of the mass strikes. Although the ideas of a past age of greater social contentment and an agrarian idyll of independent proprietor-producers can be found in Chartist poetry before 1842, the notion of 'Merry England' rarely appears. Yet between 21st May and 16th July 1842, 'Merry England' becomes a regular theme in the poetry column with F.'s 'The People Shall Have Their Own Again' and 'To England', the anonymous 'Merry England', and G. Sheridan Nussey's 'Happy Land'.

'The People Shall Have Their Own Again' (set to the Jacobite tune 'The King Shall Possess His Own Again') reads like a versified summary of Cobbett as it connects lost political rights with economic and national security.

> Time gone the Suffrage was possessed by every man,
>   And Old England then was a happy land to see;
> It was joyful in the hall, and in the cottage small,
>   And the poorest man could merry, merry be,
>
> Then gladsome was the sound as the yule went round,
>   Of the song and the glee at Christmas time;
> And happy as the day were our firesides gay,
>   For the rich thought the mirth of the poor no crime.
>
> No red coats had we then to threaten honest men,
>   But the people guarded their homesteads free;
> And their challenge was, woe to the tyrant or foe,
>   Who dares set foot on our isle of the sea.[56]

The key economic demand, for a practical sufficiency rather than a theoretical equality, recurs in both 'Merry England' and 'Happy Land'. Similarly, in all three poems economic well-being manifests itself through the emotions of mirth and joy. In all these poems a generosity of spirit, an overflow of warm feeling is contrasted with the pinched, calculated

---

[56] *Northern Star*, 21 May 1842.

watchfulness engendered by poverty. Poverty and wealth are understood to be emotional as well as economic states. The condition of 'Merry England' is one in which shared human pleasures transcend class boundaries and cement national unity.

> Once thou wert 'Merry England,' and thy fruitful soil was blest;
> Thy daughters then knew happiness, and thy sons had food and rest;
> The blighting gusts of poverty and want were then unknown,
> And the peasant seemed as happy as the monarch on his throne.
>
> Anon, 'Merry England'[57]

> O, once 'merry England!' where now are the pleasures
>   That solaced the peasant, and hallow'd his hearth,
> When they looked without envy on wealth's gaudy treasures,
>   Content with his comforts, a stranger to dearth?
>
> G. Sheridan Nussey, 'Happy Land'[58]

In 'The Favoured Land', Jesse Hammond complains 'Mammon now mocks the starv'd Englishman's sigh, / The oligarch laughs at gaunt poverty's tear'. For Chartist writers, economic suffering is exacerbated by the wealthy's callous disregard for individual dignity. In the world governed by the New Poor Law, poverty threatened familial and individual integrity (and thus identity) in a way which struck at the core of working-class masculinity. The husband and father unable to provide for his wife and children lost the key co-ordinates of his identity: the complexity of his being (worker, husband, father) reduced to that of 'pauper'. The effective criminalisation of poverty within the workhouse regime only increased the sense of injustice, which Carlyle recognised as the worst aspect of poverty – 'the real smart is the soul's pain and stigma, the hurt inflicted on the moral self'.[59] The importance of dignity and self-respect explains the commitment to agrarianism in these poems. In the Chartist imagination, 'Merry England' is inhabited by 'peasants' because it is only through the figure of the peasant proprietor (who owns the land that he cultivates) that the Chartist poet can imagine economic and political independence, and thereby the means of securing both the respect and self-respect necessary to maintain human dignity. The subsequent popularity of the Chartist Land Plan amply demonstrates the perceived attractions of the position of independent, peasant proprietor.

The figure of the independent proprietor-producer is, of course, implicitly masculine and it is noticeable that women barely feature in the 'Merry England' poems. The anonymous 'Merry England' poem contrasts

---

[57] *Northern Star*, 25 June 1842.   [58] *Northern Star*, 16 July 1842.   [59] Carlyle, 'Chartism', 177.

a past when 'Thy daughters then knew happiness, and thy sons had food and rest;' with a present wherein 'thy sons, though toiling fruitless, would conceal the gloomy truth, / Whilst thy daughters in the fact'ries spend for nought the hours of youth'. Similarly, the destruction of female beauty and health is identified by G. Sheridan Nussey in 'Happy Land', 'The rose from the cheeks of thy maidens hath vanish'd! / They wither like lillies – as lovely and pale!' In both examples, extra-domestic work is represented as damaging to working-class women's health, thereby making Chartist poetry consistent with one of the key ideological themes in the discussions over working-class women's labour.[60]

It is clear that the call for the restoration of 'Merry England' involves a return to the idyll of the household as the fundamental economic as well as social unit, demonstrating the essentially 'nostalgic' nature of Chartist literature. In Zlotnick's account, male Chartist writers are rendered incapable of embracing capitalist industrialisation due to their benighted belief in a lost golden age, their 'distaste for modernity' and their fear of an independent female factory workforce.[61]

The central weakness of Zlotnick's 'nostalgia' thesis resides in its essentially postmodern theorisation of nostalgia as a form of false memory. The past which is represented in nostalgic memory is understood never to have really existed, thus nostalgia becomes associated with infantile regression, the refuge of those unwilling or unable to meet the challenges of the modern world.[62] Yet, as Ann C. Colley has shown in *Nostalgia and Recollection in Victorian Culture*, the postmodern notion of 'nostalgia without memory' is not necessarily applicable to Victorian culture.[63] To take a very simple example, when the handloom weavers (one of Chartism's most important constituencies) of the 1840s recall a time when their wages were worth two or three times as much in real terms, they are no more indulging in wistful nostalgia than a British academic who recalls a time when undergraduate seminars consisted of 4–8 students (or fewer) rather than 15–20 students (or more). Both cases describe a process of accurate historical memory which is also a necessary starting point for a critique of the present.

---

[60] For an overview of these debates see Susan Zlotnick, *Women, Writing, and the Industrial Revolution* (Baltimore: John Hopkins University Press, 1998), 168–95.

[61] *Ibid.*, 175–95.

[62] Raphael Samuel notes the tendency of critics to '[treat] nostalgia as a contemporary equivalent of what Marxists used to call "false consciousness" and existentialists "bad faith" ', *Theatres of Memory* (Verso: 1996), 17.

[63] Ann C. Colley, *Nostalgia and Recollection in Victorian Culture* (Basingstoke: Macmillan, 1998), 4–5.

The 'Merry England' poems can be seen as a distillation of both Chartism's values and aspirations and of the historical understanding it had acquired since 1838. In formal terms, they deploy those structural antitheses which Timothy Randall, amongst others critics, has identified as a distinctive feature of Chartist verse.[64] These antitheses can operate at the level of the individual line, as in one of Benjamin Stott's 'Song for the Millions', 'We have slavery behind us, and freedom before us, / We have truth against falsehood, and right against wrong!' (*NS*, 10 December 1842), as well as structuring stanzas and entire poems. Yet within the 'Merry England' cluster these binaries are subordinated to a tripartite structure. Each poem opens by recalling, or lamenting the loss of, the time when 'Merry England' existed; it juxtaposes this lost time with England's degraded present before calling for the restoration of those same lost rights. Each poem enacts a classic dialectical process in which thesis (England favoured) clashes with its antithesis (England degraded) before yielding a synthesis (England restored).

The interplay between structural antithesis and tripartite form provides a possible clue as to the nature of the agency possessed by these poems. The structural antitheses replicate the fundamental logic of identity – the a/not-a dyad – whilst the tripartite structure repeats the logic of the Oedipal complex by re-orienting the primary dyad around a newly introduced third co-ordinate. Similarly, 'Merry England' itself with its overflowing comforts and absence of dearth can be seen as figuring a form of plenitude – there is certainly little sense of any gap between wish and fulfilment. To extend the psychoanalytical analogy, the present is clearly marked by lack and the concomitant operation of desire which finds a fantastic satisfaction in its imagined future (which closely resembles the original site of plenitude).

However, before concluding that these poems are simple expressions of fundamental psychic drives, it is necessary to note the ways in which their formal and thematic structures resist any direct mapping in terms of such drives. Most noticeably, the lost idyll is identified with the name of the father rather than the body of the mother. The past in these poems was the time of manly independence whilst the present is a time of dependence which is implicitly figured in feminine terms of weakness, passivity and tears, as in the sixth verse of 'Merry England':

---

[64] See the discussion of Randall's work in Chapter 2.

Thou'rt no longer 'Merry England', but a spectre-smitten form,
With thy bosom left uncover'd to endure the piercing storm;
While chills of want and misery are breathed in every gale –
The widow'd and the fatherless their hapless lot bewail.

The use of 'sons of toil' as a popular mode of address in Chartist poetry throughout 1842 suggests the importance of this identification – the Chartist becomes the post-Oedipal son, fighting for his rightful inheritance in the name of the father. The Charter, therefore, becomes identified with a patrimony and the historical logic of lost rights merges with basic psychic drives – thus allowing us to glimpse the forces which underpin the tenacity of this tradition within English radicalism. This alignment of the historical and the psychic undoubtedly provides the basis for a very powerful (because experienced as coherent) series of identifications and thus a coherent sense of identity.

The reading experience which these poems offer can be seen as a variation of the Chartist 'double poem' form discussed in Chapter 1, in that each poem charts a recursive journey which takes the reader from an initial state of contentment (the past) into a time-space of suffering and disorder (the present) before finishing with an invocation of a transformed future which clearly resembles the past. The poems utilise the most fundamental narrative structure (original state/disturbance/restoration), whose close associations with the folk-tale form may offer a clue to its origin and operation within Chartist poetry. It is possible that the use of a familiar narrative structure increases the ideological effectiveness of these poems. If so, then these poems are confirmatory rather than revelatory. Within these poems the three stages of the journey are not accorded equal textual weight; the emphasis is placed on past and present rather than on the future. Historical memory, in conjunction with the belief in a lost golden age, underpins a temporal politics in which a superior past guarantees a better future, which in its turn will redeem present suffering. In the poetic equivalent of Minerva's owl taking flight at dusk, the agrarian golden age enjoys a last moment of historical visibility, precisely at the time of the decisive transition to industrial capitalism.[65]

---

[65] 'It is now possible to appreciate that the turning point in the British economy was not the late forties but 1840–2', J. Saville, *1848. The British State and the Chartist Movement* (Cambridge University Press, 1990), 58.

CHAPTER 6

'The future-hastening storm': Chartist poetry in 1848

> Ye whom the future-hastening storm drove far with victory heated,
> June-heroes of the Paris fight – ye conquerors though defeated!
>> Ferdinand Freiligrath, 'The Dead to the Living'

Within Victorian Studies '1848' remains a signifier of mythic proportions. The year of European revolutions, the 'springtime of the peoples', also witnessed a remarkable efflorescence of British fiction with *Wuthering Heights*, *Jane Eyre*, *Vanity Fair*, *Dombey and Son* and *Mary Barton*, to name the most significant novels associated with this historical moment.[1] In addition, 1848, or even more precisely the Kennington Common meeting of 10th April 1848, has often been offered as the quintessence of Chartism – the messy complexities of history distilled to the simplicities of a morality play in which sincere but misguided enthusiasts foolishly threaten violence, are subdued by the integrity of the middle classes, realise the error of their ways and commit themselves to the peaceful pursuit of piecemeal reforms thereafter. This is a remarkable historiographical achievement because in Chartist terms, 1848 was an atypical year – the only year when its history was dominated by the international context, especially events in Ireland and France.[2]

Yet the task of understanding Chartist poetry in 1848 depends on evading the pressure exerted by the subsequent construction of the centrality of 10th April. In particular, it is important to recover a sense of the unease and uncertainty, the excitement and possibility which informed the prevalent 'structure of feeling' throughout that year. For it was only retrospectively and at some distance in time that '1848' marked the decisive defeat of Chartism and, as John Saville has shown, this same construction

---

[1] Raymond Williams discusses the significance of this conjuncture in 'Forms of English Fiction in 1848', *Writing in Society* (Verso: no date), 150–65.
[2] John Saville, *1848. The British State and the Chartist Movement* (Cambridge University Press, 1990), 15.

166

of '1848' was part of a deliberate attempt to consign Chartism to historical and ideological oblivion.[3] For although the British state was confident that it had neutralised Chartism's immediate threat by the end of August 1848, there nonetheless remained a widespread feeling that a decisive class conflict had been postponed rather than resolved. 'A Trifle from Brighton', a poem first published in *Punch* and reprinted in the *Northern Star*'s poetry column for 23rd December 1848, illustrates this sense of an impending social collision:

> It was Capital a-preaching, out of plump and prosperous men,
> And Labour's hundred hungry throats refusing their 'Amen:'
> When Riches mentioned 'Industry', Rags answered with 'Despair',
> And Fustian rapp'd a curse out, when Broadcloth talked of prayer.
> I dropped the TIMES to look upon the Cliff with all its life,
> And that stern sea, that now 'gan curl its white waves as for strife –
> And I felt to seek for appetite from the briny, 'twas in vain,
> And so took my place for London by the earliest fast train.

The editorial commentary which the *Northern Star* appends to these lines indicates the ambivalent hopes and fears constituting this structure of feeling. This political uncertainty finds a formal analogue in the commentary's mixed registers, where the apocalyptic, millenarian and catastrophic jostle in biblical cadences tinged with a 'red republican' rhetoric.

> How long will the ocean waves of Democracy be content to 'chafe' and 'moan'? When will the almighty waters pass over and cleanse the pestiferous soil of the land of Privilege?
> There is one consolation – the sea of human misery *mines* while it moans! Think of that, ye
>
> > 'Gentlemen of England
> > Who live at home at ease!'
>
> Ye may say 'after us the deluge', but unless you are utterly indifferent to the happiness of your children, you will put from you any such selfish reflection, and will forthwith set about taking the necessary means to prevent that deluge. Do you say 'our soldiers, our policemen, our spies, our lawyers, our judges and *our* jurors, are the means we depend on to protect us from the inundation of revolutions'. – Then be assured, you or yours, perhaps both, will suffer the just penalties of your wilful blindness.[4]

---

[3] 'Chartism was finally broken by the physical force of the state, and having once been broken it was submerged, in the national consciousness, beneath layers of false understanding and denigration.' *Ibid.*, 202.

[4] *Northern Star* 1 January 1848, 3.

Despite beginning with the established Chartist image of the cleansing flood and insisting on the continual nature of working-class resistance ('the sea of human misery *mines* while it moans!'), the *Northern Star* seeks to persuade its opponents of the need to avert the deluge. Revolution is certain, revolution can be averted, revolution ought to be averted: this triad of contradictory expectations was widespread in Victorian culture in the immediate aftermath of 1848, its structuring presence informing texts as politically distinct as Marx's *Communist Manifesto*, Carlyle's *Latter-Day Pamphlets* and Mill's *Principles of Political Economy*.[5]

Yet for all this ambivalence, 1848 does mark a watershed. Within the Chartist movement the emergence of a new 'red republican'/proto-socialist analysis (and its accompanying poetic) marks the definitive historical exhaustion of the older radical analysis and its poetic. In addition, as was shown in Chapter 3, 1848 was also a lean year for Chartist poetry with over 50 per cent of the poetry column's contents provided from outside the movement and a considerably diminished number of Chartist poets compared with the column's heyday. Indeed, 1848 can be said to mark the end of the Chartist poetic project insofar as thereafter it makes more sense to focus on the continuing activity of a limited number of individual Chartist poets rather than the poetry column itself.

The poetry column for 1848 begins on a note of aggressive despondency, with the editor's preface to his 'New Year's Wreath' repeating the medical profession's fears that the influenza outbreak of 1847 is but 'the precursor and herald of the still more dreaded cholera'.[6] In a clear challenge to 'pythogenic' theories of epidemiology the *Northern Star* calls for better housing, employment, clothing and food for the poor as the best way of preventing cholera.[7] It continues by identifying a call and response relationship between the Irish famine (then entering its third year) and economic conditions on the British mainland: 'the wail of despair' from the former finding 'a frightful response in the choking cry and muttered curse of the starving millions of Great Britain'. It predicts that without fundamental economic and social change the people will begin a 'terrible agitation . . . for objects even more startling than the Charter' and cites the French Revolution of 1789 as an example of what

---

[5] Both Marx and Carlyle predict the return of class conflict, the first as promise and the second as threat, whilst Mill's famous chapter on 'The Probable Futurity of the Working Classes' can be seen as an attempt to avert such a crisis.

[6] *Northern Star*, 1 January 1848, 3.

[7] A. Susan Williams, *The Rich Man and the Diseased Poor in Early Victorian Literature* (Macmillan, 1987), 1–38.

happens when a nation is 'goaded to madness by [its] sufferings'.[8] Significantly, the *Northern Star* welcomes neither cholera nor revolution, expressing its hope that both may yet be averted.

Indeed, the same poetry column sets out the terms under which Chartism would be prepared to enter into an alliance with the middle classes. Its publication of E. S. Wilkinson's 'The Prince and the Peasant' (a largely unremarkable anti-game law poem, wherein each stanza is preceded by a capitalised word which when taken together reads ('HE WHO FEEDS THE PHEASANT AND STARVES THE PEASANT IS A TYRANT') is accompanied by an editorial comment which advises Chartism's 'middle-class friends [to] take a hint' from Wilkinson's example. The *Northern Star* continues:

They might take for their themes the abominations of class-legislation and the necessity for the Charter; or the evils of land-monopoly and the advantages of the Chartist Land Plan; or the folly of war and 'national glory': and the true glory of international fraternity. By taking this course they might popularise their 'wares', fill their tills, and accelerate the progress of justice, freedom, fraternity, truth, and public happiness.[9]

Of these three central demands for working-class political and economic independence and an end to militarism, the latter was the least contentious to middle-class radicalism which was conscious of the cost of military expenditure and suspicious of the prestige which military glory conferred on an aristocratic officer caste.[10] Throughout 1848 the *Northern Star* reprinted many poems on foreign affairs from a range of middle-class journals indicating the extent of the agreement between middle-class and working-class radicalism in this area.[11] However, the almost complete absence of such borrowings on domestic economic and political matters indicates the difficulties which middle-class radicalism faced in restoring its leadership of the popular bloc.[12]

---

[8] *Northern Star*, 1 January 1848, 3.   [9] *Ibid.*

[10] As John Saville notes, 'anti-militarism and opposition to colonial wars remained a minority theme of middle-class radicalism throughout the nineteenth century', *1848*, 55.

[11] In addition to the five poems on French affairs reprinted from *Puppet Show* (which will be discussed later in this chapter) the poetry column also reprints: A Miner, 'Latest News from Mexico' (*Philadelphia Saturday Courier*), *Northern Star*, 8 January 1848, and Anon., 'Abd-El-Kader at Toulon; or, The Caged Hawk' (*Punch*), *Northern Star*, 22 January 1848.

[12] Indeed, it can be argued that the subsequent hegemony of Victorian liberalism was only possible once the economic and political demands of Chartism were placed in abeyance by the prolonged period of economic growth from the Great Exhibition to the onset of the 'Great Depression' in 1873. The repeated borrowings from middle-class radicalism which pepper the *Northern Star*'s poetry column demonstrate the existence of a shared language of 'radical humanitarianism' which

The *Northern Star*'s prediction of the conjunction of Irish and British distress continues Feargus O'Connor's strategy of seeking to unite English and Irish radicals discussed in the previous chapter. Following the death of Daniel O'Connell in 1847 there had been a number of realignments within Irish nationalism and by the end of February 1848, English Chartists and Irish Confederates were beginning to co-operate closely, much to the alarm of the British government.[13] Signs of the burgeoning rapprochement are evident in the inclusion of two 'Famine' poems in the first poetry column for 1848. The anonymous 'The Irish Mother' (reprinted from the *New York Tribune*) describes the death of an entire family from starvation. The horror and desperation of the famine finds expression in the poem's second verse in which the eponymous mother opens her veins in an attempt to feed her youngest child. The following verse condemns an indifferent and profligate aristocracy which feeds its hounds before its tenants, while the final stanza literally curses Britain ('That country with curses should ever be smitten') as the author of Ireland's woes.

'The Irish Mother' is followed by 'An Appeal for Ireland' by Thomas Martin Wheeler, intended (as the editor states in his prefatory remark) to 'convince our Irish brethren that the English Chartists are their true friends'. Wheeler's poem begins by acknowledging the scale of Irish suffering and contextualising it in terms of her history:

> There's a scream of despair from Erin's isle,
> A nation's tear and a nation's wail.
> It tells of long oppressions and guile,
> . . .
> Starvation stalks her plains among
> . . .
> Whilst thousands pine and die away.[14]

The second stanza asks who will save Ireland and echoes 'The Irish Mother' in its condemnation of landlords who:

> . . . spend in luxury the peasant's gain,
> Whilst they who till their native soil
> Are dying fast from hunger's pain.

Verse three mocks the 'assistance' offered by the House of Commons, 'Coercion first! and then the grave!', and implores 'Heaven' to 'Save this

---

will serve as one of the bases for Gladstonian liberalism, once it has been separated from or emptied of any specifically Chartist economic and political content.
[13] Saville, *1848*, 73–4.   [14] *Northern Star*, 1 January 1848.

wronged people from the tomb'. The poem's final stanza calls on 'the English patriot band, / [to]Disclaim your senate's fiendish howl!' and to rally to the support of 'O'Connor and the brave few' who had voted against the Coercion Bill.[15]

Both poetically and politically Wheeler's poem continues the strategy of demonstrating the affinities between Chartism and nationalism. Both face a common antagonist in the form of an unrepresentative Parliament, both experience economic hardship represented by the customary trope of the inverse relation between labour and reward. That this affinity was by no means obvious to Irish nationalism is encoded in the editorial conditional ('should persuade') which prefaces Wheeler's poem.

The construction of a radical-nationalist alliance required painstaking political labour. Some of this work was undertaken by the poetry column, which sought through verse to make the aspirations of each side intelligible to the other. The main aim of the *Northern Star* was to identify the Chartist aspects of nationalism to the Chartist constituency and to explain the nationalist implications of Chartism to the nationalists. An example of this dual process is provided by the extended engagement with the work of Francis Davis, the 'Belfast Man', who published his work in the *Nation* (the leading journal of the 'Young Ireland' movement, owned by Gavan Duffy the founder of the Irish Confederation). In its 'New Year's Wreath', the *Northern Star* reprints seven poems by Davis; 'A Song for True Men', 'My Ulick', 'Thoughts for the Present', 'Irish Frieze', 'Nanny', 'My Betrothed' and 'Request', accompanied by an extensive editorial commentary dealing with both poetry and nationalism.

At first sight there appears to be a great deal of common ground between Chartism and nationalism. Like many Chartist poets, Davis insists that his cause is divinely sanctioned, inspired by 'the word and the will of an upright God' ('Thoughts for the Present'), and his poetry abounds in calls for popular unity – 'We rose to blend our every creed / In sacred union' ('A Song for True Men'). In 'My Betrothed' (which the *Northern Star* describes as 'one of the most magnificent lyrics ever penned') the register of romantic love simultaneously encodes a nationalist politics, whilst in 'My Ulick' the eponymous lover arrives at his beloved's house on a wintry evening and proceeds to talk politics with her father, 'They talked of our isle and her wrongs, / Till both were as mad as starvation'. Political commitment generates an emotional bond between the father and Ulick whose 'hearts melted into each other' and this consolidates the romantic

---

[15] Saville, *1848*, 73.

bond between Ulick and his beloved who by the end of the poem has 'confessed' her love for him.

In addition to these common ideological features, Davis's poetry shares a number of poetic features with Chartist verse. Both use natural metaphors to encode political struggle, such as 'tempest' and 'thunder' ('A Song for True Men') or the image of clouds dispelled by light ('My Betrothed'). Apocalyptic images – 'crashing towers and creaking thrones' ('My Betrothed') – are also common to both traditions. Similarly, it is possible to trace the influence of Burns in poems such as 'My Ulick' whose domestic setting is redolent of 'The Cotter's Saturday Night'. Likewise 'Irish Frieze', with its insistence that it is a man's essence, his heart, rather than his outward garments which matter:

> 'Tis not the coat, 'tis not the hue,
> Its texture, cut, or red or blue,
> The might of mind can show
> Or tell the deeds the arm can do,
> For mankind's weal or woe;

reads as a more belligerent assertion of the central claim of 'For A' That and A' That'. Even Davis's championing of frieze resembles Feargus O'Connor's invocation of 'fustian' as the cloth of honour.

However, in spite of these similarities the relationship between Chartism and nationalism had traditionally been fraught. In particular, the experience of, and attitudes to, violence differed sharply between the two movements. The difficulties which Chartism had in imagining, much less countenancing, insurrectionary (as opposed to retaliatory) violence has been a constant theme throughout this study. In contrast, the violence and brutality practised by both the colonising power and its long resistant subjects had produced a situation in Ireland where, in the words of John Saville, 'in many areas violence was a matter of daily occurrence, and the degree of brutality practised by both the forces of law and the masses they confronted had no counterpart elsewhere [in Britain].'[16] One consequence of this was a much less inhibited attitude towards violence within Irish nationalism, and the sanguinary nature of Davis's poetry marks a major point of difference between Chartist and nationalist poetics. In places Davis's poetry becomes positively steeped in gore as, for example, in 'Irish Frieze' where the Irish landscape is described as 'That fee-blood nourish'd green!' and Irish history becomes the story of those who 'have

---

[16] *Ibid.*, 33.

fought, and thus have bled / In coats of Irish frieze!' At times, Davis's poetry is marked by the presence of an eroticised violence which has no counterpart in Chartist poetry prior to 1848. In 'My Betrothed', for example, the violence of total war is likened to the delights of early courtship:

> And to hear my love in his wild mirth sing
> To the flap of the battle-god's fiery wing!
> How his chorus shrieks through the iron tones
> Of crashing towers and crashing thrones,
>   And the crumbling of bastions strong!
> Yet, sweet to my ear as the sigh that slips
> From the nervous dance of a maiden's lips,
> When the eye first wanes in its love eclipse,
>   In his soul-creating song!

This association of violence (however necessary in historical terms) and pleasure is one which is almost unthinkable in Chartist poetry.

In the commentary which prefaces the selection of Davis's poetry, the *Northern Star* sets out its objections to nationalism. Condemning the 'nationality humbug' as 'the grossest of delusions', it denies that there is any necessary connection between national and popular freedom, and cites Russia and France as examples of countries possessing 'undisputed nationality' (that is national sovereignty) but whose peoples remain unfree. Whilst recognising the right of subjugated nations such as Poland and Italy (and by extension Ireland) 'to seek the recovery of their national power', the *Northern Star* insists that in such cases it supports the nationalist struggle only as a necessary phase in a broader movement for full human liberation, and declares 'if we thought that 'nationality' was to be the only end of Polish and Italian struggles, we would never again write or utter another word in favour of either'.

The *Northern Star* continues by acknowledging the skill of the *Nation*'s poets who 'write with true poetic fire', whilst criticising them for the 'misapplication' of their talents:

Our quarrel with the NATION poets is, that they have laboured madly, if not wickedly, to lash their countrymen into a fury against England, whilst at the same time, they have done nothing to teach the people how to win real liberty, or preserve it when won.[17]

For the *Northern Star*, nationalist poetry functions only as a destructive or negative force. It might be able to destroy the Union by exciting anti-English

---

[17] *Northern Star*, 1 January 1948.

feeling but it offers no positive knowledge of 'real liberty'.[18] By implication, therefore, the task of Chartist poetry becomes the provision of
positive political knowledge and the construction of international
working-class solidarity. The *Northern Star* suggests that the nationalists
have been seduced by 'the theatrical paraphernalia of nationality' and are
thus blinded to the class origins of social oppression. Returning to its
earlier claim that nationality does not automatically constitute freedom,
the *Northern Star* this time cites England as an exemplum. England not
only has its flag but also possesses 'a mighty navy, a brave army, innu-
merable colonies'; in short, England has everything 'the NATION poets
hope for'. Yet England's power and wealth:

are monopolised by a privileged few. The mass of the people of England are
politically and socially disinherited, and possess neither political power nor social
comfort. Now what guarantee will the NATION poets give to us, that when they
have made Ireland a 'nation', Irishmen will be better off than Englishmen are?
Nationality may co-exist with the vilest slavery, as Englishmen know full well.

The *Northern Star* continues by probing the limits of national exclu-
sivity. Praising Davis's 'laudable desire' to unite all Irishmen irrespective
of creed and religion the *Northern Star* regrets that 'his fraternal sympathies
should stop there'. In a prescient objection to nationalism the *Northern
Star* comments that 'the "patriot" whose one idea is the exaltation of his
own country, only requires the aid of favourable circumstances to make
him the scourge of mankind'.[19] In May the *Northern Star* reprints J. F. M.'s
'King Rigmarole Alive Again!' from the *United Irishman*. In the following
lines, the nature of 'Mr B's' sceptical interventions suggest that some of
the *Northern Star*'s reservations concerning nationalism had been heard
by the *United Irishman*:

FRIENDS,   we will wear our gold-laced coats –
MR B: *But what about the people's votes?*
FRIENDS,   we will all be mighty grand –
MR B: *But how about the poor man's land?*[20]

---

[18] Somewhat ironically, Chartism's critique of Irish nationalism, as a 'destructive' force capable of destroying a corrupt social order but incapable of building a just social order in its place, is similar to Carlyle's critique of Chartism.
[19] This analysis of the limitations of nationalism is almost certainly influenced by Harney's involvement with the Fraternal Democrats, and its call for labouring-class unity across national boundaries anticipates the final rallying cry of arguably the most famous textual embodiment of 1848 – Marx's *Communist Manifesto* (which also had its origins in the milieu of the Fraternal Democrats).
[20] *Northern Star*, 20 May 1848.

From February to May the poetry column seeks to consolidate the burgeoning alliance between the Chartists and the nationalists, publishing another poem from Francis Davis, 'A Winter Chant', on 5th February, and Thomas Moore's 'The Minstrel Boy' the following week. 'A Winter Chant' offers a meditation on the political significance of the seasons which rather unexpectedly identifies winter as the most propitious for popular hopes. Davis rejects spring as a cold-hearted deceiver, declares summer to be 'too brilliantly starr'd / To be lumbered with love for a democrat bard', while autumn is portrayed as a fickle coquette. Winter, however, embodies the qualities of the working-class patriot, 'sincere', 'undisguised', 'proud, honest, and rough' with a 'grasp of a hand like a patriot's lance'. Once again Davis celebrates destructive force; winter is 'so wild and so fiercely sublime' that it arouses the poet's sense of freedom. However, this destructive force is closely aligned with anti-Englishness at two points in the poem. In verse four, Davis proclaims 'Old Winter's a bard' whose music causes consternation amidst 'the tottering oaks', whilst the final verse also celebrates the destruction of England's national tree:

> Then hurra for the bard of the world-sweeping wing,
> And hurra for the harp of the earth cleaving sting!
> And hurra for the waltz, and the whirl, and the wheel,
> Of the uprooted oaks, crossed and tossed in the reel![21]

Moore's 'The Minstrel Boy' similarly associates poetry with national resistance as the captured minstrel breaks his harp rather than sing in captivity:

> 'Thy songs were made for the brave and free,
> They shall never sound in slavery!'[22]

In March and April, English poets emboldened by events in France renew their calls for Anglo-Irish unity. Edwin Gill's 'Vive la Republique' repeats the *Northern Star*'s earlier strictures concerning the 'nationality humbug', represents the O'Connellite agitation as a literal dead end and by deft use of the image of the shamrock calls on the Irish to realise their true national identity through the politics of unity rather than separatism.

> How long shall false friends with their 'blarney' deceive ye,
> While want and disease fill the cup of thy woes?
> Like thy own native shamrock – three leaves upon one stem,
> Unite with the thistle, the rose, and the leek;[23]

---

[21] For a discussion of the significance of the oak as a symbol of English identity, see P. Corrigan and D. Sayer, *The Great Arch: English State Formation as Cultural Formation* (Oxford University Press, 1991).
[22] *Northern Star*, 12 February 1848.   [23] *Northern Star*, 11 March 1848.

A few weeks later, Alfred Fennell's 'The Chartist Tricolour' treats this unity as an established fact, announcing that the eponymous flag 'Display[s] in its varied sheen, / The red, the white, with Erin's green' (*NS*, 8 April 1848).

However, the most telling poem in support of Chartist–Irish unity is John Skelton's 'The Respond to Liberty' (*NS*, 22 April 1848). Published almost a fortnight after the supposed fiasco of the Kennington Common meeting, Skelton's poem offers evidence in support of Saville's contention that Chartist morale was barely affected by the events of 10th April.[24] In addition, 'The Respond to Liberty' celebrates aggression in a manner reminiscent of Francis Davis's poetry but which had previously been rare in Chartist verse. Skelton begins by calling on 'both *Saxon* and *Celt*' to recognise the historical possibility inherent in the present moment: 'the hour has arrived for the blow to be dealt, / Then strike it, 'tis worthy the brave'. However, the poem is also haunted by the fear that both Saxon and Celt have become 'so degraded through serfdom and pain / That we never can rise to our manhood again'. As with a number of the 'Newport' poems, physical force is linked to an authentic masculinity and to the full exercise of freedom. The insurrectionary message of 'The Respond to Liberty' is accompanied by a linguistic energy and vigour which makes it, in formal terms, one of the more interesting poems to be published in the *Northern Star* in 1848. Skelton's quintains adopt an *abaab* rhyme scheme and are generally dominated by a trochaic metre whose sense of driving urgency is compounded by the stanza's oscillation between hexameters (the *a* lines) and tetrameters (the *b* lines).

By July the situation in Ireland had become so acute that 'the Whigs found their political options narrowing to the single area of coercion'. On 8th July, the nationalist leaders, Gavan Duffy, Meagher, Dohney and McGee, were arrested. On 25th July *habeas corpus* was suspended in Ireland and an attempted insurrection by the 'Young Ireland' movement was quickly suppressed.[25] Following this failure, which coincided with similar victories for the established order in Britain and the European mainland, Ireland features as part of the poetry of defeat which begins to fill the *Northern Star*'s poetry column. The first such poem, 'The Lament of O'Gnive' by Jeremiah Joseph Callahan is based on a literal translation of an original Irish poem and appears in the poetry column for 19th August. It records a catastrophic Irish defeat at the hands of the Saxon invader which brings slavery and subjugation to Ireland. The poem turns on the contrast between Ireland's ancient heroes – Gollamh, O'Neill,

[24] Saville, *1848*, 119.   [25] *Ibid.*, 158–61.

Con, Brehon – and her degraded present. The invocation of heroism no longer serves to inspire present resistance but rather acts as a measure of shame: 'Arise not to shame us, awake not to weep!' the poet implores the named heroes.

A similar sense of catastrophic defeat is found in Thomas Moore's 'Weep On, Weep On' which appears in the following week's poetry column (*NS*, 26 August 1848). However, unlike Callahan, Moore offers historical consolation rather than condemnation, expressing the hope that the future will revalue the present, 'When many a deed may wake in praise / That long hath slept in blame'. The next week sees another Moore poem, 'A Lament for Erin' (also known as "Tis Gone and For Ever') which sounds a more complex note in its treatment of the defeat of revolutionary expectations.[26] Defeat is figured as the loss of light and truth from the world, and the memory of their presence serves only to 'deepen the long night of bondage and mourning, / That dark o'er the kingdoms of earth is returning'. The danger here is of inculcating a profound and disabling sense of loss which fixes its readers in a state of permanent melancholia. Usually in Chartist poetry this is avoided by the promise of return and renewal but Moore's poem rejects this strategy. Instead, he insists that the revolutionary moment possessed an intrinsic value which is unaffected by its defeat, 'Oh, never shall earth see a moment so splendid!' The poem ends on a note which might be styled one of either suspended optimism or averted despair: the intrinsic value of the revolutionary moment is affirmed, despite its defeat and irrespective of its return:

> Then vanish'd for ever that fair, sunny vision.
> Which, spite of the slavish, the cold heart's derision,
> Shall long be remember'd, pure, bright, and elysian,
>   As first it arose, my lost Erin, on thee.

Just as events in Ireland were partly conditioned by events in France, so too do Chartist strategy and tactics need to be understood in the context

---

[26] The *Northern Star* substitutes four lines of asterisks for the first four lines of the final verse which read:

> But shame on those tyrants who envied the blessing!
>   And shame on the light race unworthy its good,
> Who, at death's reeking altar, like furies caressing
>   The young hope of Freedom, baptized it in blood!

Presumably, these lines were omitted because they were considered too inflammatory given the recent events in Ireland.

of the two French revolutions of 1848.[27] For Harney, the editor of the *Northern Star* and a great enthusiast for the 1789 revolution, the temptation to interweave '1848' with '1789' proved irresistible. The first poetry column after the February Revolution contains an anonymous translation of 'The Marseilles Hymn' (*NS*, 26 February 1848), while the next brings Edwin Gill's 'Vive la République'. This celebrates the French example – 'All honour and praise to the brave sons of Gaul / Who have crumbled the throne of a tyrant to dust' – and calls upon his Chartist audience to emulate it, 'Raise the cry of the Charter! *Vive la République*'. However, Gill's poem stops short of advocating insurrection. Its final stanza rehearses the long-held fantasy that popular unity will be sufficient to gain victory, whilst hinting at ulterior measures if Chartism's just demands are resisted:

> Thus united, base faction will quail at our might,
>   And be pleased to give that which our power could obtain,
> A repeal of all grievances, and the just right,
>   To live on the wealth that our energies gain.
> But should they insanely in pride spurn our prayer,
>   And bid us in other lands liberty seek,
> One loud and deep echo will ring through the air,
>   *Vive la République! Vive! Vive la République!*[28]

Gill's poem shares the column with William Roscoe's 'The Day Star of Liberty', a poem originally published in 1789. A fortnight later, a veteran radical sends in another song by William Roscoe simply titled 'Song. – Written in 1789' which he remembers singing 'in full chorus' in that year of revolution. Both of Roscoe's poems are organised around a series of moral binaries; freedom, reason and virtue confront oppression, superstition and terror, and political rights rather than economic interests form the basis of the anti-aristocratic bloc.

Furthermore, the initial response of middle-class radicals to the February Revolution must have encouraged Chartists to think that the restoration of the old alliance of the 'productive classes' against the aristocracy was once more possible. Certainly, the *Northern Star* was sufficiently impressed by the response of the satirical magazine *Puppet Show* to reprint five of its poems on continental politics between the last week of March and the

---

[27] In particular, the chance of a successful nationalist uprising was adversely affected by the refusal of the French provisional government to offer any form of encouragement or material support. Saville, *1848*, 80–7.
[28] *Northern Star*, 11 March 1848.

first week of June.[29] The first of these, the anonymous 'A Welcome to
Louis-Philippe', interprets the February revolution as God's judgement
on a morally bankrupt regime:

> Though tyrant Kings are false and strong,
>   Humanity is true,
> And Empire based upon a wrong,
>   Is rotten through and through.
>
> Though falsehoods into system wrought,
>   Condensed into a plan,
> May stand awhile, their power is nought –
>   There is a God in man.
> His revolutions speak in ours,
>   And make His justice plain.[30]

There is much here that would find ready assent with a Chartist audience
accustomed to similar critiques of kingcraft – although the most ideologically perceptive readers would note that the critique is specifically
directed at Louis-Phillipe (rather than kingcraft in general) and that the
linkage of divine justice and revolutionary success carries the clear
implication that failed revolutions indicate divine support for the existing
authorities (which ultimately would become the definitive middle class
interpretation of 1848).[31]

The other poems borrowed from *Puppet Show* indicate the extent of
the ideological common ground which Chartism both contested and
shared with middle-class radicalism. The anonymous 'King Smith', for
example, not only describes the socially corrosive effects of tyrannical
government (which can only rule by a combination of bribery, corruption
and military force) but also deploys flood imagery familiar from Chartist
poetry to describe the desired social change – 'The Virtue scorned, the
Truth denied, / Surged o'er the land in a living tide' (*NS*, 1 April 1848). In
similar fashion, 'Fraternity' (since 1789 one of the Revolution's watch-
words and a sufficiently charged term for the Christian Socialists to be
accused of subversive tendencies when identifying 'Brotherhood' as one of
their core values) proclaims the self-same virtue to be grounded in the
Judeo-Christian tradition and an absolute necessity for the achievement
of universal peace. 'The Brotherhood of Nations' (based on a Beranger
poem) evinces a strong desire for world peace which brings agricultural

---

[29] The five poems reprinted from *Puppet Show* appeared on the following dates: 25 March, 1 April, 29
April, 20 May and 3 June. One further poem, an anti-Louis Napoleon satire, was reprinted from
Puppet Show on 18 November. For full details of all these poems see Appendix B.
[30] *Northern Star* , 25 March 1848.   [31] Saville, *1848*, 221–37.

plenty and contentment in its train, as it does in so many Chartist poems: 'Peace, the fair mother of each bounteous year, / Dropped corn and wine on the prolific lands' (*NS*, 20 May 1848). Finally, 'The Warning Bell' is an optimistic poem about the inevitability of human progress. Its appeals to justice and unity, its image of 'Freedom's light' dispelling the darkness and its confidence that 'a People hand-in-hand / Can make this a better land' find many counterparts in Chartist verse (*NS*, 3 June 1848). Although Ian Haywood's *The Revolution in Popular Literature* describes *Puppet Show* as an 'anti-radical satirical magazine' based on its lampooning of Chartism in August 1848, its presence in the *Northern Star*'s poetry column suggests that in the first half of 1848 it was not perceived as either an anti-radical or an anti-Chartist publication; rather the *Northern Star* detected a degree of ideological affinity.[32] However, it is noticeable that the *Puppet Show* disappears from the poetry column after 3rd June; like many other middle-class publications it moved 'right' as events in France moved 'left'.[33]

In the build-up to the 10th April demonstration, the poetry column regularly brought the example of the French revolution to its readers' attention. The 1st April column offered translations of the 'Marseillaise Hymn' and 'Mourir pour la Patrie!' (also known as the 'Chorus of the Girondists') both taken from *Howitt's Journal*. Brian Maidment identifies *Howitt's Journal* as belonging to the category of 'popular progress' periodicals (magazines under middle-class control but which sought to appeal to an artisanal readership) and it is possible, therefore, that the inclusion of material from its pages in the *Northern Star* is a further indication of the attempt to build bridges with middle-class radicalism.[34]

The following week the column contains two further translations of these songs, both by Ernest Jones (entitled 'The Marseillaise' and 'Chorus of the Girondists') as well as Alfred Fennell's 'The Chartist Tricolour'.[35] The importance accorded these French revolutionary anthems is highlighted by a letter which appears in the 'Notes to Readers' column in the same issue of the *Northern Star* which carries Jones' translations. As was noted in Chapter 3, a Chartist correspondent calling himself simply 'A Republican' wrote suggesting that the Chartist Executive should organise

---

[32] Ian Haywood, *The Revolution in Popular Literature* (Cambridge University Press, 2005), 225.

[33] Saville traces this movement through a study of the coverage of French events in the *Illustrated London News, 1848*, 96–7.

[34] Brian Maidment, 'Magazines of Popular Progress and the Artisans', *Victorian Periodicals Review*, 17(3) (1984), 83–93. See also Haywood, *The Revolution in Popular Literature*, 195–7.

[35] Another translation of 'The Marseillaise' had appeared as part of the 'Songs for the People' series on 26 February 1848.

a competition to find a British equivalent to 'The Marseillaise' and 'Hymn of the Girondins'. Although the editor indicates his thorough approval, no such competition was ever instituted by the National Charter Association.[36]

Jones' contributions are offered to the *Northern Star*'s readers as 'another translation of the "Marseillaise" and "Mourir pour la Patrie"' which suggests that the poetry column's editor saw them as complementing rather than replacing the translations from *Howitt's Journal*. However, a closer analysis of the two sets of translations reveals a number of differences, both poetic and political, which under the pressure of subsequent events would divide middle-class radicalism from its working-class counterpart. A comparison of the respective translations of verse four of 'The Marseillaise' highlights many of the salient differences:

> Ye tyrants tremble, false and cruel,
>> Ye curse and shame of all mankind!
> Your parricidal schemes, ye crafty,
>> Their proper fate, at length, shall find!
> And if in deadly contest closing,
>> Our noble, youthful heroes fall,
>> The earth fresh thousands forth shall call,
> And rouse herself your power opposing!
>>>> *Howitt's Journal*

> Tremble, tyrants! traitors! Tremble,
> Plague spots of the factious few!
> Plot, conspire, betray, dissemble,
>> You shall not escape your due!
> You shall not escape your due!
> For we'll be soldiers one and all
> If hundreds die – fresh thousands stand –
> Every death recruits a band
> Vowed to crush you or to fall.
>>>> Jones' translation

The archaic language and convoluted syntax of the *Howitt's* version compares unfavourably with the urgent, concise contemporary language of Jones' translation. The greater energy of the latter is underscored by its use of seven- and eight-syllable lines as opposed to the eight- and nine-syllable lines of the former. Similarly, where the *Howitt's* translation is clotted with adjectives, Jones' version barely contains any and instead is

---

[36] Three weeks after this letter the 'Notes to Readers' column records the rejection of 'The lines entitled "The English Marseillaise"' submitted by an unnamed Cheltenham Chartist. In addition it is possible that John Skelton's 'National Song for the People', which did appear in the poetry column at the end of April, was a response to this suggestion.

dominated by verbs and nouns. Elsewhere, Jones' translation possesses greater intensity and precision: where *Howitt's* warns that 'the ruffian foe / . . . comes your homes to overthrow', Jones offers 'hirelings fierce for brutal strife / . . . outrage in your very arms, / The hope – the partners of your life'. Similarly, the nationalism of *Howitt's* is replaced by Jones' internationalism as the 'sons of France' become the 'Sons of Freedom'. Where *Howitt's* concentrates on the 'bonds ignoble / Those fetters forged in ancient time', Jones emphasises the breaking of those same bonds, 'We broke their manacles before'.

Howitt's archaisms serve to historicise the French Revolution, to consign it to the past. It is an event worthy of commemoration but its lessons are not directly applicable to the current British situation. In contrast, the contemporaneity of Jones' language insists on the relevance of the French Revolution. The predominance of verbs and nouns makes it a poem of actions and agents. The directness of Jones' warning to the tyrants – 'You shall not escape your due!' contrasts with the passivity of *Howitt's* prediction that the tyrants 'Their proper fate, at length, shall find!' For *Howitt's*, the glorious upheaval of the French Revolution belongs to the past, for Jones it cries out to be realised in the present: this difference between liberal gradualism and revolutionary expectation would soon divide middle-class radicalism from militant Chartism.

If the purpose of these repeated translations was to inspire an irresistible demonstration of the nation's will on 10th April then they must be judged to have failed. However, that they contributed to the creation of revolutionary expectations is suggested by Sir Charles Greville's triumphalist response to those events:

We have displayed a great resolution and a great strength, and given unmistakeable [*sic*] proofs, that if sedition and rebellion hold up their heads in this country, they will be instantly met with the most vigorous resistance, and be put down by the hand of authority, and by the zealous co-operation of all classes of the people. The whole of the Chartist movement was to the last degree contemptible from first to last . . . The Chartists are very crestfallen, and evidently conscious of the contemptible figure they cut; but they have endeavoured to bluster and lie as well as they can in their subsequent gatherings, and talk of other petitions and meetings, which nobody cares about.[37]

Elsewhere in the British government a sense of satisfaction at the outcome of 10th April was tempered by the realisation (suggested by Greville's closing remarks) that the Chartist movement had not been decisively

---

[37] Philip Morrell (ed.), *Leaves from the Greville Diary* (Eveleigh Nash & Grayson, 1929), 576–7.

broken, or as Palmerston wrote to the Earl of Clarendon (the Lord Lieutenant of Ireland), 'the snake is scotched, not killed'.[38] The mixed nature of Palmerston's assessment finds an asymmetric reflection in the *Northern Star*'s poetry column throughout April, May and June, where the dominant tone is one of revolutionary expectation (particularly when discussing European events) with an undercurrent of anxiety when the focus falls on domestic politics.

As if regrouping, the poetry column falls silent for two weeks after 10th April before returning on 22nd April with three unmistakably militant poems; W. C. Bennet's 'The Horrid Metamorphosis, Not from Ovid', David Knox's 'Lines on the Present Movements' and John Skelton's 'The Respond to Liberty'. The contrast with the poetry column's defensive response after the Newport insurrection is striking here. Bennet's poem takes as its starting point Louis-Philippe's flight from France on a passport made out in the name of Smith. The metamorphosis from sovereign to citizen as a symbol of the new democratic order had similarly attracted the satirists at *Puppet Show* and their offering, 'King Smith', had also appeared in the poetry column for 1st April. Bennet's poem demonstrates a familiarity with French politics and offers a sophisticated analysis of the forms of power deployed by Louis-Philippe throughout his reign. It traces the process whereby the monarch's reliance on his 'charisma' and personal popularity (namely his not being a Bourbon) is replaced by the practices of gagging the press and rigging elections, before finally resorting to military force in a futile attempt to subdue the popular mood. The poem's final stanza predicts that other monarchs will be similarly dispensed with.

'Lines on the Present Movements' eschews satire in favour of concentrating on the emotional excitement of revolution. The poem's first four verses contrast the 'hope' experienced by the 'suffering masses' with the 'fears' that now fill the tyrants' souls. In these opening stanzas hope is always accompanied by images of light which serve to indicate 'the growing might / Of truth and right'. Victory is seemingly assured in this poem, a matter of historical inevitability rather than human agency, with knowledge securing the return of the golden age:

> As the early sun, with enlivening beams,
> Revives the fruitful plain,
>> Lo, the march of truth
>> Brings back earth's youth,
> And freedom wakes again![39]

---

[38] Saville, *1848*, 120.   [39] *Northern Star*, 22 April 1848.

The new social order ushered in by this pacific revolution is characterised by peace and plenty, by 'equity' defined as a just economic
reward for labour, and virtue and love; in short, a wish-list which had
barely altered since Chartism's inception, and whose realisation would,
as the final line of the tenth stanza makes clear, 'Make earth a dream
of heaven'. However, the poem does not end on this utopian note.
Rather it turns its attention to the otherwise occluded middle term
which mediates between current degradation and redeemed future.
The poem's four closing stanzas warn tyranny against resisting the
march of freedom for fear of unleashing an indiscriminate revolutionary
violence:

> Let reigning power not seek to crush
> Progression's peaceful band,
>   Lest . . .
>   . . . wrongs long nursed
>   May indignant burst,
> And make a dread revenge!

Although the poem insists that the tyrants will be morally responsible
('bear the shame') for such violence, it is also clear that it both recognises
and imaginatively recoils from its horrors.

In structural terms, the poem offers a new narrativisation of revolution.
As previous chapters have shown, prior to 1848, Chartist poetry tended to
present linear narratives in which current degradation was either contrasted with future prosperity or transformed into that prosperity by
means of political resistance. Sometimes this took the form of a bipartite
narrative (degradation/prosperity; degradation/resistance) and sometimes
the form of a tripartite narrative (degradation/resistance/prosperity). In
all cases a strict linearity prevailed. Knox's poem resists such linearity,
transposing the transformation process and the transformed society, such
that the latter precedes the former. Thus, 'Lines on the Present Movements' affirms ends before means. More accurately, it affirms its desired
end before disavowing certain means (or at least hoping that their use will
prove unnecessary). This self-interrupting structure uncannily anticipates
Marx's account of the proletarian revolution in *The Eighteenth Brumaire
of Louis Bonaparte*:

Proletarian revolutions, on the other hand, like those of the nineteenth century,
criticise themselves constantly, interrupt themselves continually in their own
course, come back to the apparently accomplished in order to begin it afresh,

deride with unmerciful thoroughness the inadequacies, weaknesses and pal-
trinesses of their first attempts.[40]

Another kind of anxiety informs the final poem in the column, John
Skelton's 'The Respond to Liberty'. Despite its opening exhortation to,
'Arouse from your thraldom, both *Saxon* and *Celt*', the poem is dominated by the fear not only that the Anglo–Irish alliance will not occur but
also that neither party will make even a separate bid for liberty. Posed as
a series of rhetorical questions clearly intended to elicit the contrary
response (which is given in the final stanza), Skelton strives to awaken his
readers to a sense of their daily degradation:

> Has the storm of vitality died in the vein?
> The fire ceased to burn in the soul?
> Have we sunk so degraded through serfdom and pain,
> That we never can rise to our manhood again,
> Responsive to liberty's call?[41]

The loss of vital fluid, which in earlier Chartist poems represented economic exploitation, now extends inwards to connote a form of spiritual
death. The passive acceptance of the prevailing conditions amounts to
the surrender of human dignity and the right to be considered a man.
The semantic density of the poem (partly achieved through continual
reiteration) seeks to stimulate a corresponding intensity of response in the
reader. However, the very fact that the poem strives so hard for effect also
betrays its anxiety. Although Skelton's poem styles itself as a response to
'the whirlwind' sweeping Europe, it is clear that it fears the absence of
revolutionary fervour in Britain and Ireland.

The following week's poetry column contains yet another poem by
John Skelton, 'National Song for the People', which calls for a popular
uprising – 'To strike for home and England dear' (*NS*, 29 April 1848).
However, not only is the poem haunted by the fear that the moment will
be lost, it also reverts to the 'older' revolutionary metaphysics in which
the mass assembly of the nation will be sufficient to obtain freedom
instantaneously. Thus in spite of its insurrectionary beginnings the poem
ends on a note of optimistic voluntarism:

> Fear makes us weak and courage strong;
> Resolve the deed – one rush – 'tis done!

[40] K. Marx, 'The Eighteenth Brumaire of Louis Bonaparte', in R. C. Tucker (ed.), *The Marx-Engels Reader* (New York: W. W. Norton, 1978), 597.
[41] *Northern Star*, 22 April 1848.

> Great God! the fight of freedom's won!
> Huzza! huzza! one thrilling cheer,
> For KINDRED, HOME, and ENGLAND dear!

However, an emergent structure of feeling is discernible in another offering from the same poetry column, 'Address to Britons' by Geo. Tweddell. Tweddell shares with Skelton the image of freedom as an innate flame which can only be extinguished with the death of the human (either the physical death of the subject or the spiritual death which attends the acceptance of slavery). Unlike Skelton, however, Tweddell's poem emphasises process rather than instant in its account of historical change. Indeed, 'Address to Britons' offers an intriguing assessment of the role of individual agency within the historical process. For Tweddell, inspiration can be drawn from historical example:

> But those who battle for the right,
> In Freedom's oft unequal fight
> Their history fills us with delight,
> Their actions when we read.

Thus he exhorts his readers 'to emulate / The actions of the truly great' by becoming active participants in the battle against oppression. This is represented as a simple ethical-moral choice – 'But let us do what good we can / To our oppressed fellow-man' – and is offered without guarantee of immediate success. Over the course of three quatrains, human agency builds from the ethical-moral, through the political ('Then raise up those who're sunken low, / With much oppression, want, and woe') to the revolutionary ('the cheering cry, / . . . The funeral knell of Slavery'). Tweddell then retraces his steps and, in another example of a non-linear narrative structure, contemplates the resistance historically offered by tyranny. Frost and Emmett are invoked as exemplary patriotic martyrs as 'Address to Britons' reminds its readers that collective victory is purchased at the cost of individual suffering and even death. In striking contrast to the end of Skelton's 'National Song', Tweddell's poem ends with a dream of international peace and fellowship, 'And all mankind will then appear / One common brotherhood so dear'.

The new structure of feeling which informs 'Address to Britons' will shortly be named as 'red republicanism'. In essence, it marks the point at which the antagonism between the proletariat and the bourgeoisie is explicitly theorised as irreconcilable and becomes for some trends within radicalism the starting point for a new strategy and new economic demands. The rupture with the older forms of radicalism was not absolute – certain values, aspirations and ideas retained their validity, others retained their familiar names but became infused with new content, and in places new signifiers (such as 'proletarian' and 'bourgeois') began to emerge. In part, as Harney recognised, the new analysis was born out of emotional as well as political necessity. Writing for an edition of the poetry column dedicated to the French poet Beranger, Harney explained the factors governing the adoption of the red flag:

Under the Republican tricolour of 1848, the men who by their valour and blood made the revolution, have been swindled out of its fruits, and given over to proscription and massacre. Under that flag, too, Poland has been abandoned, Italy betrayed, and the honour of France basely truckled away for the advantages (?) of the English alliance. The tricolour is now as obsolete as the colourless rag of worn-out Legitimacy. Henceforth for the democracy, the red flag is the symbol of struggle, the emblem of hope, and the presage of victory. (*NS*, 30 September 1848)

The first poet to find a way of rendering this new analysis in poetic form was Ernest Jones. It appears in 'Our Trust', the last poem to be published by Jones in the *Northern Star* prior to his arrest on 6th June. This poem calls for working-class unity in the face of capitalist and aristocratic aggression and warns against the presence of *agents provocateurs* within the Chartist ranks:

> Working men, working men – stand by your order!
>   Treason is growing – deception at hand:
> Not only gold king and titled marauder –
>   Foes can be found in the heart of your band.[42]

The poem preserves the voluntarism of earlier radicalism, insisting in its second stanza that the answer to the questions of 'How?' and 'When?' the Charter will be obtained is to be found in 'your own hearts, your own hands, and your reason'. Similarly, the poem appears to subscribe to the theory of instantaneous change rather than transforming process, declaring in stanza four, 'Now is the crisis, when none may gainsay thee: / Oh! seize on the moment, for swiftly it flies'. However, the next stanza refines this by calling for action to be undertaken at the appropriate time, and representing the crisis as the culmination of a long historical process rather than an unpredicted irruption:

> Not in disorder, nor 'mid insurrection,
>   Thy sun, Revolution, is winning its noon.
> The fruit of long ages is reaching perfection,
>   But hands are uplifted to pluck it too soon!

---

[42] *Northern Star*, 27 May 1848.

In this stanza a teleological view of history (inexorable natural progress towards 'perfection') is complicated by the assertion that misdirected human agency might jeopardise the whole process. The next three stanzas develop this idea of contingency warning that the 'fruits' of the struggle may be plucked by 'The soft, silken hand of the vile profit monger' rather than the 'horny hand' of the 'brave children of hunger'. History, Jones warns, can be ironic as well as heroic:

> What! Shall your struggle – your strength – your distresses
> End but in making *their* order secure.

'Our Trust' emphasises the importance of precise calculation to political strategy. The older Chartist poetic which subscribed to a providential metaphysic that guaranteed success (the spontaneous and infallible cleansing of the flood, the decisive intervention of the God of Battles) is conspicuously absent from this section of Jones' poem. However, such political realism also has its agitational limits and the penultimate stanza sees the return of the rhetoric of certain victory with its prediction of 'Success for the valiant'. Yet, the final stanza makes clear that this is not a straightforward return to the providential metaphysic by emphasising the role of human agency:

> Do you ask me to name you the day of your power?
> Organise – organise – organise, still!
> *Then* I'll tell you the day – nay, I'll tell you the hour:
> You'll just gain the Charter, *whenever you will.*

Towards the end of May the poetry column turns its attention to the other European revolutions. The anonymous 'Hurrah-Hurrah-We Move. A Triumph!' which appears in the poetry column for 20 May integrates the revolutionary wave into its verse structure, tracing the progress of the revolution from France (v.2), to Italy (v.3), to Prussia (v.4), to Poland (v.5), to Bohemia (v.6). The poem is saturated with natural metaphors particularly that of 'the rending storm' which 'sweeps' the continent in stanzas four and five. However, these natural metaphors are no longer the straightforward, transparent signs of power of earlier Chartist poetry but are now associated with the 'ruse of nature', as in the poem's first stanza:

> It moves – it moves – Earth hath not slept –
> It crouched but for its spring;
> Of silence is the thunder born,
> And winters harvests bring;
> It did but palsied weakness feign,

> The more its strength to prove;
> 'Tis bounding for the goal again;
> Hurrah-Hurrah- we move.[43]

The increased sophistication of the handling of such metaphors is partly signalled by the verbal dexterity of the poem with its uses of both pun ('spring' may be both verb and noun) and paradox ('Of silence is the thunder born').[44]

'Hurrah-Hurrah-We Move!' shares the poetry column with another anonymous poem – 'German Student's Song' (taken from *Howitt's Journal*) – which rather in the manner of 'Chorus of the Girondists' extols the willingness of the nation's youth 'For Fatherland to combat and to die!' In the following week's column, W. W.'s 'The Holy Cause' ends with a similar 'country or death' cry, now transferred to Britain (*NS*, 27 May 1848). In June the focus shifts to Italy with two poems, 'Address of Tomaso Aniello' by George Tweddell and 'Italian Patriot Song' translated by William Cullen Bryant, appearing in the poetry column for 17th June. Both poems are decidedly martial in tone, and both end with a call for patriotic blood-sacrifice, '*Death – death, or – Liberty!*' and 'Better die bravely, than live to be slaves'. In these poems, the *Northern Star*'s earlier critique of the limits of nationalism seems to have dissolved in the enthusiasm of May and June, for the nation is not only conceived of as the agent of its own liberation, but also represented as being without its own internal social divisions.

Yet the celebration of the continental insurrections is accompanied by an anxiety regarding the apparent unresponsiveness of the British. The reprinting of Robert Burns' 'The Tree of Liberty' (*NS*, 10 June 1848) reminds the *Northern Star*'s readers that their historical situation is not unique. Burns' poem, which praises the fruits of the tree of liberty (planted by the French Revolution), ends by expressing the hope that 'Auld England may / Sure plant this far-famed tree, man'. The fear that a historic opportunity may be lost is also evident in 'Hurrah-Hurrah-We Move!', which contrasts English lethargy with continental action in the final stanza:

---

[43] *Northern Star*, 20 May 1848.

[44] However, there is an incipient danger that the attribution of cunning to nature – 'It did but palsied weakness feign, / The more its strength to prove' – may over time become a form of self-deception. Certainly, Chartist verse of the 1850s offers many examples of signs of weakness and defeat being constructed as signs of impending victory. For a more detailed discussion of the political significance of such natural force metaphors, see M. Sanders, 'Poetic Agency: Metonymy and Metaphor in Chartist Poetry 1838–1852', *Victorian Poetry*, 39: 2 (Summer 2001), 111–35.

> And England sleeps; – Bohemia stirs –
> Stirs too the fiery Hun;
> The Lombard rends the Austrian's heel, –
> Milan hath freedom won;

This anxiety finds its clearest expression in 'The Song of Freedom' by 'One of the People' which appears in the poetry column for 24th June. This poem begins with two verses celebrating the continental revolutions, but its third stanza asks

> Shall ENGLAND tamely stand and see
> Young FREEDOM's glittering lights,
> Now raise the watchword – LIBERTY,
> Our CHARTER and our RIGHTS?

The emphatic typography (which is unusual for the poetry column) only serves to underline the rhetorical rather than the substantive aspect of the question. Similarly, the poem's repeated insistence that 'We will be slaves no more!' is evocative rather than actual; as if the poet is seeking to summon up those very forces which the poem knows to be absent. Indeed, the poem is an exercise in both poetic and ideological reiteration. Its refrain 'We will be slaves no more!', its insistence that freedom is achievable by means of 'one resistless stroke' and its identification of the nation as an irresistible force ('Who can withstand a nation's might, / Impassioned, pure, and strong'), all mark this poem's adherence to the older poetic.

An elegiac note indicating an awareness of the ebbing of the revolutionary tide first begins to sound in the poetry column in mid July, with Elisa Lee Follen's 'To the Martyrs of Freedom'. Its appearance followed the trial and conviction of Ernest Jones and coincided with the beginnings of insurrectionary plotting.[45] 'To the Martyrs of Freedom' is a post-revolutionary poem, not just in its acknowledgement of the temporary triumph of reaction – 'When on pure honour, simple right, / The brood of human vipers feeds', but in its need to wrest consolation from defeat, to interpret current setbacks as stations on the way to eventual victory. It achieves this by deploying the trope of postponed success which itself is associated with the very long perspective of eternity in verse four:

> In the cloud-tent of distant skies,
> Truth calmly waits, with balance true,

---

[45] For details of Ernest Jones' trial, see M. Taylor, *Ernest Jones, Chartism and the Romance of Politics 1819–1869* (Oxford University Press, 2003), 115–20. For details of the insurrectionary plotting see, Edward Royle, *Revolutionary Britannia?* (Manchester University Press, 2000), 131–4.

> Casts off traditionary lies,
>> And gives to Justice homage due.
> Reason proclaims eternal laws;
>> Mad mobs and tyrants, in their hour –
> May, for whole ages, hurt her cause,
>> But never can destroy her power.[46]

The proffered consolation here is philosophical and rests on a quasi-Platonic-Hegelian view of history in which pre-existing eternal forms ('Truth', 'Justice' and 'Reason') struggle towards realisation in the phenomenal world.

Follen's poem sternly emphasises the likelihood and necessity of present martyrdom. Indeed, the poem begins by offering martyrdom rather than hope to its intended addressees:

> Still trust, all ye who are oppressed!
>> Though hope no ray of light may shed,
> . . .
> Yet springing from your graves, we see
>> The amaranth wreath that never dies.

In a manner which anticipates Clough's 'Say Not, the Struggle Nought Availeth', Follen insists on the value of dutiful endurance even unto death. If anything, Follen's vision is even more austere than Clough's; in her poem friends rather than foes flee the field, and the darkness of death rather than dawn awaits her protagonists:

> When for the rights of man you fight,
>> And all seems lost and friends have fled,
> Remember, in misfortune's night,
>> New glories rest on Virtue's head;
> Duty remains, though joy is gone;
>> On final good then fix thine eyes;
> Disdain all fear, and though alone,
>> Stand ready for the sacrifice.

The poem ends with a twofold consolation; martyrdom serves to encourage future generations of activists, it 'Acts with a new, immortal power, / Inspires each heart, and nerves each hand', whilst history itself holds out a promise, 'Oppression has a transient date, / Eternal Justice has no end'. However, this promise of ultimate victory is of less moment than the poem's insistence that the martyrs of its title presage rather than inhabit

---

[46] *Northern Star*, 17 July 1848.

the promised land: 'Ye shall be heralds of the dawn, / But ye must know the darkest hour'. This negative affirmation is indicative of a newly complex sense of the historical process and of the role of individuals and generations within it. It is also accompanied by a reconfiguration of the movement's political temporality, as the idea of the future increasingly comes to dominate both past and present in the Chartist imaginary.

At times, the poetry of defeat occupies an arrested psychic space characterised by postponed (rather than disavowed) political desires and redolent of a kind of limbo, as in 'The Old Standard' by Beranger. The poem is set during the reign of the restored Bourbons and is spoken by a veteran Republican soldier who keeps the tricolour hidden beneath his 'lowly bed'. The hidden flag serves as a reminder of the Republic's past glories and as an embodiment of future aspirations. Although it can no longer be displayed openly, neither is it disavowed by its votary who literally holds on to it as the embodiment of his hopes:

> Come, press my heart and glad my eyes,
>   And staunch a veteran's falling tears;
>   . . .
>   Yes, from the dust behold it free
>   That dimmed its noble colours three![47]

In England the idea of lost rights, of a vanished 'Merry England', fulfilled a similar role to that of the lost Republic and was equally capable of sustaining sentimental, yet politicised, poetry. For example, 'When This Old Cap Was New', described as coming from 'an eminent writer well known in the north of England' (and which appears in the 'first wreath' of 1848's 'Christmas Garland') laments the loss of 'Merry England'. Like Beranger's poem it is organised around the contrast between then and now. For its author, the past was a time of plentiful harvests, foaming ale, the correct observation of age distinctions and of properly organised (namely domestic) labour, whilst the present is characterised by the malt tax, the blurring of age distinctions and the dominance of the factory system. Beranger's tricolour is replaced by the old cap of the poem's title which carries a less obvious political charge, but which is equally associated with lost rights and present resistance:

> New caps must follow old;
>   Yet bless our country's name,
>   And may we live to cure

---

[47] *Northern Star*, 30 September 1848.

>   Her present woe and shame;
>   Our ancient rights restore,
>   Our hellish foes subdue,
>   And make them what they were,
>   When this old cap was new.[48]

Further evidence of changing attitudes is provided by K. W. M.'s 'To the People', which effects a significant re-working of the natural force metaphors inherited from early Chartist poetry. 'The wind that shakes the trembling leaf' (the poem's opening line) does not anticipate or represent 'the voice of the people' (as it does, for example, in W. H. C.'s poem of the same name from 4th December 1841); nor is it the harbinger of the cleansing storm, rather it 'Gives health and vigour to the stem'. In short, as well as representing the movement's strength, natural force metaphors now also encode the setbacks which paradoxically have become a necessary part of the movement's progress. The problematising of the metaphor corresponds to a problematic thickening of the historical process in which the relationship between event and outcome has become opaque and indirect:

>   So freedom's onward course may seem
>   To wear the low'ring aspect dim,
>   But be prepar'd to help the stream,
>   And on the tide to sink or swim.[49]

Like Follen, K. W. M. calls on his/her readers to perform their duty even at the cost of their own lives. As if recognising the unattractiveness of this vision the second half of the poem reverts to the confident predictions and assertions of imminent victory of earlier Chartist verse ('The glorious day shall soon appear'). However, such proclamations sound hollow and formulaic in comparison with the greater complexity and density of the poem's first three stanzas.

Poems such as 'To the Martyrs of Freedom' and 'To the People' share a number of similarities with the apocalyptic/millenarian verse of Gerald Massey which forms the subject of the next chapter. These can be dangerous energies both in poetic and political terms. In particular, the dual emphasis on the possibility of individual extinction in pursuit of the cause and the unpredictability of the moment of triumph can become transformed into the kind of nihilistic desire for oblivion which informs Beranger's poem 'The Comet of 1832' (which appears, in a translation by

---

[48] *Northern Star*, 23 December 1848.   [49] *Northern Star*, 29 July 1848.

Colonel Thompson taken from the *Westminster Review*, in the poetry column for 30th September). Beranger's poem begins apocalyptically by imagining the effects of a comet's collision with the earth. The resulting devastation is described without regret and the final line of the opening stanza (which becomes the poem's refrain) – 'Enough – enough – the world is all too old' – seems to welcome the prospect of oblivion.

The second stanza continues the theme of the cosmic irrelevance of human life, envisaging the planet as a 'kite ... with a broken string' moving aimlessly through the universe until it is dashed 'Against some sun'. The origins of this world-weariness are revealed in the following verse which is filled with an overwhelming sense of disgust at the state of the world:

> Are we not tired of fools and foolish things,
> Errors, abuses, desolation, war,
>   *Of nation lacqueys, and of lacquey Kings*
> Tired of the future's disappointing dreams –
>   *Of plaster-idols shaped in meanest mould.*[50]

The eschewal of a redemptive future is particularly striking here and the succeeding verse similarly rejects the bourgeois myth of progress, the assumption of continual improvement based on technical innovation where utopia is only a generation away:

> I hear youth say – 'Man's prospect daily brightens,
> 'Each files his fetter surely – silently;
> 'The press illumines, and the gas enlightens;
> 'The glorious steam-boat speeds across the sea.
> 'Another twenty years – and then – and then!

This complacent optimism is undercut by the 'poet's' retort, 'Oh! I have waited thirty years in vain'. The poem ends with a death-wish which the *Northern Star* attributes to Beranger being 'almost heart-broken at the miserable failure of the February revolution', before concluding, 'we trust that better, brighter days are in store, and that . . . the poet will live to see 'the good time coming'.

A similar sense of paralysed hopelessness occasioned by catastrophic defeat pervades the poetry written in the aftermath of the failed Irish revolution which dominates the poetry column from mid-August to early September. Mindful of the fatalism which might be encouraged by such poetry, the *Northern Star*'s poetry column also carries a number of poems

---

[50] *Northern Star*, 30 September 1848.

which either threaten continued resistance to tyranny or, whilst clearly registering the fact of historical defeat, nonetheless predict the return of revolutionary energies. A typical example is provided by Edwin Gill's 'The Roman Tyrant', which shares the poetry column with J. J. Callahan's 'The Lament of O'Gnive'. The poem begins by ventriloquising the voice of the titular tyrant determined to exact vengeance following a failed revolt:

> Dash to the earth the failing serf,
> That dared our mandates brave.
> Drown in blood his clamour for food,
> To dungeons bear him away.[51]

However, the third and final verse records the ultimate overthrow of 'Tarquin's race of despots brave' by the 'people's might'.

Three weeks later Charles Cole's 'The Spirit of Wat Tyler' (*NS*, 16 September 1848) records an encounter with one of the earliest English radical heroes. In Christ-like fashion, Tyler appears displaying his wounds and recounts his own failed attempt to liberate England: '*We rose at once, like men inspired, / And burst the links that bound us!*' Tyler chastises his countrymen for failing to follow his example and for being content to live as slaves, citing 'PETERLOO...WEXFORD...MERTHYR' as the 'Reward of self abasement!' In the next verse, Tyler offers a litany of martyred heroes, 'CADE...MUIR...FITZGERALD...EMMET', whilst the poem's penultimate stanza identifies the necessity of reviving the spirit of such heroes. Although the martyr's grave is referred to, it is not yet the major focus which it becomes in later Chartist poetry. The historical magnitude of the defeat is registered by Tyler's fear that 'freedom's ever banished' and the poem ends with its speaker reiterating Tyler's call for a revival of the spirit of resistance, expressed as conditional hope rather than confident prediction:

> Many kindred spirits still survive,
> To rouse for coming glory;
> Till not a Briton but will strive
> To profit by His [Tyler's] story.

Elsewhere in the poetry column the tone is one of defiance. In David Wright's 'Ye Labourers of Britain' history also furnishes 'Exemplars' in the form of Tell, Wallace and Washington, whilst 'universal nature shows / True types of Liberty' (represented by 'soaring' eagles and 'bounding' torrents). History and nature here serve as straightforward inspiration to

---

[51] *Northern Star*, 19 August 1848.

present action, they do not mark its absence as in Cole's poem, and they issue in a confident call for one final push for liberty:

> Let 'Freedom' be your watchword,
>   And bid the trumpet sound,
> To call the millions, in their might,
>   To freedom's battle ground;[52]

Sadly, the 'millions' remained unmoved by Wright's call for them to 'rally round the good old cause' and with the exception of Ferdinand Freiligrath's 'The Dead to the Living' the poetry column published no further poems on the subject of the European revolutions until the first week of December, when another poem of defiant commitment, 'The Legionist' by Cassimir Brodswecki (translated by Dr Bowring), appears (*NS*, 2 December 1848).[53]

Freiligrath's 'The Dead to the Living' appeared in the poetry column in the first week of November, and is the most striking example of the new revolutionary poetry. An editorial preface informs readers that Freiligrath had recently been tried and 'triumphantly acquitted' on a charge of high treason for the publication of this poem, and it is not difficult to understand why the poem caused the German authorities such consternation. It is voiced by the martyrs of 1848, who complain that the revolution has been betrayed by a treacherous king and self-interested politicians, and who call on the people to 'perfect unto the whole the half-formed revolution!'

It is also a poem unlike anything which had previously been published in the *Northern Star* and as such serves to illustrate many of the differences between the respective imaginaries of Chartism and the continental

---

[52] *Northern Star*, 21 October 1848.
[53] In this poem, the Legionist of the title asks an Italian if he knows the whereabouts of the Polish Legion. The Italian tried to persuade the Pole to abandon his quest, accept historical reality (the loss of his nation), marry and settle in Italy and exchange his doomed political commitment for cultural and religious consolation. This counsel of submission is rejected by the Polish patriot who insists that nations only fall when their citizens accept the death of liberty:

> And is the life-tide of my country past?
> And is her death-knell sounded? No! No! No!
> The fires of freedom in our bosoms glow;
> We watch the hour; – we sleep not – Rome's proud heirs
> Fell, but they fell not while one spark was theirs
> Of freedom.

The poem ends with the Legionist setting off to join his comrades, much to the Italian's bemusement.

revolutionaries. This difference is apparent from the opening lines of the poem which confront the reader with the physical horror of revolution as the dead recall their transformation from corpses into martyrs:

> With bullet wounds in every breast, with foreheads gashed and rifted,
> You placed us on the bloody plank and high in air up lifted!
> With horrid cries uplifted, that each pain-contorted gesture
> To him who caused our death, should cling a curse-inflicting vesture![54]

Such an emphasis on wounds and physical suffering is rarely found in the poetry column of the *Northern Star*, and it is accompanied by a bitter, unforgiving tone equally rare in Chartist poetry. Freiligrath's dead desire that their sufferings should be ever present to their murderer:

> That he should see them night and day, as sleeper or as waker –
> . . .
> That mid his death-pain should come back each sob from grief now
>   wrenched.
> That each dead hand against his head should even then be clenched –

In these lines the desire for vengeance becomes identified with the revolutionary spirit in a manner which not only anticipates Benjamin's insistence on the necessity of remembering 'enslaved ancestors', but which also carries an uncomfortably sadistic charge, as the desire to inflict suffering threatens to overwhelm the desire for retribution.

If the dead desire to be ever present to their murderer, they are equally insistent on keeping themselves before the reader, and refuse to be interred for the first twenty-two lines of the poem. Thereafter, the dead recall their original willingness to be buried in the belief that through their sacrifice a final victory had been won:

> We thought, 'the cost indeed is great, but the prize has well repaid us!'
> And therefore without murmuring upon our biers we laid us.

However, subsequent events have revealed the assumption of victory to be premature:

> Now woe to you, we are deceived! Four moons have waxed and waned,
> And through your cowardice is lost all that we bravely gained!

The lines which follow record the multiple betrayals of the revolution; the Danish war, the massacre at Posen, the return of the standing army and the voluntary disbanding of the popular militia, the restoration of the

---

[54] *Northern Star*, 4 November 1848.

prince and the return of corrupt factions to the political process, and worst of all:

> . . . the breach of all alliance,
> Ah! even with you who from your graves breathe glory and defiance,
> Ye whom the future-hastening storm drove far with victory heated,
> June-heroes of the Paris fight – ye conquerors though defeated!

In response to this series of betrayals, the dead call for 'War, second war,' to reclaim the lost 'Commonwealth!' and demand their own exhumation – 'there now is need that you once more from earth displace us!' – as a necessary part of this process. In a macabre sequence the dead demand that their corpses should once again be paraded through the country and then brought before the Senate. In their imagined address to the senators, the dead lament the betrayal of the revolution and warn that not only will their rage not abate but that it will ultimately revive and complete the revolution:

> . . . in our rebuke doth consolation waken!
> You had already done too much, too much for you was taken;
> For you each passing day is felt such scorn, such detestation,
> That trust the dead, who cannot lie, that hate has no cessation!
> It lives for you; yes it awakes – will awake for execution –
> And will perfect unto a whole the half-formed revolution!

In a grim dialectical inversion, the spirit of the revolution is awakened by the concrete, material presence of the dead martyrs, who confidently predict future victory:

> The *red flag* o'er the barricades of liberty is breathing!
> The *red flag* leads the burgher-guard – it sets the troops in motion;
> Ascending flame consumes the throne – the kings fly to the ocean –
> . . .
> The people, the true Sovereign, themselves their future fashion!

However, this is another 'interrupted' poem which does not end on this image of the revolution triumphant. Instead it returns to the present and calls on the people to remember the 'tribulation' of the dead in order to prepare themselves for the forthcoming struggle. The poem ends with the dead imploring the living to disprove their fear that the revolution is permanently betrayed, 'That you were free, but now again are slaves – and slaves for ever!' This finale is criticised by the *Northern Star*'s editor, who expresses both his regret that the poem did not end six lines earlier (with the image of the people making their own future) and his fear that the actual ending may be misread as a prediction of perpetual slavery.[55] Nonetheless, despite these reservations, the *Northern Star* offers Freiligrath 'the thanks of the Democracy of England for his magnificent poem'.

The nature of Freiligrath's poem also prompts speculation as to the debt of gratitude which might be owed it by the editor of another radical newspaper, namely the *Neue Rheinische Zeitung*. For Freiligrath's poem reads as a remarkable anticipation of the famous opening section of Marx's *The Eighteenth Brumaire of Louis Bonaparte*. In particular, 'The Dead to the Living' opens with the dead wanting to weigh 'like a nightmare on the brain of the living', and closes with a recognition that only the success of the revolution will allow the dead to rest. This bears a strong family resemblance to Marx's observation that '[i]n order to arrive at its content, the revolution of the nineteenth century must let the dead bury their dead'. Furthermore, the poem's central trope, the revivified bodies of the dead, is a striking anticipation of Marx's analysis of the uses of revolutionary retrospection:

The awakening of the dead in those revolutions therefore served the purpose of glorifying the new struggles, not of parodying the old; of magnifying the given tasks in imagination, not of taking flight from their solution in reality; of finding once more the spirit of revolution, not of making its ghost walk again.[56]

Finally, Freiligrath's insistence on futurity (the 'future-hastening storm' of the June revolution and the people's ability to 'their future fashion') itself foreshadows Marx's prediction that the 'social revolution of the nineteenth century cannot draw its poetry from the past, but only from the future'.[57]

At the end of December the poetry column's 'Christmas Garland: Wreath II' offers a range of political and emotional moods all of which are intended to convince a movement traumatised by defeat that recovery is possible. 'The Day of Small Things' by the American poet James Russell Lowell traces the emergence of a mass movement (in this instance, abolition) from small beginnings and celebrates the power of the conscientious and morally courageous individual to effect change:

> Oh! small beginnings, ye are great and strong,
> 　　Based on a faithful heart, and weariless brain!
> Ye build the future fair, ye conquer wrong,
> 　　Ye earn the crown, and wear it not in vain.[58]

---

[55] 'Unless the last six lines of the poem are carefully read, the reader will probably mistake the poet's meaning as expressed in the last line of all.' *Northern Star*, 4 November 1848, 3.
[56] Marx, 'Eighteenth Brumaire', 595–6.　[57] *Ibid.*, 597.
[58] *Northern Star*, 30 December 1848.

Another poem in the same column from an American, 'The Bondsmen Waking' by W. M. C. Hosmer, also rehearses the growth of the movement towards human freedom. The poem portrays a process wherein the bondsman first attains awareness of his situation as a slave, next becomes conscious of 'Great, equal Nature' and finally confronts the tyrant. The poetry column's editor describes these lines as 'not inappropriate to the present state of Europe and the prospects of the coming year'.

By the end of 1848 there is a sense of a pressing need to interpret the year's events in order to plan future strategy. Edwin Gill's 'Farewell to the Year Forty-Eight' is one such attempt to distil the year's historical lessons. It begins by hailing the 'strange, eventful year,' in which 'every land with liberty was rife'. 1848 is represented in quasi-apocalyptic terms as a time when 'Thrones tottered'; its advent greeted 'with rapture'. Yet this religious language is accompanied by a new vocabulary of class struggle; in France, Gill informs us:

> . . . the proletarians wove
> And wore the sacred wreath of liberty,
> Destroyed in June by the false *bourgeoisie*.[59]

The poem also celebrates the struggles of the Sicilians and the Viennese, singling out the leadership and heroism of Blum for special praise. Indeed, the martyred Blum becomes either the object or subject of sacrificial atonement as the reader is told 'crimson tears / Wash out his last indignity'. Gill affirms that 1848 'Hath taught a lesson, which after years / Shall turn to good account'. The nature of that lesson is expressed in somewhat abstract terms:

> . . . When man is rife
>   For freedom, he'll scorn each tyrant's fears,
> And teach the lesson he hath dearly bought,
> Till all his woes be on the oppressor wrought.

As the immediate context describes the ruthless betrayal and violent crushing of the revolution, the implicit lesson is of the historical necessity of proletarian violence. The poem's closing stanzas focus on a Britain which has become a place of intense political repression and human suffering. While the poem ends on a determinedly optimistic note, predicting an imminent 'day of reck'ning' and enjoining Chartists 'By deeds, not words, [to] prove their sincerity', the actions which it then depicts are defensive

---

[59] *Ibid.*

rather than aggressive: 'Support the class-made victims, and command / Success by being worthy liberty'. Thus it remains unclear whether Britain will have to experience the violence which accompanied political trans- formation in mainland Europe.

The final poem to appear in the poetry column for 1848 is the ano- nymous 'Better Times'. It is preceded by a short editorial commentary which illustrates the ambivalences and uncertainties which surround Chartist assessments of the year's meaning:

Farewell, then year of heroic deeds and terrible calamities – bright hopes and bitter disappointments! Thy seasons have witnessed many a battle for man's rights 'lost and won' – many a glorious victory succeeded by a death-dealing defeat of freedom's dauntless defenders.

. . .

May the year 1849 witness the completion of the good work commenced in 1848 – the good work of mankind's political and social regeneration. (*NS*, 30 December 1848)

'Better Times' opens with an unmistakable image of defeat, 'the desolate chief' who, as either fugitive or exile, offers the toast to better times, 'Though the signs of their coming grow faint and depart'. Despite this, the poem insists on the tenacity of hope which undergoes a temporal relocation to the distant future. In an image which anticipates Massey, 'tears' become the medium through which both present defeat and future victory are recognised:

> But concord and victory rise to his sight
>   Through the deluge of tears and of crimes,
> And he sees his hope's banner still float in the light
>   Of those future and far 'better times!'

The poem ends on a complex emotional note compounded of defi- ance, muted optimism, uncertainty and a sense of stoic endurance which teeters on the brink of fatalism. Although its final stanza begins by reminding readers that the movement has recovered from similar defeats in the past, it also countenances the possibility that the current defeat is complete and that previous political activities have been pointless, before ending with a defiant (but not necessarily convincing) assertion of the restoration of the movement's fortunes. Once more, this prediction belongs to the register of hope rather than anticipation or expectation:

> 'Better times!' – we have watched for their march to begin,
>   When the skies were as wintry as now;
> But it may be the world was less weary within,

And the toil-marks less deep on the brow.
'Better times!' – we have sought them by wisdom's calm ray;
We have called them with folly's gay chimes;
But they came not, and hope by the watch fire grows grey,
Yet to each and to all – 'better times!'

CHAPTER 7

Constellating Chartist poetry: Gerald Massey, Walter Benjamin and the uses of messianism

Thinking involves not only the flow of thoughts, but their arrest as well. Where thinking suddenly stops in a configuration pregnant with tensions, it gives that configuration a shock, by which it crystallizes into a monad. A historical materialist approaches a historical subject only where he encounters it as a monad. In this structure he recognizes the sign of a Messianic cessation of happening, or, put differently, a revolutionary chance in the fight for the oppressed past. He takes cognizance of it in order to blast a specific era out of the homogeneous course of history – blasting a specific life out of the era or a specific work out of the lifework.[1]

In his 'Theses on the Philosophy of History', Walter Benjamin enjoined Marxist critics to 'constellate' rather than 'tell' history, by bringing a threatened past into a meaningful relationship with an equally endangered present.[2] This chapter is both excursus and exemplum of the Benjaminian method in that it seeks to constellate the work of the Chartist poet, Gerald Massey, with that of Benjamin himself.[3] It will demonstrate that Massey's messianic vision of history anticipates many aspects of Benjamin's own messianism. Both, for example, will be shown to turn on the opposition between the 'homogeneous, empty time' of capitalist modernity and the charged potentiality of *Jetztzeit* ('the time of the now').[4] In addition, the chapter will demonstrate that, like Benjamin, Massey conceives of past and present as containing 'temporal indices' which refer to redemption,

[1] Walter Benjamin, Thesis XVII, 'Theses on the Philosophy of History', *Illuminations* (Fontana Press, 1992), 252–3. All further quotations from this work are taken from this edition and will be cited by reference to individual thesis, for example, W. Benjamin, Thesis IV.
[2] W. Benjamin, Thesis XVIIIA.
[3] An earlier draft of this chapter was presented at a *British Association of Victorian Studies* conference and I am grateful for the suggestions, comments and advice received at that event. I should also like to thank Professor Simon Dentith who encouraged me to pursue the comparison between Massey and Benjamin.
[4] W. Benjamin, Thesis XIV.

and that his task as a poet is to produce a 'constellation', a meaningful temporal alignment (of past and present) which allows those scattered 'chips of Messianic time' to be gathered together, thereby endowing the present with sufficient power 'to blast open the continuum of history' and usher in a new, just, social order.[5] Finally, the chapter also explores the poetics of social transformation with a particular emphasis on the relationship between forms of temporal understanding and political activity.

Gerald Massey was born on 29th May 1828 in Tring, Hertfordshire, the son of an illiterate father, William, and a semi-literate mother, Mary. Both his working life and poetic career began relatively early. Aged eight, he was sent to work in a local silk mill and some ten years later he published (by subscription) the improbably titled *Poems and Chansons by a Tring Peasant Boy.*[6] Massey's involvement with the Chartist movement began in 1848 when he joined the Uxbridge Young Men's Improvement Society. There he met John Bedford Leno with whom, in 1849, he founded the *Uxbridge Spirit of Freedom*, a short-lived radical periodical which nonetheless garnered praise from the leading Chartist newspaper, the *Northern Star*.[7] Indeed, between 1849 and 1851, Massey became the most published Chartist poet in the *Northern Star*'s poetry columns. In addition, throughout 1850 his poetry was frequently printed and reprinted in *The Red Republican* and *The Friend of the People* (both edited by G. J. Harney) and *Cooper's Journal* (edited by Thomas Cooper), making Massey the most important Chartist poet in the immediate aftermath of the continental revolutions of 1848.

By 1850, as a result of his friendship with Harney, Massey had become a serving member of the committee of the Society of Fraternal Democrats (an organisation of English and émigré, mainly German and Polish, socialists) and secretary to the committee of the *Red Republican* (which published the first English translation of Marx and Engels's *Communist Manifesto*). At the same time Massey was involved in the Christian Socialist movement where he found paid employment as secretary of the Working Tailors' Association (WTA).[8] However, Massey's Christian Socialist employers, unhappy at his involvement with the 'red republicans', told him to choose between the WTA and the *Red Republican*. Massey 'chose' paid employment with the WTA but continued to write for the *Red*

[5] W. Benjamin, Thesis XVI.
[6] D. Shaw, *Gerald Massey: Chartist, Poet, Radical and Freethinker* (Buckland Publications Ltd, 1995), 16–24.
[7] *Ibid.*, 26–29.   [8] *Ibid.*, 31–9.

Republican using the pseudonyms 'Bandiera' and 'Armand Carrel' whilst simultaneously writing for the *Christian Socialist*.[9]

In 1851 Massey published a shilling volume of his poetry, *Voices of Freedom and Lyrics of Love*, to generally favourable reviews in the radical press.[10] The following year he became, briefly, the literary editor of the *Star of Freedom* (formerly the *Northern Star*). However, by the end of 1852 Massey's active involvement with Chartism had ceased and thereafter he pursued a career as a poet, journalist, writer and lecturer. As a poet he enjoyed critical and commercial success with *The Ballad of Babe Christabel: together with other Lyrical Poems* (1854) which sold 5,000 copies in under a year. His journalistic appointments included a stint as editor of the *Edinburgh News* (1855–57) and another as poetry reviewer for the *Athenaeum*, as well as working for *All The Year Round, Good Words, Cassell's Magazine* and *Punch*. When familial and financial problems forced him to apply for a civil list pension in 1861, his application was supported by Carlyle, Ruskin, Browning, Tennyson, Thackeray and Landor. From the late 1860s onwards Massey became increasingly involved with spiritualism and embarked on a long study of ancient religions and myths.[11]

Massey's historical situation is, indeed, central to any understanding of his Chartist poetry, as Massey himself recognised later in his career when, in his *Collected Poems*, he styled these works 'Cries of 1848'.[12] As was noted earlier, Massey joined the Chartist movement in 1848, a year of revolution on the European mainland and of 'tumults and disturbances' throughout the British Isles.[13] Thus his entry into organised radical politics coincided with a period of revolutionary optimism and reactionary alarm. Likewise, his departure occurred as the fragmentation of Chartism signalled its collapse as a mass political movement.[14] The emotional intensity of the Chartist experience from 1848 to 1852, as the movement oscillated between euphoria and despair, with radical expectation modulating into

---

[9] *Ibid.*, 47.   [10] *Ibid.*, 51.   [11] *Ibid.*, 57–125.

[12] G. Massey, *My Lyrical Life: Poems Old and New* (Kegan, Paul & Tench, 1889). Unless otherwise stated, all quotations from Massey's work are taken from this edition. Publication details for those poems which appeared in the Chartist press are given in the body of the chapter. It should be noted that there are a number of differences (some significant, others less so) between the earlier and later versions of these poems. Differences which are directly relevant to this chapter will either be noted in the text or by way of footnote.

[13] John Saville, *1848. The British State and the Chartist Movement* (Cambridge University Press, 1990), 218.

[14] For a brief account of Chartism's decline after 1848 see E. Royle, *Chartism*, second edn. (Longman, 1986), 48–53. For a more detailed account of the movement's fragmentation see M. Taylor, *Ernest Jones, Chartism, and the Romance of Politics 1819–1869* (Oxford University Press, 2003), 137–94.

dogged resignation, finds its corollary in the heightened emotionalism of Massey's poetry.

Furthermore, it is this matrix of historical circumstance and its attendant emotional vectors which generates the messianism underpinning both Massey's poetics and his politics. Messianism, which generally emerges at moments of historical crisis, is a complex, sometimes contradictory, intellectual and emotional structure. It expresses a critical attitude towards the existing social order (the profane world which stands in need of redemption) and affirms a belief that a truly just society will, ultimately, be established. Yet despite its commitment to both social critique and social justice, messianism can engender and sustain political quietism as well as militancy. Similarly, it can be charged with either hope or despair. These contradictions (militant hope versus quietist despair) can be traced back to a fundamental antinomy within messianism concerning the question of agency. Within the messianic tradition, one strand insists that it is the Messiah alone who brings redemption, whilst the other argues that it is human activity that will initiate the messianic era with 'the arrival of the Messiah [serving as] the a posteriori signal that redemption has come'.[15] Therefore, messianism contains an optimistic and a pessimistic view of both human agency within, and human responsibility for, history. Messianism also displays a similar uncertainty as to the nature of the redeemed world. For example, in *Fragments of Redemption*, Susan A. Handelman, notes the very different ideal polities imagined by 'restorative' and 'apocalyptic' forms of messianism:

> The restorative tendency in the messianic idea envisions the return of a past condition remembered as ideal, the time of the First Temple and the Davidic Kingdom . . . But the utopian tendency presses forward to the vision of a future state, a condition which has never yet existed.[16]

However, it should be emphasised that these contradictions are only apparent at the level of critical reflection on the messianic tradition. Within messianism these contradictions co-exist. Indeed, it is possible that it is precisely the radical uncertainty of messianism with regard to agency which gives it its historical valency. Messianism, in short, allows the historical subject to feel both hope and despair, optimism and pessimism, agency

---

[15] E. Jacobson, *Metaphysics of the Profane: The Political Theology of Walter Benjamin and Gershom Scholem* (New York: Columbia University Press, 2003), 6.

[16] S. A. Handelman, *Fragments of Redemption* (Bloomington: Indiana University Press, 1991), 516. Handelman's distinction between 'restorative' and 'apocalyptic' forms of messianism is drawn from her reading of the work of Gershom Scholem.

and powerlessness, as constituent parts of a unitary historical process rather than as conflicting drives which in the very process of their apprehension threaten to rend that same subject. Furthermore, messianism can, perhaps, be understood as the process whereby the historical subject moves from hope to despair without needing to renounce the former or even, perhaps, without being aware of the move except retrospectively.

It is not difficult to understand messianism's appeal to Massey. Raised by a Calvinist mother, the biblical tropes and cadences of messianism would already be sufficiently familiar to provide him with a repertoire of images with which to imagine and represent radical social change.[17] Furthermore, that strand of messianic thinking which, in effect, assigns to human activity the power of summoning the Messiah imparts point and purpose to political activity especially at times of social upheaval, while its companion trend which gives 'all historical responsibility' to the Messiah provides a consoling optimism during periods of political quiescence.[18] It might even be suggested that messianism's central antinomy (the question of agency) is analogous to the unresolved strategic dilemma facing the Chartist movement. In this case, messianism would not only be psychologically and emotionally familiar (thus making itself a ready vehicle for the 'transcoding' of political problems) but it might also be sufficient to mask this radical uncertainty in the minds of Chartists themselves. Similarly, messianism's 'restorative' and 'apocalyptic' forms structurally resemble two key trends within late Chartism. The Land Plan may be seen as essentially restorative whilst the emergent republican/socialist trend can be thought of as apocalyptic.[19] Finally, the emphasis on collective redemption which is a distinguishing feature of Jewish messianism provides a further cognitive fit with Chartism.[20]

Benjamin's oeuvre contains two major reflections on messianism, the 'Theological-Political Fragment' (1921) and the better known 'Theses on the Philosophy of History' (1940). My main interest in these works stems from their analysis of the connection between agency and time in relation to redemption. Although in the 'Theological-Political Fragment',

---

[17] Shaw, *Gerald Massey*, 19.   [18] Jacobson, *Metaphysics of the Profane*, 25.
[19] On the Chartist Land Plan see Malcolm Chase, *The People's Farm: English Radical Agrarianism, 1775–1840* (Oxford: Clarendon Press, 1988).
[20] Emmanuel Levinas observes that Judaism has no equivalent to the Christian conception of individual salvation and, therefore, that Jewish messianism aims at the collective redemption of an entire society. E. Levinas, 'Messianic Texts', *Difficult Freedom: Essays on Judaism* (Athlone Press, 1990), 59–96. J. F. C. Harrison observes that the idea of collective as opposed to individual salvation is also a distinguishing feature of millenarianism, *The Second Coming: Popular Millenarianism 1780–1850* (Routledge & Kegan Paul, 1975), 8.

Benjamin's central concern is with the role of human agency in summoning the Messiah, there are some suggestive hints concerning the nature of messianic time. At one point, Benjamin proposes the following thesis:

the Kingdom of God is not the telos of the historical dynamic; it cannot be set toward a goal. Historically seen, it is not a goal but an end.[21]

Thus at an early stage of his intellectual development Benjamin sees redemption as the cancelling of history rather than its fulfilment. Redemption here is not a future state rather it involves the radical suspension of temporality.

By the time of 'Theses on the Philosophy of History' it is clear that Benjamin not only understands messianism as a reordering of human conceptions of temporality but is also alive to the ways in which such conceptions exert a profound influence on human agency. The fourteenth of the 'Theses on the Philosophy of History', famously contrasts the 'homogeneous, empty time' of capitalist modernity with *Jetztzeit* or the 'time of the now' which is shot through with 'chips of Messianic time'. As Benjamin makes clear, not only is the idea of progress inseparable from that of 'empty time' but the critique of the latter is a necessary precondition for the critique of the former. Terry Eagleton argues that for Benjamin 'empty time' is the time of the commodity, and this identification allows us to understand that 'empty time' is time without a future.[22] In 'empty time' the future is merely an intensified repetition of the present – the future is always simply 'improved' rather than 'new', to adapt the most revealing of capitalist modernity's articles of faith.

Against this unreal future Benjamin posits a real historical past. His second thesis contains a series of important claims:

The past carries with it a temporal index by which it is referred to redemption. There is a secret agreement between past generations and the present one. Our coming was expected on earth. Like every generation which preceded us, we have been endowed with a *weak* Messianic power, a power to which the past has a claim.[23]

The past too, it seems, contains 'a temporal index' ('chips of Messianic time') which indicates the presence of redemptive power. Moreover, there exists a 'secret' relationship between past and present based on the

---

[21] W. Benjamin 'Theological-Political Fragment' in Jacobson, *Metaphysics of the Profane*, 20.
[22] T. Eagleton, *Walter Benjamin or Towards a Revolutionary Criticism* (Verso, 1981), 29.
[23] W. Benjamin, Thesis II.

presence of 'a *weak* Messianic power' in every generation. Finally, because the messianic redemption of history must encompass the past as well as the present, the former has a 'claim' on the latter. The idea that the past 'has a claim' on the present generation contains an implicit rejection of unilinear, unidirectional time and opens the possibility of a properly reciprocal relationship between past and present.

Elsewhere, Benjamin stresses the extent to which the past can be a powerful, motivating force in present political struggles. Thesis XII, for example, assigns more power to images of 'enslaved ancestors' than to 'liberated grandchildren'. For Benjamin, it is historical memory (or remembrance) which alone is capable of seizing those 'chips of Messianic time' with which the past is studded and fusing them with the '*weak* Messianic power' of the present in order to create the portal or 'strait gate through which the Messiah might enter'.[24] Unlike 'empty time' which seeks to obliterate the past and negate the future, historical memory represents a desire to bring present and past into meaningful alignment thereby creating the conditions for redemption, which is envisaged as the cessation of time rather than the initiation of the future.

A similar, though not identical, 'constellating' process can be found in Massey's Chartist poetry written in the aftermath of 1848. Like Benjamin, Massey conceives of revolution as primarily a transformation of temporality (the political and social changes usually associated with revolution are seen as the necessary consequences of this prior, and fundamental, transformation), characterised by the replacement of 'homogeneous, empty time' by *Jetztzeit*. Both regard the past as carrying 'a temporal index by which it is referred to redemption' and emphasise the importance of 'remembrance' as a means of augmenting the '*weak* Messianic power' of the present. However, Massey and Benjamin part company on the question of the future, where Benjamin's scepticism contrasts with Massey's much more optimistic attitude towards the possibility of redemption through an idea of the future. This, in turn, accounts for their rather different conceptions of revolutionary possibility as the 'Messianic cessation of happening' (Benjamin) and an equally messianic inauguration of a redeemed future (Massey).

Massey's poetry, therefore, not only attempts to chart the relationships between past, present and future, but also to bring these three temporal states into a politically meaningful alignment. The clearest example of such a constellation in Massey's work is found in 'The Three Voices'

[24] W. Benjamin, Thesis XVIIIB.

(published originally in *Cooper's Journal*, no. 5, 2 February 1850),[25] which allocates one of the temporal states to each of its three stanzas. Thus the whole poem is an attempt to figure (both literally and poetically) the relationships between past, present and future. It begins with a decidedly non-heroic past represented as a site of oppression, and characterised through a series of baleful and inharmonious sounds:

> Like a sound from the Dead Sea all shrouded in glooms
> With breaking of hearts, fetters clanking, men groaning,
> Or chorus of Ravens that croak among tombs,
> It comes with the mournfullest moaning:
>   'Weep, weep, weep!'
> . . .
> 'Tis the Voice of the Past: the dark, grim-featured Past,
> All sad as the shriek of the midnight blast:

The voice of the past calls its listeners (addressed as 'Yoke-fellows', suggesting that solidarity is to be built on the basis of a shared economic and

---

[25] Massey, *My Lyrical Life*, 268–70. In the *Cooper's Journal* version the quoted lines read:

> Like a sound from the Dead Sea shrouded in glooms,
>   With breaking of hearts, chains clanking, men groaning,
> Or chorus of ravens that croak among tombs,
>   It comes with a mournful moaning,
>   Crying, 'Weep!'
> . . .
> 'Tis the voice of the Past – the dark, guilty Past,
> Sad as the shriek of the midnight blast.

Other changes include: the single (as opposed to the triple) iteration of 'Tearfully' and 'Fearfully'; 'Weep tears, to wash out the red, red stains' for 'Tears . . . terrible stain'; 'Be free! – and then work for the freedom of others' rather than 'Be Freemen: and then for the freedom of others / Work, work, work'. Massey also makes numerous small changes to the final verse which reads:

> There cometh another voice sweetest of all,
>   Cheerily,–
> And the heart leapeth up to its god-like call,
>   Merrily,–
> . . .
> It comes like a choir of the seraphim harping
>   Their gladsomest music around us –
> . . .
> To the voice of the Future, the sweetest of all,
> That makes the heart leap to its god-like call:
> Brothers, step forth in the Future's van,–
>   For the worst is past,–
>   Truth conquers at last,–
> And a better day dawns upon suffering man,
>   Hope, hope, hope!

political situation) to a mournful recollection of wrongs inflicted and sufferings endured, repeating its injunction to 'Weep, weep, weep'. However, the poem also holds out the possibility that these acts of remembrance might also provide the basis of redemption – 'Tears to wash out the terrible stain'.

The second stanza deals with the present and although its opening words, 'Another Voice', suggest difference, the emphasis initially falls on the continuities which exist between present and past. The present too is characterised by emotional and physical suffering, and its voice issues,

> Tearfully, tearfully, tearfully!
> From hearts which the scourges of Slavery rend,
> Fearfully, fearfully, fearfully!

The object of the address ('Yoke-fellows') also remains unchanged. However, the stanza suggests that the present differs from the past in a number of important ways. Most importantly, active inspiration replaces passive recollection. For example, where the past saw 'Yoke-fellows, listen, / Till tearful eyes glisten', the present sees 'Yoke-fellows, listen / Till *earnest* eyes glisten' (my emphasis), as the poem moves from passive pessimism to focused resolve. Not only has the injunction itself changed from '*Weep, weep, weep!*' to '*Work, work, work!*' but the meaning of 'work' is itself transformed within this stanza. When this refrain is first used, in connection with 'Mine, Forge, and Loom', its economic meaning is predominant. However, each time it is repeated it refers to political rather than to economic activity, and hence to the transformation of social relationships:

> Be Freemen: and then for the freedom of others
> Work, work, work!

The third stanza focuses on an already transformed future which is represented by a series of harmonious sounds:

> There cometh another Voice sweetest of all,
>> Cheerily, cheerily, cheerily!
> And my heart leapeth up at its clarion-call,
>> Merrily, merrily, merrily!
> . . .
> It comes like a choir of Celestials, harping
>> Their gladsomest music around us:

This imagery both recalls and redeems the images of inharmonious sounds used in the first stanza. In other words this is a future which exists in a determinate relation to its own past. In addition, this future exists in a complex relation to the present of the poem, for it is capable of inspiring the present and through such inspiration it secures its own realisation:

> The Voice of the Future, the sweetest of all,
> Makes the heart leap to its clarion-call.
>   Hope, hope, hope!
> Be of good cheer and step forth in the van;
>   For serfdom hath passed,
>   And labour at last
> Shall enter the Brotherhood common to Man:
>   Hope, hope, hope!

'The Three Voices' offers an example of the politically meaningful constellation of past, present and future, in which both past and future can possess agency in the present. The three time-states are conceived as comprising a sequence of discrete yet continuous stages, with each stage capable of transforming both itself and its contiguous state.

This conception of time is expressed in terms of both the form and content of the poem. In formal terms the three stanzas embody the three discrete time-states whilst the structural repetition-with-difference of each voice's injunction ('Weep', 'Work', 'Hope') and the reaction to each voice ('tearful', 'earnest', 'gleeful') combined with the simple repetition of 'Yoke-fellows, listen,' embodies the principle of continuity. History is conceived of as both a teleological and a voluntaristic process.[26] The past conditions the present and, thereby, the future. However, the past's influence on the present is multivalent: the inequalities and sufferings of the past *are* reproduced in the present but the conscious and sorrowful apprehension (or remembrance) of past sufferings can alter not only their significance, but also their consequences.

Thus, there is a sense in which the present may retroactively structure the very past of which it is the product. A similar complexity attends the relation of present to future. The future is made in the present and is, therefore, in one sense part of the fabric of the present itself. In another sense the future exists as a separate state beyond the present. However, it is in this second state that the future is capable of inspiring, which is to say restructuring, the present and thus pre-structuring itself. In this model of time, while the present provides the pivotal moment, neither past nor future can be ignored. Ideally, as in this poem, the three temporal states cohere in an alignment which sees the present transform itself into (but

---

[26] In this poem the historical process is teleological insofar as it has an intended destination, but also voluntaristic because the realisation of that intention ultimately depends on human activity.

also by means of) a future capable of redeeming the suffering of the past. However, Massey's poetry is also haunted by a fear that such an alignment will prove impossible.

Stated simply, Massey represents the present in dualistic terms as both a site of oppression and domination and as a site of resistance and change. It is the multiple relations generated both within this temporal estate and between it and its preceding and succeeding temporal states which impart a particular dynamism to Massey's poetry. Significantly, where Massey constructs the present as a site of domination the emphasis falls on the control of *space* rather than time. For example in 'The Battle-Call' (originally published as 'A Call to the People' in *The Red Republican*, vol. 1, no. 2, 29 June 1850) he writes, 'There's not a spot in all this dear land, / Where Tyranny's cursed brand-mark is not seen'.[27] Similarly in 'The Earth for All', in an image which connects the economic, political and gendered dimensions of oppression and exploitation, the present is understood in terms of spatial domination:

> Behold in bonds your Mother Earth;
> The rich man's prostitute and slave!
> Your Mother Earth, that gave you birth,
> You only *own* her for a grave![28]

Graves, both literal and metaphorical, provide a central image in this period of Massey's poetic career. One reason why the grave should feature so prominently is that it provides an exemplary image of working-class existence as negation. From William Benbow's *Grand National Holiday* onwards, this conception of working-class life as defined by its absences had long provided working-class radicals with both theory and theme for their social analysis.[29] It is a theme which Massey makes extensive use of in 'Anathema Maranatha' (published in *The Red Republican*, vol. 1, no. 18, 19 October 1850):[30]

---

[27] Massey, *My Lyrical Life*, 228–32. In *The Red Republican* the quoted lines read, 'There's not a spot in all this flowery land / Where Tyranny's scatheful footwork has not been'.

[28] Massey, *My Lyrical Life*, 232–3.

[29] 'For many years the people have done nothing for themselves. They have not even existed, for they have not enjoyed life. Their existence has been enjoyed by others; they have been, as far as regards themselves, *non-entities* . . . What working man can say he lives? Unless he says he lives when he is pining away piecemeal, producing with an empty stomach and weary limbs what goes to make others live . . . The existence of the working man is a *negative*.' William Benbow, *Grand National Holiday, and Congress of the Productive Classes* (Benbow, undated [1832]), 4–5.

[30] Massey, *My Lyrical Life*, 243–5.

> Love is the Crown of all life, but ye wear it not;
> Freedom, Humanity's palm, and ye bear it not;
> Beauty spreads banquet for all, but ye share it not;

and which he summarises succinctly in 'God's World Is Worthy of Better Men', 'Prepare to die? *Prepare to live! / We know not what is living*'.[31] The grave then stands as a summative image of the 'death-in-life' which, for Massey, constitutes the essence of working-class existence under the prevailing political and economic conditions.

Despite tyranny's dominance the present is rarely represented as a moment of despair. (Significantly the two poems which arguably offer the bleakest vision of the present, 'Anathema Maranatha' and 'Hope On, Hope Ever' (the latter originally published in the *Uxbridge Spirit of Freedom* and twice reprinted in the *Northern Star*, 8 September 1849 and 3 May 1851),[32] are poems which record an activist's sense of increasing frustration with and alienation from a 'people' who no longer seem interested in liberty.) This is largely due to the fact that the present is also represented as possessing a variety of restorative forces. For if the present is marked by negation in Massey's poetry it also holds the key to its own transformation, as is made clear by the fifth stanza of 'This World Is Full of Beauty' (published in *Cooper's Journal*, no. 14, 6 April 1850):[33]

> We hear the cry for bread with plenty smiling all around;
> Hill and valley in their bounty blush for Man with fruitage crowned.
> What a merry world it might be, opulent for all, and aye,
> With its lands that ask for labour, and its wealth that wastes away!
> This world is full of beauty, as other worlds above;
> And, if we did our duty, it might be as full of love.

This stanza not only figures the present as a series of absences – of bread, of labour, of wealth – but contrasts these absences with the abundance of nature. The implication of these lines is clear: scarcity and want arise from the existing political and social arrangements and not as the result of a deficient natural order. Again, the implied political lesson is plain to see, the realisation of a decent standard of living will require the transformation of those existing social and political structures.

Massey's poetry oscillates between a view of change as something which is either actual or latent within the present, and another, more millenarian vision, where change results from a miraculous intervention which occurs outside of time. It is the former view of change, as time-bound and already

---

[31] *Ibid.*, 271–3.   [32] *Ibid.*, 267–8.   [33] *Ibid.*, 273–8.

underway in the present, which dominates the final stanza of 'The People's Advent' (originally published in the *Uxbridge Spirit of Freedom* and reprinted in both the *Northern Star* 7 April 1849 and *The Red Republican*, vol. 1, no. 5, 20 July 1850).[34]

> Aye, it must come! The Tyrant's throne
>   Is crumbling, with our hot tears rusted;
> The Sword earth's mighty have leant on
>   Is cankered, with our best blood crusted.
> Room for the men of Mind! Make way
>   You Robber Rulers! – pause no longer!
> You cannot stay the opening day!
>   The world rolls on, the light grows stronger –
> The People's Advent's coming!

This contrasts with 'The Battle-Call' where change is represented as latent, yet also inexplicably unrealised, in the present:

> Immortal Liberty! We see thee stand
>   Like Morn just stepped from heaven upon a mountain
> . . .
> O! when wilt thou draw from the People's lyre
>   Joy's broken chord?

A noticeable difference between these two poems is that the latter privileges space, albeit abstractly conceived, over time, and that this emphasis somehow appears inimical to the poem's political aspirations. In Massey's poetry, transformed time seems much more imaginable than transformed space; it affirms as certain the realisation of 'liberty' in time whilst finding its realisation in space almost inconceivable.

The fact that Massey finds it easier to imagine and represent transformed time rather than transformed space helps, perhaps, to account for the significant roles played by both past and future in his poetry. As was noted earlier, the past in Massey's work prepares the way for both present and future. One of the ways in which the past achieves this is by providing an alternative to the dominated present. The contrast between heroic past and degraded present provides a theme for many Chartist writers and Massey is no exception to this general rule. The opening stanza of 'After the Struggle' focuses the contrast between active past and quiescent present by means of a metaphor of natural process – the loss of

---

[34] *Ibid.*, 226–8. *The Red Republican* version reads 'Kings, priests, and rulers' rather than 'You Robber Rulers!'

foliage in the autumn. The metaphor crystallises that sense of a falling off
of political activity:

> There's little left us now, Old Friend,
>   To cheer the Patriot's heart.
> The Altars where we knelt, Old Friend,
>   Grow desolate and cold;
> The faith is faint they felt, Old Friend,
>   In valiant days of old.[35]

However, such an overtly elegiac tone is rare in Massey's poetry which
usually emphasises the role of the past as a source of alternative, positive
values which are capable of present realisation. In 'The Battle-Call' he
invokes notions of 'Merry England' (third stanza) and of a lost Golden
Age (ninth stanza) as yardsticks against which the dominated present can
be measured. However, the aspect of the past which Massey values above
all else is the legacy of the struggle against tyranny. For him, it is the
image of 'resisting' rather than 'enslaved' grandfathers which will best
motivate Chartist struggle.

These past acts of resistance are the equivalent in Massey's work of
Benjamin's 'chips of Messianic time', and it is precisely these instances of
'*weak* Messianic power' which Massey seeks to collect and concentrate in
his poetry.[36] The sixth stanza of 'The Battle-Call' offers a good example
of such a concentration:

> Where is the spirit of our stalwart Sires,
>   Who rose and wrung their Rights from Tyrannies olden?
> Great Spirits have been here, for Freedom's fires
>   Live in their ashes, to earth's heart enfolden;
> The mighty Dead lie slumbering around,-
>   Whose names thrill through us as Gods were in the air;
> Life leaps from where their dust makes holy ground:
>   Their deeds spring forth in glory,- live all-where,-
>   But we are Traitors to the Trust they bade us bear.

Although this stanza opens by contrasting heroic past with degraded
present, the tone here is far from elegiac because Massey does not want to
represent a past which is hermetically sealed off from, and therefore
irretrievable to, the present. Rather, Massey is concerned with constellating
past and present in order to reactivate past values in the present. Indeed,

---

[35] Massey, *My Lyrical Life*, 254.
[36] Handelman likens the monad (or achieved constellation) to Benjaminian memory insofar as both
are produced by 'an act of *compression* which releases an otherwise unavailable meaning', *Fragments
of Redemption*, 172.

this stanza abounds in images of an ever present power which is, as yet, only intermittently actualised in the present ('Freedom's fires / Live in their ashes', 'Life leaps from where their dust makes holy ground: / Their deeds spring forth in glory, live all-where'). Additionally, in a striking anticipation of Benjamin, Massey acknowledges the past's claim on the '*weak* Messianic power' of the present, castigating the present generation as 'Traitors to the Trust' bequeathed them by their heroic ancestors.

The political challenge for Massey is to find a means of making the current generation conductors of the past's messianic power, and it is memory (conceived of as 'remembrance' in Benjamin's sense) which he considers capable of fulfilling this task. For Massey, memory is not simply a matter of recalling a past event or hero. Rather, it is to re-incarnate the political energies stored in the past, thereby producing a situation in which the names of the 'mighty Dead . . . / . . . thrill though us'. This image of the present generation as literal conductors of past political energies also occurs in 'The People's Advent' where Massey writes 'The lightning of their living thought / Is flashing through us, brain and bosom'. It is the immediacy of the union of past and present which is particularly striking as Massey depicts the regeneration of the revolutionary tradition through a form of apostolic succession, wherein the flame of rebellion is transferred immediately across generations. Similarly, in 'Our Martyrs' (published in *The Friend of the People*, no. 1, 14 December 1850)[37] the dying breath of the slain seems immediately to infuse the lungs of the present generation:

> They are gone!
> Yet 'tis well to die up-giving
> Valour's vengeful breath,
> To make Heroes of the living,

Unsurprisingly, the image of the martyr's grave recurs frequently in Massey's Chartist poetry. In poems such as 'The Battle-Call', 'A Cry of the People', 'After the Struggle' and 'It Will End in the Right',[38] the martyr's grave is simultaneously a sign of past political defeat and (as a focus for 'remembrance') a source of present political inspiration. The importance of the grave as a central trope in Massey's work is underscored by its metaphorical deployment to figure political states. For example, in 'The Battle-Call' not only is 'Tyranny' described as having 'Wedded our living hopes unto the grave' ('Wedded our living thoughts to the dark

---

[37] Massey, *My Lyrical Life*, 255–6.   [38] *Ibid.*, 264–6.

grave' in *The Red Republican* version), but the poem also asks its readers,
'O! how long will ye make your hearts its [Liberty's] living graves?'

Thus the grave is a decidedly polysemic image in Massey's work. As an
emblem of the 'death-in-life' status of working-class existence and a literal
representation of the death of the revolution, the grave is Massey's
equivalent of Benjamin's 'homogeneous, empty time' – the lifeless present of capitalist modernity which admits of no political change. Yet the
grave is also represented as a liminal, as well as a terminal, space; a portal
through which revolutionary energies may be transmitted. In this latter
aspect it is informed by an eschatological scheme drawn from Christianity
in which both the resurrection and second coming of Christ are used as
'types' of the revolution itself. As such, it is the equivalent of 'the strait
gate through which the Messiah might enter' in Benjamin's formulation.

However, despite providing a source of inspiration for current struggles, the past ultimately proves incapable of redeeming the present.
Massey's own historical logic comprehends the dominated present as the
result of failed previous liberation struggles. Past failure and present
impasse thus increase the importance of the future in Massey's poetry. As
was noted earlier, it is Massey's belief in a redemptive futurity which
constitutes the sharpest difference between his temporal politics and those
of Benjamin. Benjamin's primary objection to the idea of redemptive
futurity is that it rests on an idea of 'historical progress' which induces a
facile optimism and an enervating complacency in the putative agents of
historical change that is politically catastrophic.[39] Benjamin's thinking
here is informed by the failure of the German left to prevent the rise
of Nazism (and, additionally perhaps, by the earlier capitulation of the
Second International at the outbreak of the First World War). He
attributes this failure to 'the politicians' stubborn faith in progress' allied
to their conviction that they already represent the future which will arrive
as promised by the 'historical process' (see Theses X and XI). For Benjamin such a conception of the future can only produce an intensified
version of the present catastrophe.[40] Implicit in Benjamin's analysis is a
critique of the smooth unfolding of history, of the possibility of a seamless
(and painless) transition from one historical epoch into the next.[41] He

---

[39] W. Benjamin, Theses XII, XIII and XVIIIB.
[40] See, in particular, Benjamin's interpretation of Klee's 'Angelus Novus' in Thesis IX.
[41] Edward Bernstein's *Evolutionary Socialism* (1899) exemplifies this 'revisionist' trend within German
    Social Democracy. For a fuller discussion see D. McLellan, *Marxism After Marx*, second edn.
    (Macmillan, 1980), 20–56.

recognises that such an idea of redemptive futurity ultimately denies human agency. Not only will the future arrive as required, thereby obviating the need for human action, but the meaning of history will also be unveiled in its realisation. Against this Benjamin insists on the need for collective human action as the maker of both history and its meaning: 'Not man or men but the struggling, oppressed class itself is the depository of historical knowledge'.[42]

Occasionally Massey's poetry exhibits the facile optimism denounced by Benjamin, which asserts the inevitability of the desired historical outcome, as in the final stanza of 'Hope On, Hope Ever':

> Hope on, hope ever! after darkest night
>   Comes, full of loving life, the laughing Morning;
> Hope on, hope ever! Spring-tide, flushed with light,
>   Aye crowns old Winter with her rich adorning.
> Hope on, hope ever! yet the time shall come,
>   When man to man shall be a friend and brother;
> And this old world shall be a happy home,
>   And all Earth's family love one another!
>   Hope on, hope ever.

This stanza depicts a future which will be radically different from the present but there is little sense of human agency here. Instead there is a surfeit of natural metaphors (with all their attendant political ambiguities) as the poem affirms the desirability of social change but sees no way of securing it. A similarly insubstantial sense of agency informs 'The Chivalry of Labour'.[43] Like 'The Three Voices' this poem also seeks to bring past, present and future into politically meaningful alignment. Unlike 'The Three Voices', however, 'The Chivalry of Labour' identifies 'Beauty' rather than memory as the force capable of connecting past and present and of transforming the present into the future. As in 'Hope On, Hope Ever', social change occurs in a miraculous fashion by means of divine, external intervention, as Beauty ('Earth's crowning miracle!') transforms the present into a world of superabundance and harmony.

However, these poems are atypical and elsewhere Massey's poetry demonstrates the necessity of a redemptive futurity as a way of making present sacrifice and suffering meaningful. This idea receives its most powerful expression in 'To-day and To-morrow' where the first five stanzas

---

[42] W. Benjamin, Thesis XII. [43] Massey, *My Lyrical Life*, 278–81.

not only turn on the opposition between defeated present and victorious future but, in the manner of 'The Three Voices', posit a vital, reciprocal connection between the two temporal states: present struggle is a necessary precondition of the victorious future, but the idea of such a future is equally necessary to sustain current struggles:

> 'Tis weary watching wave by wave,
>   And yet the Tide heaves onward;
> We climb, like Corals, grave by grave,
>   That pave a pathway sunward;
> We are driven back, for our next fray
>   A newer strength to borrow,
> And where the Vanguard camps To-day
>   The Rear shall rest To-morrow![44]

The penultimate stanza also offers an image of how the present may not only project into, but also connect with, its preferred future: 'To many a heaven of Desire / Our yearning opes a portal'.[45]

In poems such as 'The People's Advent', 'The Battle-Call', 'After the Struggle' and 'The Three Voices' this redemptive future is portrayed as the culmination of a teleological process, usually figured as the actual fulfilment of humanity's potential. In 'The People's Advent', Massey writes '[the People] shall write the Future's page / To our Humanity more truthful'. However, this should not be confused with a commitment to the notion of 'progress' (in Benjamin's sense). Massey's poetry rarely offers a seamless transition from present into future. Instead, his verse emphasises rupture and discontinuity, with the bridge between present and future often provided by the trope of revolution figured as Christian apocalypse. In 'The Battle-Call', for example, Massey (alluding to Matthew 27:51) writes, 'Earthquakes leap in the Temples, crumbling Throne and Power'. Similarly, the version of 'Our Martyrs' published in *The Friend of the People* unambiguously identifies the revolutionary with the (Christian) messianic; the fallen foot-soldiers of the revolution are described as 'Murdered where for Right they stood! / Murdered, Christ-like, doing good', and their bodily sufferings echo Christ's agony:

---

[44] *Ibid.*, 281–3.
[45] Massey's lines here anticipate the work of Franz Rosenzweig, an important influence on Walter Benjamin. In his discussion of Benjamin's 'Theological-Political Fragment', Eric Jacobson observes that Benjamin (under Rosenzweig's influence) is particularly interested in the power, inherent in human activity, to create a 'portal, through which redemption makes its entrance', *Metaphysics of the Profane*, 31.

And hands are agony-clencht!
See them! Count their wounds! ha! Now
There's a glory where the plough
Of Pain's fire-crown seam'd each brow.[46]

Although, it might appear that Benjamin and Massey disagree on the possibility of a redemptive futurity, I want to suggest that the disagreement is purely one of terminology. Both writers are searching for ways of expressing an alternative temporality which is capable of redeeming both past and present. Similarly, both agree that this alternative temporality can only be achieved through the negation of 'homogeneous, empty time' by *Jetztzeit* and, in turn, that this depends on a constellation which augments the 'weak Messianic power' of the present with that of the past. Both insist on the necessity for collective human agency and envisage messianic change in terms of an absolute rupture, which is nonetheless produced within, and as a result (by no means inevitable) of the historical process.[47]

For both Benjamin and Massey there is no contradiction between a belief in the messianic properties of revolution and a commitment to human agency. However, the messianism of both writers is ghosted, as it were, by millenarianism.[48] The key difference between the messianic and the millenarian (in the sense in which these terms are being used here) is

---

[46] This equating of the travails of the activist with the sufferings of Christ also occurs in 'The Kingliest Kings' (originally published as 'The Kingliest Crown' in *Cooper's Journal* no. 8, 23 February 1850 and reprinted in the *Northern Star*, 21 June 1850), *My Lyrical Life*, 266–7. Equally audaciously, Massey ventriloquises God as revolutionary agitator in 'The Earth for All':

> *Thus saith the Lord:* You weary me
> With prayers, and waste your own short years:
> Eternal Truth you cannot see
>   Who weep, and shed your sight in tears!
> In vain you wait and watch the skies,
>   No better fortune thus will fall;
> Up from your knees I bid you rise,
>   And claim the Earth for All.

[47] Although Benjamin describes this change as 'a Messianic cessation of happening' whilst Massey emphasises what might be described as a 'Messianic inauguration of being', this should not be allowed to obscure the fact that both descriptions unmistakably refer to a radical transformation of temporality.

[48] For a fuller discussion of millenarianism and its relationship to radical politics in the first half of the nineteenth century see Harrison, *Second Coming*, and E. P. Thompson, *The Making of the English Working Class* (Harmondsworth: Penguin, 1980), especially 'The Chiliasm of Despair' section in Chapter 11.

that the former can be thought of as possessing desire and agency whilst the latter consists of desire alone. Benjamin's 'Theses on the Philosophy of History' signals his awareness that under the pressure of historical circumstance the messianic can be displaced by the millenarian. Indeed his analysis of the failings of German social democracy can be read as an account of just such a displacement and its consequences. However, Massey does not consciously differentiate between the messianic and the millenarian in his poetry. This is a function of Massey's historical situation, in that his Chartist poetry is written, initially, at an unmistakable moment of *Jetztzeit* (the revolutionary wave of 1848) whose resonances and reverberations persist (with varying degrees of intensity) for a number of years thereafter. At the same time, Massey is writing during a moment of profound historical defeat, which his verse also, in places, apprehends. The messianic impulses in his work signal the presence of revolutionary expectations whilst the millenarian provides Massey with a means of managing historical disappointment by allowing the deferral of such expectations to some unspecified future time (or, in the case of Spiritualism, future state).[49]

'Hope On, Hope Ever' provides the clearest example of a millenarian poem and, therefore, allows us to identify the crucial differences between millenarianism and messianism. Perhaps the most noticeable feature of this poem is the narrowness of its temporal horizons. Its main focus is on the present, and the past only appears as the immediate personal past of the poem's speaker and its addressee. There is no sense of a collective history in the poem. Furthermore, whilst a redeemed future appears in the closing lines of the third and fourth stanzas, it is a future which is 'coming' ('shall come') but which is not generated in the present. Thus, 'Hope On, Hope Ever' offers its readers a redeemed future which is essentially disconnected from the present, and a present which enjoys no vital connection with the past.

The sense of disconnection extends from the temporal to the political. The poem emphasises the isolation of the activist, whose 'loneliness' is increased by the apparent absence of any wider movement – 'thou must toil 'mong cold and sordid men, / With none to echo back thy thought or love thee'. The sense of isolation is underscored by the uncharacteristic use of the poetic 'I' by Massey. In similar fashion, God, the guarantor of

---

[49] For further details of the relationship between radicalism and spiritualism in the post-Chartist period see Logie Barrow, *Independent Spirits: Spiritualism and English Plebeians 1850–1910* (Routledge, 1986).

ultimate victory in this poem, exists apart from the movement ('God is over all') and is no longer identical with it as in poems such as 'Our Martyrs', 'The Earth for All' and 'It Will End in the Right' which proclaims 'be our God revealed / In our lives, our works, in our warfare for man'. Equally tellingly, the desired transformation is achieved without apocalypse or rupture. Tears rather than blood mark the site of the conflict which itself is cast in abstract terms as a contest between 'Error' and 'Truth', 'That Error from the mind shall be uprooted, / That Truth shall flower from all this tear-dewed dust'.

In the preparatory sketches for his 'Theses on the Philosophy of History' Benjamin noted, 'Three moments must be made to penetrate the foundations of the materialist view of history: the discontinuity of historical time; the destructive power of the working class; the tradition of the oppressed'.[50] It is precisely the absence of the first two moments and the attenuated presence of the third which distinguishes the millenarian 'Hope On, Hope Ever' from Massey's messianic poetry. Millenarianism encodes a crisis of agency, doubly figured as absence of violent rupture and the concomitant presence of 'homogeneous empty time' which prevents political change. Under the pressure of this crisis the desired social transformation becomes a matter of personal wish or fantasy (rather than the object of a collective project), exemplified by the third stanza of 'Hope On, Hope Ever':

> Yet from Earth's cold Real
> My soul looks out on coming things, and cheerful
> The warm Sunrise floods all the land Ideal;[51]

In contrast, the messianic is marked by the presence of all three moments. Massey's insistence on the necessity of producing a politically meaningful alignment of past, present and future testifies to the 'discontinuity of historical time'. Moreover, while Massey's method of constellating past and present in order to re-activate past acts of resistance and fuse them with current struggles attests to 'the tradition of the oppressed'; his use of martial and apocalyptic imagery clearly acknowledges 'the destructive power of the working class'. Finally, the image of the grave serves, in

---

[50] Cited in R. Wolin, *Walter Benjamin: An Aesthetic of Redemption* (New York: Columbia University Press, 1982), 261. For the 'tradition of the oppressed', see W. Benjamin, Thesis VIII, and Eagleton, *Walter Benjamin or Towards a Revolutionary Criticism*, 48 and 73.

[51] This was originally the second verse of 'Hope On, Hope Ever', see *Voices of Freedom and Lyrics of Love*, 29.

Massey's poetry, as a concentrated trope of the messianic: simultaneously registering past resistance and present violence, and in so doing creating the temporal conditions which will inaugurate the redeemed future; wherein, as Massey reminded his readers in *The Red Republican*, the people 'shall write the Future's page / To our Humanity more truthful'.[52]

---

[52] G. Massey, 'The People's Advent', *My Lyrical Life*, 226.

Appendix A: Three Chartist Poems

CHARLES DAVLIN, 'ON A CLIFF WHICH O'ERHUNG'
(*NORTHERN STAR*, 5 OCTOBER 1839, 7)

On a cliff which o'erhung the huge billows that hove
    Their white foam, to the war waging skies;
Sat Britannia consulting the daughter of Jove,
    Rebel faction, how best to chastise.
When Minerva, soft tuned as the lute on the gale,
Said the gods had decreed hence that justice prevail,
That the millions, whose pacific arguments fall,
    Shall for death or for liberty rise.

Whilst contemn'd and despised are the lion and crest,
    Shall the late laurell'd Queen of the waves
Boast her millions so long, so exclusively blessed,
    So remote from the bondage of slaves?
Shall her time-serving tools still continue to sing,
Of her famed Constitution, Lords, Commons, and King,
While a Church and Statemongrel, hermaphrodite thing,
    That loud long-boasted, lion outbraves?

Shall hoarse Neptune's proud daughter, whose menace was fate,
    Deign to plead, but with scorn to be heard,
And her famed royal brute, by mere monkeys of state,
    Be audaciously pluck'd by the beard?
Ere that the lion should long thus in torpitude sleep,
Or thyself thus degraded, degenerate weep,
Be thy last crumbling atoms dispers'd through the deep,
    Nor the tomb of thy mem'ry be rear'd.

That fell hydra, which preys on thy heart's inmost core,
Still around thee whose coils vilely hang
That political tape-worm, from darkness of yore
    And the law primogeniture sprang.
Now the mandate of Jove and of justice obey,

Spurn the paltry, proud, profligate, impotent sway,
From thy blood-yielding pelican bosom away,
    Pluck the lazy legitimate fang.

But the curse that hath clouded the children of men,
    Immemorially, near and afar,
Superstition must die, ere the mountain and glen,
    Bid adieu to the echoes of war;
Ere the blood-crimson'd shore, the incarnadined wave,
The fell stripes of the tyrant, the tears of the slave,
Or those terrors, that erst have encompass'd the grave,
    Cease the bliss of life's being to mar.

Hast thou heard not the last cry of Poland, and hast
    Thou not blush'd, all inactive, to see
The first people on earth by the hurricane blast,
    Swept away all unaided by thee?
E'en the all-flaming Mars crimson'd heaven with a blush,
On beholding the Autocrat's demonic rush,
With his million of carnage-dyed bayonets to crush
    The brave legions, who died to be free.

Yet the Poles are immortal! though victory crown'd
    Not those heroes to mem'ry enshrined;
They have burst that vile cobweb, the bandage that bound
    The more recreant part of mankind.
Though the tower-shielded tyrant may boast his defence,
From the soldier and slave, cannon, sabre, and lance,
The declension of Empire was dated from thence,
    Europe's purple-robed ruffians shall find.

'Twere delusion to deem e'er that freedom divine,
    Blessed thy Peer and thy priest-ridden shore,
That the cause dear to Poland was equally thine
    Which bedrench'd her in patriot gore,
Is a fact she exclaim'd as revolting as true!
Go remember the feats of the fam'd Peterloo;
When on air-cleaving pinions, like Mercury flew,
    The celestial of light and of lore.

CHARLES DAVLIN, 'QUESTIONS FROM THE LOOM'
(*NORTHERN STAR*, 28 JULY 1838, 7)

    Oh, tell me ye tyrants of earth!
    Ere arrive the retributive hour,
Tell the millions degraded, the butt of your mirth,

What distinguishes noble from ignoble birth?
  Whence arises, what constitutes power?
Now your bark is at sea, and your mariner's sleep,
Tho' the dark gloom of thunder half shadows the deep.

    Oh, where is your pilot, and where
    Are your means, whence to buffet the storm?
Now the dark gulf beneath you behold and beware,
From the sea rifted wreck who would shoreward repair,
    Can but reach by the raft of reform.
Fate frowns dark on your windward, rocks rise on your lee,
Leave the hulk of your hopes or ye founder at sea.

    Ye who scoff when a nation complains,
    When all mangled it bleeds at the core!
How, when millions in bondage shall sever their chains,
Bidding war's brazen trump banish peace from you plains,
    Will you silence the cannon's dread roar?
Or behold undismayed and with pitiless eyes
Desolation's dark columns ascend to the skies?

    Shall those bastiles of famine late built
    For divorce – child bereavement – and woe
Blast the land of our fathers, and cold-blooded guilt
Stay the gripe of the torch and the dagger's dark hilt
    In revenge? fell despair answers no.
For the mob on those *grounds* you their franchise refuse
Having nought to protect can have nothing to lose.

    Yet that mob or what else you may please
    They from whom you your grandeur derive;
Who the battle field brave, the deep mine and seas;
But to nurture your pride aggrandizement and ease
    Could expel every drone from the hive;
Where the check of populationists find with alarm
That improvident marriages cumber the swarm.

    Ye despoilers o'er earth, of your kind,
    All your hope blighting prospects were vain,
Were you still, to the times so besottedly blind
As to deem that the mob whom your manacles bind,
    Cannot burst the vile bondage in twain.
Inoffensive shall fall the red blade of your trust
And your cloud-cleaving citadel crumble to dust.

    They whose thousands have passively died
    Ere a death wound to *patience* was given,
As a power long insulted by impatient pride

Shall the millions to whom due redress is denied
   Make appeal to their strength and to Heaven.
Is that *source* whence your wealth and your mightiness come,
Restitution to reap at the roll of the drum?

   Beard no more sleeping vengeance with deeds;
   Such as yet you might vainly deplore;
Tho' with judgement suspended morality pleads
And with patience e'en carnal omnipotence bleeds,
   Dread the burst of an Etna the more.
For the darkness of yore superseded shall be
By the effulgence of reason the light of the free.

   Yes: the night of delusion is by
   And the heart gladd'ning glimpses of man
Make the clouds of corruption dissolve as they fly;
   Glows the life-beam of ages unborn!
When fell wars cease to crimson green earth and blue wave,
And alike shall unknown by the tyrant and slave.

P. B. TEMPLETON, 'TO THE 'DEAR LITTLE DEAD'
(*NORTHERN STAR*, 19 JANUARY 1839, 7)

Sleep! sleep little babes on your ocean pillow!
   Sleep 'mid the foam of your watery bed!
Sleep, 'mid the rage of the stormy billow,
   That entombs the young and the hoary head!

Dark was the dawn of your earthly morning;
   Hidden your sun, and cloudy your sky!
No bright solar rays your horizon adorning;
   You lived, but 'twas only to breathe and die!

Deep in the depths of the fathomless ocean –
   Deep is the grave where your ashes repose!
Deep 'midst that darkness – that ceaseless commotion,
   Whose long-hidden secrets no tongue can disclose!

On your grave the fond eye of a mother's affection
   Ne'er shall gaze, – nor the tear of pity be shed;
For no sod marks the spot where the sad recollection
   Might restore to her bosom the dear little dead.

Rest! rest little babes on your ocean pillow!
   Rest 'mid the foam of your watery bed;
Rest, till the rage of the stormy billow
   Shall have spent all its fury – then yield up the dead.

Then wake, little babes, from that ocean pillow;
    Wake from the foam of that watery bed;
Wake to contemn the stormy billow,
    And rise to mingle no more with the dead.

Rise to re-join your affectionate mother,
    And unite in the melodies angels shall sing;
Where the friend and the father, the sister and brother,
    Their songs to the throne of Jehovah shall bring.

Leeds, Jan. 14, 1839

The occasion of these lines is the death of three lovely children who left Leeds, with their mother, in August last, for Canada, and who, dying on their passage, were committed to the deep. The mother of the children was the sister of the writer, and the only remaining member of his family in England.

Appendix B: Details of Poetry published in the poetry column of the Northern Star

1838

6 January 1838	John Smithson, 'Working Men's Rhymes – No. 1'
13 January 1838	B. Smith, 'The Tear of Beauty'
20 January 1838	J. B. Walker, 'Plaint of the Wandering Irish Peasant'
3 February 1838	B. T., 'Answer to Beauty's Tear'
	T. B. Smith, 'Lines on the Conviction of the Glasgow Cotton Spinners'
17 February 1838	A. L., 'The Slaves: Address to British Females'
	L., '[Two] Sonnets Addressed to a Certain Lord'
3 March 1838	T. B. Smith, 'The Smile of Beauty (A Counterpart to the Tear of Beauty)'
	J. B. Walker, 'The Portrait of Arthur O'Connor'
24 March 1838	J. Gower, 'New Poor Law Rhymes: The Wanderer'
	L. S., 'Lines on Factories'
31 March 1838	Robert Dibb, 'The Victim of the Lash'
7 April 1838	Philo-Beranger, 'Do Kings or Nobles Care for Us?' (reprinted from *Tait's Magazine*)
14 April 1838	Joseph Middleton, 'The Bonnie Green Banners'
	Mrs Wallworth, 'The Last Journey' (reprinted from *Blackwood's Magazine*)
28 April 1838	T. B. Smith, 'Anti-Poor Law Rhymes No.1: Gradual Oppression of the Labourer'
	'L-d M-dst-ne', 'Leeds Conservative Festival'
	Anon., 'Song (Sung by Lords Wharncliffe and Maidstone at the Close of the Easter Festivities)'
5 May 1838	S. Gower, 'The Wanderer's Death Bed'
12 May 1838	Robert Dibb, 'The Death of Lucy Ashton, or, The Factory Girl's Last Hour'
19 May 1838	F. Saunderson (A Female Cottager), 'Spring Reflections'

26 May 1838	Robert Dibb, 'The Standard-Bearer: A Tale of the Wars'
	J. H. M., 'On the Inequality of the Lot of Man'
2 June 1838	Robert Buchanan, 'Black and White Slavery'
	Robert Dibb, 'The Gathering of the Great Northern Union'
23 June 1838	Pumkin Vine, 'An American Hit at Fopism'
	Anon., 'To Mr and Mrs S–'
30 June 1838	Anon., 'Soliloquy, of one of the Banished Cotton Spinners Written by one of the Trade'
7 July 1838	John Taylor, 'To the Memory of Augustus Harding Beaumont'
14 July 1838	Morian, 'The Labourer's Orison at Sunrise'
28 July 1838	T. B. Smith, 'Oh Tell Me Not'
	Charles Davlin, 'Questions from the Loom'
11 August 1838	Thomas Campbell Esq., 'The Parrot, a Domestic Anecdote'
18 August 1838	T. Lister, 'Sunset Musings in Milan'
25 August 1838	L. S. T., 'The Harrogate Visitor's Excursion Guide'
1 September 1838	Aristides, 'Sacred Lyrics No. XII, The Dying Republican to his Comrades'
22 September 1838	J. Hutchinson, 'Sonnet – The Old Soldier'
	Anon., 'The Mob and the People'
6 October 1838	G. W., 'To the Queen'
	T. B. Smith, 'England Arise!'
13 October 1838	Robert Dibb, 'The Song of Liberty for the Great Northern Union'
27 October 1838	Robert Dibb, 'Gilbert Weldon: Or the March of Crime'
	Robert Southey, 'Inscription'
3 November 1838	Robert Dibb, 'Grace Darling'
10 November 1838	T. S. L., 'The Voice of Liberty!'
	Robert Southey, 'Inscription'
	Anon., 'The Patriot's Prayer' (reprinted from the *Scotch Reformer's Gazette*)
17 November 1838	C. Tunnicliffe, 'The Value of Liberty Illustrated by Napoleon's Plaint to a Swallow, when in Exile'
	T. B., 'A Lyric Poem. Who Are My Friends?'

24 November 1838	John Goddwin Barmby, 'The Briton's Fatherland'
	Anon., 'The Impressed Sailor's Child'
	Anon., 'Alexander the Great!!'
1 December 1838	Robert Nicoll, 'I Am Blind'
8 December 1838	Christian Reflector, 'Dying Speech of a War-Horse to a Prince'
	Robert Southey, 'Inscription'
15 December 1838	C. N. S., 'To an Infant Daughter'
22 December 1838	A. S. G., 'What is a Peer?'
	Anon., 'The Sailor's Orphan Boy'
	Anon., 'The Free Torch Beam'
29 December 1838	David Mawson, 'The Orphan and the Lord' and 'On the Death of a Poor Highland Soldier'

1839

5 January 1839	T. Z. Y., 'The Contrast'
12 January 1839	T. B. Smith, 'An Acrostic'
	Anon., 'A Familiar Epistle to the Queen'
	Anon., 'The Holy Alliance of Nations'
19 January 1839	P. B. Templeton, 'To the Dear Little Dead'
26 January 1839	T. T., 'Lost to the World and to Me. To * * *'
	Peter, 'The King's Evil'
	T. B. Smith, 'The Nativity. Stanzas for Christmas Day'
2 February 1839	Lacon, 'Cock-Fighting'
	A. S. G., 'Lines on Finding A Tennis-Ball'
9 February 1839	T. T., 'Restored to the World and to Me. To * * *'
16 February 1839	Anon., 'Evening'
23 February 1839	Swing, 'Captain Swing to Lord Howick' (reprinted from the *Northern Liberator*)
	Peter Thimble, 'Peter Thimble to Lord Durham' (reprinted from the *Northern Liberator*)
2 March 1839	John Peacock, 'Conventional Hymn' (Air: 'Rule Britannia')
	J. N. J., 'The Governor's Request Not Granted'
9 March 1839	Anon., 'The Lament for the Lost' (reprinted from the *New Monthly*)
16 March 1839	T. W., 'The Tricolour'
	Anon., 'Hymns for the Unenfranchised No. III'
23 March 1839	Anon., 'Lord P-LM-ST-N's Vision' (reprinted from the *Morning Herald*)

30 March 1839	Anon., 'The M.P.' (reprinted from the *Northern Liberator*)
6 April 1839	Robert Dibb, 'On the Birth of My Son' Anon., 'A State'
13 April 1839	Percy Bysshe Shelley, 'To the People [from *The Masque Of Anarchy*]' (reprinted from *The National*)
20 April 1839	Mary Howitt, 'Nature Versus Malthus' Raleigh, 'On Death' D., 'Beauty'
27 April 1839	Percy Bysshe Shelley, 'To the Men of England' Cowper, 'Cowper, Versus Tory-Whiggery' (from *Winter: Morning Walk*)
4 May 1839	T. Moore Esq., 'Song' ('To those we love we've drank tonight') T. H., 'Liberty' and 'The Day Star of Freedom'
11 May 1839	Alex Laing, 'Jock, Rab and Tam; or, Natural Requisites for the Learned Professions' (reprinted from *Whistle-Binkie*) Gardener's Gazette, 'The Violet's Spring Song' Moore, 'Song of the Freeman'
18 May 1839	E. H. (A Factory Girl of Stalybridge), 'On Joseph Rayner Stephens'
8 June 1839	Anon., 'Linger Not Long' (reprinted from the *Birmingham Journal*) Eliza Cook, 'Song of the Worm'
22 June 1839	Anon., 'Printing Office Melody. The Pressman' (reprinted from the *York Paper*)
29 June 1839	Anon., 'Lines by a Factory Operative'
6 July 1839	T. B. Smith, 'The Seals'
13 July 1839	Two Ultra-Radical Ladies, '[Two] Songs for the People' Anon., 'Fall, Tyrants, Fall!' (Sung on Lillsley Hill, at the Great Demonstration Gloucester, near Stroud)
20 July 1839	Percy Bysshe Shelley, 'The Arguments of Tyranny' (from *The Revolt of Islam*)
3 August 1839	Anon., 'The Future Life' Anon., 'Stray Rhymes on Woman'
10 August 1839	Caroline Bowles, 'Youth, Manhood, and Old Age' Revd H. Alford, 'How Fare the Dead?'

17 August 1839	Bayley, 'The Love of Woman' (reprinted from the *Birmingham Advertiser*)
31 August 1839	W. McDouall, 'Lines for the 'Star''
7 September 1839	T. B. Smith, 'The Wish'
14 September 1839	Anon., 'My Old Coat' (from the French of De Beranger)
	H. Drapier, 'Chartist's Appeal to the Queen'
21 September 1839	Cecini, 'Death of Chatterton'
28 September 1839	Eliza Cook, 'The King of the Air'
	Anon., 'The Loves of the Plants'
5 October 1839	Charles Davlin, Untitled ('On a cliff which o'erhung the huge billows that hove')
	Anon., 'The Working Man's Song' (reprinted from *Tait's Magazine*)
12 October 1839	Anon., 'Chester Gaol'
19 October 1839	Wm. Calder, 'The Destiny of Man'
	A Phrenologist, 'Night Thoughts'
	Anon., 'From the French of Victor Hugo' (reprinted from the *Court Circular*)
26 October 1839	Trimbush, 'An Admirer of the New Poor Law'
	Mrs Leigh Cliffe, 'The Aconite'
	Leigh Cliffe, Esq., 'Epigrams'
2 November 1839	Percy Bysshe Shelley, '[Extract from] Queen Mab'
	Thomas Watson Jun., 'The Fair One'
9 November 1839	Anon., 'The Right Divine'
	Bryant (An American Poet), 'The Winds'
23 November 1839	A. Park, 'Philosophical Links' (an extract from *Blindness*)
30 November 1839	Anon., 'Crumbs of Comfort for the Single Ladies of Anywhere, Affectionately Presented to them by the Married Ladies of Somewhere' (reprinted from an Old Newspaper)
7 December 1839	M., 'Prospects, Present and Future' (from *John Bull*)
14 December 1839	Anon., 'Lord Tomnoddy; or, The Execution. A Sporting Anecdote'
21 December 1839	Anon., 'Advertisement and Sale Extraordinary' (reprinted from *John Bull*)
	T. N., 'A Railroad Song' (reprinted from the *Morning Chronicle*)

28 December 1839	Anon., 'Song from the German' (reprinted from *Tait's Magazine*)
	Gateshead Observer, 'The New Grievance. – The Church Forgotten'

1840

4 January 1840	John Goodwin Barmby, 'The Irish Fatherland' and 'The Mechanics of Young England – a Berangeism'
25 January 1840	Edward Thomas, 'Sonnet to Fame'
	G. M., 'Sonnet. – The Poet's Solitude'
1 February 1840	Anon., 'God'
	P. W. B., 'Acrostic' (John Frost)
8 February 1840	Anon., 'The Judges Are Going to Jail' (reprinted from *John Bull*)
15 February 1840	The Corn Law Rhymer [Elliott?], 'Epithalamium on The Marriage of Queen Victoria The First'
22 February 1840	Sigma, 'The Maid of Warsaw'
	W. McDouall, 'Now Wide and Far the Tyrant's Power Prevails'
	Philip Bevan, 'The Covenanters'
29 February 1840	R. M. B., 'Nursery Rhymes. Little Jack Horner Sat in a Corner. New Reading'
	J[ohn] W[atkins], 'Sheriff Wheelton to the House of Commons'
	William S. Villiers Sankey M. A., 'Ode' ('Men of England, ye are slaves')
	Anon., 'The Bishop and the Bible'
7 March 1840	J. L., 'The Vision of Liberty' [poss. John Lefevre?]
	Philip Bevan, 'Frost'
	Anon., 'Privilege (A Few Lines after Pope)'
14 March 1840	Anon., 'Cabinet Resolutions to Satisfy the Country'
28 March 1840	Jonathan Lefevre, 'The Enslaved'
	J[ohn] W[atkins], 'Swarthone'
	W., 'To My Melancholy'
4 April 1840	Eliza Cook, 'The Tree of Death'
	Sylvan, 'Lines Suggested By Daniel O'Connell's Visit to the Anti-Corn Law Dinner, at Manchester'

13 June 1840	James French, 'Lines: In Answer to Enigma for Radicals'
	P., 'The True Hero'
	John Cook, 'Address to Erin'
	W. G., 'The Swallow'
20 June 1840	Harold, 'Lines' ('O! let me tread the mountain path where slave')
	A Devonian, 'Sonnet to Knowledge'
	Anon., 'Air' ('Swearing death to tyrant King')
	Aneurim, 'Cambria'
27 June 1840	Samuel Whitlock, 'Lines to Feargus O'Connor, Esq.'
	Spartacus, 'Green Tails; A Weaver's Song' (Air: 'The Roast Beef of Old England')
	Iota, '[2] Sonnets Devoted To Chartism'
4 July 1840	[Feargus O'Connor], 'Untitled' ('From East to West, From North to South')
11 July 1840	[Feargus O'Connor], 'Looking-Glass Poetry from York Castle'
25 July 1840	Anon., 'The Queen Dowager at Leeds'
	Anon., 'Groan Again, My Bonny Neddy, a Parody by the Queen Dowager'
	Anon., 'The Lament of our Beloved Captive, John Frost, Esq.'
	Anon., 'The Captive's Dream'
1 August 1840	George Binns, 'John Frost' (Tune: 'The Gallant Hussar')
	J[ohn] W[atkins], 'Lines on Mulgrave Castle, The Seat of the Marquis of Normanby'
	Iota, '[4] Sonnets Devoted to Chartism'
8 August 1840	L. T. Clancy, 'Scraps for Radicals. No. I, Farewell to Erin, and No. II, My Native Land'
15 August 1840	E. La Mont, 'The Land of the Brave and the Free'
	John Mills, 'A Patriot's Reflections'
	Iota, '[2] Sonnets Dedicated to Chartism'
22 August 1840	Z., 'On the Projected Union. Erin – Or the Maid I Love'
	Anon., 'Chester Gaol'
29 August 1840	Don Juan, 'Who Stole the Rugs' (reprinted from the *Sun*)

	Z., 'Ode to Benevolence' (reprinted from the *Beauties Of The Press*)
5 September 1840	Argus, 'Daniel O'Wheedle. A Portrait Drawn from Life'
12 September 1840	Anon., 'How to be a Great Lord' (reprinted from the *Beauties Of The Press*)
	Anon., 'Brougham'
	J[ohn] W[atkins], '[2] Sonnets, Composed on Seeing the Flag Flying at Mulgrave Castle in Token that the Marquis of Normanby Was at Home'
19 September 1840	J[ohn] W[atkins], 'Wellington' and 'Lines'
26 September 1840	E. La Mont, 'Universal Liberty – The Chartist Reaction'
	J[ohn] W[atkins], 'Lines on Shell, Killed at Newport'
	J. V., 'Sonnet to Freedom'
	R. C. R., 'Sonnet, Inscribed to James Bronterre O'Brien'
3 October 1840	J. M., 'To Feargus O'Connor, Esq., Prisoner for the Cause of Truth in the Land of Bibles and Church Accommodation'
	Anon., 'The Pauper's Death-Bed'
	J[ohn] W[atkins], 'Lines'
10 October 1840	E. La Mont, 'Thoughts by Moonlight. A Simile'
	Argus, 'Reynard Maule. A Portrait Drawn from Life' and 'The Movement'
	Anon., 'Ah, Sure A Pair!'
17 October 1840	J[ohn] W[atkins], '[2] Sonnets to Feargus O'Connor Esq.'
	J. Watkins, 'The Yorkshire Hills'
	E. P., 'Lines'
	Anon., 'Nursery Rhymes'
24 October 1840	J. V., 'A Sonnet to Feargus O'Connor, Esq.' and 'Sonnet to Father Matthew'
	T. Gow, 'To the Lords of the Soil'
	T. H., 'The Arising of the Nations'
	J[ohn] W[atkins], 'The Gentry of Whitby Intend to Cure All the Sin and Misery they Cause in the Town, by Building a New Church'
31 October 1840	Will Watch, 'The Foxes Foiled'
	Argus, 'The Cabinet Council Chaunt'

7 November 1840	Argus, 'Liberty – Universal Liberty'
	Thomas Haig, 'Feargus O'Connor'
	W. McDouall, 'The Refuge of Freedom. A Sonnet'
14 November 1840	W. V. Sankey M. A., 'Rule Britannia!'
	James Vernon, 'On Astronomy'
	Quiz, 'An Epistle to ' "The Brave"' (Air: 'The Shamrock')
21 November 1840	Joseph Radford, 'The War-Cry'
	Amicus, 'Lines to Messrs. White and Collins'
28 November 1840	W. S. Villiers-Sankey M. A., 'To Working Men of Every Clime'
	John A. Lawson, 'The Irish Exile's Address to his Country on Hearing of the Progress of Temperance'
5 December 1840	Anon., 'The Expectancy and Rose of the Fair State'
	J[ohn] W[atkins], 'Chartism – A Fragment'
	B. [a prisoner], 'Unite' and 'A Chartist Song' (Air: 'Mary La More')
	J[ohn] W[atkins], 'Prologue to a New Drama, Entitled 'John Frost, Or the Insurrection at Newport'
12 December 1840	Anon., 'Nursery Rhymes'
	W. J., 'Morning Walk'
	E. A., 'Enigma'
	J. Vernon, 'Sonnet to Lovett and Collins'
	Argus, 'Whig Malignity – A Simile'
19 December 1840	B. [a prisoner), 'Lines on Seeing a Young Lady Shed a Tear as She Left Me in Prison'
	John A. Lawson, 'Freedom to the Slave. Humbly Inscribed to the Members of the Late Convention'
	Argus, 'One Word for Louis Phillipe, First Crown-Craft and Royalty'
	Anon., 'The Devil and Owen O'Connelly: or The New Irish Chancellor. A Romantic Ballad'
26 December 1840	Wm. Hick, 'Shout for the Charter and Freedom Is Near'
	J. C. E. Blyth, 'Answer to an Enigma in the *Northern Star* of December 12th, 1840'
	Wm. Jones, 'Lines Addressed to the Princess Royal'
	James Syme, 'Labour Song'

1841

2 January 1841	Joseph Radford, 'The Charter'
	Argus, 'Invocation to the Memory of Sir Wm. Wallace'
	J[ohn] W[atkins], 'Extracts from the Play of John Frost'
16 January 1841	Wm. S. Villiers Sankey, M. A., 'The Chartists' Address to Ireland' (Air: 'Away with this pouting and sadness')
23 January 1841	James Vernon, '[2] Sonnets. To the Mind' and 'Sonnet. To the Incarcerated Chartists'
30 January 1841	W. A. Thompson, 'Lines to Williams and Binns, on their Return from Prison'
	J. Vernon, 'A Fragment'
6 February 1841	Anon., 'O'Connor – Chartist Song' (Air: 'I sing the British seaman's praises')
13 February 1841	James Vernon, 'Sonnet on a Wheel Chair (Gratuitously presented to the writer by Mr Smith, tanner, of this town)' and 'Sonnet to Williams and Binns' and 'Sonnet to Oastler'
	Democraticus, 'The Rights and Duties of Man' (Tune: 'Ben Block')
	E. P. Mead, 'A New Chartist Song' (Tune: 'The Bay of Biscay, O!')
20 February 1841	C. Westray, 'To the Chartists'
	Alexander Huish, 'The Radical's Litany'
	W. C., 'Engima'
27 February 1841	'Look at the Clock!' (taken from *The Ingoldsby Legends* in *Bentley's Miscellany*)
6 March 1841	Robert Peddie, 'Spirit of Freedom!'
	Anon., 'The Brighton Chartist Meeting'
20 March 1841	W. C., 'Answer to Engima'
27 March 1841	William Hick, 'Teetotal Chartist Song' (Tune: Millers' 'We're soldiers fighting for our King')
	W. E., 'A Chartist Song'
3 April 1841	Basanitas, 'The Bank Screw'
	Wm. Rider, 'The League'
	A. W., 'The Sons of Toil'
10 April 1841	W. Mann, Sen., 'The Charter Hymn'
	Anon., 'Chartists and Liberty'

Anon., 'A Sonnet, A' but Twa Lines. On Seeing A Wretched-Looking Beggar Turn Away from a Palace Door he Had Essayed to Knock at, but Refrained'

24 April 1841 Aliquis, 'A Lecture to Chartists'
J. Vernon, 'Sonnet on Truth and Honesty' and 'Sonnet to Justice'
J. C. Elliot, 'An Enigma'

1 May 1841 Thomas M. Wheeler, 'Answer to J. C. Elliot's Enigma'; 'The Cause' and 'Here's to the Man, &c.' (Tune: 'Brave Old Oak')
Blackwood, 'Little John Finality'
J. L., 'Freedom'

8 May 1841 E. P. Mead, 'Chartist Song' (Tune: 'March to the Battle Field') ('Hark! 'tis the trumpet call)
Robert Peddie, 'Ode to Freedom'

15 May 1841 Argus, 'The National Anthem' (Air: Rule Britannia) and 'The Past. – The Present. – The Future. A Prophecy'
Thomas Wheeler, 'Freedom and the Charter!' (Tune: 'Bright are the beams of the morning sky')
J. C. Elliot, 'A Charade'
Arthur Boon, 'The Inquisition. Chorus of Imps.'

22 May 1841 Thomas M. Wheeler, 'Answer to J. C. Elliot's Charade'
John Mulholland, 'The Exile's Farewell'
Wm. Hick, 'A Fragment for the Labourer'
E. M., 'Feargus O'Connor'

29 May 1841 James Clarke, 'Acrostic' ('Liberty')
Rhilo, 'Answer to Elliot's Charade'

5 June 1841 William Hick, 'The Presentation of the National Petition, and the Motion of Mr Duncombe'
J. R. K., 'The Friends of the Charter, God Bless 'Em' (Tune: 'The King, God Bless Him')
John A. Lawson, 'Temperance' and 'The Drunkard's Grave. (From Fact)'

12 June 1841 Anon., 'Transportation of John Frost' (Air: 'Not a Drum Was Heard') (From the *Wreath of Liberty, or Gem of Chartism*, a work preparing for the press.)

Thos. M. Wheeler, 'The O'Connor Welcome' (Tune: 'Gaily the Troubadour Touched his Guitar')

Edward Polin, 'The Toilers' Homes of England!' [introduced as a response to F. E. Hemans, 'Homes of England']

4 September 1841	David Wright, 'The Sons of the North'
	David Cassedy, 'Arthur O'Connor's Farewell to his Country'
11 September 1841	Joseph Turner, 'Parody on "Begone Dull Care"'
	E. La Mont, 'Life's Dream'
	Anon., 'The Lion of Freedom'
	Edward Polin, 'Address to the Enslaved Millions'
18 September 1841	W. X., 'On the Release of Mr O'Connor'
	W. J., 'The Government's Address to the Working Classes'
25 September 1841	Anon., 'The Patriot' (Air: 'In a cottage near a wood')
	L. T. C[lancy], 'Scraps for Radicals [no. III, and no. IV 'To Those Who Can Best Understand Them']'
	Anon., 'A Song for the Ladies' (Tune: 'Farewell to the Mountain')
2 October 1841	J. P., 'A Glee for the Millions' (Tune: 'Scots wha hae')
	David Wright, 'To Feargus O'Connor, Esq.'
	James Vernon, 'Stanzas'
9 October 1841	L. T. Clancy, 'Scraps for Radicals [no. V, 'Whig pay, and patriotic perfidy!', and no.VI, 'Song. Commemoration of the Caged Lion's Liberation from York Castle']'
	Anon., 'Irish Absenteeism'
16 October 1841	E. P. Mead, 'Address of E. P. Mead, of Birmingham, to the Chartists of Great Britain and Ireland'
	Eliza Cook, 'King Death'
23 October 1841	James French, 'The Land! The Land!' (A Parody on 'The Sea! The Sea!')
	Thomas Gillespie, 'O'Connor's Welcome' (Sung by Mr Bryce in the Great Hall of the Bazaar, on the Evening of the Demonstration for O'Connor)

6 November 1841	Anon., 'The Law and the People'
	F., 'To Erin' ('Taken (with a few alterations) from an old Irish Magazine')
13 November 1841	James Vernon, 'On the Late Demonstrations'
	J. H., 'O'Connor's Lament' ('Taken (with a few alterations) from an old Irish Magazine')
20 November 1841	Anon., 'Feargus O'Connor at Kirkcaldy'
	J[ames] V[ernon], 'Sonnet to Knowledge' and 'Sonnet to Wisdom'
27 November 1841	Anon., 'Song' (Air: 'Scots wha hae!') ('By our brave O'Connor's zeal')
	F., 'To Democracy'
	Harold, 'Lines' ('Man is his own enslaver: if he will'd')
	John Horne Tooke, 'Pitt's Ten Commandments'
4 December 1841	John A. Lawson, 'The Briton's Fatherland'
	L. T. Clancy, 'Scraps for Radicals [nos. VII and VIII]'
	W. H. C., 'The Voice of the People'
	James Vernon, 'A Sonnet. to the Humane and Benevolent'
11 December 1841	Walsingham Martin, [Untitled] ('Father, look up and see that flag')
	Benjamin Stott, 'Songs for the Millions' ('Great famine rides rampant o'er all the land')
18 December 1841	J. H., 'The Irish Immigrants' Grave' (reprinted from the *Baptist Herald, Jamaica Paper*)
	Ion, 'The Voice of Freedom'
	James Vernon, 'A Sonnet. – On the Treatment which is Necessary for me to Undergo Ere I Can Attain a Cure', and 'A Sonnet' ('To raise the means I'll try the easiest plan')
24 December 1841	Anon., 'Lyrics From A "Sussex Farmer" Not One Hundred Miles from Goodwood'

1842

1 January 1842	Thomas Moore, 'Poetry for Ireland'
	Benjamin Gough, 'Poetry for Ireland'
	James Vernon, 'A Sonnet. to Mr Engall, of the University College'
	J. Watkins, 'The Corn Laws and Emigration'

8 January 1842	Anon., 'The Old Year'
	John Watkins, 'Corn Laws and Emigration'
15 January 1842	Anon., 'Last Words of Emmett'
	James Vernon, 'A Sonnet'
22 January 1842	J. R., 'The Goodness of Nature Withheld from the Poor'
	R. Stewart, 'Teetotalism'
29 January 1842	John Watkins, 'Address. Written by request, on the Strike of the Masons from the New Houses of Parliament, &c., &c.'
	Anon., 'Truth'
	James Vernon, 'Stanzas. To the Poets of the Northern Star and its Musical Readers'
5 February 1842	Anon., 'The Pauper's Drive'
	Anon., 'Who Stopp'd the Clock? A South Saxon Legend'
12 March 1842	Benjamin Stott, 'Song for the Millions' ['How long will the millions sweat and toil']
19 March 1842	Anon., 'The Blessings of Instruction'
26 March 1842	Benjamin Stott, 'Song for the Millions' ['A shout for freedom: be it loud and long,']
	Anon., 'The Evil Spirit'
	Anon., 'Label for a Gin Bottle'
2 April 1842	Jesse Hammond, 'The Favoured Land'
9 April 1842	John Watkins, 'Sonnet' ['Chartists! What strive ye for? for liberty!']
	G. Sheridan Nussey, 'The Emigrant's Song'
16 April 1842	Benjamin Stott, 'Song for the Millions' ['Old England! They call thee the land of the free']
23 April 1842	L. T. Clancy, 'Scraps for Radicals: IX. 'The Land of Repeal and the Charter My Boys!' (Air: 'Sprig of Shillelagh and Shamrock so green')' ['O, blest be the Island which Brien the brave']; X. 'Farewell to Cambria' (Air: 'Napoleon's Farewell to France'); XI. 'Sarmetia'
7 May 1842	J[ohn]W[atkins], 'Sonnet' ['Awake, St. John! arise ! we need thee now']
	Anon., 'What is a Peer?'
21 May 1842	Thomas Brown, 'Britannia's Appeal to Englishmen on behalf of the Temperance Reformation'

F., 'The People Shall Have Their Own Again'
(Tune: 'The King Shall Possess His Own Again')

Benjamin Stott, 'Song for the Millions' ['We will
be free! the millions cry']

4 June 1842   F– , 'To England'

S. J., 'Presentation of the National Petition' (Song –
'The Chartist Gay Day')

Caroline Maria Williams, 'Self Conceit'

11 June 1842   Benjamin Stott, 'Song for the Millions' ['Our God
is good, his works are fair']

18 June 1842   John Frazer, 'The New "Shoy Hoy"' (Air: 'Pity
Poor Jarvey')

J. S., 'A Bard's Address to the Chartists. Song II.
Chartists We Are'

25 June 1842   F. G., 'To Feargus O'Connor, Esq' [Acrostic]

J[ohn] W[atkins], 'To My Infant Daughter'

F., 'One and All'

Anon., 'Merry England'

2 July 1842   L. T. Clancy, 'Scraps for Radicals No. XIII. Song
of the Irish Absentees' (Tune: 'The night before
Billy's birth-day')

Benjamin Stott, 'Song for the Millions' ['Beware!
ye white slaves of old England, beware!']

9 July 1842   S. J., 'Pilgrim of Chartism'

David Wright, 'The People's Charter'

L. T. Clancy, 'Scraps for Radicals. No. XIV. Elegiac
lines on the death of Samuel Holberry, who
died a Martyr to Democracy, June 21st, 1842,
aged 27'

E. P. Mead, 'The Star' (Tune: 'The Brave Old
Oak')

16 July 1842   G. Sheridan Nussey, 'Happy Land'

E. P. Mead, 'Address to the Starving Millions'

23 July 1842   Sir E. Bulwer, 'The Song of the Emigrants'

F., 'Hymns for Chartist Camp Meetings. No.I'
['Great God, we call on thee!']

E. P. Mead, 'A New Chartist Song' ['O, for a pilot
to weather the storm']

30 July 1842   L. T. Clancy, 'Scraps for Radicals. No. XV
Napoleon'

	John Sixty, 'Cheltenham. O'Connor's Demonstration'
6 August 1842	John Sixty, 'Cheltenham. O'Connor's Demonstration'
	L. T. Clancy, 'Scraps for Radicals. No. XVI' ['Let the harp of my country now slumber']
	Eliza Cook, 'A Home in the Heart'
13 August 1842	F., 'Hymns for Chartist Camp Meetings. No. II' ['Great are thy works, O God of all']
	Thomas MacQueen, 'Thomas MacQueen's Farewell to Britain'
27 August 1842	G. Sheridan Nussey, 'The Tory Advent'
	Benjamin Stott, 'Song for the Millions' ['God of the world! in mercy bend thine ear']
3 September 1842	George Lindsay, 'The Charter'
	J[ohn] W[atkins], 'Chartist Lines for Recitation'
	D. C., 'Oppression'
17 September 1842	Old Commodore [E. P.] Mead, 'Address of the Old Commodore to his Chartist Friends'
	F., 'Lines. Written at Midnight, September the 10th, 1842'
24 September 1842	Benjamin Stott, 'Song for the Millions' ['Friends of Freedom, swell the strain']
	Ebeneezer Elliot, 'Labour's Woes and Triumph'
1 October 1842	Edwin Gill, 'An Invocation to the Spirit of Holberry'
	J[ohn] W[atkins], 'Chartist Song', ['I said to my father a Chartist I'd be']
	Clutha, 'The Scottish Patriots Invocation to Freedom'
8 October 1842	W. Thom, 'A Chieftain Unknown to the Queen'
15 October 1842	G. J. H., 'Song for the Chartists' ['Britannia's sons, arise, arise'] and 'Hail! Noble O'Connor, our chieftain, we'll greet thee'
22 October 1842	Benjamin Stott, 'Song for the Millions' ['The Britons may boast of their sea-girt Isle']
	J[ohn] W[atkins], 'Lines on the Death of my Father'
29 October 1842	S. J., 'Song of Freedom. Nine Cheers for the Charter'

	Thomas Wilson, 'A Song for those Who Like to Sing it'
	Edwin Gill, 'The Charter For Ever Shall Weather the Storm'
	Wm. Rider, 'The Welcome'
	Anon., 'The Tory Squire'
5 November 1842	Bradshaw Walker, 'The Banner of Green'
	Anon., 'The Chartist Hearts of Oak. A Parody' (Written in Kirkdale Prison)
	C. Westray, 'The Voice of Freedom'
12 November 1842	J[ohn] W[atkins], 'The Charter. An Ode'
	Anon., 'An Acrostic. Written in Warwick Gaol, November 1842' ['Feargus O'Connor']
	Benjamin Stott, 'An Ode to Liberty'
19 November 1842	W. McDowall, 'I Will Have Mercy and Not Sacrifice'
	H. H. H., 'Lines on Seeing the Account of the Meeting of Ellis with his Family in the *Northern Star* of Nov 5th, 1842'
26 November 1842	James Montgomery, Esq., 'The Press'
3 December 1842	M. K., 'We May, We Will, We Must, We Shall Be Free'
10 December 1842	J. M., 'An Acrostic. Written in Stafford Gaol' ['William Hill']
	Benjamin Stott, 'Song for the Millions' ['Let us sing a glad song in sweet liberty's praise']
17 December 1842	J. W. C., 'Rally Again Boys'
	J. Bishop, 'Tyranny and Oppression' (Tune: 'Scots wha hae wi' Wallace bled')
31 December 1842	Benjamin Stott, 'Song for the Millions' ['It comes! it comes! the glorious day']
	John Watkins, 'An Address' ('Written by John Watkins, and Spoken by Mr Saville, at the Royal Victoria Theatre, on Wednesday, December 7th, 1842, for the Benefit of the Orphan of the late William Thomas, Stone Mason.')

1843

| 7 January 1843 | J[ohn] W[atkins], 'The System' |
| 14 January 1843 | J. S. B., 'A Revolutionary Ode' (From *Tait's Magazine*) |

21 April 1843	J[ohn] W[atkins], 'Stanzas for Music' (Air: 'The Thames!')
	W. Rider, 'Friend Sturge'
28 January 1843	M. K., 'Enigma'
4 February 1843	Patrioticus, 'The Disinterested Chartist'
	F. Goodfellow, 'To Chartist Lecturers'
11 February 1843	L. T. Clancy, 'Scraps for Radicals. No. XVII. The Soldier's Bride, or La Heroine de Francais' and 'No. XVIII. Fall of Warsaw'
	Edward P. Mead, 'The Steam King'
	Benjamin Stott, 'Praise to the Deity'
	Anon., 'The Shoemaker'
18 February 1843	Schiller, 'The Words of Belief'
	Thomas M. Wheeler, 'Answer to M. K.'s Enigma'
	Anon., 'The Wish'
25 February 1843	Anon., 'Parting Lines on an Old Fount of Type' ('Extract from a note to a friend, published in an American paper.')
4 March 1843	Benjamin Stott, 'A Song of Freedom'
18 March 1843	Mrs Abdy, 'The Press'
25 March 1843	L. T. Clancy, 'Scraps for Radicals. XIX. The Mountain, Nymph Liberty'; 'XX. For Freedom! For God!! And For Right!!!' and 'XXI. Impromptu'
	T. Rankin, 'Inscription for a Scientific Lecture Room'
22 April 1843	Benjamin Stott, 'The Patriot's Prayer'
	Edwin Gill, 'An Ode' ['Oh, shame to the land of the free']
	Samuel Bamford, 'Hymn to Spring'
29 April 1843	S. J., 'A Reply to Dr Bowring's Free Trade Flourishes. Spoken by himself at the Drury-Lane Theatre'
6 May 1843	A Poor Chartist, 'The Poor Man's Prayer'
	Crito, 'Ode to Liberty'
13 May 1843	F. M. F., 'The Mind of the Past, the Present, and the Future'
20 May 1843	W. H. Clifton, 'To Liberty'
27 May 1843	F., 'To the Chartists of Shropshire'
3 June 1843	Commodore Mead, 'To the Rescue, Chartists!!!'

10 June 1843	Z., 'On the Projected Union. Erin – Or the Maid I Love' (From *The Beauties of the Press*, an Irish Newspaper devoted to the people, prior to the establishment of the Act of Union)
	F.-, 'To the Chartists of Wales'
17 June 1843	Anon., 'Written on Presenting a Female Infant with a Green Top-Knot, on her Birth-Day, 1797'
24 June 1843	Anon., 'Erin. To Its Own Tune' (from *The Press* an Irish newspaper, suppressed by Government to carry 'Union')
	John Rayson, 'The Calm and Temperate Mind'
1 July 1843	Anon., 'The Fatal Battle of Aughrim. Translated from the Irish' (from *The Press* an Irish newspaper, suppressed by Government to carry 'Union')
	T. B. Smith, 'The Appeal' ('Written at the request of a father to be spoken by his little daughter at a public meeting.')
8 July 1843	Thebor, 'The London Pride and Shamrock. A Fable' (from *The Press* an Irish newspaper, suppressed by the government to carry 'Union')
	John Rayson, 'Social Cup of Tea'
15 July 1843	Z., 'Ode To Benevolence' (from *The Press* an Irish newspaper, suppressed by government to carry 'Union')
	Eliza Cook, 'Song of the Haymakers'
22 July 1843	Sarsfield, 'An Ode' ['Hark! heard ye not those dreadful screams?'] (from *The Press* an Irish newspaper, suppressed by government to carry 'Union')
	Benjamin Stott, 'To Thomas Slingsby Duncombe, Esq., M.P.'
5 August 1843	Allen Davenport, 'Repeal and the Charter'
	Anon., 'Song' ['Up – up with our flag; shall our courage be shown']
12 August 1843	Mrs Crawford, 'Irish Song. The Chieftain of Erin'
	Wm. Rider, 'The State Tinkers'
19 August 1843	Anon., 'A Lament for the Whigs' [reprinted from the *Sun*]

2 September 1843	The Old Commodore [Mead], 'To The Chartists of Great Britain and Ireland. Lines on reading the new plan of organisation'
	Eliza Cook, 'Song of the Blind One'
	Elijah Ridings, 'I Would Go to Your Church'
9 September 1843	Anon., 'Cap Fit – Cap Wear' [from *Dublin Freeman's Journal*]
	Anon., 'The Patriot's Grave'
23 September 1843	W. Rider, 'Thoughts on reading the puerile remarks in the *Leeds Times*, of Saturday last, on Mr Hill's account of the state of Chartism in Scotland, as given in the *Star* of the previous week'
	Benjamin Stott, 'Stanzas. From *Freedom*, an unpublished poem'
30 September 1843	David Ross, 'A Call to the People'
	Mr George Binns, 'Lines. (Written on board of the Bombay, on a passage to New Zealand, August, 1842)'
7 October 1843	Frances Brown, 'Trees'
	Washington Alston, 'America to England'
14 October 1843	Anon., 'O! The Days of Romance Are Not Over' (*Cork Examiner*)
	Anon., 'The Cry of the Children' (*Blackwood's Magazine*)
21 October 1843	Eliza Cook, 'Song of the Hempseed' (*New Monthly Magazine*)
28 October 1843	Anon., 'Marco Bozzaris'
4 November 1843	Anon., 'The Absent Father' (From a Work entitled *The Miller of Deanshaugh*)
	Eliza Cook, 'Rhymes by the Roadside'
11 November 1843	Eliza Cook, 'Birds'
18 November 1843	Benjamin Stott, 'No Surrender'
25 November 1843	Samuel Bamford, 'God Help the Poor'
	Anon., 'What are the Repealers?' (Air: 'Tipperary O!') (from the *Nation*)
2 December 1843	J. McKowen, 'Birds' ('Answer to Eliza Cook's poem on birds')
	Eliza Cook, 'Old Songs' (Abridged from the *Forget-me-Not* for 1844)

9 December 1843	Henry Moon, 'The Good Old Plough'
	Charles Dickens, 'A Word In Season'
16 December 1843	Anon., 'The Newspaper'
	J. Booth, 'To the Friends of Freedom'
23 December 1843	'A Christmas Garland' comprising:
	Jesse Hammonds, 'A Lay for Winter'
	Anon., 'Old Winter Is Come'
	[Thomas Hood], 'The Song of the Shirt'
	Burns, 'A Man's a Man for A' That'
	Robert Nicol, 'We'll Mak the World Better Yet'
	Charles Mackay, 'A Song after a Toast'
30 December 1843	Anon., 'The Pauper's Christmas Carol' (from *Punch*)
	Anon., 'New Year's Day' (*Charnock's Poems*)
	Eliza Cook, 'Song of the Old Year'

1844

6 January 1844	E. P. Mead, 'The Brave Old King' (Air: 'The Brave Old Oak')
	Anon., 'Friar Tuck's Chaunt'
13 January 1844	Anon., 'From Beranger' ['In spite of what sages repeat,'] (*Nation*)
	E. Mantz, 'A Nation's Will'
20 January 1844	Jas. McKowen, 'Lines to a Snowdrop'
	Anon., 'Old Winter'
27 January 1844	Robert Nicol, 'Stanzas on the Birthday of Burns'
	Bryant (American Poet), 'The Poet's Grave'
3 February 1844	T., 'The Union Workhouse'
	Channing, 'The Poor'
	James Taylor, 'The Poor Man's Complaint'
10 February 1844	J. M'Owen, 'Father! Who Are the Chartists?'
	Herweg, 'A German War Song: The Hymn of Hate'
	Anon., 'Very True'
17 February 1844	Eliza Cook, 'Song of the Spirit of Poverty'
	Anon., 'German War Song'
24 February 1844	[Thomas Hood], 'The Lady's Dream' (*Hood's Magazine*)
	Anon., 'The Old Green Lane'
2 March 1844	Ebenezer Jones, 'Song of the Kings of Gold'
	Frances Brown, 'The First Valentine' (*Hood's Magazine*)

	James Thom, 'St. Paul's Day' (Tune: 'Old England on the lea')
9 March 1844	W. B., 'To the Poets of America'
	Monckton Milnes, 'The Eastern Woman'
	James Montgomery, 'Robert Burns'
16 March 1844	James B. Syme (Edinburgh), 'Lines on the Death of John O. La Mont'
	James Henderson (Glasgow 29 February 1844), 'Stanzas to Freedom'
	Tam Webster (Arbroath 4 February 1844), 'Sonnet' ['O rank oppression . . .']
	William Thom, 'The Mitherless Bairn'
23 March 1844	Anon., 'The Cry' (*Times*)
	Eliza Cook, 'Many Happy Returns of the Day'
	Shelley, 'Liberty'
30 March 1844	Camilla Toulmin, 'The Death of the Pauper Peasant' (*Ainsworth's Magazine*)
	Robert Nichol, 'Wild Flowers'
	Anon., 'Beautiful Eyes'
	Anon., 'American Stripes'
6 April 1844	Mrs James Gray, 'The Dwellings of the Poor'
	Eliza Cook, 'My Old Companions'
	James M'Kowen (Lambeg), 'Song' ('Sing, sing, "banish dull care"')
13 April 1844	Anon., 'The Circassian War Song' (*Blackwood's Magazine*)
	Eliza Cook, 'Love On'
	Schiller, 'The Sharing of the Earth' (trans. Bulwer Lytton)
20 April 1844	Frances Brown (28 February 1844), 'The Ancient Tombs'
	John Fergusson (Sunderland), 'To The Memory of Byron' (Tune: 'Loch na Garr')
	Anon., 'Creep Afore ye Gang'
27 April 1844	C. Swaine, 'Let Us Love One Another'
	John Fergusson, 'Now Burns Is Gane' (Tune: 'Adieu, a heart warm fond adieu')
	David Lister Richardson, 'Sonnet – Evening at Sea' and 'Sonnet – To a Child'
	W. Cross, 'Oppression'

4 May 1844	Sir William Jones, 'Ode' ('What constitutes a state?')
	Prince, 'There is Beauty on Earth'
	Frances Brown, 'The Lesson of the Louvre'
11 May 1844	Anon., 'True Dignity' (*New York Subterranean*)
	Anon., 'The Gallows-Goers' (*The Irish Citizen* (US))
18 May 1844	Thomas Jenkins, 'To Poland'
25 May 1844	Thomas Campbell, 'Field Flowers'
	Barry Cornwall, 'Within and Without: A London Lyric'
	Anon., 'Song of Liberty' (Air: 'Colleen O'ge') (*The Nation*)
1 June 1844	Frederika Bremer, 'The Polka; or, the Bohemian Girl to her Lover [A National Ballad]'
	Anon., 'The Bridegroom to his Bride'
	Jas. Henderson (Glasgow, May), 'Hope On'
8 June 1844	Charles Mosley Kennedy, 'Shakspere' [*sic*]
15 June 1844	Eliza Cook, 'The Happy Maid'
	Anon., 'The English Girl' (*Punch*)
22 June 1844	Beranger, 'The Garret'
	James Henderson (Glasgow, June 1844), 'Sonnets [2] – To the Stars'
	James M'Kowen (Lambeg), 'The Old Irish Jig'
29 June 1844	G. Burt, 'Lines to T. S. Duncombe Esq., M. P.'
	Desmond, 'The Voice and Pen' (*The Nation*)
	E. S., 'The Death Song of Chatterton'
6 July 1844	Clericus, 'The Tyrant's Welcome'
	R. J., 'London Improvements'
	S. R. G. (London, June 8, 1844), 'Dreams of the Past'
13 July 1844	Barry Cornwall, 'The Fate of the Oak'
	Anon., 'A Yankee Song. The Working Men's League' (Tune: 'Old Dan Tucker')
	Thomas Muir, 'The Exile's Adieu'
20 July 1844	Anon., 'To the Reformers of England' (*American Democratic Review*)
	F. W. N. Bayley, 'She Gathers a Shamrock'
	John Fisher Murray, 'The Seaman's Light'
27 July 1844	Anon., 'The Advent of Steam' (*Illuminated Magazine*)
	Joan Combe, 'Her Eyes Were as Blue as the Ocean Bed'

3 August 1844	Barry Cornwall, 'The Poor Home'
	Thomas Haynes Bayly, 'You Remember It – Don't You?'
10 August 1844	Frances Brown, 'On the Death of Thomas Campbell'
	Anon., 'A Ballad of Freedom' (*The Celt*)
17 August 1844	Anon. ['A Poor Irish Girl'], 'The Burns' Festival' (*Ayr Advertiser*)
24 August 1844	Alexander Smart, 'To the Sons of Burns'
	Spartacus, 'On the Birth of Another Guelph'
31 August 1844	John Keats, 'The Capelocracy' (From *Isabella*)
	James M'Kowen, 'The Hawthorn Tree'
	Charles Swain, 'Loving and Forgiving'
7 September 1844	George Sydney Smythe M.P., 'The Jacobins of Paris'
14 September 1844	Anon., 'Stanzas to the Memory of Burns' (*New Monthly Magazine*)
	Samuel Lover, 'Song. The Emigrant Mother the Night Before She Sails from Ireland'
	Anon., 'Career of a Fashionable Poet' (*Fraser's Magazine*)
21 September 1844	Delta, 'Stanzas for the Burns' Festival' (*Blackwood's Magazine*)
28 September 1844	Anon., 'The Marriage Vow'
	S. P., 'A Dialogue Between the Steeple and the Brig, Ayr'
5 October 1844	M. J. B., 'The Broken Violin. (From Beranger)'
	William Wallace, 'Thomas Campbell' (*New York Sun*)
12 October 1844	Placido, 'To God: A Prayer'
	James M'Kowen, 'The Hour That I Love Best'
19 October 1844	Percy B. Shelley, 'A King'
26 October 1844	Irish Girl, 'The Auld Aik Tree'
	Adelaide [A Lowell factory girl], 'The Tomb of Washington'
2 November 1844	Reprints 'The Auld Aik Tree' and 'The Tomb of Washington' from the previous issue
9 November 1844	Anon., 'A Bard's Request'
	Eliza Cook, 'My Old Straw Hat'

16 November 1844	Anon., 'Sir Walter Raleigh's Last Adventure'
	N. Mitchell, 'The Harem Favourite'
	Anon., 'The Girls on Annexation'
23 November 1844	John Kennedy (Gateshead, 4/11), 'Lines addressed to William Thom, Inverury'
	Anon., 'The Auld Wife's Plaint'
	The Miller of Deanhaugh, 'My Cottage Maid'
30 November 1844	Anon., 'Hymn to Liberty'
7 December 1844	Benjamin Stott, 'To the Spirit of the *Northern Star* on its Removal to the "Great Wen"'
	Anon., 'The Pheasant's Eggs'
14 December 1844	Anon., 'The Blue-Eyed Angel' ('From the French of Beranger') (*Edinburgh Weekly Register*)
	Anon., 'Song of the Cheap Customer' (*Punch*)
21 December 1844	'A Christmas Garland' comprising:
	Miss Sheridan Carey, 'A Warning Cry'
	Henry Ware, 'Oppression Shall Not Always Reign' (*Boston Labourer*)
	Anon., 'The Mistletoe'
	Charles Mackay, 'Tubal Cain'
	Beranger, 'Woman and Wine'
	Anon., 'A Christmas Carol' (*Punch*)
28 December 1844	'A Christmas Garland: Wreath II' comprising:
	Eliza Cook, 'Christmas Song of the Poor Man'
	Mrs E. S. Craven Green, 'The Grey Goose Quill'
	Freiligrath, 'Our Freedom and Right'
	James M'Kowen, 'A Christmas Song'

1845

4 January 1845	J. (Bristol), 'The Commission of Genius'
11 January 1845	Jesse Hammond, 'Glee – The Men of Kent'
	A Footman, 'Anacreontic' (*Hood's Magazine*)
18 January 1845	Charles Mackay, 'Little Fools and Great Ones'
	An Englishwoman, 'Our Home and Fatherland'
25 January 1845	Cecil Harbottle, 'Repudiation. – An Old Song to a New Tune' (*Literary Gazette*)
	Thomas Mills, 'Sons of Albion Wake to Glory'
1 February 1845	David Ross (Stamford-Street, Leeds), 'The Charter and No Surrender!'
	Tate, 'Sonnets' [2]

8 February 1845	Anon., 'Royalty and Buckingham' (*Satirist*)
15 February 1845	A Serf, 'The Rogues Are Met'
	J. C. Prince, 'Vision of the Future'
22 February 1845	Anon. ('Imitated from Beranger'), 'The Holy Alliance of Nations'
	Anon., 'Never Give Up'
1 March 1845	Anon., 'A Labourer's Thoughts on St. Valentine's Day' (*Douglas Jerrold's Magazine*)
15 March 1845	Anon., 'Harrow Reminiscences – Peel and Byron' (*Chronicle*)
22 March 1845	Anon., 'A Striking Remedy: Or, Merciful Maxims, a la Grantley Berkeley' (*Great Gun*)
29 March 1845	Curlew, 'Young Kate of Glenkeen' (*Nation*)
5 April 1845	Anon., 'April Fools' (*Jerrold's Shilling Magazine*)
12 April 1845	W. S. L., 'A Case at Sessions' (*Douglas Jerrold's Shilling Magazine*)
19 April 1845	'The Feast of the Poets' comprising:
	W. C. (Glasgow), 'The Poet's Feast'
	David Ross (Leeds), 'Ode to Spring'
	Anon., 'Address to the Ocean. By the author of 'The Voice of Nature'
	J. McKowen, 'Fanny Williamson'
	James Emslie Duncan, 'Hymn of Liberty'
	William Jones (Leicester), 'Toil On'
	John Peacock (Glasgow), 'Song of Freedom'
26 April 1845	'The Feast of the Poets: Part Two' comprising:
	Caroline Norton, [extracts from] 'The Child of the Islands' (*Literary Gazette*)
	Frances Brown, 'We Are Growing Old'
	Eliza Cook, 'Summer Is Nigh'
	F. M. S., 'Woman's Prayer'
	Anon., 'The Americans' Apostrophe to Boz' (*The Great Gun*)
	John Greenleaf Whittier, 'Stanzas for the Times'
	G. Hervegh, 'Song of Liberty'
	Beranger, 'The Wandering Outcast'
	Mrs James Gray, 'The Use of Poets'
3 May 1845	Anon., 'The Song of the Gallows' (*Great Gun*)
10 May 1845	Anon., 'The Social Flower' (*Jerrold's Magazine*)

17 May 1845	Anon., 'A Voice from the Pauper Union' (*Great Gun*)
	Anon., 'The *Small* Difference Between Rich and Poor' (*Joe Miller the Younger*)
24 May 1845	Anon., ' "The Old Straw Hat's" Address to its Owner'
31 May 1845	Laman Blanchard, 'Lines'
7 June 1845	Anon., 'The Melancholy Month of May' (*Cruikshank's Table-Book*)
14 June 1845	H. B. K., 'My Mither's Kist' (*Edinburgh Weekly Register*)
21 June 1845	George S. Nussey, 'The Emigrant'
28 June 1845	'The Feast of the Poets' comprising:
	William Jones (Leicester), 'The Tyrant's Death'
	D. Wright (Aberdeen), 'Nature and Freedom'
	Anon. [USA], 'Down with the Landlords'
	Anon. [USA], 'Freedom's Call. – 1775'
	Wm. Lloyd Garrison, 'The Triumph of Freedom'
	John Greenleaf Whittier, 'The Christian Slave'
	T[homas] D[oubleday], 'Mob Melodies'
	Byron, '[Extract from] Prophecy of Dante', and '[Extract from] Childe Harold'
5 July 1845	'The Feast of the Poets: Part Two' devoted to Ferdinand Freiligrath and comprising: 'The Greek Girl at the Fair', 'Flowers', 'Good Morning', 'When?', 'The Two Flags', 'It chanced the other day in Heaven...' and 'Freedom and Right'
12 July 1845	Beauties of Byron I, 'On the Death of a Young Lady'
	J. McKowen, 'An Invitation'
19 July 1845	Beauties of Byron II, 'When I Roved a Young Highlander'
	Hon. Mrs Norton, 'Summer'
26 July 1845	Beauties of Byron III, 'To a Lady'
	Simrock (a German Poet), 'The Mysterious Mask'
2 August 1845	Beauties of Byron IV, 'The Prayer of Nature' and 'A Fragment' ('When, to their airy hall ...)
9 August 1845	Beauties of Byron V, '[Extracts from] English Bards and Scotch Reviewers'

	T[homas] D[oubleday], 'Mob Melodies: The Hymn of Glencalvie'
16 August 1845	Beauties of Byron VI, '[Extracts from] English Bards and Scotch Reviewers' and '[Extracts from] Don Juan' and 'Poem in Memory of Kirk White'
	J. McKowen, 'Stanzas'
23 August 1845	Beauties of Byron VII, '[Extracts from] English Bards and Scotch Reviewers'
30 August 1845	Beauties of Byron VIII, '[Extracts from] Childe Harold'
	Anon., 'Food for the Poor. Song of the Andover Union' (*Joe Miller*)
6 September 1845	Beauties of Byron IX, '[Extracts from] Childe Harold'
13 September 1845	Beauties of Byron X, '[Extracts from] Childe Harold'
20 September 1845	'The Feast of the Poets' comprising:
	Beauties of Byron XI, '[Extracts from] Childe Harold'
	Thomas Cooper, '[Extracts from] The Purgatory of Suicides'
	J. McK[owen], 'The Gloamin' Hour'
	George S. Nussey, 'Sea-Side Thoughts'
	William Jones (Leicester), 'Autumn's Departure'
	Thomas Jones (Liverpool), 'Lines Addressed to John Frost, Esq.'
	The Last Bard of Breffni, 'The Pleasures of Home'
27 September 1845	'The Feast of the Poets' comprising:
	Beauties of Byron XII, '[Extracts from] Childe Harold'
	Thomas Cooper, '[Extract from] The Purgatory of Suicides'
	John Peacock, 'To the Memory of Robert Tannahill'
	Thomas Doubleday, 'The Factory Child' (Tune: 'Langolee') and 'The Poacher'
4 October 1845	Beauties of Byron XIII, '[Extracts from] Childe Harold'
11 October 1845	Beauties of Byron XIV, '[Extracts from] Childe Harold'

18 October 1845	Beauties of Byron XV, '[Extracts from] Childe Harold'
25 October 1845	Beauties of Byron XVI, '[Extracts from] Childe Harold'
1 November 1845	Beauties of Byron XVII, '[Extracts from] Childe Harold'
	George Herwegh, 'Against Rome'
8 November 1845	Beauties of Byron XVIII, '[Extracts from] Childe Harold'
15 November 1845	Beauties of Byron XIX, '[Extracts from] Childe Harold'
22 November 1845	Beauties of Byron XX, '[Extracts from] Childe Harold'
29 November 1845	Beauties of Byron XXI, '[Extracts from] Childe Harold'
6 December 1845	Beauties of Byron XXII, '[Extracts from] Childe Harold'
13 December 1845	Beauties of Byron XIII, '[Extracts from] Childe Harold'
20 December 1845	'A Christmas Garland' consisting of:
	Anon., 'Welcome Christmas – Welcome, Christmas'
	Anon., 'The Shelterless Poor'
	Anon., 'Starving'
	William Johnson (Knaresborough), '[Extract from] Christmas Ode to Liberty',
	Amos Horseman, The Mill Boy, 'The Working Man's Christmas Complaints and Hopes'
	F. P. Palmer, 'A Song of a Pleasant Old Woodman and his Wife Joan, at a Christmas Fire' (*Dublin University Magazine*)
27 December 1845	'A Christmas Garland: Wreath II' consisting of:
	Eliza Cook, 'We'll Sing Another Christmas Song' [The rest of the garland is given over to extracts from Dickens' *The Cricket on the Hearth*]

1846

| 3 January 1846 | 'A New Year's Wreath' consisting of: |
| | Thomas Cooper '[Extracts from] The Baron's Yule Feast. A Christmas Rhyme' |

John McCrea, 'A New Song' (Tune: 'Woo'd an'
married an' a'')

Anon., 'A Word of Apology'

J. Greenleaf Whittier, 'Our Countrymen in Chains'

Charles Mackay, 'The Voice of the Times'

Hugh MacDonald, 'A Gude New Year I Wish Ya
A'' (Air: 'Gude nicht, and joy be wi' you a'')

10 January 1846	Beauties of Byron XXIV, '[Extracts from] Childe Harold'
17 January 1846	Beauties of Byron XXV, '[Extracts from] The Giaour'
	Songs for the People: Thomas Spence, 'The Land'
24 January 1846	Beauties of Byron XXVI, '[Extracts from] The Giaour'
	W. L. Warren, 'Byron Defended'
	Songs for the People: Percy Bysshe Shelley, 'To the Men of England'
31 January 1846	Beauties of Byron XXVII, '[Extracts from] The Giaour'
	Songs for the People, 'The Marseilles March'
7 February 1846	Beauties of Byron XXVIII, '[Extracts from] The Siege of Corinth'
	Songs for the People: The Last Bard of Breffni', 'The Light of the *Northern Star*'
14 February 1846	Beauties of Byron XXIX, '[Extracts from] The Siege of Corinth'
	Songs for the People: Robert Nicoll, 'Honour to the Champions of Freedom'
21 February 1846	Beauties of Byron XXX, '[Extracts from] The Bride of Abydos'
	Songs for the People: J. A. Leatherland, 'The Standard of Truth'
28 February 1846	Beauties of Byron XXXI, '[Extracts from] The Bride of Abydos'
	Songs for the People: J. A. Leatherland, 'We Will Be Free'
7 March 1846	Beauties of Byron XXXII, '[Extracts from] The Corsair'
	Songs for the People: Anon., 'Masniello's Call to the Neapolitans'

14 March 1846	Beauties of Byron XXXIII, '[Extracts from] Lara'
	Songs for the People: Edward Decker, 'Invocation to Poland'
21 March 1846	Anon., 'The Polish Insurrection' (*Illustrated London News*)
28 March 1846	Campbell, 'On the Downfall of Blood'
	Songs for the People: Anon., 'Fall, Tyrants, Fall!'
4 April 1846	Beauties of Byron XXXIV, '[Extracts from] Parisina'
	Songs for the People: J. A., 'A Greek War Song' (*Tait's Magazine*)
11 April 1846	'The Feast of the Poets', consisting of:
	John Peacock, 'An Address to the Toiling Millions'
	John Ackroyd (Thornton, near Bradford), 'Man Shall Cease to be a Slave'
	Allen Davenport, 'The Poet's Hope' (March 30th, 1846)
	J. K. Smith, 'The Polish Patriots'
	H. D., 'Cead Mile Failte! The Hundred Thousand Welcomes' (*The Examiner*)
	John Swain, 'Tidings of the Battle'
	Beranger, 'La Mort du Diable'
	Freiligrath, 'To the Darklings'
	George Herwegh, 'The Song of Hate' (*Nation*)
	Charles Mackay, 'The Watcher on the Tower' (*Daily News*)
18 April 1846	'The Feast of the Poets. Part II', consisting of:
	William Thom, 'To My Flute', 'Dreamings of the Bereaved', 'Oh Mary! When You Think of Me' and 'Willie'
25 April 1846	'Feast of the Poets', consisting of:
	William Thom, 'My Heather Land'
	Allen Davenport, 'Ireland in Chains' (Air: 'Marseillaise Hymn')
	J. G. Whittier, 'To Ronge' (*Democratic Review*)
	C[harles] M[ackay], 'Old Opinions'
	Georgiana C. Munro, 'The Gold Mines of the West' (*Simmond's Colonial Magazine*)
2 May 1846	Beauties of Byron XXXV, '[Extracts from] The Prisoner of Chillon'

	Songs for the People: John Peacock (Greenock), 'The Land! The Land For Me!'
9 May 1846	Beauties of Byron XXXVI, 'Beppo'
	Songs for the People: Charles Cole, 'The Strength of Tyranny'
16 May 1846	Beauties of Byron XXXVII, '[Extracts from] Mazeppa'
	R. F., 'On the Young and Beautiful Countess Pluter' (*Literary Gazette*)
	Songs for the People: Ernest Jones, 'Our Summons'
23 May 1846	Songs for the People: Moore, 'Forget Not the Field' (Air: 'The Lamentation of Aughrim')
	Songs for the People: Alfred Fennell, 'On the Polish Insurrection'
30 May 1846	Beauties of Byron XXXVIII, '[Extracts from] The Island'
	Songs for the People: Anon., 'The Beauty of Liberty'
6 June 1846	Songs for the People: Ernest Jones, 'A Chartist Chorus'
	Songs for the People: Hugh McDonald, 'Gudesake Let's Agree' (Air: 'The Miller of Dee' (*People's Journal*)
13 June 1846	Beauties of Byron XXXIX, '[Extracts from] Manfred'
	Songs for the People: Ernest Jones, 'A Chartist March'
20 June 1846	Songs for the People: Thomas Cooper, 'We'll Rally Around Him'
	Songs for the People: J. Harkness, Edinburgh, 'The Chartist Exiles'
27 June 1846	'The Feast of the Poets' consisting of:
	F. M. S., 'To Summer' (*Brighton Herald*)
	W[illiam] H[owitt], 'Where are the Spring Flowers?' (*People's Journal*)
	Ernest Jones, 'The Corn Field and the Factory'
	Allen Davenport, 'The Land, the People's Farm'
	Charles Stewart (Shettleston), 'Ode to Scotia' (Air: 'Exile of Erin')
	Aurora (Glasgow), 'Temperance Song'
	Alfred Fennell, 'A Song' ('We raise no battle axe nor brand')

D. Wright (Aberdeen), 'We Are Not Men of War'
J. Edwards, 'The Voice of Freedom'

4 July 1846   'The Feast of the Poets: Part II' consisting of:
Ernest Jones, 'England's Greatness'
Allen Davenport, 'The Iron God'
J. Harkness, 'Song' ('Let princes and potentates talk of their grandeur')
Ferdinand Freiligrath (trans. By Mary Howitt, 'Requiescat' (Written expressly for the *People's Journal*)
Anon. ('an English lady'), 'Washington'
S. F. Key, 'Star-Spangled Banner'
Anon., 'The American Star' (Tune: 'Humors of Glen')
Anon., 'Ode – For the Fourth of July'
Henry W. Longfellow, 'The Arsenal at Springfield'
Charles Mackay, 'France and England' and 'The Three Preachers'

11 July 1846   Songs for the People: Robert Nicoll, 'The Honest and True'
Ernest Jones, 'Our Destiny'

18 July 1846   J. Mck[owen?], 'Wild Flowers of Summer'
Songs for the People: T. R. Smart (Leicester), 'The God's of St. Stephen's' (Air: 'To Anacreaon in Heaven')
Ernest Jones, 'Britannia'

25 July 1846   Anon., 'Lines on the Bandiera'
Songs for the People: Ernest Jones, 'Liberty'

1 August 1846   Ernest Jones, 'Our Warning'
Songs for the People: John Arnott (Somers Town, 'The People's First Estate'

8 August 1846   Ernest Jones, 'Our Cheer'
Songs for the People: T. R. Smart (Leicester), 'The Land and the Charter' (Air: 'Death of Wolfe')

15 August 1846   Songs for the People: Ernest Jones, 'A Song for the Road!'
Songs for the People: J. Harkness (Edinburgh), 'The People's Jubilee' (Tune: 'Donald Cord's come again')

22 August 1846	Songs for the People: Ernest Jones (Kirkstall Abbey, August), 'The Blackstone-Edge Gathering: on the 2nd of August, 1846' (Air: 'The Battle of Hohenlinden')
29 August 1846	Allen Davenport, 'O'Connorville'
	Songs for the People: Alexander Yates, 'The Land'
5 September 1846	Ernest Jones, 'The Better Hope'
12 September 1846	Ernest Jones, 'The Two Races (Part I. The Old; Part II. The New)'
19 September 1846	Songs for the People: John Arnott (Somers Town, Sept.), 'A Song addressed to the Fraternal Democrats'
	Songs for the People: Julian Harney, 'All Men Are Brethren. A Song for the Fraternal Democrats'
26 September 1846	Anon., 'A Yankee's Notion About Enlisting in the Mexican War' (*People's Journal*)
3 October 1846	Beauties of Byron XL, 'Wellington'
	Songs for the People: An Irish Chartist (Killaloe, Limerick), 'Song of the Irish Chartists'
10 October 1846	Ernest Jones, 'The Maid of the West'
	Songs for the People: Tom Pen, 'A Stave about the Quack Patriot and his Repeal Delusion' (Tune: 'O'Rowland McFigg')
17 October 1846	Ernest Jones, 'Onward and Upward!'
	John Arnott (Somers Town), 'An Acrostic [Ernest Jones]'
	Songs for the People: S. D., 'The Field of Morat' (*Tait's Edinburgh Magazine*)
24 October 1846	Alfred Fennell, 'On the Flight of the Son of Schamyl, the Brave Chief of the Circassians, to Join his Father and his Brothers in his Native Mountains'
	M. M. T., 'A Dream'
	J. Shaw (24 Gloucester-street, Commercial-Road East), 'Acrostic on William Howitt the Patriot Writer'
31 October 1846	Songs for the People: T. R. Smart (Leicester), 'The March of Liberty' (Air: 'Jesse of Dumblin')

Beauties of Byron XLI, '[Extracts from Southey's *Vision of Judgement* contrasted with Byron's *Vision of Judgement*]'

7 November 1846   Ernest Jones, 'Through'
Beauties of Byron XLII, '[Southey contrasted with Byron]

14 November 1846   Beauties of Byron XLIII, '[Extracts from] Heaven and Earth'
Songs for the People: T. R. Smart (Leicester), 'The Past and the Present' (Air: 'Nancy Dawson')

21 November 1846   P. Smyth (Killaloe, Ireland), 'A Conversation between Dan and his Son John'
Songs for the People: Ernest Jones, 'Our Cheer'
Walter Savage Landor, 'To Michelet, on his "People"'

28 November 1846   Alfred Fennell, 'On the Annexation of Cracow to Austria'

5 December 1846   A Brother Bard and Shoemaker, '[2] Sonnets on the Death of Allen Davenport'

12 January 1846   W. I. L., 'The Spirit of Konarski'

19 December 1846   'A Christmas Garland' consisting of:
Mrs L. H. Sigourney (Boston, USA), 'The Snow-Storm'
Robert Southey, 'The Complaints of the Poor'
Lewis M. Thornton (Agard-Street, Derby), 'A Sigh for the Poor'
W. G. J. Barker, 'A Lyric for Christmas'
Ferdinand Freiligrath, 'St. Nicholas' (*Dublin University Magazine*)
J. G. Whittier, 'The Reformer'

26 December 1846   'A Christmas Garland: Part II' consisting of:
George William Wheeler, 'Winter'
G. Linnaeus Banks, 'Hurrah for Old Christmas'
Frances Brown, 'The Last Year's Cup'

1847

2 January 1847   Lady Dufferin, 'The Gates of Rome – The Gates of Heaven' (*Fisher's Drawing Room Scrap Book, 1837*)

9 January 1847   G. H., 'The Annexation of Cracow' (*Morning Advertiser*)
William Thom, 'The Hameless'

16 January 1847	Ernest Jones, 'The New Year's Song of Our Exile'
23 January 1847	Ernest Jones, 'England'
	Anon., 'Liberty'
	Anon., 'Song – (Johnny Bright)'
30 January 1847	Ernest Jones, 'To the Queen'
	Anon., 'Up For Free Land'
6 February 1847	Anon., 'Erin' (*The Labourer*)
13 February 1847	Ernest Jones, 'The Factory Town' (*The Labourer*)
20 February 1847	Anon., 'English Subscriptions and Irish Landlords' (*The Examiner*)
27 February 1847	Ernest Jones, 'Poland's Hope'
6 March 1847	Alfred Fennell, 'On the Illness of Prince Metternich'
13 March 1847	John Arnott (Somers Town), 'A Song' [sung in honour of T. S. Duncombe, M. P.] (Air: 'With Helmet on his Brow')
20 March 1847	A Sympathiser, 'The Patriot Pensioners'
	A Manchester Operative, 'Just Instinct and Brute Reason' (*Howitt's Journal*)
	William Howitt, 'An Early Spring Picture'
27 March 1847	Mary Howitt, 'Coming Spring' (*Howitt's Journal*)
3 April 1847	Speranza, 'France in '93. A Lesson from Foreign History' (*The Nation*)
	Alexander Huish, 'An Easter Offering'
10 April 1847	Ferdinand Freiligrath, 'Ireland' (trans. Mary Howitt, *Howitt's*)
17 April 1847	William Thom, 'Fasting for Fun'
24 April 1847	'Feast of the Poets' consisting of:
	T. R. Smart (Leicester), 'Labour's Holiday' (Air: 'Lucy, thy Fav'rite Bird')
	M. W. Trumble, 'A Weeping Mother to a Sleeping Child'
	John Peacock, 'The Voice of the Slave'
	J. Harkness (Edinburgh), 'Song' ['The millions toil – the millions starve'] (Tune: 'A Man's a Man for a' that')
	Michael Segrave (Barnsley), 'To Erin'
	J. Blackaby, 'Moral Musings'
	J. Edwards (Derby), 'The Might and March of Intelligence'

1 May 1847	'Feast of the Poets: Part II' consisting of:
	Ernest Jones, 'The Working-Man's Song'
	Colonist, 'Storm on a Forest Lake'
	T. Denham, '[Extracts from] Priestcraft', '[Extracts from] Wha think ye is the greatest slave?', and 'Blue Bell Braes'
	John Niven, 'The Sweetest Flower on Athol Braes' (Air: 'Oh, Nanny, wilt thou gang wi' me?'), and 'The Land of Liberty' (Air: 'Scotland Yet')
	John Watkins, '[Extracts from] *Griselda; or Love and Patience*' [a verse drama]
8 May 1847	'Feast of the Poets: Part III' consisting of:
	Thomas Hood, 'Spring. A New Version'
	Anon., 'Lines to the Stars'
	Joseph H. Butler (Bristol, April), 'The Human Mind'
	Soyer's Poetical Scullion, 'The Soyer Soup-Feeders'
	John Peacock (Greenock), 'The Spirit of Freedom'
	John Ackroyd (Thornton nr. Bradford), 'The Land. A Song'
	Anon. (Shettleston), 'Song of an Old Scotch Chartist'
	Ernest Jones, 'A Song for May' (*Labourer*)
15 May 1847	Samuel Langley, 'Odd Notions' (*Howitt's Journal*)
22 May 1847	Ernest Jones, 'A Song of the Starving'
29 May 1847	Michael Segrave (Barnsley), 'England's May-Day'
5 June 1847	Ernest Jones, 'The Slave-Song' (*The Labourer*)
	J. Harkness (Edinburgh), 'Song – For the Emancipated'
12 June 1847	Ernest Jones, 'The Battle' (*The Labourer*)
19 June 1847	Charles Mackay, 'The Little Moles' (*People's Friend*)
26 June 1847	'Feast of the Poets' consisting of:
	Frances Brown, 'The Song of Summer'
	Mary Howitt, 'Lyrics of Life'
	Samuel Kydd, 'Lines Suggested by a Letter from a Friend'
	Joseph H. Butler, 'Selected Fragments'
	William Motherwell, 'Jeanie Morrison' (*Tait's*)
	Beauties of Byron, 'Waterloo'

3 July 1847	'Feast of the Poets: Part II', dedicated to American poetry, consisting of:
	John G. Whittier, 'A Dream of Summer'
	Anon., 'Our Aborigines'
	Lydia Huntley Sigourney, 'Indian Names'
	Anon., 'Song of the Vermonters'
	J. G. Whittier, 'Yorktown'
	Anon., 'The Slave-Dealer'
	Thomas L. Harris, 'A Hymn of Liberty'
	W. C. Bryant, 'The Evening Wind'
10 July 1847	'Feast of the Poets: Part III', dedicated to American poetry, consisting of:
	A Mechanic, 'Appeal for Justice'
	Anon., 'Opening Ode'
	I. B., 'Awake! Ye Sons of Freedom Rise'
	Anon., 'To Feudal Lords'
	R. W. B., 'The Working Man's Dream'
	John St. John, 'Rise'
	Anon., 'The Agrarian Gathering' (Air: 'Hunters of Kentucky')
	Anon., 'Downfall of Feudalism'
	Revd J. G. Lyons, 'The Heroine Martyr of Monterey'
	J. G. Whittier, 'The Angels of Buena Vista'
17 July 1847	An Irishman [Henry Gracchus] (London), 'The Apotheosis'
	J. H. Bramwich, 'God Never Made A Slave' (Tune: 'New Crucifixion')
24 July 1847	An Irishman [Henry Gracchus] (London), 'The Land and the Charter. An Epistolary Eclogue, Addressed to Feargus O'Connor, Esq.'
	Mrs B. F. Foster, 'Song of the Emigrant'
31 July 1847	Shelley, 'Song to the Men of England'
	Henry Gracchus, Gentleman (London), 'The Broken Harp'
	T. R. Smart (Leicester), 'Song for the Million' (Air: 'Scots wha hae')
14 August 1847	Henry Gracchus, Gentleman (London), 'The Battle'
	Alfred Fennell, 'On the Visit of the Archduke Constantine to England'

21 August 1847	Mrs B. F. Foster, 'The Broken Stile – A Ballad'
	Henry Gracchus, Gentleman (London), 'The Victory'
	Rambler (Glasgow), 'Victoria's Visit to Scotland'
28 August 1847	Beranger (trans. W. Anderson), 'Were I A Little Bird'
	Henry Gracchus, Gentleman, 'Lowbands'
4 September 1847	Mrs B. F. Foster, 'My Old Home'
11 September 1847	Thomas Almond (Horseley Fields, Wolverhampton), 'Song to Feargus O'Connor, Written at the Request of an Irish Female'
18 September 1847	Henry Gracchus, Gentleman (London), 'Thomas Muir, the Scottish Martyr'
	John Arnott (Somers Town), 'A Song for the Fraternal Democrats'
25 September 1847	Henry Gracchus, Gentleman (London), 'The Chieftain'
	Alfred Fennell, 'The Italian Summons'
2 October 1847	Edwin Gill (Manchester), 'The Power-Loom Weaver'
	Mrs B. F. Foster, 'A Chartist Song'
9 October 1847	Charles Mackay, 'Eternal Justice' (*The Family Herald*)
	Mrs B. F. Foster, 'Let Us Be Sober (written for the *Northern Star*)
16 October 1847	W. C. Bennet (Greenwich), 'To The Right Hon. The Earl of —. A Humble Epistle Touching Scorn of Low Birth' (*Tait's Edinburgh Magazine*)
23 October 1847	Robert Findlay, 'Aberdeen's Welcome to F. O'Connor, M.P.' (Air: 'Dainty Davie')
30 October 1847	Charles Mackay, 'Baron Braemar'
13 November 1847	A Working Man (Manchester), 'Give it us now!'
20 November 1847	Beranger (Paris), 'The Deluge'
27 November 1847	Henry Gracchus (London), 'A Sketch of the Past, and the Present'
4 December 1847	Ernest Jones, 'The Age of Peace'
18 December 1847	Dr Mackay, 'Retractions and Repentance for Having Called Louis- Philippe an Honest Man'
25 December 1847	'A Christmas Garland' consisting of:
	Robert Burns, [Extract beginning] 'It's Hardly in a Body's Power'

S. T. Coleridge, [Extract Beginning] 'O! Ye
  Numberless,/Whom Foul Oppression's Ruffian
  Gluttony'
Anon., 'The Cottage and the Palace'
William Thom, 'Old Father Frost and his Family'
Anon., 'A Song for Christmas'
Robert Nicoll, 'Steadfastness' and 'The Honest and
  True'
Anon. [US poet], 'Flour in Ireland Ten Dollars per
  Barrel – Soldiers in Mexico Seven Dollars per
  Month'
George W. Light, 'Go Ahead'
Moore, 'Oh, the Sight Entrancing' and 'One
  Bumper at Parting'

1848

1 January 1848	'A New Year's Wreath' consisting of:
	Ernest Jones, 'A New Year's Cup'
	Anon., 'The Respectable Man' (*Comic Almanac*)
	Anon., 'The Irish Mother' (*New York Tribune*)
	Thomas Martin Wheeler (O'Connorville), 'An Appeal for Ireland'
	E. S. Wilkinson, 'The Prince and the Peasant. A Game Law Ditty'
	John Jones, 'To the People of England'
	Francis Davis (the 'Belfast Man'), 'A Song for True Men': 'My Ulick': 'Thoughts for the Present': 'Irish Frieze': 'Nanny': 'My Betrothed': 'A Request' (All 7 poems taken from F. Davis, *Miscellaneous Poems and Songs*)
8 January 1848	A Miner, 'Latest News from Mexico' (*Philadelphia Saturday Courier*)
	Sarah Parker (The 'Irish Girl'), 'Address to the New Year'
15 January 1848	Ernest Jones, 'The Blind Boy's Song'
	George Morrison, 'Caledonia'
22 January 1848	Songs for the People: J. A. Leatherland, 'We Will Be Free'
	Anon., 'Abd-El-Kader at Toulon; or, The Caged Hawk'

29 January 1848	Ernest Jones, 'The Patriot's Test'
	Songs for the People: John Rathbone, 'Our Native Land'
5 February 1848	'The Belfast Man' [Francis Davis], 'A Winter Chant'
12 February 1848	Anon., 'Louis Philippe's Valentine to the Queen of Spain' (*Punch*)
	Charles Mackay, 'Street Companions'
	Songs for the People: Thomas Moore, 'The Minstrel Boy'
19 February 1848	'The Belfast Man' [Francis Davis], 'A Lay of Labour'
	Songs for the People: Anon., 'Masaniello's Call to the Neapolitans' (Air: 'The Queen, God Bless Her')
26 February 1848	Songs for the People: Anon., 'The Marseilles Hymn'
	George Binns, 'The Doom of Toil'
11 March 1848	Edwin Gill, 'Vive La Republique'
	William Roscoe, 'The Day Star of Liberty', [First written in 1789]
18 March 1848	Ernest Jones, 'The March of Freedom' (*The Labourer*)
25 March 1848	William Roscoe, 'Song. – Written in 1789' ('Unfold, father Time, thy long records unfold')
	John Arnott, 'Lines on seeing a portrait of the Duke of Wellington displaced by one of Ernest Jones'
	Anon., 'A Welcome to Louis-Philippe' (*The Puppet Show*)
	Ernest Jones, 'Gratitude to the Martyred Poet of the People'
1 April 1848	Anon., 'Translation of the Marseillaise Hymn' (*Howitt's Journal*)
	Anon., 'Mourir Pour la Patrie! For Our Country to Die!' (*Howitt's Journal*)
	Anon., 'King Smith' (*Puppet Show*)
8 April 1848	Ernest Jones (transl.), 'The Marseillaise' (*The Labourer*) and 'Chorus of the Girondists', [translation of 'Mourir Pour La Patrie!]
	Alfred Fennell, 'The Chartist Tricolour'

	John Arnott (Somers Town), 'The Northern Star. An Acrostic'
22 April 1848	W. C. Bennet (Osborne Place, Blackheath), 'The Horrid Metamorphosis, not from Ovid'
	David Knox (Glasgow), 'Lines on the Present Movements'
	John Skelton, 'The Respond to Liberty'
29 April 1848	Geo. Tweddell, 'Address to Britons'
	Spartacus, 'Felony'
	John Skelton (London), 'National Song for the People' (Air: 'The Fishermen' from the opera of Masaniello)
	Anon., 'Fraternity' (*Puppet Show*)
20 May 1848	Anon., 'The Brotherhood of Nations' (*Puppet Show*)
	Anon., 'Hurrah-Hurrah-We Move'
	Anon., 'German Student's Song' (*Howitt's Journal*)
	J. F. M., 'King Rigmarole Alive Again!' (*United Irishmen*)
27 May 1848	Ernest Jones, 'Our Trust'
	W. W., 'The Holy Cause'
3 June 1848	Speranza, 'Attendite Popule' (*Nation*)
	Anon., 'The Warning Bell'm (*Puppet Show*)
10 June 1848	Robert Burns, 'The Tree of Liberty'
17 June 1848	George Twedell, 'Address of Tomaso Aniello'
	Anon., 'Italian Patriot Song' (translated by William Cullen Bryant)
24 June 1848	One of the People, 'The Song of Freedom'
	J. K. (Dublin, 40 Bride's-street), 'God Forbid' (Tune: 'Bang it up')
1 July 1848	Edwin Gill, 'The Felon' (Air: 'Scots wha hae')
8 July 1848	Hosea Biglow, 'The Pious Editor's Creed' (*Anti-Slavery Standard*)
15 July 1848	Eliza Lee Follen, 'To the Martyrs of Freedom'
	P. B. Shelley, 'Song to the Men of England'
22 July 1848	Mrs Hemans, 'Burial of William the Conqueror, at Caen in Normandy, 1087' ('A lesson for land-robbers')
	Edwin Gill, 'Emigration; or Here and There'

29 July 1848	K. W. M., 'To the People'
	Anon., 'Huzza for the Rule of the Whigs!' (Air: 'Old Roisin the Beau')
5 August 1848	Thomas Moore, 'The Harp that once through Tara's Halls'
12 August 1848	Thomas Moore, 'Let Erin Remember the Days of Old'
19 August 1848	Jeremiah Joseph Callanan, 'The Lament of O'Gnive'
	Edwin Gill, 'The Roman Tyrant'
26 August 1848	Thomas Moore, 'Weep On, Weep On'
	Charles Mackay, 'The Light in the Window'
2 September 1848	Thomas Moore, 'A Lament for Erin'
9 September 1848	James Elmslie Duncan, 'The Murdered Chartist' ('An epitaph for inscription upon the tomb of Henry Hanshard, a young weaver, who, having attended a Chartist meeting, on Sunday, June the 4th, 1848, in Bethnal-green, was attacked by the police, and received blows which caused his death')
16 September 1848	Charles Cole, 'The Spirit of Wat Tyler'
23 September 1848	'Poetry for the People' consisting of:
	Beranger, 'The Tailor and the Fay' (*Dublin University Magazine*); 'The Garret' (Thackeray's 'Paris Sketch Book'); 'The Will-O'-The-Wisps'; 'The Blind Mother'; 'The Coronation of Charles the Simple' (*Westminster Review*) and 'The Devil's Death' (*Westminster Review*)
30 September 1848	'Poetry for the People' consisting of:
	Beranger, 'Nature', 'Overflowing Love', 'The Old Standard', 'The Old Beggar' (*Tait's Magazine*), 'James', 'The Swallows', 'If I Were A Little Bird', 'The Comet of 1832' (*Westminster Review*), and 'An Imaginary Voyage'
14 October 1848	Spartacus, 'The Lament of the Present' [Linton, *The Republican*]
21 October 1848	J. G. Whittier, 'The Shoemakers'
	David Wright (Aberdeen), 'National Song. Ye Labourers of Britain' (Air: 'Ye Mariners of England')

28 October 1848	Shelley, '[Extracts from] Queen Mab'
4 November 1848	Ferdinand Freiligrath, 'The Dead to the Living' (trans. Mary Howitt, *Standard of Freedom*)
11 November 1848	Samuel Whitelocke (Bridgeton, Glasgow), 'The Song of the Land'
18 November 1848	Anon., 'The Unprecedented President' (*Puppet Show*)
25 November 1848	Anon., 'What Is a Peer?' (*Midland Progressionist*) J. W. King (Sheffield), 'A Tribute of Respect to the memory of the late Mr Councillor Briggs of Sheffield, an uncompromising Advocate of the People's Rights'
2 December 1848	Cassimir Brodzinski, 'The Legionist' (trans. By Dr Bowring)
23 December 1848	'A Christmas Garland. Wreath I' consisting of: Anon., 'A Trifle from Brighton' (*Punch*) Barry Cornwall, 'The Poor House' Anon., 'When this Old Cap was New' F. Monckton Milnes, Esq., M. P., 'The Violet Girl' Edwin Gill, 'The Free English Working Man'
30 December 1848	'A Christmas Garland. Wreath II' consisting of: Anon., 'Address to Winter' John Swain, 'The Last Year's Hymn' Frances Brown, 'The Last Year's Cup' D. W. (Aberdeen), 'A Social Song for Hogmanay' Burns, '[1 verse from] The Twa Dogs' Edwin Gill, 'Farewell to the Year Forty-Eight' Miss A Samsuda, 'Carol for the New Year' W. H. C. Hosmer, 'The Bondsman Waking' James Russell Lowell, 'The Day of Small Things' Anon., 'Song for a Cheapener' (*Standard*) Anon., 'Better Times'

1849

6 January 1849	Beauties of Byron. Second Series I: '[Extracts from] Ode to Napoleon Bonaparte'
13 January 1849	Beauties of Byron. Second Series II: 'Ode from the French'
20 January 1849	Beauties of Byron. Second Series III and IV: 'Prometheus' and 'Windsor Poetics'

27 January 1849	Anon., 'Thomas Paine'
	Anon., 'The Rights of Man' (Tune: 'God Save the King')
3 February 1849	Beauties of Byron. Second Series V: 'To Belshazzar'
	Anon., 'The Fallen' (*Dublin University Magazine*)
10 February 1849	W. C. Bennet, 'A Word to Kings' (*Birmingham Mercury*)
	Anon., 'The Kirkdale Prisoners'
17 February 1849	Mrs Mary M. Maxwell, 'Freedom's Lyric'
24 February 1849	Ernest Jones, 'The Marseillaise' and 'Chorus of the Girondists: (Mourir pour la Patrie')
3 March 1849	Thomas Watson (Pollokshaws), 'The Bairns O' The Mill' (Air: 'Calm Dewy Mornin')
	Michael Doheny, 'To My Country' (Air: 'Gra ma c'ree') (*Cork Examiner*)
10 March 1849	Duganne, 'The Acres and the Hands' (*Mark Lane Express*)
	Revd J. C. Lord, D. D., 'Kings and Thrones are Falling' (*The National Reformer and Pittsburgh Saturday Mercury*)
17 March 1849	Campbell, 'Retribution' [an extract from *Pleasures of Hope*]
24 March 1849	George White, 'Lines on Liberty'
	Tipperary, 'Acrostic', [Thomas Francis Meagher]
31 March 1849	Dodsley, 'Ode to Human Kind' (Extracted from *Pig's Meat for the Swinish Multitude*)
7 April 1849	Gerald Massey, 'The People's Advent' (*The Uxbridge Spirit of Freedom*)
14 April 1849	Anon., 'California' (*New York Tribune*)
21 April 1849	C. H. Hitchings (Rome), 'The Two Wishes' (*Athenaeum*)
28 April 1849	W. H. C. Hosmer, 'Tasso' (*New York Tribune*)
	G. White (Kirkdale Gaol), 'A Chartist Prison Rhyme. To Spring'
5 May 1849	Dr P. M. McDouall, 'Labour!' [Extract from *A Poetical petition to Queen Victoria*]
12 May 1849	J. M. L., 'Song of the Speaker' (*Examiner*)
19 May 1849	Anon., 'The German Fatherland'
26 May 1849	Anon., 'Hungary' (*Birmingham Mercury*)

2 June 1849	Thomas Gerald Massey, 'To The People' (*Progressionist*)
9 June 1849	Humanitas, 'Hungary'
16 June 1849	T. Gerald Massey, 'Oh, Listen in your Palaces'
	James French (Newcastle, Staffordshire), 'Acrostic' [Ernest Charles Jones]
23 June 1849	'Feast of the Poets' consisting of:
	Anon., 'Prison Lays'
	Michael Doheny, 'To My Wife'
	Thomas Dillon, 'The Song of the Exile'
	Charles Gavan Duffy, 'Address of St Lawrence to Irish Chiefs' and 'The Irish Chiefs'
	T. Gerald Massey, 'Kings Are But Giants Because We Kneel'
	Alfred Fennell, 'The Struggle'
	John H. Mackay (Glasgow), 'The Song of the Red Republican'
30 June 1849	Wm. Lyle (Annfield Pottery, Glasgow), 'Robert Blum's Farewell to his Wife, An Hour Previous to his Execution'
7 July 1849	T. Gerald Massey, 'Saith the Voice Truly' (*Uxbridge Spirit of Freedom*)
14 July 1849	Anon., 'The Kings of the Soil'
	William Taylor, 'To France'
21 July 1849	James Harkness (Edinburgh), 'The Spirit's Flight'
	Anon., 'Congratulatory Ode to the French on their Triumph at Rome'
28 July 1849	Spartacus, 'Rome Shall Be Free'
	James Harkness (Edinburgh), 'A Voice from the Bastile'
4 August 1849	Spartacus, 'For Rome, June, 1849' (*Democratic Review*)
	Gerald Massey, 'We Are Many, Our Tyrants Are Few'
11 August 1849	S. B. M. Wildman (Bradford), 'A Tribute to the Brave Hungarians, By One who had not a Sovereign, But Gives them a Song' (*Sun*)
18 August 1849	J. P. Dougflas (Maryport), 'God Speed Thee, Gallant Hungary!' (*Sun*)

25 August 1849	J. Clarence Mangan, 'Watch the Clock!'
1 September 1849	Herwegh, 'The Song of Hatred' (trans. Clarence Mangan)
8 September 1849	Gerald Massey, 'Hope On, Hope Ever' (*Uxbridge Spirit of Freedom*)
	John Arnott (Middlesex-place, Somers Town), 'An Acrostic to the Memory of Henry Hetherington'
15 September 1849	Charles J. Smith, 'Freedom'
22 September 1849	J. G. Whittier, 'Impromptu on receiving an Eagle's Quill from Lake Superior'
29 September 1849	T. Gerald Massey, 'The Martyrs of 1848–49'
6 October 1849	Robert McQueen, 'The March of Intellect' (*Democratic Review*)
	George Tweddell (Middlesbro-on-Tees), 'Sonnet to Byron'
13 October 1849	Wardrop (Dumfries), 'Rhyme for the Times'
	G. W. Wheeler, 'Acrostics on Joseph Williams and Alexander Sharp, who died in Tothill-Fields Prison, on the 7th and 14th of September, 1849'
20 October 1849	Eugene (October 2nd), 'There is no Peace' (*The Reasoner*)
27 October 1849	Dr P. McDouall, 'The Old Handloom Weaver'
3 November 1849	W. P., 'The Baker's Doom' (*Baker's Gazette*)
10 November 1849	Gerald Massey, 'Hold On, Hold On, in the World's Despite' (*Uxbridge Spirit of Freedom*)
17 November 1849	W. T. Gallagher, '[Extracts from] The Promise of the Present'
	Eugene, 'Sonnet [To the Memory of Count Bathyany Murdered by Haynau]' (*Reasoner*)
24 November 1849	Edgar A. Poe, 'The Bells'
1 December 1849	James Harkness, 'A Rural Home for Me' (*Democratic Review*)
8 December 1849	Leigh Hunt, 'On Receiving a Crown of Ivy from John Keats'
	Gerald Massey, 'Struggle on Bravely' (*Uxbridge Spirit of Freedom*)
15 December 1849	T. Hempstead, 'The Sound of the Drum'

22 December 1849	'A Christmas Garland' consisting of:
	Scott, '[Untitled 18-line extract]' and 'Christmas in the Olden Time'
	Frances Brown, 'The Bright Houses of Memory'
	Thomas Hood, 'Those Eyes that were so Bright, Love' and 'A Toast'
	Tom Moore, 'Drink of this Cup'
	Anon., 'A Word for Christmas'
	Anon., 'The Invitation to the Dance' ('A Popular Magyar Melody')
	Edwin Gill, 'Song' ('Fill, fill to the brave and free')
29 December 1849	'A Christmas Garland: Wreath II' consisting of:
	James Harkness (Edinburgh), 'December'
	E. L. Hervey, 'The Old Man's Song of the Old Year's Dying'
	Barry Cornwall, 'The Leveller'
	Edwin Gill, 'A Prologue to the Year Forty-Nine'
	Alfred Tennyson, 'The "Last New Year"'
	Spartacus, 'The Temple of Janus'

1850

8 January 1850	Anon., 'The Snow'
	George Tweddell (Middlesbro'-on-Tees), 'Percy Bysshe Shelley'
12 January 1850	Wansbeck, 'Poland and Hungary'
19 January 1850	C. D. Stuart, 'Noblemen'
	J. R. McKenzie, 'Lines' ['What mean those proud and haughty terms']
26 January 1850	James Harkness (Edinburgh), 'A Voice from the Ocean. John Mitchel to his Country'
2 February 1850	Eugene, 'The Hopes of '48'
9 February 1850	Gerald Massey, 'God's World Is Worthier Better Men' (*Spirit of Freedom*)
	A Glove-Maker, 'Song of the Future'
16 February 1850	Pasquin, 'Nothing To Do! A Song for Parliament'
	Wansbeck, 'Song of the British Slaves'
23 February 1850	J. R. McKenzie, 'A Tribute of Respect to the National Association of United Trades'
	William Whitmore (Leicester), 'To Mazzini and Kossuth' (*Cooper's Journal*)

2 March 1850	Gerald Massey, 'The Kingliest Crown'
	Pasquin, 'A Lay for Lord Grey'
9 March 1850	Pasquin, 'Exeter Hall'
16 March 1850	Gerald Massey, 'A Lay of Love'
23 March 1850	J. Lemon, 'The Patriot's Grave. Suggested on Visiting the Tomb where Andrew Hardie is Interred'
	Feargail, 'A Malediction'
30 March 1850	F. S. O., 'The Return' (*New York Tribune*)
	Walter Savage Landor, 'Kossuth'
6 April 1850	A member of the Oxford Farmers' Club, 'Sir Charles Wood and his Budget' (*Oxford Journal*)
13 April 1850	Anon., 'The Lament of O'Gnive'
	Anon., 'Love in the Country'
20 April 1850	John Alfred Langford (Birmingham), 'Sonnet: To Mazzini' and 'Sonnet: To Kossuth' (*Cooper's Journal*)
	J. R. McKenzie, 'We May Yet See Happier Days'
27 April 1850	Anon., 'Ministers Won't Go! A Tory's Lament'
	McQueen, 'Kings and Priests'
4 May 1850	Anon., 'The Popular Creed' (*American Paper*)
	J. M. D., 'The Soldier to the Sunburst' (*The Irishman*)
11 May 1850	Anon. ('Written in Newgate, by a Chartist Prisoner'), 'Chartist Song ['The Charter! thy principles never shall founder]' (Air: 'Old England for ever shall weather the storm')
25 May 1850	James Harkness (Edinburgh), 'The Popular Prints'
	J. R. McKenzie, 'The Heart's The Approving Place'
1 June 1850	George H. Boker, 'A Ballad of Sir John Franklin' (*Sartain's (American) Magazine*)
8 June 1850	W. M. Oland Bourne, 'Lady Jane Franklin's Appeal to the North' (From an American Paper)
15 June 1850	William Jones (Leicester), 'The Hawthorn Bush in Bloom'
22 June 1850	Eliza Cook, 'The Heart's Charity'
29 June 1850	D. W., 'The Irish Felon'
6 July 1850	Anon., 'Nobody Kens Ye'
	Henry Lestar Harrison, 'The Better Land' (*National Instructor*)

13 July 1850	Gerald Massey, 'The Red Banner' (*Red Republican*)
20 July 1850	Leigh Hunt, 'Ode to the Sun'
27 July 1850	Leo Penney, 'Ireland as she Was, Is, and Will Be' (Air: 'The Old Irish Gentlemen') (Composed and printed for the 'Knights of Erin')
3 August 1850	Anon., 'The Commonwealth' (*McDouall's Journal*)
10 August 1850	Anon., 'The Hungarian Heroine'
17 August 1850	Anon., 'Welcome As Flowers in May'
	C. D. Stuart, 'The True Man'
24 August 1850	John G. Whittier, 'The Slaveholders and their Allies. An American Poet'
31 August 1850	Anon., 'The Great Mistake'
7 September 1850	Anon., 'Uninscribed Tomb of Emmet' (*Dublin Comet*)
14 September 1850	Butler, '[Extract from *Hudibras*] 'The Swinish Multitude!'
	L. M. Thornton, 'A Word in Season'
21 September 1850	John Goodwyn Barmby, 'The Communists' Hymn'
28 September 1850	A. J. H. D., 'The Exodus of the People'
	Frances Brown, 'Our Early Loved'
5 October 1850	Ben, 'General Haynau and Judge Lynch. A New Song to an Old Tune' (Air: 'The Mistletoe Bough')
12 October 1850	Anon., 'To Emigrants' (*New York Tribune*)
	Mrs J. H. Lewis, 'Flowers! Fresh Flowers!'
19 October 1850	Etna, 'The Genius of Poverty'
	Anon., 'There's Something Good in Every Heart'
26 October 1850	Eliza Cook, 'The Poor Man to his Son'
2 November 1850	Anon., 'Uninscribed Tomb of Emmett'
	Anon., 'To a Bee. Straying in London Streets'
9 November 1850	Anon., 'Autumn Wild Flowers'
16 November 1850	C. H. B., 'Our Future'
23 November 1850	O., 'Oh! the Weary Ages' (*The Lever*)
30 November 1850	Gerald Massey, 'God's World Is Worthy Better Men' (*The Leader*)
7 December 1850	Anon., 'The Poor Man's Sabbath' ('By the author of 'The Omnipotence of the Deity', 'Leisure Hours' and other poems')
14 December 1850	T. Westwood, 'Love Her Still'

| 21 December 1850 | A. M. P., 'A Christmas Carol' |
| 28 December 1850 | Anon., 'The Poor Man's Temple' ('By the author of 'The Omnipotence of the Deity', 'Leisure Hours' and other poems') |

1851

4 January 1851	G. Cole, 'Who Made the Poor?'
11 January 1851	Longfellow, 'Life Is Real'
18 January 1851	Anon., 'Mother Church and the Cherry Trees'
25 January 1851	Edwin Gill, 'Throw Away the Apple'
	Anon., 'How to Confess'
1 February 1851	Thomas Martin Wheeler, 'To Rome'
8 February 1851	Anon., 'The Toiler's Dream'
15 February 1851	D. F. McCarthy, 'The Voice and the Pen'
22 February 1851	Anon., 'The Warning'
	C. Chauncey Burr, 'Time's Watch Word'
1 March 1851	Anon., 'The Cry of the Lawful Lanterns' (*Bennett's Poems*)
8 March 1851	Anon., 'The Press'
	Emily Varndell, 'The Dust of Dead Man's Graves'
15 March 1851	J. Barker, 'Pebbles in the Sea'
22 March 1851	Charles Swain, 'What is Noble?'
29 March 1851	Anon., 'Who is my Neighbour?'
	Anon., 'The Labourer'
5 April 1851	Anon. [Charles Kingsley], 'A Rough Rhyme on a Rough Matter' (*Yeast*)
12 April 1851	T. Gerald Massey, 'The Lords of Land and Money'
19 April 1851	William Cullen Bryant, 'Antiquity of Freedom'
26 April 1851	A Wrangler of Trinity College, Cambridge, 'Columbus' (*Poems of Earlier Years*)
3 May 1851	Gerald Massey, 'Hope On, Hope Ever' (*Voices of Freedom*)
10 May 1851	Mrs Barrett Browning, 'Life in London' (*Poems*)
17 May 1851	Anon., 'Earth's Wrongs'
24 May 1851	Anon., 'Education'
31 May 1851	Anon., 'Labour's Social Chivalry'
7 June 1851	Ernest Jones, 'Earth's Burdens' (*Notes and Poems*)
14 June 1851	Mrs Browning, 'Peace'
21 June 1851	Gerald Massey, 'The Kingliest Kings' (*Voices of Freedom and Lyrics of Love*)

28 June 1851	Anon., 'True Progress'
5 July 1851	Anon., 'Ohne Hast, Ohne Rast' (*Leader*)
12 July 1851	G. Meredith, 'London by Lamplight' (*Poems*)
19 July 1851	Anon., 'The Low Born' ('From the French of P. J. de Beranger)
26 July 1851	Anon., 'The New Aristocracy'
2 August 1851	Ann Moss, 'Who are the Great'
9 August 1851	W. B. (Potteries), 'Caligula's Example'
16 August 1851	Anon., 'Sunrise Comes To-morrow' ('From a small volume of Poems entitled *Reverberations*')
23 August 1851	Anon., 'The Cloud' ('Imitated from the German') (Harpur's *Wild Bees of Australia*. From the *People's Advocate*, Sydney)
30 August 1851	Gerald Massey, 'Our Fathers Are Praying for Pauper Pay' (*Voices of Freedom and Lyrics of Love*)
6 September 1851	Anon., 'Education' (From *Poems*, by Fritz and Liolett), [Previously published 24 May 1851]
13 September 1851	Charles Swain, 'Song for Thinkers'
20 September 1851	E. B. P., 'To Louis Kossuth'
27 September 1851	[W. J. Linton], 'The Mechanic' (*English Republic*)
4 October 1851	Anon., 'True Progress' (From *Poems*, by Fritz and Liolett) [Previously published 28 June 1851]
11 October 1851	Gerald Massey, 'A Song of Welcome to Kossuth' (*Voices of Freedom and Lyrics of Love*)
	[W. J. Linton], 'Rhymes and Reasons Against Landlordism: The Parks' (*English Republic*)
18 October 1851	Walter Savage Landor, 'Kossuth. To The President of France'
25 October 1851	W. Jones (Leicester), 'Welcome Kossuth'
1 November 1851	Charles Kingsley, 'A Thought from the Rhine' (*Christian Socialist*)
	Tennyson's, 'The Bugle-Song' (*The Princess*)
8 November 1851	Walter Savage Landor, 'To Meschid, The Liberator of Kossuth'
15 November 1851	A. H. L., 'A Word to the Wise' (*Christian Socialist*)
	William Oland Bourne, 'Speak Boldly'
22 November 1851	Anon., 'The Voice of the Exile' (*Punch*)
29 November 1851	Frances D. Gage, 'The Sounds of Industry'

6 December 1851	W. E. P. Haskell, 'Yankee Doodle Did! On England and America in 1851. A Ballad of the Times' (*Chelsea Telegraph*, United States)
13 December 1851	John Booker (Sheffield), 'The Upward Pathway'
20 December 1851	J. F., 'Too Poor to Pay' (*New York Tribune*)
27 December 1851	J. E. B., 'Ode on the Late Coup D'Etat' (*Spectator*)

1852

3 January 1852	Gerald Massey, 'Love's Fairy Ring'
10 January 1852	Anon., 'Lines to Brother Jonathan' (*Punch*)
17 January 1852	Anon., 'The Flesh-Pots of the Navy' (*Punch*)
24 January 1852	Anon., 'Battle On Bravely'
31 January 1852	Gerald Massey, 'Labour's Social Chivalry'
7 February 1852	Anon., 'Flecti, Non Frangi – Bent, but not Broken' (*The British Journal*)
14 February 1852	Gerald Massey, 'God's World Is Worthy Better Men'
21 February 1852	J. Burbudge, 'Never Fear'
28 February 1852	John Booker (Sheffield), 'Love Each Other'
6 March 1852	Anon., 'Progress'
13 March 1852	Anon., 'Keep in Step!'
20 March 1852	Anon., 'The Roebuck and Coppock Controversy' ('Air: 'Oh! no we never mention him')
3 April 1852	Thomas Cooper, 'The Time Shall Come' (Air: 'Canadian Boat Song')
10 April 1852	John Booker (Sheffield), 'The True Heart'
17 April 1852	Gruntwig, 'The Mother-Tongue' (Translated in Howitt's *Literature and Romance of Northern Europe*)
24 April 1852	Gerald Massey, 'Fragments from "My Scrap Book"'
8 May 1852	'Our May Garland' by 'Critic' and 'Poet' consisting of: Tennyson, 'May Queen' Anon., [Untitled: 'O, the World goes by'] Anon., [Untitled: 'O, the Merry, Merry Lark was up and Singing']

George Meredith, 'Song' ('I Cannot Lose Thee for a Day')

'Poet' [Massey?], 'Song' ('Ah! 'tis like a Tale of Olden')

Hood, 'Song' ('O Lady, Leave thy Silken Thread')

Lowell, '[Extract from] Vision of Sir Launfal' and 'Stanzas On Freedom'

Freiligrath, [Untitled: 'On manhood's tree, springs crowding flower on flower']

Alton Locke, [Untitled: 'Weep, weep, weep, and weep / For pauper, dolt, and slave']

Louis Napoleon, 'Idées Napoléoniennes'

15 May 1852   Obadiah Bind-Their-Kings-in-Chains-and-their-Nobles-With-Links-of- Iron (Sergeant in Ireton's Regiment), 'The Battle of Naseby'

29 May 1852   Walter Savage Landor, 'On the Death of M. D'Ossoli; and his Wife Margaret Fuller'

5 June 1852   Spartacus, 'The Man Who Slew Wat Tyler'
Anon., 'The Song of the Serf'

3 July 1852   Charles Kingsley, 'Epicedium on the Death of the Journal of Association'

Bibliography

Place of publication is London unless otherwise stated.

PRIMARY SOURCES

Adams, W. E., *Memoirs of a Social Atom* (New York: Augustus M. Kelley, 1968 [1903]).

Benbow, William, *Grand National Holiday, and Congress of the Productive Classes* (Benbow, n.d. [1832]).

Carlyle, Thomas, 'Chartism' in A. Shelston (ed.), *Thomas Carlyle: Selected Writings* (Harmondsworth: Penguin, 1971).

The Chartist Circular

Cooper, T., *The Life of Thomas Cooper* (Leicester University Press, 1971 [1872]).

Cooper's Journal

The Democratic Review

English Chartist Circular

Disraeli, Benjamin, *Sybil* (Harmondsworth: Penguin, 1980 [1845]).

The Friend of the People

Frost, T., *Forty Years' Recollections: Literary and Political* (Sampson Low, Marston, Searle & Rivington, 1880).

Gammage, R. C., *History of the Chartist Movement 1837–1854* (Merlin Press, 1969 [1894]).

Goodridge, John (ed.), *Nineteenth-Century English Labouring-Class Poets 1800–1900* (3 vols.) (Pickering & Chatto, 2006).

Jones, Ernest, *Chartist Poems and other Fugitive Pieces* (MacGowan, 1846).

Jones, Ernest, *The Battle-Day: and Other Poems* (Routledge, 1855).

Kingsley, Charles, *Alton Locke, Tailor and Poet: An Autobiography* (Oxford University Press, 1983 [1850]).

The Labourer

Leno, J. B., *The Reformer's Book of Songs and Recitations*.

Linton, W. J., *Memories* (New York: Augustus M. Kelley, 1970 [1894]).

Lovett, William, *Life and Struggles of William Lovett* (MacGibbon & Kee, 1967 [1876]).

Karl Marx, 'The Eighteenth Brumaire of Louis Bonaparte' in R. C. Tucker (ed.), *The Marx–Engels Reader* (New York: W. W. Norton, 1978).

Marx, Karl, 'The Paris Manuscripts' in R. C. Tucker (ed.), *The Marx-Engels Reader* (New York: W. W. Norton, 1978).
Massey, Gerald, *Voices of Freedom and Lyrics of Love* (J. Watson, 1851).
Massey, Gerald, *My Lyrical Life: Poems Old and New* (Kegan, Paul & Tench, 1889).
Moore, Thomas, *Poetical Works* (Frederick Warne, no date).
Morrell, Philip (ed.), *Leaves from the Greville Diary* (Eveleigh Nash & Grayson, 1929).
The Northern Star
Notes to the People
Poor Man's Guardian
The Red Republican
Revolutionary Rhymes and Songs for Socialists, no. 1 (T. Binning, 1886).
The Trial of Feargus O'Connor (New York: Augustus M. Kelley, 1970 [1843]).
Reitzel, W. (ed.), *The Autobiography of William Cobbett* (Faber, 1967).
Somerville, A., *The Autobiography of a Working Man* (MacGibbon & Kee Ltd, 1967 [1848]).
Trial of John Frost for High Treason (2 vols.) (New York: Garland, 1986 [1840]).

SECONDARY SOURCES

Althusser, Louis, *Essays on Ideology* (Verso, 1984).
Andrews, James R., 'The Passionate Negation: The Chartist Movement in Rhetorical Perspective', *The Quarterly Journal of Speech* 59: 2 (April 1973): 196–208.
Armstrong Isobel, *Victorian Poetry. Poetry, Poetics and Politics* (Routledge, 1996).
Armstrong, Isobel, *The Radical Aesthetic* (Oxford: Blackwell, 2000).
Ashraf, P. M., *Introduction to Working Class Literature in Great Britain. Part One: Poetry* (East Germany: unknown, 1978).
Ashton, Owen, R. Fyson and S. Roberts (eds.), *The Duty of Discontent: Essays for Dorothy Thompson* (Mansell, 1995).
Ashton, Owen and S. Roberts, *The Victorian Working-Class Writer* (Cassell, 1999).
Ashton, Owen R. Fyson and S. Roberts (eds.), *The Chartist Legacy* (Rendlesham: Merlin, 1999).
Ashton, Owen, R. and Paul A. Pickering, *Friends of the People* (Merlin, 2002).
Baldick, Chris, *The Social Mission of English Criticism 1848–1932* (Oxford University Press, 1983).
Barrow, Logie, *Independent Spirits: Spiritualism and English Plebeians 1850–1910* (Routledge, 1986).
Barthes, Roland, *Mythologies* (Paladin, 1973).
Batho, E. C. and B. Dobree (eds.), *The Victorians and After 1830–1914* (Cresset Press, 1962, 3rd revd. edn.).
Benjamin, Walter, *Illuminations* (Fontana Press, 1992).
Berg, Maxine, *The Machinery Question and the Making of Political Economy 1815–1848* (Cambridge University Press, 1982).

Blair, Kirstie, *Victorian Poetry and the Culture of the Heart* (Oxford University Press, 2006).

Boos, F., 'Working-Class Poetry' in R. Cronin, A. Chapman and A. H. Harrison (eds.), *A Companion to Victorian Poetry* (Oxford: Blackwell, 2002).

Brantlinger, Patrick, *The Reading Lesson: The Threat of Mass Literacy in Nineteenth-Century British Fiction* (Bloomington: Indiana University Press, 1998).

Burnett, John (ed.), *Useful Toil: Autobiographies of Working People from the 1820s to the 1920s* (Penguin, 1974).

Burnett, John (ed.), *Destiny Obscure: Autobiographies of Childhood, Education and Family from the 1820s to the 1920s* (Penguin, 1982).

Butler, Marilyn, *Romantics, Rebels and Reactionaries* (Oxford University Press, 1981).

Campbell, Matthew, *Rhythm and Will in Victorian Poetry* (Cambridge University Press, 1999).

Cannadine, David, *Class in Britain* (New Haven: Yale University Press, 1998).

Castoriadis, Cornelius, *The Imaginary Institution of Society* (Cambridge: Polity, 1997).

Caudwell, Christopher *Illusion and Reality* (Lawrence & Wishart, 1973 [1937]).

Charlton, John, *The Chartists* (Pluto, 1997).

Chase, Malcolm, *The People's Farm: English Radical Agrarianism, 1775–1840* (Oxford: Clarendon Press, 1988).

Churchill, R. C., *English Literature of the Nineteenth Century* (University Tutorial Press, 1951).

Clark, Anna, *The Struggle for the Breeches* (Berkeley: University of California Press, 1995).

Cole, G. D. H., *Chartist Portraits* (Macmillan, 1965).

Cole, G. D. H. (ed.), *William Morris: Collected Writings* (Nonesuch Press, 1946).

Colley, Ann C., *Nostalgia and Recollection in Victorian Culture* (Basingstoke: Macmillan, 1998).

Collini, Stefan, *Public Moralists: Political Thought and Intellectual Life in Britain* (Oxford University Press, 1993).

Collins, T. J. and V. J. Rundle (eds.), *The Broadview Anthology of Victorian Poetry and Poetic Theory* (Peterborough, Ontario: Broadview, 2000).

Corrigan, P. and D. Sayer, *The Great Arch: English State Formation as Cultural Formation* (Oxford University Press, 1991).

Cronin, R., A. Chapman, A. H. Harrison (eds.), *A Companion to Victorian Poetry* (Oxford: Blackwell, 2002).

Cunningham, Valentine, (ed.), *The Victorians: An Anthology of Poetry and Poetics* (Oxford: Blackwell, 2000).

Curtis L. Perry Jr., *Apes and Angels: The Irishman in Victorian Caricature* (Washington: Smithsonian Institute Press, 1997).

Davis, Philip, *The Oxford English Literary History. Volume 8: 1830–1880. The Victorians* (Oxford University Press, 2002).

Driver, C., *Tory Radical: The Life of Richard Oastler* (New York: Oxford University Press, 1946).

Dumbreck, J. C. and M. Beresford transl., '[Y. V. Kovalev's] Introduction to *An Anthology of Chartist Literature*' *Victorian Studies*, vol. II (1958), 117–38.

Eagleton, Terry, *Criticism and Ideology* (Verso, 1978).

Eagleton, Terry, *Walter Benjamin or Towards a Revolutionary Criticism* (Verso, 1981).

Elbourne, Roger, *Music and Tradition in Early Industrial Lancashire 1780–1840* (Woodbridge: D. S. Brewer, 1980).

Epstein, James A., *The Lion of Freedom: Feargus O'Connor and the Chartist Movement, 1838–1842* (Croom Helm, 1982).

Epstein, James A. and D. Thompson (eds.), *The Chartist Experience* (Macmillan, 1982).

Epstein, James A., *Radical Expression: Political Language, Ritual, and Symbol in England, 1790–1850* (Oxford University Press, 1994).

Erickson, Lee, *The Economy of Literary Form. English Literature and the Industrialisation of Publishing, 1800–1850* (Baltimore: John Hopkins University Press, 1996).

Faas, Ekbert, *Retreat into the Mind: Victorian Poetry and the Rise of Psychiatry* (Princeton University Press, 1988).

Finn, Margot, *After Chartism: Class and Nation in English Radical Politics, 1848–1874* (Cambridge University Press, 1993).

Flett, Keith, *Chartism After 1848* (Monmouth: Merlin, 2006).

Gagnier, Reginia, *Subjectivities: A History of Self-Representation in Britain, 1832–1920* (Oxford University Press, 1991).

Gallagher, Catherine, *The Industrial Reformation of English Fiction: Social Discourse and Narrative Form 1832–1867* (University of Chicago Press, 1985).

Gallagher, Catherine, *The Body Economic* (Princeton University Press, 2006).

Gilmartin, Kevin, *Print Politics: The Press and Radical Opposition in Early Nineteenth-Century England* (Cambridge University Press, 1996).

Gramsci, Antonio, *Selections from Prison Notebooks* (Lawrence & Wishart, 1971).

Gray, R., *The Factory Question and Industrial England, 1830–1860* (Cambridge University Press, 1996).

Hambrick, Margaret, *A Chartists's Library* (Mansell, 1986).

Handelman, Susan A., *Fragments of Redemption: Jewish Thought and Literary Theory in Benjamin, Scholem, and Levinas* (Indiana University Press, 1991).

Harrison, Antony H., *Victorian Poets and the Politics of Culture* (Charlottesville: University Press of Virginia, 1998).

Harrison, J. F. C., *The Second Coming: Popular Millenarianism 1780–1850* (Routledge & Kegan Paul, 1975).

Harrison, T., *Continuous* (Rex Collings, 1981).

Haywood, Ian, *The Literature of Struggle* (Aldershot: Scolar Press, 1995).

Haywood, Ian, *Chartist Fiction* (Aldershot: Ashgate, 1998).

Haywood, Ian, *Chartist Fiction Vol. 2: Ernest Jones, Women's Wrongs* (Aldershot: Ashgate, 2001).

Haywood, Ian, *The Revolution in Popular Literature: Print, Politics and the People, 1790–1860* (Cambridge University Press, 2005).

Hewitt, Martin, *The Emergence of Stability in the Industrial City: Manchester, 1832–1867* (Aldershot: Scolar Press, 1996).

Hobsbawm, Eric, *Labouring Men* (Weidenfield & Nicolson, 1968).

Hobsbawn, Eric, *Industry and Empire* (Harmondsworth: Penguin, 1969).

Hoggart, Richard, *The Uses of Literacy* (Harmondsworth: Penguin, 1957).

Hollis, Patricia, *The Pauper Press: A Study in Working Class Radicalism of the 1830s* (Oxford University Press, 1970).

Host, John, *Victorian Labour History: Experience, Identity and the Politics of Representation* (Routledge, 1998).

Jacobson, E., *Metaphysics of the Profane: The Political Theology of Walter Benjamin and Gershom Scholem* (New York: Columbia University Press, 2003).

James, Louis, *Fiction for the Working Man* (Harmondsworth: Penguin, 1974).

James, Louis, *Print and the People 1819–1851* (Harmondsworth: Penguin, 1978).

Jameson, Fredric, *The Political Unconscious* (Routledge, 1989).

Janowitz, Anne, *Lyric and Labour in the Romantic Tradition* (Cambridge University Press, 1998).

Jenkins, Mick, *The General Strike of 1842* (Lawrence & Wishart, 1980).

Johnson, E. D. H., *The Alien Vision of Victorian Poetry: Sources of the Poetic Imagination in Tennyson, Browning and Arnold* (Princeton University Press, 1952).

Johnson, Pauline, *Marxist Aesthetics* (Routledge & Kegan Paul, 1984).

Jones, David J. V., *The Last Rising: The Newport Insurrection of 1839* (Oxford University Press, 1985).

Joyce, Patrick, *Work, Society and Politics: The Culture of the Factory in Later Victorian England* (Brighton: Harvester, 1980).

Joyce, Patrick, *Democratic Subjects* (Cambridge University Press, 1994).

Joyce, Patrick (ed.), *Class* (Oxford University Press, 1995).

Kanth, R. K., *Political Economy and Laissez-Faire: Economics and Ideology in the Ricardian Era* (New Jersey: Rowman and Littlefield, 1986).

Kirk, Neville, *The Growth of Working Class Reformism in Mid-Victorian England* (Croom Helm, 1985).

Knott, John, *Popular Opposition to the 1834 Poor Law* (Croom Helm, 1986).

Kossick, K. (ed.), *Nineteenth-Century English Labouring-Class Poets 1800–1900. Volume II 1830–1860* (Pickering & Chatto, 2006).

Kovalev, Y. V., *An Anthology of Chartist Literature* (Moscow: Foreign Languages Publishing House, 1956).

Kuduk, Stephanie, 'Sedition, Criticism and Epic Poetry in Thomas Cooper's *The Purgatory of Suicides*', *Victorian Poetry* 39: 2 (2001): 165–89.

Landry. D., *The Muses of Resistance: Laboring-Class Women's Poetry in Britain, 1739–1796* (Cambridge University Press, 1990).

Langbaum, Robert, *The Poetry of Experience: the Dramatic Monologue in Modern Literary Tradition* (Chatto & Windus, 1957).

Levinas, E., 'Messianic Texts', *Difficult Freedom: Essays on Judaism* (Athlone Press, 1990).

Lloyd, A. L., *Folk Song in England* (St Albans: Paladin, 1975).

Lown, Judy, *Women and Industrialisation: Gender at Work in Nineteenth-Century England* (Cambridge: Polity, 1990).

Maidment, Brian, 'Magazines of Popular Progress and the Artisans', *Victorian Periodicals Review* 17(3), (1984), 83–93.

Maidment, Brian *The Poorhouse Fugitives* (Manchester: Carcanet, 1992).

Mather, F. C., *Public Order in the Age of the Chartists* (Manchester University Press, 1966).

Mays, K. J., 'Subjectivity, Community and the Nature of Truth-telling in Two Chartist Autobiographies' in O. Ashton, R. Fyson and S. Roberts (eds.), *The Chartist Legacy* (Rendlesham: Merlin, 1999).

Mays, K. J., 'Slaves in Heaven, Laborers in Hell: Chartist Poets' Ambivalent Identification with the (Black) Slave', *Victorian Poetry*, 39: 2 (Summer 2001), 137–63.

McCalman, Iain, *Radical Underworld: Prophets, Revolutionaries, and Pornographers in London, 1795–1840* (Oxford University Press).

McLellan, D., *Marxism After Marx,* 2nd edn. (Macmillan Press, 1980).

Miles, A. H. (ed.), *The Poets and the Poetry of the Century* (Hutchinson, 1891–7).

Morris, M., (ed.), *From Cobbett to the Chartists* (Lawrence & Wishart, 1948).

Morton, A. L. and G. Tate, *The British Labour Movement 1770–1920* (Lawrence & Wishart, 1956).

Murphy, Paul T., *Towards A Working-Class Canon: Literary Criticism in British Working-Class Periodicals 1816–1858* (Ohio State University Press, 1994).

de Nie, Michael, *The Eternal Paddy: Irish Identity in the British Press 1798–1882* (Madison: University of Wisconsin Press, 2004).

Norman, Edward, *The Victorian Christian Socialists* (Cambridge University Press, 1987).

Parker, Andrew and Eve Kosofsky Sedgwick (eds.), *Performativity and Performance* (Routledge: 1995).

Paul, R., ' "In Louring Hindostan": Chartism and Empire in Ernest Jones's *The New World*', *Victorian Poetry*, 39: 2 (Summer 2001), 189–204.

Pickering, Michael, *History, Experience and Cultural Studies* (Basingstoke: Macmillan, 1997).

Plummer, Alfred, *Bronterre* (George Allen & Unwin, 1971).

Ranciere, J., *The Politics of Aesthetics* (Continuum, 2004).

Randall, Timothy, 'Chartist Poetry and Song' in O. Ashton, R. Fyson and S. Roberts (eds.), *The Chartist Legacy* (Rendlesham: Merlin, 1999).

Read, Donald and Eric Glasgow, *Feargus O'Connor* (Edward Arnold, 1961).

Rendall, Jane, *The Origins of Modern Feminism: Women in Britain, France and the United States, 1780–1860* (Basingstoke: Macmillan, 1985).

Reynolds, Matthew, *The Realms of Verse 1830–1870. English Poetry in a Time of Nation-building* (Oxford University Press, 2001).

Roberts, Stephen, 'Who Wrote to the *Northern Star*?' in Owen Ashton *et al.* (eds.), *The Duty of Discontent: Essays for Dorothy Thompson* (New York: Mansell, 1995).

Roberts, Stephen (ed.), *The People's Charter: Democratic Agitation in Early Victorian Britain* (Merlin Press, 2003).

Rogers, Helen, *Women and the People. Authority, Authorship and the Radical Tradition in Nineteenth-Century England* (Aldershot: Ashgate, 2000).

Roll, E., *A History of Economic Thought* (Faber, 1973).

Rose, Jonathan, *The Intellectual Life of the British Working Classes* (New Haven: Yale University Press, 2001).

Royle, Edward, *Chartism* (Longman, 1986).

Royle, Edward, *Revolutionary Britannia?* (Manchester University Press, 2000).

Rule, John, *The Labouring Classes in Early Industrial England 1750–1850* (Longman, 1986).

Russell, Dave, *Popular Music in England, 1840–1914* (Manchester University Press, 1987).

Sammons, Jeffrey L., *Heinrich Heine: A Modern Biography* (Manchester: Carcanet, 1979).

Samuel, Raphael, *Theatres of Memory* (Verso: 1996).

Sanders, M., 'Poetic Agency: Metonymy and Metaphor in Chartist Poetry 1838–1852', *Victorian Poetry*, 39: 2 (Summer 2001). 111–35.

Saintsbury, G., *A History of Nineteenth Century Literature (1780–1895)* (Macmillan, 1896).

Saville, John, *1848: The British State and the Chartist Movement* (Cambridge University Press, 1990).

Schwab, Ulrike, *The Poetry of the Chartist Movement: a Literary and Historical Study* (Dordrecht, Netherlands: Kluwer Academic Publishers, 1987).

Schwarzkopf, Jutta, *Women in the Chartist Movement* (Macmillan, 1991).

Scrivener, Michael, *Poetry and Reform: Periodical Verse from the English Democratic Press 1792–1824* (Detroit: Wayne State University Press, 1992).

Seccombe, Wally, *Weathering the Storm: Working-Class Families from the Industrial Revolution to the Fertility Decline* (Verso, 1993).

Shaaban, Bouthaina, 'Shelley in the Chartist Press' *Keats-Shelley Review* 34 (1983): 41–60.

Shaaban, Bouthaina, 'The Romantics in the Chartist Press' *Keats-Shelley Journal* 38 (1989): 25–46.

Shaw, David, *Gerald Massey: Chartist, Poet, Radical and Freethinker* (Buckland, 1995).

Shiach, Morag, *Discourse on Popular Culture* (Oxford: Polity Press, 1989).

Slinn, E. Warwick 'Dramatic Monologue' in R. Cronin, A. Chapman and A. H. Harrison (eds.), *A Companion to Victorian Poetry* (Oxford: Blackwell, 2002).

Slinn, E. Warwick, *Victorian Poetry as Cultural Critique: The Politics of Performative Language* (Charlottesville: University of Virginia Press, 2003).

Smith, F. B., *Radical Artisan: William James Linton, 1812–97* (Manchester University Press, 1973).

Smith, Sheila M., *The Other Nation* (Oxford University Press, 1980).

Stafford, William, *Socialism, Radicalism and Nostalgia* (Cambridge University Press, 1987).

Taylor, Barbara, *Eve and the New Jerusalem* (Virago, 1983).

Taylor, Miles, 'The Six Points: Chartism and the Reform of Parliament' in O. Ashton *et al.* (eds.), *The Chartist Legacy* (Rendlesham: Merlin, 1999).

Taylor, Miles, *Ernest Jones, Chartism and the Romance of Politics 1819–1869* (Oxford University Press, 2003).

Thomas, W., *The Philosophic Radicals* (Oxford University Press, 1979).

Thompson, Dorothy, *The Early Chartists* (Macmillan, 1971).

Thompson, Dorothy, 'Ireland and the Irish in English Radicalism before 1850' in J. Epstein and D. Thompson (eds.), *The Chartist Experience* (Macmillan, 1982).

Thompson, Dorothy, *The Chartists: Popular Politics in the Industrial Revolution* (Aldershot: Wildwood House, 1986).

Thompson, Dorothy, *Outsiders: Class, Gender and Nation* (Verso, 1993).

Thompson, E. P., *The Poverty of Theory* (Merlin, 1978).

Thompson, E. P., *The Making of the English Working Class* (Harmondsworth: Penguin, 1980).

Thompson, Noel, *The Real Rights of Man. Political Economies for the Working Classes 1775–1850* (Pluto Press, 1998).

Tucker, R. C. (ed.), *The Marx-Engels Reader* (New York: W. W. Norton, 1978).

Vernon, James (ed.), *Re-reading the Constitution. New Narratives in the Political History of England's Long Nineteenth Century* (Cambridge University Press, 1996).

Vicinus, Martha, *The Industrial Muse: A Study of Nineteenth Century British Working-Class Literature* (Croom Helm, 1974).

Vickers, R., 'Christian Election, Holy Communion and Psalmic Language in Ernest Jones's Chartist Poetry', *Journal of Victorian Culture*, 11: 1 (2006), 59–83.

Vincent, D. (ed.), *Testaments of Radicalism: Memoirs of Working Class Politicians 1790–1855* (Europe Publications, 1977).

Vincent, D., *Bread, Knowledge and Freedom. A Study of Nineteenth-Century Working Class Autobiography* (Methuen, 1982).

Vines, S., *100 Years of English Literature* (Gerald Duckworth, 1950).

Walker, H., *The Literature of the Victorian Era* (Cambridge University Press, 1910).

Wilks, Ivor, *South Wales and the Rising of 1839* (Beckenham: Croom Helm, 1984).

Williams, David, *John Frost A Study in Chartism* (London: Evelyn, Adams & Mackay, 1969).

Williams, A. Susan, *The Rich Man and the Diseased Poor in Early Victorian Literature* (Macmillan, 1987).

Williams, Raymond, *Writing in Society* (Verso: no date).

Williams, Raymond, *Marxism and Literature* (Oxford University Press, 1977).

Williams, Raymond, *Culture and Society, 1780–1850* (Hogarth Press, 1990).

Wolin, Richard, *Walter Benjamin. An Aesthetic of Redemption* (New York: Columbia University Press, 1982).

Wyatt, A. J. and H. Clay (eds.), *English Literature of the Nineteenth Century* (University Tutorial Press, 1912).
Yeo, Eileen, 'Some Practices and Problems of Chartist Democracy' in J. Epstein and D. Thompson (eds.), *The Chartist Experience* (Macmillan, 1982).
Zlotnick, Susan, *Women, Writing, and the Industrial Revolution* (Baltimore: John Hopkins University Press, 1998).

UNPUBLISHED THESES

Timothy Randall, 'Towards A Cultural Democracy: Chartist Literature, 1837–1860', PhD thesis (University of Sussex, 1994).
Vickers, Roy, 'The Gospel of Social Discontent. Religious Language and the Narrative of Christian Election in the Chartist Poetry of Cooper, Jones and Linton', PhD thesis (Liverpool John Moores University, 2005).

Index

CAMBRIDGE STUDIES IN NINETEENTH-CENTURY
LITERATURE AND CULTURE

General editor
Gillian Beer, *University of Cambridge*

Titles published